The Gift
A voice from the Shadows

Meredith Gresham

First published by Busybird Publishing 2022

Copyright © 2022 Meredith Gresham

ISBN
Hardcover Print: 978-1-922691-44-6
Softcover Print: 978-1-922691-58-3

This work is copyright. Apart from any use permitted under the *Copyright Act 1968*, no part of this publication may be reproduced, stored in a retrieval system or transmitted in any form or by any means, electronic, mechanical, photocopying, recording or otherwise, without the prior written permission of Meredith Gresham.

The information in this book is based on the author's experiences and opinions. The author and publisher disclaim responsibility for any adverse consequences, which may result from use of the information contained herein. Permission to use any external content has been sought by the author. Any breaches will be rectified in further editions of the book.

Cover Image: Merrie Gresham

Cover design: Busybird Publishing

Layout and typesetting: Busybird Publishing

Busybird Publishing
2/118 Para Road
Montmorency, Victoria
Australia 3094
www.busybird.com.au

Contents

Prologue	1
Chapter 1 - The early days: 1942–1947	7
Chapter 2 - Chargot, Barrington, Tasmania	13
Chapter 3 - Roman Catholicism	24
Chapter 4 - Rowella	31
Chapter 5 - Restless years: change and turmoil	35
Chapter 6 - Nursing training days	42
Chapter 7 - Freedom, here I come	55
Chapter 8 - The shark and the flying fish	59
Chapter 9 - Nursing days in London	65
Chapter 10 - Enter Douglas	72
Chapter 11 - Our first home	90
Chapter 12 - Tasmania to Perth	112
Chapter 13 - Perth, Western Australia	120
Chapter 14 - Daddles	143
Chapter 15 - Trials and adjustments, Homes in WA	154
Chapter 16 - Tasmania, homeward bound – again	163
Chapter 17 - Merriedale Farm	171
Chapter 18 - New outlooks	194
Chapter 19 - Around the world in sixty-three days	200
Chapter 20 - Moving on, time of change	218
Chapter 21 - Yachting and a fifth child	229
Chapter 22 - Hyun Joo Choi	241
Chapter 23 - Ringarooma	250

Chapter 24 - Time to move again — 263

Chapter 25 - Rathvinden house, 1993 — 270

Chapter 26 - Pandora's box — 281

Chapter 27 - Rathvinden ministries — 291

Chapter 28 - Wendy's story — 309

Chapter 29 - Interesting people, interesting times — 315

Chapter 30 - Stage, TV and film — 331

Chapter 31 - Narnia in film — 337

Chapter 32 - Relocating – again — 347

Chapter 33 - Malta – our new location — 362

Chapter 34 - Making connections — 373

Chapter 35 - Today: 29th October 2020 — 386

Chapter 36 - Balance points — 406

Epilogue — 409

Prologue

28th April 2020

Most people call me Merrie; when they get to know me even better, I'm simply referred to as Mompska, a name that seemed to have evolved when I had four small children. I've been the wife of Douglas Gresham for the last 54 years. He gets called Daddles by his family and many of his closest friends.

Up till quite recently I have always remembered my early beginnings from the emotional viewpoint of an immature child, a teenager or a fledgling adult who was thrust into the world, ill-equipped to handle life.

Looking through these lenses, I saw nothing but my own emotional pain of rejection, which left me with a very low self-worth and self-pity. But recently my understanding has changed. I began to see people and circumstances through the eyes of a somewhat wiser mature adult of seventy-eight years, who has embraced the teachings of Jesus Christ. As C.S. Lewis said, "I believe in Christianity as I believe that the Sun has risen, not only because I see it, but because by it I see everything else."*

So now at last I can write about the people, places and circumstances that have made me into the person I am today, without being a totally self-absorbed bore. I have had the privilege of living with and being taught and helped by some amazing and extraordinary people. The greatest of which would have to be the man I have shared my life with. You will read a lot about him in the pages of this book.

I am writing this story of my life as I remember it; some people might remember events differently as I know my memory of facts and events may be defective. It's not meant to be an autobiography as such, but a telling of the trials and tests of a woman, a wife and a mother who overcame many of the difficulties that a lot of us face during life. Looking back from a vantage point of seventy-eight

---
* - C.S. Lewis *The Weight of Glory* (Macmillan, 1980), 92

and as a grandmother to eleven grandchildren, I realise that I have thought and behaved differently in a lot of those situations than may be normal. People often destroy their own lives and leave other people's lives shipwrecked and bereaved by the way they handle life's circumstances.

For many years now, people have been asking me to write my life story. Well, for me, it's just how life was, but many find my telling of different aspects of my life – my early years, and then later, my life shared with Douglas Gresham – totally fascinating. I often thought about writing but I never had the time to write because, as you will find out, I have lived a very busy life swamped by fascinating people, and endless household chores: cooking, gardening and church activities, and the onset of old age that seemed to accelerate time and make every job take longer.

Doug and I are in the habit of spending three months of every year in Australia where we have three married sons and ten grandchildren. This year, 2020, I decided to only stay for six weeks. I came back to Malta via Dubai on the 16th of February, leaving Doug to spend the remaining six weeks at our lovely tropical beach front property on the coast of Queensland.

Shortly after I got home Covid-19 threw the whole world into a lockdown. Airports were closed and some still are. (As I write, it is now the 28th of April). No public gatherings were allowed, and businesses that weren't considered 'essential' – shops, schools, universities and even churches – were shut down worldwide. The pandemic had brought the world to a standstill with most businesses now being run from peoples' homes using computers. My local government in Malta issued an order for every person over sixty years of age to not leave their homes. All this was to keep the numbers of seriously ill people – those who needed hospitalisation and a ventilator – to a manageable level. Many people were dying because there simply weren't enough hospital beds or ventilators to go around.

So, I found myself shut up in my beautiful house with no one to look after except myself. Just prior to all this, when visiting my son James on his beef farm in northern New South Wales, he again tried to persuade me to write my story. He gave me a writing pad and sat me down in a comfortable chair to jot down a few memories. Little did I know that I would soon have so much time to write. Today, no one can tell you how long this pandemic is going to last. All I know is that it has been the longest time Doug and I have been apart since our marriage 54 years ago. We have both shed many tears over it.

So now I've written this book *The Gift,* for you to read.

I dedicate this book first to my Redeemer, Jesus Christ, whom I made my managing director and the Lord of my life, because He saved me from myself, and he gave me a code of ethics to live by. I eagerly look forward to receiving all He had promised me. And secondly to my husband, Douglas Gresham, who has always loved me and been there for me through thick and thin over the period of those 54 years.

Chapter 1

The early days: 1942–1947

My full name is Meredith Agnes Llewella Gresham, daughter of Geoffrey and Ermyntrude Conan-Davies, and these are my memories. To begin, let me tell you about my gentle father and my clever and adventurous mother. Mum was born into British aristocracy in its finest era, 1907. Her name was Ermyntrude Virginia St Lo Malet, the oldest child of Lieutenant-Colonel Sir Harry Charles Malet, DSO OBE and Lady Mildred Malet. The home she grew up in was Wilbury House, Wiltshire, England. It is a massive country house and estate which is now owned by the Guinness family.

When my mother lived there it was fully managed by butlers, ladies in waiting, cooks, cleaners, and grooms. The grounds, spacious gardens and stables were maintained by staff of most likely dozens of people, and she was schooled by a governess in that grand home. The house is well worth looking up if you have the time. Later, the family moved to a smaller house in Luxborough, Somerset, called Chargot Manor House. It was in this house many years later that I first got to know my mother's family and met my husband.

My mother trained as a nurse in St Thomas' Hospital in London. To train there in those days, one apparently had to have a pigtail and a pedigree – she had both. She went on to do midwifery training at the Radcliffe Infirmary in Oxford. When she was twenty-one, she joined an Anglican order of nuns, and was sent somewhere in East Africa. It was there that she learnt Swahili. However, she soon became disillusioned with the order and left it to return to England. Mum had a talent for languages, speaking both French and German fluently and later Latin as well as English and Swahili. She translated *Alice in Wonderland* into Swahili, illustrating it herself, depicting Alice and other characters as Africans. She wrote it under her maiden name, Ermyntrude St Lo Malet. Recently my husband searched the internet for a copy of her Alice rendition. It turns out this book is still in print and is used today in schools in East Africa as a child's early reader. I now have a brand-new copy on my bookshelf.

Back in the UK, she realised that she had grown to love Africa and so she applied for a nursing job in the then British colony of Tanganyika (now Tanzania) with the government medical service, arriving again in Dar es Salaam on the 28th of July 1936. There she met and married my father, Geoffrey Win Severn Conan-Davies, at Minaki St Andrews on the 14th of May 1937. He was a Welshman, the son of an Anglican minister in Worcestershire. At the time they met he was Assistant District Commissioner in Tanganyika, a British public servant.

My oldest brother, Stephen, was born in England, but the subsequent four babies were born in Africa. My sister Bliss was born in Shinyanga where the pink diamond in Queen Elizabeth's crown came from. A third baby was born, and my parents called him Quintin. Sadly, that baby died of cot death at eight months old.

Then came me. My mother always told me that I was born in Masasi, in a mud hut where she had a parrot as a midwife. Apparently, the house for the Assistant District Commissioner wasn't ready to live in so my parents had to temporarily sleep in a mud hut without a door and that's where I decided to make my not-so-grand entry into the world. No midwife was available to help with the birth, but there was a parrot on the end of her bed. The fourth baby, or should I say fifth, was born in Abercorn, Zambia: another boy, who she named Quintin again, after her lost child. This child somehow got the nickname Tinker during his childhood, but he later adopted the name Tim.

After ten years in Tanganyika and after the Second World War, my parents uprooted the family and immigrated to Tasmania, the island state off the south coast of Australia, for the sake of its climate and English language. There they turned their hand to farming. However, my mother soon deserted my father and her four children and in 1958 returned to Tanganyika. There she lived as an anchoress at Mbinga, remaining there until 1966. My mother had loved Tanganyika in her youth, but it may have been her youth that she loved, a psychological phenomenon that clouds the memory of most of us as we age, for she found it very changed when she had returned in 1958. She no longer enjoyed the place, once telling me, 'It was not the Tanganyika I left.'

My early memories of Africa are mainly from photos and the many stories my parents told us. Photos are great memory-joggers, and my mother took lots of them. She also kept a weekly handwritten record of her life in Africa, about eight large volumes with illustrations and accompanying photos. My sister, Bliss, has them in Melbourne. It was no easy feat to master the workings of a camera in those days. Aperture, depth of field and light had to be accurate. Not like today's point and shoot camera phones. My brother, Stephen, bought me my first camera when I was sixteen; it was an Agfa Silette. I had to use a separate exposure meter and get the distance spot-on to get a decent photo.

Those early photos of us children growing up in Africa are imprinted on my memory, reminding me of many things. Tousi Binti Simba, for instance, was our *Ayah*, or Nanny. A tall and very soft ebony black lady with shiny white teeth. She always wore a colourful sarong, held up by her soft ample bosom. It is strange that here in Malta, where I now live, whenever I see a black lady in a sarong amply endowed, I always want to go up to her and hug her. Tousi had a disabled sister, Mahella, whom she cared for. Mahella would always be sitting on the floor, a perfect delight for small children to climb on, and she would entertain us with games and African rhymes.

Tousi would plait our snowy blonde hair into multiple braids and carry the babies around on her back in a sling while tending to her chores. Every morning our shoes (*tackies*, my mother called them) would have to be sewn on around our ankles. This was to prevent us from taking them off and going barefoot on the soil. There were parasites that the natives called *jiggers* which were a type of hookworm carrying a disease called bilharzia. These burrowed through the skin and would find easy access into the soft feet of a small white child.

Malaria was also a constant worry. There were no antimalarial drugs in those days. My bottom is still dimpled to this day with many life-saving quinine injections – quinine was an early form of malaria treatment. Today it is used mostly for flavouring tonic water, oddly enough. It was these types of things that made my mother realise that Africa wasn't a suitable place to raise children. But she didn't want to return to war-torn England which was still on rationing. Her criteria for a home were that the spoken language was English, and she preferred the climate at the European latitude of about 45 degrees. So, what she did was to run her finger around a globe of the world at 45 degrees south latitude and her finger bumped into Tasmania. It was the only place that qualified and so that's where we all eventually went.

All of us only spoke Swahili in Africa. English wasn't used much – even by our parents. Today I still use some words and phrases that my parents never exchanged for English. Phrases like *shut the door* became *funga mlango*, and a bad tasting medicine was *karli dower*. And many other words I still have in my vocabulary. When we arrived in Australia, I spoke not a word of English.

There is a photo of the three little older Conan-Davies children, taken in Africa, with satchels on our backs, waving goodbye as we went off to Lishoto School. Baby Quintin was left behind crying.

'When are the *chooloons* coming back?', he would ask.

I don't remember anything about that school, just the photo, but that was the first of eight schools I attended during my schooling years.

Our eventual government homes in various parts of Africa were gracious and spacious, with lovely gardens cared for by gardeners. There was a Dobi, the laundry man, and there were cooks and cleaners as well as Tousi and Mahela. As a result, my mother had plenty of time to create amazing tapestries and embroideries. One such work of art, called the *Gustasp*, is about 5-feet high and 6-feet long. It depicts a large dragon, covered with sequins for its scales. The dragon is in combat with a white stallion and rider. The rider has jewelled armour on. This masterpiece now hangs in my niece Mary-Anne's home in Hobart, Tasmania.

Mother learnt various African crafts from the local women, such as making baskets and raffia carry bags. I still have some of them.

Tousi was like a mother to me. I bonded deeply with her, so much so that at the age of five – when it came time to relocate to Tasmania – I caused a great deal of stress to the other passengers on the steamship with loud non-stop crying for hours on end. I'm told that the ship's doctor even suggested that he give me a general anaesthetic to stop the noise. Tousi was also my mother's friend, companion, and helper – she loved Tousi dearly and regularly sent her money from Tasmania. Tousi couldn't read or write so we never got a reply. It was always an unanswered question whether she got that money.

Little ebony statues of elephants and African warriors adorned our various homes in Tasmania. Some not so little. *Mgeni*, meaning guest, was a 3-foot-high ebony statue of a man carrying a tray, which was handy to put a vase of fresh flowers on. There were also two very heavy black elephants. It used to be a challenge to see which child could lift them.

Chapter 2

Chargot, Barrington, Tasmania

We departed Africa in 1947 on a steamship of *The Blue Funnel Line* from Durban in South Africa, to Fremantle in Western Australia, and then on to Beauty Point, near the city of Launceston on the north coast of Tasmania. I was immediately placed in a girls' boarding school called Methodist Ladies College, not speaking a word of English and only five years old. My visual memory kicks in around this time. I remember the headmistress. I even remember her name which was Miss Madder. I cried a lot, especially at night, so Miss Madder put me in her own bed to sleep and read me illustrated books. I didn't understand a word, but I can clearly remember the pictures. All the little girls depicted in the book had very short wide legs with small feet. I found this confusing and thought, *the children here are not the same.*

I never attended class and spent my days trying to catch a litter of small kittens who had made their home in a pile of old building timbers.

My parents then caught the Tasman Limited steam train to Hobart – a good four-hour journey – to drop my older brother Stephen at The Friends' School. Bliss was placed with a family called Cook in Trevallyn in Launceston till the end of term. Now they only had to look after three-year-old baby Quintin and Mum and Dad began house hunting.

During this period, my parents stayed in Devonport at the Elimatta Hotel guest house on The Strand. They had chosen to concentrate their efforts on the north-west sector of Tasmania because of its rich, red-soiled farming land. The hotel guest house was on a beautiful wide tree-lined road which ended at the bluff and a beach playground. On the few occasions that we children were with our parents, my father would often walk us to the bluff, but it was mid-winter at the time and far too cold to paddle in the sea.

On the 8th of July 1948 our parents signed an agreement to buy a partly cleared 80-acre farm in Barrington, Tasmania. It was 14 miles from Devonport and all on gravel roads. They named the farm "Chargot Barrington" after Mum's last home in Somerset England. The house was a very typical Tasmanian farmhouse. It was weatherboard clad with a tin roof, a water tank to catch the rainwater, and a paling fence closely around it. A very different home from what we had all been accustomed to in Africa, and so different from the grand estate houses my mother had lived in in England. But it was home and it was so exciting. There were rabbits, wallabies and very brightly coloured birds everywhere. The rosella parrots would make such a *kelele* (Swahili for noise) as they flew overhead, as if to say, 'Who are you, and why are you invading our territory?'

My childhood days spent on the farm were wonderful – the four of us children were together again. We rode our bikes to the primary school in Barrington in all weathers, with our satchels on our backs containing sandwiches wrapped in greaseproof paper from the Weetbix packets. With the flexible mind of a child, I had, by this stage, learned to speak English.

The roads were all made of gravel, often with very uneven surfaces. I regularly crashed my bicycle and had knees and elbows washed by Mum and sprinkled with sulfonamide powder. Mum loved that stuff; it was a new invention back then.

Once I crashed into a deep snow drift while trying to keep on the snow-covered road and I lost my gloves in the snow. I remember feeling so ashamed for losing them. In summertime it was quite common to come across a squashed rabbit on the road, full of maggots. If the carcass had dried, it was such fun to pick it up by the hind legs and shake the maggots out on one of your siblings who would protest loudly and try to get you back.

At our school, the year levels from kindergarten to grade six were schooled in two classrooms. Miss Mason taught the younger ones, and Mr Archer, the headmaster, taught the older children. If you have ever had the joy of reading the poem by the Australian author John O'Brien, called *The Old Bush School*, then you have a very good description of that school in those pioneer days.

My parents made that house, the gardens and the whole farm into a showpiece – it was even displayed to school children as a model farm. But first let me tell you what my mother did to the house and gardens all by herself, with no hired help. She was an amazing woman.

The house was originally timber weatherboards but she clad over them with white cement and bedded black boards into it so as to resemble a Tudor-style English house. She also ordered *wunderlich* roofing tiles from England. When workmen came to re-roof the house, they left the original tin roof still in place and put up the timber framework that was to support the tiles. My mum was up on the roof helping them. She watched closely while they laid the first tiles, then dismissed the men and completed the job herself!

The garden was also landscaped by my mother using a spade and wheelbarrow, first by flattening a large expanse in front of the house under the big picture window and planting it down with lawn. She left the lowest section as it was and built thick concrete walls which she heaped the soil against and made a swimming pool for us. The front door had a porch built onto it and she laid a cement crazy paving area down for cars to drive on. We imprinted our hand and feet prints into the wet cement, along with other things like African coins, glass eyes out of a doll and badges.

A statue that she made from cement had a plaster cast of Bliss' face on it; it held a lamp to light up the forecourt. There were rows of rambler roses on trellises and every flower you could imagine. My favourite flowers were very large full-bloomed poppies varying from shades of deep pink to reds and purples. The poppies would self-seed themselves every year and had a habit of even invading the roadside and surrounding farm buildings.

Inside, the floors of the house were covered with a green woollen carpet with red roses that she specially imported from England. We were constantly reminded that it was a £100 carpet, 'So don't let your pet rabbits run around on it!' A big picture window was put in place looking out on farmlands with Mount Roland beautifully framing the background.

She re-modelled the kitchen with red Laminex (a new material then) on the counter tops and the walls were pale grey trimmed with white. A Thor dishwasher doubled up as a laundry machine, by just lifting the centre plate rack out. Tinker once dropped a kitten into it when it was on the spin dry cycle and killed it stone dead. That was a terrible day. We never got smacked for being naughty, but we were justly made to feel very ashamed of our conduct.

When Mum's parents died, a very large chest arrived from England full of the crested family silverware, grand trays and tea pots and coffee pots with matching sugar bowl and milk jugs. Now our home was adorned not only with ebony African warriors and animals, but with extravagant silverware as well. These items were in constant use, not displayed behind locked glass. Sadly, these precious inherited family heirlooms were all given to the nuns in the Carmelite Monastery in Longford when my mother became a Catholic – which is something I'll discuss later on. Jewellery also came in that chest. One such piece was a necklace with eight opals suspended from gold chains. Inside the case was a note handwritten by Lady Mildred Malet, my grandmother, saying, 'This opal necklace belongs to Meredith.' Years later that necklace was stolen twice by different people, and believe it or not, twice recovered.

When I had my own family home and garden in Ringarooma, Tasmania, many years later, it was the self-seeding poppies from my mother's garden that I remembered and longed for. In Ringarooma, I had a small greenhouse and, as you can imagine, a large garden which was my delight and joy. But I couldn't forget those poppies from my childhood. I had never seen them since.

It was at the farm in Ringarooma that I came to a full understanding of what it actually means to be a real Christian. At the time, I was forty years old and bursting with excitement for my newfound faith in Jesus. One day I was in a little green house with Dig, my eight-year-old son, when I saw a small pale-green plant with only four leaves developed. I knew instantly it was a poppy like those in my memory, and I knew it was a gift from God and I told Dig as much.

All over the north-east of Tasmania farmers grow plain light pink opium poppies as a commercial crop, and occasionally one would pop up in an unexpected place. They are all the same species, but I knew the one in my greenhouse was different. The plant grew and grew, becoming very large and had very considerable buds which finally burst open to display huge vivid red poppies. I thanked God for that gift He gave me and named them Hosanna poppies. Of course, I carefully collected all the seeds and in a few years my garden was also covered with them.

When our next-door neighbours John and Stella Wade's house burnt to the ground, I sprinkled Hosanna poppy seeds all over the charred remains. Two years ago, in 2018, my husband Doug and I paid the Wades a surprise visit. They had rebuilt their home but not on the original site. There, to my utter delight, was a brilliant display of those poppies in full bloom. John and Stella had always remembered when I had sowed those seeds on their destroyed home and kept that area free for these flowers to bloom and reseed themselves, year after year.

Now back to my childhood home in Barrington. The drive into the house was overhung with large fir trees and Mum had planted thousands of daffodils along the drive. There was a fountain in the garden which she had made, and a paved sunken garden with a sundial in the centre and a large productive vegetable garden, laid out with concrete paths. Wow, what a woman! In only a few years she had transformed a dull little farmhouse with no garden into a paradise, where brightly coloured butterflies and we kids frolicked and played.

When we moved in, the house had no hot water, but it did have electricity and as soon as it became available, we had a telephone installed – I remember our number was 23. I also remember being bathed in a cattle trough; our hair washed with velvet soap and to rinse off we would climb up into the rainwater tank that fed the trough. All such fun.

I have mentioned that Mum had translated and illustrated *Alice in Wonderland* into Swahili before she was married but she also wrote and illustrated another four small books. These were bound by an amateur book binder but never got published. And I doubt whether she ever submitted them for publication. The books had each one of her four children in their own fairy story set in Africa. The first was called *Shindy and Flinders*. Shindy was Stephen's nickname, and Flinders was the name of our parrot. The second one was *Bliss and Black Fairies*. And the third, *Melody and Mermaids* was my book – they always called me Melody. The fourth book was *Quentin and Quilliam*. Quentin, as I have mentioned, was Tinker's real name, and Quilliam was a porcupine. All four books are immaculately hand illustrated. The stories themselves are fascinating adventure stories that used to captivate the minds of my own four children as well. Mum was an immensely talented woman. I still have that original handmade book here with me and am admiring it as I type.

My Father, Geoffrey Wynne Severn Conan-Davies, was the youngest child of a family of seven and born in England in the year 1904. His father was Welsh, an Anglican Minister in the County of Worcester, England, and his mother was English. Geoffrey's late arrival in the family meant that he was a passive onlooker of what already was. Although his family were never wealthy, he was loved and protected by his siblings and parents. He knew no malice or self-seeking, so he always felt secure and unthreatened. His parents must have sacrificed a lot for him, for he was sent to Oxford University and Keeble College, where he gained a Master of Arts and Administration and would proudly put the initials MA after his name on all his documents.

In 1929 he travelled to Tanganyika, in East Africa (Tanzania), where he joined the British colonial service. In 1936, still working in Tanganyika, the young British public servant met and married Lady Ermyntrude Malet, my mother. Both spoke fluent Swahili.

Much of his childhood was in the austerity of the First World War so whenever we would eat an orange in his presence, he would tell us the smell reminded him of Christmas, for when he was a little boy each child would be given an orange in their Christmas stocking as a special treat.

My father was by nature a businessman and bureaucrat. He had retired from the British colonial system on a lifelong pension from the British Government in 1948 and moved his young family to the 80-acre farm in Tasmania that I have previously described. Manual labour didn't come easily to him, but he was a perfectionist, and everything had to be done very well. His first job on his new farm was to fence the rabbits out. He built paling fences around each field. Most of the cleared fields still had the massive stumps of very large trees in them.

These had to be burnt out, as no machine then invented – and few even today – would have been able to move them. At night one could see the glow of the burning stumps. We were not allowed to go into these fields because the roots underground would also be alight and the danger of falling into a fire pit was very real. Our first farm tool was a draught horse called Daisy. Dad was terrified of horses, but he got over it and ploughed the fields with a single furrow plough pulled by Daisy.

Towards the end of his life there was a permanent look of disappointment in his eyes. He would scold me for taking so long to visit him and would scold me again for leaving. It's only now that I can understand and excuse this. At the time it offended me, especially because I had often come to see him from the other side of the planet. He eventually lived in a nursing home in Melbourne. Shortly before his death, word got to me that he was very frail and fading fast, although his mind was still 100 per cent sound. Doug and I were living in Ireland at the time. I wrote a letter to the matron of the nursing home and asked her if there was a serious Christian on the staff there. She gave me the name and address of one of her nurses. I wrote to this nurse and asked her if she would please lead my dad in a commitment prayer. I wrote something along the lines of thanking Jesus for dying on the cross for him, for forgiving his sins, and asking Jesus to come into his life, but much more detailed. I also asked this nurse to tell him Merrie asked her to do it. So, she held his hand, and he repeated the words after her.

Thereafter, Dad thought that this nurse was the greatest thing since sliced bread and would cling to her whenever she was on duty. He died shortly afterwards on the 16th of August 2002 at the age of ninety-one. One phrase he often quoted from the Bible when we were children was, 'Death, where is thy sting? Grave, where is thy victory?'

Strange. Perhaps he was trying to tell us he was unhappy?

On the farm in Tasmania, we had the first tractor in that area. It was a little grey Ferguson TEA-20 that my parents had sent over specially from England. When it arrived, Dad drove that tractor 14 miles from the dock yards in Devonport all the way to Barrington.

We also had a milking cow called Bria. I would often milk her. She was so quiet that she would stand completely still in the paddock untethered while I'd sit on a short three-legged stool carved out of a solid block of wood by an African man, milking her into a stainless-steel bucket. When it was raining, Bria would be tied up in the machinery shed to be milked. I would squirt some warm milk onto my gum boot and if I kept very still, little mice would come and lick the milk off my boots.

Sheep were, at first, our only income. For shearing them, and marking the lambs, we had to have stock yards, which Dad built. One day, I watched with fascination as my mother did a caesarean on a dying sheep. Mum knocked the poor ewe on the head and without hesitation sliced it open and released live twin lambs from the dead sheep's belly. Bottle feeding the lambs was so delightful; they quickly became so tame and so keen, wriggling their little tails like mad as they enthusiastically sucked the warm milk from the bottle.

Later on, we changed to dairy farming, milking twenty-eight cows in a new two-stall dairy parlour with an ultra-modern new-fangled milking machine. It was very up-market and a brand-new thing in the district. The dairy also had to look lovely, so it was built to resemble the house, black and white Tudor-style with a tiled roof. Many of the neighbour's scoffed at it.

The milk was passed through a cream separator. The cream was sold, and the skim milk was gravity fed to two breeding sows at the bottom of the hill. I loved the piglets, and still do love pigs. They are such charming animals, very intelligent and surprisingly clean. Do you know they only do their toilet in one spot in their field? That's if they are not penned up in a small area. And if they have a field, they need to have a ring in their nose to stop them rooting up the soil.

Chapter 3

Roman Catholicism

As a child and young adult my mother was always drawn to things spiritual. As mentioned above, when she was twenty-one, she joined an Anglican order of nuns, but became disillusioned with that order and returned to England. In her words, 'I didn't find God there.'

Much of her early days she would write poetry about spiritual things, and I still have some of these in my office. She could recite *The Hound of Heaven* by Francis Thompson all the way through. However, through my early childhood, she appeared to have discarded the whole spiritual thing and was enjoying creating her own paradise on earth. She took interest in her personal appearance, and she would curl her hair and wear floral dresses. But I never saw her with make up on – she considered that low class.

But then one tragic day, she happened to meet an Irish Catholic priest in Latrobe called Father Hanahoe. It is bringing me to tears as I remember the rape of our happy home on that farm in Barrington by Hanahoe and the Catholic Church. I see now, so clearly, how Satan destroyed our family and wounded each of us children very deeply. Especially now that I see through the eyes of a mature adult and committed Christian – that is to say, a follower of Jesus' teachings, not the teachings of some self-serving priest.

The devil must have seen Mum's unfulfilled hunger for God and deceived her into thinking that the Roman Catholic Church was the only way to heaven. The bait was using the name 'Jesus'. But having been myself a follower of that religion during my school days at various Catholic boarding schools (at the instigation of my mother), I concluded that it was a sham and one that so many churches teach. Why didn't she test everything told to her and hold onto what was true? The Word of God is true, not some man-made dogma claiming salvation through penances and adherence to the church's human dictates.

It is revealing to me that for many years, the Catholic Church insisted that the Bible was only to be available in Latin: a dead language that no one spoke – certainly it was like that when I used to attend Mass at Catholic schools which was said entirely in Latin. In bygone days simply having a copy 'in the vernacular' (plain language) could get you burned at the stake! It took one very brave young German monk by the name of Martin Luther, who could read Latin, to stand up and say, 'hang on a minute...'.

He kicked off a rediscovery of what real Christianity was about. A rediscovery that showed the Catholic Church for what it was and rendered it unnecessary. Even during my school days in Catholic schools, we were still being told we were not capable of understanding the Bible because we hadn't spent years in a seminary college studying it like the priests had.

However, Father Hanahoe's doctrine found fertile ground in the mind of my mother. She was an intelligent, stubborn, determined, and independent person. And if the road to heaven was to tick all the Catholic boxes, then she could do that, and do it better than anyone else. But lingering doubts must have haunted her. Was she a good enough Catholic? Had she ticked *all* the boxes? And ticked them well enough? The Bible simply became a prop on the stage of her salvation journey. Had she read it instead of worshiping it, she may have found, like Luther and many others, that Christ alone was sufficient, and all their doctrines and dogmas were of little value.

She pressed on, relentlessly goaded on by assorted fake Catholic 'spiritual advisors' who encouraged her in what I now see as her descent into religious madness. Hanahoe did a great deal of damage to all of us, including her. One travesty after another followed. The children were all sent far away into Catholic boarding schools so we wouldn't interfere with her journey to heaven. Bliss and I were sent to a school on the west Tamar River near Launceston, called Rowella – but there will be more about Rowella shortly. Stephen was already boarding with people in Devonport and attended the state high school there. Little Tinker? I don't know what she did with him, but he was not left at home, possibly farmed out to some other family.

She began dressing differently. Discarding her nice clothes, she now wore a brown skirt and a blouse, and her head was covered with a black scarf. She told us that she was a Discalced Carmelite Nun, whatever that meant. Intimacy with her husband now stopped. She moved out of their bedroom into a very small room which she called her oratory. She decorated it with intricate patterns, using oil pastels over white wallpaper to resemble the interior of a Gothic cathedral. The artistry was very beautiful. There she had an altar and one hard chair. No bed in the room was necessary for she did penance by sleeping on the floor with a big Old Testament wrapped in blue plastic as a pillow. This was to somehow make atonement for her sins.

Other penances she did was to make herself a vest out of a potato sack. She called this her hair shirt. She also wore an elasticised snood that had drawing pins embedded into it to hold back her hair. But the thing I hated most was a length of white polyethene pipe that also had drawing pins pushed into it, emerging through the plastic. She whipped the top of her legs with this, often so hard that her skirt would be stained with blood that would seep through. It was hidden out of reach of the children on top of her wardrobe. I found it one day, took it, and put it at the top of a tall pine tree. I knew she couldn't get it from there.

Today, I feel sorry for her. Her desire to know and please God was admirable but I think her reading of Catholic mystics and the lengths they went to to atone for their sins must have influenced her a lot. She was also utterly convinced of the Catholic Church's infallibility. Her zeal was encouraged by Hanahoe, and later taken advantage of by a Hungarian man claiming to be a priest, who only saw monetary gain for himself. We suspect he was a crook. My father must have seen this, but he did very little to stop it.

Poor Dad. I can't imagine what he went through, but being a perfect English gentleman, he never showed his emotions much. He did, however, occasionally find anaesthetic in a bottle of whisky, and would pace up and down the corridor outside her room, whisky glass in his hand, trying to reason with her. She probably saw him as the devil's advocate coming to tempt and torment her.

She began driving our little Morris Minor car 16 miles to Latrobe every morning to go to Mass and 16 miles back, all on gravel roads. She would drive 6 miles again in the evenings to a church in Sheffield and lie face down on the floor in front of a false god, a piece of white pressed flour, she called the 'Real Presence'. How can any sane person believe such nonsense? This 'Real Presence' is not found anywhere in The Scriptures.

Of course, for my father, the inevitable happened. We had a very good family friend nearby, called Verna. She was an attractive English lady who had separated from her husband, a British Colonel in the Indian colonial service living in India. To my dad, Verna must have been a touch of sanity in his life. He liked to go to her place – they were great friends. She was a brilliant pianist and a fun-loving lady who loved children. We always had great fun at her place. Of course, this caused my mother a great deal of alarm and stress, not because of her husband, but because Dad had the car, and she needed the car to go to Mass. One day when he hadn't returned early enough, she drove the tractor to Latrobe. So, a second car was bought, a Morris Oxford.

Verna had a child our age called Peter who we used to play with. But she always grieved the death of a later baby who had died of cot death shortly before we knew her. She had kept his nursery intact as a kind of shrine to his memory. I remember being taken into that room by her and quietly shown around. I felt very privileged that day.

However, Verna did have another baby, and called him Geoffrey after my father, for he was my father's child. In 1954 Verna left Tasmania and went back to India where Geoffrey was born. After four years she returned and settled in Melbourne. That child Geoffrey became a world-famous pianist. He was a child prodigy and at the age of eight performed Bach's Concerto No. 5 in F minor with the Victorian Symphony Orchestra, a concert that was televised nationally by ABC TV. He became the youngest recipient of a Churchill Fellowship award at the age of thirteen. He toured the world with his gift of music but somehow received very little recognition in Australia. A film called *The Eulogy* was recently made about his life as a brilliant pianist and the way Australia failed to recognise his talent.

Sadly, my father was unable to admit to anyone that Geoffrey was his child. Shame or pride? He was such a gentleman that I expect he couldn't admit to the fact that he had had an affair. But it wasn't really a secret, for everyone knew about it. We just could never mention it, or he would get very angry and defensive. Young Geoffrey was the one who suffered most by the fact that his father disowned him. I met him for the first time about eighteen years ago in Melbourne. He was thrilled to finally meet me. I found him to be a very sweet and loving brother. He died in 2009 aged 54, a lonely alcoholic. I grieve for that missed relationship.

However, back to life at Chargot Barrington.

My mother soon lost interest in her little corner of paradise that she had created. But the breakdown of the family was tragic and relentless. Four healthy, happy children who loved each other were now separated and became estranged. Dad also lost his children. I know he loved us dearly – we were his pride and joy.

The destructive force of my mother's misguided pursuit for eternal happiness was, and is, felt to this day as she trampled on all those who hindered her or prevented her from practicing her religion. Her youngest child was wounded the most. As an adult he eventually became a recluse, carving out for himself a lovely sanctuary amongst the tall gum trees in a remote area in the state of Victoria, where he built himself a house and became almost self-sufficient: growing his own food and lavishing his attention on his beloved horses. Today he is a sad and angry man haunted by his past and hating the very mention of anything biblical. He is a man who despises any form of falsehood, and he views a relationship with God as a pretence. He has accused me of being just like Mum who followed and worshipped a man-made religion. He refuses to entertain any discussion of the difference between Christianity and churchianity.

I was always very close to my brother Tinker. It grieves me to this day that my relationship with my younger brother was to suffer an almost fatal blow at the hands of my mother and I have only recently uncovered the cause. Sadly, our relationship has never properly recovered.

As a child, Tinker was sent to a Catholic boarding school in Hobart where he was sexually abused by the so called 'Christian Brothers', but his time there was cut short by Mum who put him, unaccompanied, on a ship bound for England at the age of only

14. He went to live with Mum's sister, our aunt, at Cothelstone Manor House in the UK where he would go to school with our cousins. The only reason he got on that boat was because he was apparently told that I would be going with him. And when his closest sister failed to board, he was told that I had changed my mind. The fact is I knew absolutely nothing about it. He has spent most of his life deeply wounded by this apparent betrayal. My much-loved brother related this story to me only recently. He told me he cried on that ship all the way to England. My heart grieves for that lovely child who was so clever and had so much potential. He was a gentle and good person, and there was no malice in him.

All this was a ploy to achieve my mother's objective, which was to be free of all her responsibilities, so she could go back to Africa. And she soon did. She went and joined a Benedictine mission in Songea and Mbinga from 1960 to 1967. However, she broke her leg while there, and was a patient in the Muhimbili Hospital in Dar es Salaam, so I flew there when I was nursing in London and rescued her. As a result, she was at our wedding – but that's a story for a later chapter.

Mum had us all christened into the Catholic Church and for a christening gift she bought us big black nun's rosary beads. It was such fun to whirl them around in the air. One day she was trying to get us all into the car to go to Sunday Mass in Sheffield. But my younger brother was nowhere to be found. Eventually he was located up a fir tree that overhung the drive. I can't help rejoicing every time I tell this story. Mum yelled that he would go to hell if he didn't go to Mass, and Tinker, perched in the tree, calmly and methodically pulled off every bead on the rosary and, one by one, threw them at her. He somehow felt deep down that what she was doing to the family was wrong and so refused to cooperate with her madness.

There is a part of me that wonders why my father let her do all this. But when I look at his gentle non-aggressive character and the love and unity that was in his childhood, I can see it was not in his nature to stand up to or oppose anyone. He was very childlike in his assessment of people and loved everyone. I have never met a gentler, kinder man. He saw only good in people and probably was a bit too trusting of the lovely woman he had originally married. I never ever heard him speak ill of her.

Our Tasmanian home, Chargot Barrington, and the farm ended abruptly with another deception, again from a Catholic Priest. I don't know how, but Mum became friendly with a Hungarian Priest called Father Tetany. This scoundrel saw in my mother an opportunity for easy monetary gain. He sang the appropriate tune and told my mum that he wanted to start a monastery and was looking for a suitable place. He spoke of the monastery being a place where the monks could be self-sufficient, grow their own food and live a holy life. Mum was delighted at the thought of our home being just that and talks about selling Chargot began.

Father Tetany would come to our house and discuss the details of the sale. Of course, we were not privy to those conversations so we would crouch outside the closed door and eavesdrop.

Soon a chorus would be heard in the room as we would shout in a loud voice, 'Bliss, stop spitting in Father Tetany's hat!' or 'I'm not spitting in Father Tetany's hat, you are.' This would be repeated as we accused one another of all manner of nasty things.

On another occasion, Father Tetany took off his fancy fur-lined boots and put on Dad's gumboots to walk around the farm, which was wet and muddy, leaving Dad to get his nice shoes filthy. We were horrified, so Tinker put a large dollop of marmalade in each of the fur-lined boots. The farm and everything on it were sold to Father Tetany. He never made it into a monastery. I'd love to know what actually became of that home of ours, but I have never found out. We were all now safely in boarding schools and only came home, to a different house, in the summer holidays.

I actually enjoyed the cleaning work, and it has been a very handy skill to have. Nowadays it seems most newly married young women haven't got a clue how to clean and tidy their homes. I found this out at my expense when Doug and I ran a large Christian ministry years later. I recruited the help of *Ministry Volunteers*, girls in their twenties to help me clean and maintain the rooms and help in the kitchen. One newcomer was given a bucket of potatoes to peel. She looked up at me and said, 'This is the first potato I have ever peeled.' *Holy cow*, I thought, *and you have come all the way from America to help me*. Many of them had little to no domestic skills.

Not only did I learn how to look after my own homes there, but we girls all had to attend a class called Domestic Science, where we learnt how to cook meals, how to set tables, sew garments, knit, do embroidery, darn a sock, and mend cloths and generally manage a household.

One of the daily jobs was to work in the steamy laundry where a big vat boiled sheets, pillowcases, and tea towels with Lux Soap Flakes. There we learnt how to iron two dozen shirts before the school bell went. But thank God for modern washing machines and advanced laundry detergents. No more need for boilers and such. I also enjoyed working with the nuns in the big boarding school kitchens. We never did any of the cooking there, only endless washing up and preparing vegetables.

That school was so cold in the winter months. The puddles outside would have ice on them all day. The classrooms were poorly heated, often by one small radiator up front and I suffered terribly from chilblains. My poor little feet and hands would have great cracks over the knuckles. At one stage if I bent my fingers, the bone could be seen at the knuckle. No one treated the wounds or helped me. But working in the laundry and kitchen provided some time to thaw out a bit.

Overall, I was desperately lonely, lost, and frightened and felt rejected and unwanted by my parents and even by my sister, Bliss, who was at that school with me.

During one of my school holidays at home I acquired a baby rabbit as a pet. I was told to let it go when the holidays finished and school started again, but I somehow smuggled that bunny back to St Mary's College. I kept him locked up in my locker, but it was soon discovered by the girl who had the locker below mine. A nasty smelling liquid had soaked through onto her schoolbooks. My bunny was taken from me and, ever after, when the boarders had curried rabbit for a meal, they always insisted that it was my poor bunny.

We only came home for the long summertime Christmas holidays. We were told we lived too far away to be coming home for the shorter holidays. The May holidays and Easter holidays we were sent to stay in another boarder's home as guests. One of the places I was sent to was in Ouse in the Central Highlands on a sheep farm, with my classmate Petita Rice and her family. But it was horribly ill-timed. Petita had a younger brother called Justin who had very recently died a tragic death by falling off the horse he was riding. His foot had caught in the stirrup, and he was dragged home at a gallop. He was dead on arrival. Justin had only recently been buried and the family was still in deep mourning over the loss of their only male child. I felt so uncomfortable being there.

Oh dear, now I'm getting to an emotional stage that I often arrive at when thinking about that period of my life. I'm going to view myself as if I am detached from being Meredith, and just an onlooker. I feel so sorry for that little girl, but somehow it doesn't feel like me. I'm sure psychiatrists would have a name for such thoughts.

Bear with me, because I'm going to speak of myself in the third person for a while, because that sad little girl wasn't really me. I felt I just lived her life for her by enduring her rejection and humiliation for her. During this time, I chose what was known as elective autism or elective mutism as a defence. Let me explain. I would dive into myself and be in a field of soft daisy-covered grasses, surrounded by little animals, rabbits, guinea pigs, lambs, and birds. I would talk with them, eat with them, and even sleep with them. That horrid cold school wasn't even remembered. Yes, to the outsider I must have seemed very weird; it's no wonder they shunned me. I would be found wandering the playing fields instead of going into class when the bell rang. The nuns would hit me on the backs of my legs with a strip of rubber linoleum. I never flinched or cried. I'd think to myself, *the worst they can do to me is kill me and that would be a relief.*

Today, I have a different attitude towards hardship. God wants us to benefit from hard times. If you deal with hard times God's way and cast all cares and anguish on Him by saying, 'Lord I can't handle this. You, please take it and deal with it Yourself.' Then Satan can't destroy you. I was a slow learner, and no one ever taught me to do this. If I had been taught, I wouldn't have been so unhappy and on the defensive for forty years of my life. God will use even the hard times that Satan puts us through to strengthen us, teach us, and to bring us to Himself. It doesn't make the hardship any better, pain is still pain. But at least you know there is light at the end of the tunnel.

However, I'll now tell you more of what that silent little girl lived through. She was a social outcast. A nervous habit of hers was to pull threads out of the sleeves of her school jumper. Her face was covered with freckles and in the summer would be burnt, peeling, and often bleeding. Her breath smelt because of poor dental hygiene due to underlying gingivitis and bleeding gums which was never treated. But worse than everything was that she had a condition that first manifested itself at that school, now known as angioedema – swelling of the mucus membrane surfaces usually of the mouth or tongue. This happened at random for no particular reason. I still suffer from it today, and no one knows what causes it.

On a long weekend holiday, the nuns would try to clear the boarding house of students, so we were often sent to stay with one of the day girls. One particular morning Meredith's tongue started to swell. It got so big that she couldn't even shut her mouth. Horribly embarrassed, she held a dirty saliva-soaked handkerchief over her face. Regardless of her condition, the nuns sent her off to her allotted family to stay for three nights. Feeling like a leper, she sat most of the time on the back veranda not able to eat or speak.

The swelling eventually went down, but the memory never fades. The feeling of being repulsive to strangers and trying to not be seen still haunts. The little girl's sister was also there but she shunned her. She was an embracement to her, for Bliss was one of the popular girls who played tennis and basketball. Meredith soon learnt not to take her troubles to her.

However, there are now drugs that arrest the swelling of angioedema quite quickly. The danger is if the oesophagus swells it can and does kill by suffocation. It's amazing that this never happened to me. I now carry an EpiPen whenever I go on a trip.

On the weekends, the prefects, about five of them, would stand in front of the other boarders and one by one would choose a girl from the group, and that girl would then go and stand with the prefect who had chosen her. Each prefect would end up with about twenty girls who would be in their charge and taken on outings often to Mount Wellington lookout, to the beach in Sandy Bay, to the Queens Domain (a large parkland on the outskirts of Hobart) or even on a bus trip to Port Arthur, which was an old convict settlement. One poor little soul called Meredith, would invariably end up a conspicuous shame-faced person, the last to be chosen, and chosen only because the prefect whose turn it was to choose a girl had no option but to call her name.

One's memory is an amazing thing. I think it must have automatic defence mechanisms that block out the most traumatic experiences, but I do remember a time that Africa came back to haunt me. I was put into the infirmary, running high temperatures and sweating profusely. A doctor was called and could find no cause. Even penicillin injections didn't help. So, as a last resort, they called my mother who I believe was living in a house in Trevallyn, Launceston. She knew what was causing the symptoms and drove the four-hour drive to Hobart. She elbowed all the nuns and doctors out of the way and jabbed a quinine injection into my bottom. I was well again very soon. Mum knew that malaria could take hold years after leaving a malaria-infected country.

I survived those years and emerged comparatively sane. I expect so because I could elect, at will, to mentally not be there. It was the last of the schools I attended. I left there suddenly at the age of sixteen. I still have the reference that the nun who was teaching me in third year secondary school wrote. She was totally unable to give me any recommendation, so simply wrote, 'Meredith is capable of doing anything she wants to do.' A very true statement indeed.

By this time my parents lived in Pedder Street in a house in New Town, a suburb of Hobart. Bliss had left school and was doing her second year at Calvary Hospital training to be a nurse. She would walk twenty minutes back and forth from that home to the hospital. A young red-headed boy used to wait in his front garden to see her pass by. He was infatuated by her beauty. Eventually he plucked up the courage to talk to her and a friendship grew. His name was David Pocock.

But Bliss was seeing a man called Gerald Breen and before long found herself pregnant with his child. Out-of-wedlock pregnancy was still very frowned upon, and Bliss was very troubled by this, yet Gerald had no intention of marrying her. Bliss poured her dilemma to David who immediately said, 'I'll marry you.' And that's exactly what he did. Bliss gave up her nursing career to mother that baby. I'm so glad she did, for this world wouldn't be the same without my niece, Mary-Anne, whom I love dearly.

Chapter 6

Nursing training days

My heart's desire was to be a nurse but my schooling days at St Mary's College had come to a premature end. I was two grades short of the required schooling to do nursing training and only sixteen years old, two years underage. The year was 1958.

Mum wanted to return to the Africa that she had loved in her youth. The only thing stopping her leaving was me. Stephen was working and studying public administration in Canberra. Bliss was living in Berridale as wife to David Pocock and mother to her new baby, Mary-Anne. As mentioned earlier, Tinker had been sent to our mother's sister, Ista, who had married Allen Stodart, an American man, and now lived with her three children in a very grand manor house called Cothelstone Manor in Taunton, Somerset, England. Poor Tinker, he hated it there and couldn't adapt to the British school or their lifestyle, which he thought was a bunged-on act of false politeness. Dad was not one to put up a fight, so he just stood back and let it all happen. He used to say it was out of his control. I was the only untied loose end as far as my mother was concerned.

Taking me with her to Calvary Hospital in Hobart, Mum, to my mortification, eventually went down on her knees in front of the matron – who was at the time Mother Isabel Guild – and implored her to take me off her hands.

'Meredith will work for you free of charge, just give her food and accommodation,' she said.

I owe my sanity and my life's security to that wonderful woman, Mother Isabel, who, against every written rule, took me under her wing. I was given a white nurse's uniform, cap and pale blue cape, and my own room in the newly built nurses' home.

Then, without any sort of farewell, my mother left one morning taking with her only a small carry-on bag and caught an Ansett plane out of Hobart, the first leg of her journey to join the staff at a Catholic Benedictine Mission Hospital in Songea and Mbinga, East Africa. Stephen found out about her quiet getaway plan and so rode his motorbike, with me on the back, out to the airport. It was a drive of about 30 miles on a cold November morning from our home in New Town. We arrived at the airport just in time to see her walking to the plane. She waved goodbye to us from the steep steps leading into the plane. Stephen took two photos of her as she left. I still have those photos.

But it was the last straw for me. From that moment on she had utterly betrayed my trust in her, and I cut her out of my life, and I never answered any of her few letters. She had broken my heart for the last time, and I deliberately put her out of my mind and forgot about her. Unforgiveness harms the unforgiving far more than the unforgiven. Both rejection and unforgiveness are deadly. I travelled a long way in my life carrying both deadly loads. So much so, that my life became a pretence of happiness. I was unable to love or to accept the love of others. No one was aware of this for I became a great pretender.

My condition was obvious to me however, for when I would open the door to a friend and they'd say, 'Hello, Merrie. How are you?', I would feel like crying for I knew I wasn't okay, and my heart was broken. But I'd smile, and greet them warmly and say, 'Come in, how nice to see you.'

But even that was a lie. It wasn't until I became a devoted Christian that I realised the seriousness of this rejection and unforgiveness. Unless I forgive, Jesus told me, then I could not be forgiven. So eventually, I told God that I forgive my mother for what she had done to me. But there was a problem that I couldn't resolve. I still carried resentment and bitterness towards her in my heart. I knew I hadn't really forgiven her, and I did not know how to rid myself of these corrosive emotions.

I worried, prayed, and stressed about this for a long time. Then a video I chanced to watch suggested that my mother was up against God's wrath for what she had done to me. I immediately was hit by a longing to plead with God on her behalf. So, I left the room, went down on my knees in my office, head on the floor, bum in the air, crying like a baby, and implored God, 'Please don't take it out on my mother for what she had done to me, let her go free.'

The heavy blanket of unforgiveness was lifted off my shoulders, the bitterness had gone. I no longer resented her, I had in fact forgiven her. No one had ever told me how to forgive. She, of course, would have to ask her forgiveness from God for herself. But I was set free from that deadly load of unforgiveness. And that was a gift from Him.

While I was no longer burdened by unforgiveness, the full healing of my broken heart came much later. Tom Jewett was a minister of an Anglican church who came to stay with us years later when we had moved to Ireland. Tom, who was accompanied by his wife, Anne, had taken on the task of teaching Christians all over the world about healing and wholeness, according to God's word. He led me through a prayer for the healing of my broken heart, using Jesus' statement from Isaiah 61, repeated in Luke's gospel.

Jesus said, 'I have come to mend the broken hearted, and set the captives free, to proclaim liberty for all those who mourn in Zion.' My heart was broken, and I was in gaol – a captive. I had put up the bars around myself. These bars were made of my refusal to love anyone or be loved by anyone – play acting, pretence, and low self-worth. If I did make a good friend or someone claimed to love me, I would always create a scenario that would drive that friend or lover away. This habit nearly cost me my husband-to-be.

Tom led me through repentance for putting up these barriers and for not casting my cares upon Him, for He cares for me (1 Peter 5:7). I was behaving in a base way, and not His way. Then Tom asked Jesus to reach into me and mend my broken heart. I then had to make Jesus the keeper of my heart and to guard my heart, for 'out of it comes the issues of life' (Proverbs 4:23). I promised Him that I would in future not try and handle emotional pain myself but would give it to Him to handle for me. Another gift had been given to me. The pretence of loving people was gone, I felt a genuine love for others and joy in being loved; I was set free and no longer was in mourning over my abusive childhood.

······································

My mother lived in Africa for nine years until 1967 when she had a fall and broke her leg, ending up in the Muhimbili Hospital in Dar es Salam. I was living in London at the time and was about to be married in a month's time, on the 20th of February.

During my time in London, I had worked in the private wing of St Thomas' Hospital and had nursed a British lady who, on hearing I was born in Tanganyika, gave me the address of a family member who lived in Dar es Salam. I contacted them and told them my intention of coming to my mother's rescue and taking her back to London with me. They offered me accommodation with them in their home. So, taking a few days off, I flew to Tanzania. It was a wonderful time with happy memories of my early childhood bubbling up.

While staying with them, one very hot night, they took me to the beach. We walked along in the shallows. The temptation to really cool off and swim was too great and having no bathers with us didn't stop us. We all stripped our clothes off, buried them in the sand lest they get stolen and raced naked into the sea. We swam and splashed around for quite some time under the cover of darkness. Panic hit us when we eventually came out and couldn't find our buried clothes! There was a lot of nervous laughter at the thought of getting back to their house naked. Eventually we did find them, and quickly put them on with a sigh of relief.

Love of one's parents usually overrides even the greatest abuse inflicted on a child when a parent is in trouble. I arranged wheelchair assistance for Mum and flew her back with me to London, putting her into St Thomas' Hospital. When she was discharged from there she came to live with Doug (my about-to-be husband) and me, in a flat we had rented on Oakhampton Road. A month later she attended our wedding in Westminster Cathedral. However, none of the wedding photos depict her being there.

She lived with Douglas and me till we had to board ship, the MV Aurelia, to Tasmania later in March at which point she went to Germany to stay with Stephen in Hamburg, where he was working as a diplomat with the Australian Embassy. From there she returned to Australia and went to live with Bliss in a caravan at the end of her garden in Berridale, Hobart.

Stephen eventually bought her a small house in the farming district of Oatlands, Tasmania. There she lived till Bliss moved to Melbourne and took her to live with her in a granny flat built and paid for by the government. She died there in 1989, a frightened old lady still unsure that she had ever done enough to win God's favour or acceptance.

That sums up very briefly the path she took after handing her sixteen-year-old daughter over to the care of Mother Isabel Guild in Calvary Hospital, Lenah Valley, Hobart. Thus, freeing herself of all her God-given responsibilities of the four children lent to her by God.

....

But back to that sixteen-year-old girl.

In January 1958 I joined the nursing staff at Calvary Hospital under the supervision of the Blue Nuns, The Little Company of Mary, who ran that hospital. I was permitted to sit in on the lectures with the new preliminary class. At the end of the year the big question was, 'What shall we do with Meredith?' I was still underage and under-schooled and should not have even been there. The decision was made to let me sit the exams.

'Let's just see how she does,' they said. Well, I did very well and passed with high marks. So, I moved onto my second year and then third year of training to be a nurse. Nursing was only a three-year course then. Usually one graduates, registers and can then carry the title of *Nursing Sister* and are employed as such. But, as I mentioned, I was still underage to register even after the three years of studying. So, I did another year and trained as a midwife. Then another year in the surgical theatre. Finally, I was twenty and could register and move on. I was a fully qualified nurse and midwife at last. It was November 1963.

I loved the practical work, but I found the theoretical subjects very challenging. I am a slow reader, and spelling posed a particular problem for me. My handwriting has always been very neat, tidy, and even artistic, but if I was not careful, I could start at the wrong side of the page and write the entire piece backwards! It was perfectly legible to me. But others had to hold it up to a mirror to read it. I had, and still have, what is now known as dyslexia. This had a terrible effect on my spelling but thank heavens for modern spell checkers.

Sister Edward was our teacher and tutor. I owe her a sincere debt of gratitude because she believed in me. She was afraid that I would fail my final exams on account of my bad spelling. But she knew that I knew the subjects better than most of the other nurses, so she arranged for me to do oral exams. Orally, I could answer all the questions and in considerable detail. But pharmacology was my weak point. All those long Latin names for drugs. Thankfully, I didn't have to spell the drug names, so I passed those exams too.

There wasn't really much interaction with the doctors. Because it was a private hospital, each patient had their own doctor visiting them once a day. The nuns would accompany the doctors to the bedside, but not the trainees. It was only when working alongside the doctors in the operating theatre that you would get to know them at all. There were no intern doctors – they would have been less formidable. We were always a little in awe of the nuns and the doctors, so we were incredibly polite and respectful. It wasn't until years later that I had the confidence and experience to scold the doctors and make them re-write what they had written as orders in the patient's notes. Why do nearly all doctors have such terrible handwriting?

The Little Blue Nuns, as they were affectionately called, were formally known as The Little Sisters of Mary. A finer bunch of dedicated women I have never met. The hospital was purely a training hospital run entirely by the Blue Nuns. The trainee nurses were constantly under their supervision, and we helped on the wards, theatres, maternity wards, and the nursery – always learning as we worked. Once you had completed your training you left. Those nuns loved me and taught me so much more than just nursing skills. Sister Edward, as mentioned above, was our tutor, and Sister Gerard was in the theatre, Sister Loretto in the nursery, and of course Sister Eugene with a stern face and a heart of gold. She was a perfectionist, and we nurses had to be perfect too. That was on second north wing, where the elite patients had their own rooms.

The girls I trained with I still remember very fondly. There was Gloria Castels, Margaret Watson, Gabrielle Williams, Brigitta Tubel (she was Hungarian and, as it happened, the niece of Father Tetany who robbed us of our farm home in Barrington). Then, there was Anne Sire, who had a car, Bernice Moore, Jennifer Healy, Kay McSherry, and a little girl from Fiji called Kasturi Bai-Reddy.

Kasturi was a bundle of fun but I'm not sure if she ever finished her training. She and I were great friends. Once a week we were all permitted to have one late pass which meant we could stay out till midnight. One night, Kasturi and I had been to a fair on the Domain, but we returned well after midnight, both giggling with nervousness that goes with the thrill of breaking the rules. To our delight we found a window open on the basement level, so we squeezed through it and navigated our way along the dark corridor to my bedroom. Only once safely inside did we dare to turn on a light. There, sitting on the end of my bed waiting for us, was Sister Edward! Kasturi let out a rapid stream of every swear word that we had gleefully taught her.

'Shit! Bum! Bugger! Blast! Bloody oath! No joke. Have a Snowball.' And she held out a crumpled bag to sister Edward with the remains of marshmallow 'snowballs' inside. Sister Edward could not refrain from laughing so was unable to scold us too much and she graciously took a snowball from the bag.

It was the era of rock and roll and crinoline, full-flared skirts held out by layer upon layer of starched frilly lace petticoats, a body-hugging top, and a wide belt pulled tightly in to exaggerate our slim waistlines and hips. We listened to The Big Bopper, Buddy Holly, and Ritchie Valens. Other nurses and I would go to the Belvedere dance hall most Saturday nights, when we weren't on duty. Buddy Holly would be singing, 'Oh Boy. All my love, all my kissin', you don't know what you've been missing, oh boy.' That song and *Peggy Sue* were among my favourites.

Suddenly, I was popular and no longer the social outcast that I had been at St Mary's College. I had my own money. It wasn't much, but it seemed like pennies from heaven to me. I was able to buy myself pretty clothes. Mostly I put purchased articles on layby, paying what I could afford each week till it was mine. I also bought material and made myself clothes on my mother's old treadle Singer sewing machine. It's amazing how educational it was for me to be amongst girls who knew how to put curlers in my hair and could advise me on how to look attractive, yet modest. Stockings with seams down the back and suspender belts were all new to me.

Modesty was important in those days. We had to wear a girdle under our nursing uniforms, so our bottoms wouldn't be seen to wiggle. The nuns would often squeeze us from behind to see if we had them on. Stockings held up by the tight-fitting girdle were the worst thing for me for I was well padded on my hips, and upper legs. Wearing a girdle and stockings that ended halfway up my thighs caused a bulge that would get sweaty and rub red-raw while walking fast up and down the corridors of the wards. It was extremely painful. Thank God for the introduction of the pantyhose years later.

I loved dancing and after lots of practise at the Belvedere on Wednesdays – the night for ballroom dancing – and the progressive barn dance and rock and roll on Saturday nights, I became very good at it. So good in fact that the boys who were skilled dancers chose me as their partner. Often, we would captivate everybody's attention. The floor would be vacated as my dance partner and I would twirl and swirl to the rock and roll music, my long hair tied with a big bow in a high ponytail. A flash of bright pink petticoats and legs as he would throw me over his shoulder and retrieve me and swirl me once again round and round. How I wish I had video or even photos of those occasions. It was the nearest I ever got to being a performing artist. However, my dancing ended when I married a man who disliked dancing and couldn't himself dance. But he did take me up in an aerobatic aeroplane and did a barrel roll or two and took me for two rides in the Concord from London to New York. I bet none of those pretty dancing boys could have done that with me.

Another thing I have always excelled at was art. I could draw and paint well and spent many leisure hours doing this. During the festive Christmas season, I was given a whole week off on full wages to decorate the hospital windows with angels, nativity scenes, holly, bells and such. The top floor of the hospital was the maternity ward and was glassed in at the top of the stairs. On this large glass partition, I would create my masterpiece. A full nativity scene, complete with angels blowing trumpets. Below is one of my pieces.

The ugly, shunned duckling had turned into a beautiful swan. The transition happened in that nursing home amidst lotions and potions, diets, curling wands, exercise, eyelash curlers and mascara, money to spend but most of all was the return of my self-confidence. But the old demon from my days at St Mary's was still there and used every opportunity to tell me I was unlovable. So, I practised the same deceit that I had mastered at school. I sought the praise of the nuns by a pretence of holiness. Probably because I was missing the affection and encouragement of my parents, so I pursued it elsewhere. I also proudly wore a badge of total abstinence from alcohol. That was again to show the nuns what a good little girl I was. But in hindsight it probably was a blessing.

When the other girls weren't on duty and were sleeping in, I got up and went to the 6.00 am Mass in the small nun's chapel. Often, I was the only nurse there; that made me feel especially good. But how I later hated myself for my hypocrisy.

··

The devil's plan, as always, is to destroy what God loves the most: His children. So, he was out to destroy me. This is how he executed that plan. It was at the height of my acceptance into the social circle that he set his first tempting trap. I was admired by the nuns, the girls liked me, and the boys looked on me as a kind of trophy if they could take me to the cinema and get a kiss goodnight when they escorted me back to the nursing home at midnight. The European boys were always my choice in men, new immigrants from Germany, Holland, Austria, and England. They had more refinement than the ocker Australian men. I avoided the Italian men – they had a blatantly one-track mind.

I resisted mens' sexual advances and felt a measure of power because of their desire for me and my ability to deny them. I, however, underestimated my own willpower and ability to resist the powerful urge of my own youthful libido.

There were two handsome young German brothers, Gunta and Rudi, that my friend Gloria and I met at the Belvedere one night. They had pooled their resources and bought a small block of land in Springfield, a new developing suburb of Hobart. Gloria and I would often catch a bus and go and see them in their temporary shack they had erected on their plot. Rudi would woo and charm me as he gently explored my secret parts. He was my first sexual encounter. It was intoxicating, so personal, intimate, and pleasurable. I had let down all my drawbridges and let him in. Believing that *this was love*.

The keeping of my newfound pleasure as a secret was also strangely pleasing to me. I doubled my religious activities, while smiling and thinking, *if they only knew what I had been up to*. However, the smile vanished when my period was late, and became even later – I realised I was pregnant.

This would mean I'd have to abandon my nursing career under a banner of disapproval and shame. My nursing qualifications were my ticket to freedom. Freedom from being dependent on others. Freedom from my parents. How could I let the nuns know I was so two-faced, pretending to be so holy while blatantly committing mortal sin? If my mother found out she would only have gloated over my misfortune and tell me, 'It serves you right for not being a good little Catholic girl.'

Rudi offered me a way out. He found an abortionist in a suburb of Melbourne who charged £60. Rudi paid for my airfare and put the £60 in my hand. No other soul knew what I was going through, even though I was on night duty and spent half the night vomiting all through my shift. They never suspected a thing.

I planned my flight to coincide with an early off, late duty time slot. It was the first time I had ever flown in an aeroplane. I was nineteen years old. The doctor's surgery was small. Two nurses greeted me warmly. I felt numb, knowing I was doing something terribly wrong, but thinking I had no other way out. The doctor hesitated when he learnt that my baby was five months gestated and tried to talk me out of my decision. But I pleaded with him, and he went through with the procedure under general anaesthetic.

When I awoke, I saw hostile disgusted looks on both the nurses' faces as they hurriedly dressed me and took my money. The smiles were gone. Even the doctor was dismissive and eager to get rid of me. I felt shame like I had never felt before. I promised God that *if I ever saw a baby on a doorstep, I'd take it in as my own*.

Back at the hotel that night I looked at myself naked in front of a full-length mirror. I'd never seen my full body naked before. I was amazed at the beauty of it. So pale-skinned, unblemished, and full. Not at all like the tanned beauties I had envied at the beach. For the first time I was able to accept and even like my pale complexion. My tummy was flat now. It was a strange emotion. I felt so relieved, almost happy. So why was I crying? I cried myself to sleep and caught the plane back to Hobart the next morning. I reported on duty at 3.00 pm and worked through till 11.00 pm. No one knew I had even been away.

I had done what my sister Bliss had refused to do and for this I admire her.

That deed done in secret has haunted me through my life. It wasn't until in 1983, when I was able to know Jesus and accept His total forgiveness, that I got peace from it. That peace did however come with divine intervention, for although I was ready to accept His forgiveness, I could not forgive myself.

I had a dream. I was standing accused of murder in front of a judge and jury in a court room. It was a straightforward case, I was tried and found guilty of first-degree murder. I knew their judgement was correct. Two policemen came and put handcuffs on me and led me off to be hung by the neck till I was dead. An ordinary looking man stepped in front of them as they were leading me out. Holding his wrists together in front of him, he said, 'Stop. Take the cuffs off her, put them on me, and let her go free. I will take her punishment for her.'

They removed my hand cuffs and clasped them on his outstretched wrists, and led him away, like a lamb about to be slaughtered for the crime I had committed. He never said a word, but I was free. Free indeed. I cried, I laughed, I fell at that man's feet, saying, 'Thank you, thank you' over and over again. It wasn't until I woke that I realised it had been Jesus Himself. And I was now able to forgive myself.

Chapter 7

Freedom, here I come

Graduation day came. It was officiated by a cardinal of the Catholic Church, the Right Reverend Monsignor Cullen in July 1963. The room was crowded with parents and relatives of the graduating nurses and the nuns who taught us. No one from my family attended. We were now in a nursing sisters' uniform with a highly starched veil perched on top of our heads as we recited our nursing pledge and were ceremoniously given our nursing certificates and state registered badges. It was the crowning climax of five incredible years of my life. I clutched my certificate closely with a measure of pride and guilt for it had been achieved at terrible expense. But I refused to think about that.

Then on a warm bright sunny morning in November 1963, I boarded a ship, the MV FairSea, bound for Southampton, England. It was to be a journey of six weeks for our first port of call was Auckland, New Zealand, then on to England. The ticket was a one-way ticket given to me by my father. Streamers of many colours connected the passengers with their loved ones below on the dock. I held a streamer with my father. I can't remember if any other members of my family were there on that exciting day. I think not.

The ship pulled away and my streamer broke, disconnecting me from my father and my life in Tasmania. All the passengers slowly walked to their cabins or to the ship's lounges, each with their thoughts, sorrows, or joys. For some a return home, for others a starting of a new adventure or chapter in their lives. For me it was freedom, mixed with fear of the unknown. I looked at my worldly possessions, a small suitcase with only a few clothes, a leather writing case with pen, paper and envelopes and a note from Stephen inside saying, 'Don't forget to write to me often.' And of course, my nursing certificates and references from the nuns of Calvary Hospital. My handbag contained my British and Australian passports and £100.

Life on board ship soon became familiar to me and I enjoyed every moment of it. Well, perhaps with the exception of one bad evening. I threw away two things on that trip. I threw away my Catholic religion with all its pretence and never went to Mass ever again. What a relief. I also threw my badge of total abstinence overboard into the Indian Ocean. My first introduction to alcohol was nearly a disaster for me. Never ever having had alcohol before in my life, I was unaware of its ways.

I was given vodka and orange. *Tastes quite nice*, I thought. A Dutch man called Jim Whybema bought me those drinks. Needless to say, I became completely intoxicated and somehow ended up in his cabin where he looked after me all night. I vomited all over his bed and disgraced myself in other ways too. Jim cleaned me up and saw to it that I didn't die of inhaled vomit. That was a lesson very well learned. I never ever wanted to repeat it. And had a healthy regard for alcohol ever after.

The ship called into Aden and Cairo in the Suez Canal. We were able to spend a few days in these ports. I saw and climbed and went inside the great pyramid and even rode on a camel. A man offered to buy me for fifteen camels, quite a high price. Thankfully my escort refused to part with me.

In mid-December we finally arrived in Southampton. Uncle Jack and Aunty Valmai, my father's sister, met me off the ship. As we drove the long distance back to their home in Malvern, Worcestershire, through many towns and villages, I noticed the mothers wheeling big English prams and fell in love with them. I made a promise to myself that I wouldn't leave England without one of those prams, married or not. I kept my promise to myself and after our wedding Doug and I went and purchased one at Harrods. They carefully crated it and put it on the ship we were to sail back to Australia on in 1967. All my children were reared in that pram, and I still have it, now fully restored to mint condition twenty years later by a pram restorer in Lincolnshire, England, rebuilt and immaculate.

I stayed with Aunty Valmai and Uncle Jack and their tall handsome son Jonathan in their beautiful English Tudor-style cottage in Cradley. Jonathan was 6-foot and 3-inches tall. Most of my relatives are very tall. I think I'm about the shortest one in that family line being only 5-foot 4-inches tall. He was so handsome and debonair. I remember that he used his eyebrows a lot to express himself which was very endearing. I used to call him Daddy Long legs and he affectionately called me Cuddles. It was a strange sight when he was at the wheel of his Morris Mini Cooper S, for he sat in the back seat having removed the front seat and extended the steering wheel column. It looked as though there was no driver. His legs were far too long to sit in the front.

Each year Jonathan put together a group of people to go skiing in Switzerland. I was invited to come along and eagerly agreed. Zermatt, nestling in the foothills of the Matterhorn, was like fairyland to me. Snow-covered, with fat ponies brightly clad pulling open sleighs which tinkled as they went along. I never mastered the art of skiing – I tried but ended up a mass of bruises from falling over constantly.

Back in England with my aunt and uncle again, I was taken around with Jonathan who would proudly show me off to his circle of friends. Tim Cash was his friend and accompanied us most places. Tim fancied himself as a car racer. Sadly, his life ended rather abruptly when he crashed on the circuit.

The weeks rolled on and the warmer weather had arrived at last. Valmai's garden was magnificent. I had no idea that all that beauty was hidden under the drabness of that winter covering. Eventually, I began feeling very strongly that I was overstaying my welcome and Aunty Valmai eventually called me to task about it, suggesting I look for a job. All alone, I set off to London by train. I had been told that there were lots of youth hostels in Tottenham Court Road. So, when I got off the train in Paddington Station, I looked for and found that road. I walked and walked searching both sides of the road for a youth hostel. I must have walked for miles. *This street must have an end somewhere,* I thought. But the road seemed to be never ending.

I knew no one. All the passers-by kept their eyes to themselves. I was gripped with shyness and terror and a feeling of being utterly lost and alone. With little or no forethought, I eventually entered a bank. Just to feel the four walls around me and not an endless road was a comfort. Not knowing what to do next I went up to a teller who stood in his booth behind glass. He looked up at me and smiled and said in an impeccable English accent, 'Yes, madam, can I help you?' I was unable to speak and simply burst into tears. He left his booth and escorted me to a quiet room. He sat me down and bought me a cup of tea and a plate of Marie biscuits.

When I was eventually able to control my sobs, I told him, 'I'm lost, I don't know where I am or where to go.' It was probably nearing the end of his working day. He took me to his place where I slept the night on his sitting room carpet. The next day he took me to a youth hostel on Tottenham Court Road. I don't know his name. But if you happen to be reading this and remember that when you were a young man working in a bank on Tottenham Court Road and a pretty little Australian girl burst into tears in front of your booth, I just want to thank you.

Chapter 8

The shark and the flying fish

The next day I was to have an interview at St. Thomas' Hospital in London. So, having had some sleep, I established myself at the hostel that the gentleman showed me to and pulled myself together. I then made my way across the biggest and busiest city I had ever been in, to the biggest hospital I had ever seen.

St Thomas's Hospital has existed as early as the year 1215 when it was named after St Thomas Becket. During the Reformation, the hospital was closed and then reopened and dedicated to the Apostle Thomas. The hospital has moved and changed several times throughout its history, but the present-day building is directly across the River Thames from the Palace of Westminster, that is, the Houses of Parliament and Big Ben. It is one of the first hospitals to be laid out according to Florence Nightingale's pavilion principle with six separate ward buildings at right angles to the river frontage linked by low corridors.

The chimes of Big Ben can be heard even in the hospital wards so there was never any excuse for being late for duty. The main corridor of the hospital on the ground floor was considered to be a mile long and I can well believe it. The entire length of the floor was covered in 24-foot strips of different floor coverings. Along the wall beside each strip was a plaque with a date and the name of the flooring material written on it. I was told it was done for the magazine *Which* where they tested different products and reported on its durability. That corridor was certainly a good testing ground. It had a lot of human traffic on it. Some even resorted to traveling on little motorised scooters. From Westminster Bridge, the hospital looked very impressive, with an ornate style of architecture – although I believe it looks very different today, having been modernised and enlarged.

Matron Isabel Turner was waiting for me in her office when I arrived. Strangely enough she had been the matron when my mother had done her training there many years before and she remembered her well. It surprised me how readily she accepted my application; she hardly glanced at my references or certificates. I learnt later that Australian trained nurses were very well thought of and sought after. The job was mine, but I wouldn't be required to start work there for another month, and was told to report back to the hospital at a certain date and time to be fitted out with a uniform, cape, and cap. I was then given a brief tour and shown my sleeping quarters-to-be.

ST. THOMAS' HOSPITAL.

Here is a poem by E.V. Rieu called *The Flattered Flying Fish* for you to ponder while I relate my next (mis)adventure.

> 'Said the shark to the flying fish over the phone,
> "Will you join me tonight? I'm dining alone.
>
> Let me order a nice little dinner for two and come as you are in your shimmering blue."
>
> Said the flying fish, "Fancy remembering me and the dress that I wore at the porpoise's tea."
>
> "How could I forget," said the shark in his guile.
> "I'll expect you at eight," and rang off with a smile.
>
> She has powdered her nose and has put on her things.
>
> She is off with one flap of her luminous wings.
>
> Ah little one, light-hearted and vain,
>
> The moon will not shine on your beauty again.'

· ·

Perhaps it wasn't the wisest thing to do, but after interviewing at St Thomas', I returned to my Aunty Valmai's home in Cradley. It wasn't long before suggestions were made that I go and do some sight-seeing.

'After all, you have come all this way, so you don't want to be sitting around here with us all the time,' they said.

With a pretence of being so brave and worldly – which I wasn't at all, how could I be? I was only twenty and knew nothing of the big bad world – I told them I would go to Paris. That show of false confidence nearly cost me my life and taught me another very valuable lesson.

Everybody told me I didn't need to speak French as everyone in Paris speaks English. Wrong! I found myself badly handicapped, and unable to communicate. Somehow, I eventually found my way from the cheap hotel I was staying to the Eiffel Tower. I stood marvelling at the panoramic view with my very long blond hair being swept off my face by a pleasant breeze. I had on the fashion of those days, a full-flared skirt, a body-hugging pink jersey tucked into my skirt and a wide black shiny belt pulled in tightly around my slim waist.

A man in his mid-thirties approached me and addressed me in English. It was so nice to chat with someone, after not being able to for so long. He introduced himself to me as Peter Mindon from Chile. He was nice; he bought me a coffee and seemed very friendly. In the days that followed, he escorted me all around Paris. We went to the Palace of Versailles, and Notre Dame, and had a cruise on the River Seine. He even took me to Le Moulin Rouge. He had moved into my hotel and had a separate room down the corridor. I was impressed that he never made any sexual advances towards me – so, he gained my complete confidence as a sort of kind friend.

I was very sad when he told me he had to go to Hamburg to see his uncle. I had another two weeks left in Paris. He suggested that I accompany him, reassuring me that I would be back in London in time to start my new job at St Thomas' Hospital. I readily agreed.

The next day, sitting next to him waiting for the train to Hamburg to pull out of the station, a plain clothed policeman asked me to follow him. I was a bit alarmed, but Peter reassured me. The policeman took me into an office where he took down the information from my two passports, Australian and British, and let me go.

I wrote a letter to my brother, Stephen, while on the train. He was working with the Australian Embassy in Cologne at the time. I told him of my adventures, and all about this very nice man called Peter Mindon who was taking me to Hamburg. I was excited to be going to Germany for I was still mildly infatuated with my ex-boyfriend (who was German) that I had left behind in Hobart. I was also keen to practice the little bit of German that I had learned at a night school when I was with him.

The train came to a slow stop at the Hamburg train station. To my irritation, before I even stepped down from the train, I was taken by the arm by another plain clothed policeman to a small office, where once again my passports were examined and handed back to me. No explanation was made to me. On my way back to join Peter I saw a box with *post brief* written on it. I recognised this to be the German for letterbox. Much to Peter's alarm I dropped my letter to Stephen inside it – Peter had been telling me that he would post the letter for me.

Peter's uncle took me to a hotel called the Donna Torum, where I left my suitcase and went on a sight-seeing trip with Peter and his uncle. They showed me the fish market, and then to a big park called Planten un Blomen where a live orchestra was playing classical music. A big fountain sent jets of water high into the sky as if dancing to the music. Occasionally a duck would be jet propelled upwards with loud duck protests. I found that very amusing. I was shown around the red-light district of Hamburg with the pretty girls loitering around at every doorway.

The next day we were to cross the River Elbe to the free port. This meant passing by a passport check point area. I was in the back of the car. The policeman peered into the back of the car and said to Peter's uncle in German, 'Und das ist ein deutsches mädchen?'

The uncle said, 'Ja, ja.'

Whereby I piped up in protest and said in English, 'I'm not a German girl.'

I was told to get out of the car by the guard and was led into the booth. The traffic was banking up behind us. Again, I was irritated. All my credentials were examined and written down. Then we were allowed to leave. The men told me to wait in the car for them while they went on board a large freighter bound for Chile. Well, I waited three hours in that car for them to return. When they did eventually get into the car, their attitude towards me had changed. Ignoring me, they spoke fast and urgently to each other. By this time, it was already getting dark, so they took me to a nightclub to eat and watch the show.

The next thing I remember, I was naked on the floor in a room behind the main entertainment area. I was cold, terrified, and sore. I hurriedly got dressed. Thankfully, my money and return train ticket were still in my handbag. When the moment was right, clasping my shoes in my hands, I made a dash through the open door into the street.

I had noticed that the train station was on the river, so I ran barefoot all along the riverbank till I came to the station. I phoned Stephen and caught the next train to Cologne where my brother was waiting for me. Before Stephen took me to his house, he took me into a picture theatre that repeated the same film over and over again. There I saw what my eventual destination could have been.

The film depicted a pretty young tourist girl being charmed on top of the Eiffel Tower, taken to Hamburg and put on a Chilean ship, drugged on heroin and a false passport given to her. She was sold and ended her days as a prostitute owned by a pimp, never to be seen or heard of again. This was the way of the white slave traffickers. It was my story and very nearly my fate. Thank God for Interpol, the International Police, they saw me as a prime candidate and tracked my every move. I was obviously too much of a risk for those two men to go through with their plans.

Later, Stephen drove to Hamburg, and fetched my suitcase from the hotel they had put me in. Thank God I was able to make my return journey to London. But I was no longer the happy chirpy person who had left London thirty days ago. Now I was silently harbouring an abuse that left me fearful and apprehensive. I told no one about it. I now see God's saving hand in protecting a very naïve, trusting child of His, who had a long way to travel before I even recognised Him.

Chapter 9

Nursing days in London

For some reason I was allocated to work in the private wing of St Thomas' Hospital. The uniform was very attractive – I wore a pin-striped, blue dress with long sleeves where there were separate white cuffs with elastic at each end. These were to secure the rolled-up dress sleeves while working on the wards. The dress was covered by a white apron, with a wide buckled belt which held the apron on. The nurses who had trained there had a black belt with a silver St Thomas' Hospital insignia on the silver buckle. A neat white nurse's cap made the uniform complete and very attractive. The cap worn by the hospital trainees differed a little from the hired staff. They wore a white lace cap with a flared piece like a dove's tail behind. I was also given a navy-blue cape with a red lining and long red straps which were crossed over the chest and secured under the cape at the back. I still have one of those uniforms hanging in my wardrobe.

I proudly pinned my light-blue Calvary Hospital badge under the white starched collar and the Australian nurse's badge that had DC engraved after my name which was attached to my cape. DC stands for Double Certificate, indicating that I was also a midwife. With my hair in a neat bun at the nape of my neck, I looked very neat and professional.

I was given a room on the basement level of one of the nurses' quarters to sleep in. The only view I had was of people's feet going past on the footpath. But it was home and my little comfort zone for the next year. The incident I had escaped from in Europe weighed heavily on me. I couldn't free myself of the trauma. But, as usual, I kept it to myself and disguised it with a happy face and a dedication to my work on the wards. However, my emotional distress manifested itself in another way. I missed two periods and underwent a horrible time of worry and uncertainty. In those days there were no pregnancy tests that one could buy at a chemist.

Eventually, in the third month, my period came, and my greatest fear was gone. I wasn't pregnant from that abuse in Hamburg after all. But I had shed many private tears fretting about that possibility.

Many of the patients I nursed were foreigners, very rich people who valued the British medical and surgical expertise. Because we were in the private sector of the hospital, we had a mixture of surgical, medical, and psychiatric patients. They all had their own spacious room with a bathroom attached. There were only about eight rooms, if I can remember correctly. As a result, one got to know and interact with the patients a lot more. Most of the patients I remember only by their conditions, but a few I remember personally.

There was one lovely lady from Greece. She had a nasty misfortune at the hands of a surgeon who performed a hysterectomy on her and nicked her urethra. However, this wasn't noticed until her dressings and bedding became soaked in urine. This went on for some days with no improvement. Feeling for this poor woman, I modified a funnel, strapped it to her tummy and rigged up tubes so that the urine drained into a bottle instead of into her bed. Later, she had the kidney removed.

A lot of the patients were Arabic. The Arabic women were very fastidious and demanding. It could take your whole morning shift to give her a bed bath. It had to be done her way, like a ritual. Fortunately, the hospital made an allowance for these demands. For me it was time consuming and frustrating – I hope my attitude never showed. Then there was a long-term patient. He had crashed his race-car and was in a coma. The nurses tended to his every bodily need. I remember intensive daily care for him. He was a credit to the nursing staff who kept him clean shaven and in excellent condition, even his muscles and limbs were exercised. He was still in a coma when I left a year later.

In my first week on the wards of the private wing I met a Dutch nurse called Yohanna Kazer. I nicknamed her Yogi. We took an instant liking to each other. We became best friends for a long time. I made her a Yogi Bear out of felt material and presented it to her while we were on-duty one day. She loved that bear and kept it in the Sisters' Station to be admired by all. I have a photo of her with it on the desk while she was writing up the patient's report book.

During my time at St Thomas', I went to nearly all the London theatrical shows and many films. The hospital was given free double tickets to be given to the staff on request. This enabled you to invite a guest. It was much appreciated by the nurses' boyfriends. Yogi and I would each pick up tickets and invite two boys to accompany us. We had some wonderful times, the two of us together with whichever boys accompanied us. Often before the show we were taken to a restaurant, wined and dined and then after the show we would all roam the streets of London as we slowly wended our way back to the hospital on foot. We avoided inviting the same boy twice. That way we avoided getting romantically involved with any of them.

Yogi and I eventually moved into a one-bedroom flat in St George's Square in Pimlico, SW1. The flat was very central to many places of interest in London. It was within walking distance to St James' Park and Buckingham Palace, Westminster Cathedral, Horse Guards Parade, and even Trafalgar Square. One end of the square butted on to the Thames Embankment and Lambert Bridge. Dressed in our smart hospital uniforms, Yogi and I would walk to work along the embankment to St Thomas' Hospital, crossing the Thames on Westminster Bridge, which is near the Houses of Parliament and Westminster Abbey.

The square itself was spacious with trees and a garden which was enclosed with a decorative wrought-iron fence. All the houses on both sides had the same architectural feature of tall white columns forming the entrance, up a few steps on to a covered porch, leading to a large, heavy, carved wooden door, with a brass door knocker. Our flat was easy to find because, for some reason, it was the only one with black painted pillars instead of white. Our flat was on the ground floor. The large drawing room had a big oval table under the window that looked out onto the square. I used to love seeing the bluebells and daffodils which grew in profusion in early spring. There was one bedroom and a small kitchen at the back which we seldom ever cooked in. Attached to the kitchen was a very small room, where we put a small bed for any guests.

The flat was expensive so to make it affordable we took in two more flatmates. The four of us shared one bedroom. The four beds fitted neatly around the walls, leaving only the doorway and the centre free. Our clothes were kept in the large front sitting room's ornate lounge room dressers and sideboards. Our flatmates came and went. However, some of them had to be told to leave. This was usually an unpleasant job that Yogi made me do. We didn't tolerate smoking, sexual activities or uncleanliness in our flat – with four of us in a small bedroom that would be very unpleasant.

Later, Yogi and I left St Thomas' Hospital and joined the Finchley Private Nursing Agency. This meant that we would be sent to private homes all over London, and to many different hospitals who needed a nurse for a special patient or were short of staff. Private agency nurses were paid almost double the wages of a regular hospital nurse. Some of the private homes I was called to nurse in were amazing. One such house had a night watchman standing guard all night over a large painting, Thomas Gainsborough's *The Blue Boy*. I got to work in many of London's elite hospitals. These patients would have many expensive baskets of fruit, flowers or chocolates given to them, most of which was handed onto the nurse, so I was never short of fruit, flowers, and chocolates. In Guy's Hospital I nursed Leslie Grade, the owner of ITV, a British television network.

I preferred doing night duty. Often, I was given a bed to sleep in and was only required to answer the patient's bell at night and attend to their needs. When that was the case, I would also do a day job as well.

I worked in nursing homes, Paddington Eye Hospital, cancer clinics, and even spent some time in the casualty rooms at a Selfridges department store on Oxford Street. That was interesting. I worked with three other nurses there and mainly dealt with staff with period pains or other minor ailments like headaches, sore throats, panic attacks and even hiccups. The difficult ones were the shoppers who purposely injured themselves in the store with the idea of making money from their 'accident'. There was so much red tape, forms, and even calling up a doctor sometimes to verify the extent of the trauma, but I loved working at Selfridges. The wages were better than the hospitals and being in charge gave me an air of importance.

We could also dictate to the agency when we were available to work. Yogi and I would work solidly for weeks till we had saved up enough money to go to Europe. And we would only return when our money ran out. Our record was three months away on £50 each. We became experts at not spending money. Our luggage consisted of a backpack, in which we had a small child's tent, a canvas washing up dish, a saucepan and a small metho stove. And only one change of clothes. I had an Australian flag sewn onto my jeans and Yogi had a Union Jack on hers. Our mode of transport was the thumb, hitching a lift with the big semi-trailer trucks. We knew they were safer because they were delivering a load and couldn't go off the main roads. These men, usually two in each truck, were great fun and would buy us food at the truck stops, while singing and entertaining us with stories of their lives. Only occasionally did we get into a private car.

Yogi spoke fluent Dutch, German, Italian and some French, but we would never let the drivers know this. This meant that they thought they could speak to each other freely and think they were not being understood. If their intentions were to use us dishonourably, Yogi and I had agreed on a secret hand movement that indicated danger and the necessity for us to make an escape at the first opportunity. This we did on one occasion only.

We had hitched a ride with two Italian men, who spoke freely in Italian. Yogi started frantically making our secret hand signal as the men discussed their plan of action to sexually abuse us. When they stopped to get petrol for their car, we pretended we had to use the loo and we managed to squeeze ourselves through a small window in the back of the building and ran through a field and into the woods. Another safety precaution we had was a small aerosol tear gas spray that looked like a lipstick. Fortunately, we never had to use it.

We made several of these European adventures, and I think we visited most of the countries in Europe. We even caught a boat in Brindisi, Italy, to Greece. We slept under the stars on the Acropolis. In Greece we ran very short of money, so we sold our blood. Giving blood in Greece was not a free gift.

For a while, we stayed in absolute luxury with the lady I had nursed in St Thomas' Hospital, who I mentioned earlier. Her huge marble villa was in the countryside amidst olive groves, and vineyards. To me it was like paradise. We were treated like royalty there. Mrs A. held me in high regard for my care of her in London even though all I had done was to invent a crude way of keeping her and her bed dry after her operation. I would have loved to stay there longer but Yogi was determined to see all the ancient mythological places in Greece.

In Holland we stayed with Yogi's parents in The Hague. Their house was in a row of semi-detached houses each with a window looking out onto the street. A mirror set at an angle outside each window allowed the occupant to have a view of anyone walking along the pavement. Her parents were big, warm, and friendly. Each meal was set on a table clad with a blanket under the tablecloth. The food was often cold sliced meats, yoghurt in large amounts and a variety of cheeses, breads, and cakes. Being in Holland I just had to hire bikes – much to Yogi's disgust – and join the hundreds of other bikers on the designated bicycle paths. We peddled those bikes all over The Hague and even went to Madurodam – a miniature city made in minute detail by amazing craftsmen. We visited the tulip farms in flower and saw windmills and canals and the dykes that claimed extra land from the sea.

On our last day in Holland, we went to a fishing port of Scheveningen. We had been told that we could get a lift in a herring transporting truck bound for Hamburg, Germany. My brother, Stephen, was still working for the Australian Embassy there. It wasn't hard to find such a lift. The two Dutch drivers were great fun and looked after us well but, my goodness, the smell of herrings was so strong. Our clothes and hair stunk of herrings for weeks. I taught Yogi to sing the Australian song *Waltzing Matilda*. The truck drivers thought it was hilarious and made us sing it over and over again.

My brother Stephen and his Swiss wife, Ursula, with their baby, Michael, welcomed us into their home. Yogi had to return to England, but I spent several extra weeks with my brother before following her.

Chapter 10

Enter Douglas

Yogi had a fascination for the British aristocracy and would take on their mannerisms and way of speech so much so that she often fooled many people. She had completely discarded any trace of a Dutch accent. When I arranged a trip to Chargot in Somerset to visit my mother's brother, Colonel Sir Edward St Lo Malet, 8th Baronet, my Uncle Daily and his wife, Lady Malet, or Aunt Iki, Yogi asked if she could come with me. Uncle Daily was so nicknamed because as a child he always looked forward to The Daily Mail newspaper with his favourite cartoon character, Teddy Tail of the Daily Mail. We caught a train to Taunton where my cousin, Harry Malet, known as Hazi, met us. It was spring of 1964.

Hazi had brought along with him a young lad by the name of Douglas Gresham, who was getting some practical farming experience on their sheep and cattle farm, prior to going to study at Harper Adams Agricultural College in Shropshire. This young lad took one long look at me as I stepped down off the train along with the other passengers who were alighting and turned to Hazi and said, 'Hazi, do you see that girl over there?'

'Which one?' said Hazi, to which Doug replied, 'The blonde girl with the ponytail.'

'Yes, what about her?'

'That's the girl I'm going to marry!' said Douglas determinedly.

Hazi looked at him and said, 'Don't be daft, that's my cousin.'

He had told Douglas a few days earlier that his cousin, who was coming to visit, was the biggest flirt. Well, I never thought Hazi would say that about me. He certainly seemed to enjoy my company. But, yes, I expect I was a bit of a flirt. It was my way of interacting with people. I certainly was very under-schooled and underread and knew nothing of politics or world affairs. I cultivated charm and sweetness as my way to be accepted.

But this young man, Douglas, was in earnest. Even at the tender age of eighteen he knew what he wanted. Apparently, he always had a mental image of the girl he was to marry. When he was a child, the girl was the same age as himself. As he grew older, the girl also grew older. But she was always the same girl. And, that day, his vision of his bride-to-be stepped off that train. To tell you the truth, I hardly noticed him. I was aware that he was very young, slight in stature and scruffy. He had on a shapeless floppy jumper that was way too big for him and rather comical. When he would sit down, he sat in it, then it would stick out at the back when he stood up.

Chargot House itself was large, set apart, and nestled amongst the tree-clad rolling hills of Somerset. The fields were surrounded by ancient cut and layered hawthorn hedges, providing shelter for the sheep from the icy winds of winter and to keep the livestock in. The network of little lanes were all edged with these hedges as well, and were so narrow that two cars often couldn't pass each other. But there was always a handy gateway or clearing to back into. Rhododendron bushes were a big feature of the area, and if you were blessed and came to Chargot when they were in bloom, it was breathtakingly beautiful with hues of pinks and purples giving the place the look of a fairyland. I think they must have been self-seeded, for they were everywhere.

The spacious, gently sloping lawn in front of the house had no fence to mar the view. Instead, it had a *ha-ha* – this was where the slope of the lawn had been cut into and the soil spread on the upper slope. The bank it created was faced with a stone wall to secure the step down. As a result, from the house, the lawn ended, and the paddock started with no obvious demarcation. Animals could not climb up into the garden, but the view was totally uninterrupted.

None of the family were gardeners so the house and grounds blended into the surroundings as if it had just grown there.

Inside the house was, for me, like stepping into a bygone era of antiquity. The first thing you saw if you entered through the front door was a big wide staircase on top of which was hanging the Durbar painting by Thomas Daniell. It was enormous and almost covered the entire wall being about 6 feet high and 9 feet wide. It depicts Sir Charles Warre Malet signing a treaty in 1790 with the Peshwa Madhavrao II of the Maratha Empire in India. It now hangs in the Tate Gallery in London.

Although the artifacts in the house could be considered valuable quality antiques, there was nothing that felt sacred. Most things were in everyday use. The whole atmosphere inside was welcoming and homely, despite the house containing countless ancestral paintings in large gold painted frames and many other fine pieces of art and statues. There was even a large pale-blue and gold urn about 4-feet high given to Sir Edward by Kaiser Wilhelm II, with the Kaiser's bust on one side. This side was always jokingly turned to the wall.

There was always a welcoming fire alight in the large fireplace. Loisy, a short busy little Austrian lady who used to be Lady Malet's governess in Austria, would bring us all afternoon tea on a trolley in front of the fire. The first person who would be served was the sheepdog. He would have his own cup-shaped bowl on the floor and milk warmed with tea from the silver teapot poured into it. Many a cosy rainy afternoon was spent in front of that fire. If I were to describe the whole house there wouldn't be room for the rest of my story to be told. It was a fascinating place but badly in need of repairs. Despite the grandeur, money wasn't something that was in abundance.

Uncle Daily was 6-foot 8-inches tall. He was my mother's younger brother, the owner and manager of the Chargot Estate and was an amazing man in many ways. He studied at Dover College and later Christ Church, Oxford, and was, for many years, a military man in the family regiment, the 8th King's Royal Irish Hussars. He fought in the Palestine campaign and in several theatres of the Second World War, particularly in the deserts of North Africa where he developed the sun compass, a device mounted on jeeps and trucks for navigating in the deep desert.

After the war, Uncle Daily was Chief Civil Affairs officer in the canal zone in Egypt where his humanity to 'the enemy' was well recognised. At one stage he was put in charge of ordering the surrender of a police post that was harbouring numerous terrorists, but the post refused to surrender so he brought up tanks and threatened to open fire. A journalist asked if he considered the Egyptian Commanding Officer as an enemy, to which he replied that, on the contrary, he regarded him as a 'very gallant gentleman.' The remark made headlines in newspapers all around the world and had a huge positive impact on Anglo-Egyptian relationships, inspiring President Nasser of Egypt to send a personal Christmas card to Uncle Daily at Chargot every year thereafter.

He was awarded the Order of the British Empire (OBE), in 1953 and held the office of High Sheriff of Somerset in 1966. Sir Edward had married an Austrian Baroness, Baroness Maria Joanna Benedicta Von Maasburg, my Aunt Iki. They had three children: Sir Harry Douglas St Lo Malet, 9th Baronet, known to me as cousin Hazi, Mary-Jane St Lo Malet and Micaela Elizabeth St Lo Malet.

Despite Uncle Daily's high breeding and accomplishments, he was the most gentle and loving man I had ever met. His clothes were always old and patched, not because he never had decent clothes but because he gave his decent clothes away. It was impossible to give him a new coat or a jumper because he very soon found someone he considered poorer than himself and would give it to them. Once when I was there, his family bought him a lovely new warm dressing gown and he gave it away in a matter of days. It used to infuriate his family. He was a Godly man who loved the Scriptures – he was a saint. He always had a ready smile on his face, and I loved him dearly – so did Douglas.

Everything about that place was soft. No cutting words or sharp tones, your gumboots were found clean and neatly placed on the boot rack in the morning. The job was done by Hall who used to be the groom in charge of the horses. There was no fear of rejection or disapproval of your ignorance or youth. You were accepted and loved. If ever you have felt like having a break from the world, that was the place to do it, especially if you felt like an alien in a world you were ill-equipped to handle.

Later, having been in hospitality myself, I know how touching it is that, while your guests are out, that you put fresh flowers in their room, or return their laundry, washed, ironed and neatly folded, straightening their crumpled bed and prepared a meal ready for them when they returned that evening. Little things that a thousand words couldn't express. I learnt a lot of that at Chargot. Uncle Daily died in 1990 and my eldest son was able to represent our family at his funeral. A sad loss to the world, and to us.

I loved being at Chargot. The farm, the animals, the people, and the house itself, were all a fascinating playground for me and I loved to show off my farming skills that I had learned as a child in Tasmania. Now also I had the added delight of being able to show Yogi around. Many of the people who worked there were the original staff who were there when my mother had lived there, though now elderly. They had felt it their lifelong duty to care for this family who had been so good to them in the past.

Surnames were used by the members of the family when addressing the staff as if it were a Christian name. Mr Hall, who knew my mother when she was a child, was simply called Hall. But Hall addressed the family members by their title, Sir Edward, or Lady Malet. I was a little taken aback when he addressed me as Lady Meredith. Actually, I was tickled pink – especially for Yogi to hear him call me that.

The bedroom I was always given had a four-poster bed which stood higher than usual off the floor. Douglas would come into my room every morning and bring me a cup of tea and sit on the bed and talk to me. I noticed how Douglas would always try to dominate the conversation when sitting with the family in front of the fire in the evenings. Iki would roll her eyes and smile at her husband. I pointed this out to Douglas and told him that when I noticed him doing it, I'd twiddle my thumbs. I also told him to ask questions and to not endlessly talk about himself, for these people had lived very full, interesting and active lives compared to his few years as an adult.

Another irritating thing that troubled Uncle Daily about him was that he would always return to the house not having finished his assigned job and I knew why this was. He disliked being alone, for it wasn't too long ago that his mother had died of cancer in July

1960 and his father had contracted cancer of the tongue and taken his life only two years later in September 1962. Then his stepfather died a year later in November 1963. Doug experienced too many losses of all that he had held dear. The loss caused great loneliness in him, akin to fear. He would always return to the house with the job half done, and some feeble excuse. But he listened to my advice and acted upon it and loved me for it.

It was irritating, but also quite charming to see how smitten Douglas was with me. He would follow me around like a puppy and was always looking for an excuse to hold my hand down a slippery slope or when climbing over a fence. On one occasion when Yogi wasn't with us, we found a comfy spot to relax, in the hay loft of a barn that was on the side of the road. Unfortunately, the village postman saw the open barn door and, thinking it had been left open by accident, he looked in and found us there. I remember how embarrassed we both were when he found us in the loft. We had no reason to be embarrassed for neither of us had been in the slightest way intimate with each other at this stage. But we expected the postman thought otherwise.

Yogi and I must have been great company and help to Douglas for we accompanied him on most of his farm jobs. We often went with him on the little Fordson Dexta tractor with Douglas driving and Yogi and I sitting on the big back mud guards to feed hay to a flock of sheep on Langham hill. One day I expressed a desire to drive the tractor. As a child growing up on my parents' farm, I used to drive our grey Ferguson tractor. After much persuasion he agreed to let me drive.

This time our seating arrangement was different; I sat on the front edge of the tractor seat, Yogi sat behind me on the same seat and Douglas was on the mud guard. The terrain was rough. I was trying to look confident and probably going a bit too fast, when I hit a bump in the track which lifted me off the seat. Yogi slid forward into the seat and my feet landed on the clutch and the brake. Well, the tractor came to a very sudden stop and Douglas was propelled into the air, landing in front of the tractor. I sat back down and took both feet off the pedals. The throttle was still well open, so the tractor leapt forward. Douglas narrowly missed getting run over by me – he leaped out of the way just in time. It's a story he loves to tell, but his version is slightly different than mine.

So began a three-year-long pursuit by Douglas to win over my affection and love, and to persuade me to marry him. To me, he seemed to be a very unsuitable lifelong marriage partner. He was three years younger than I, had no qualifications, no money, and no family support system. Both his parents were dead and his older brother, David, was very strange and Douglas insisted he was dangerous. Douglas refused to let me meet him and did not let David know about me. Douglas was obviously afraid of him and told me that he had always destroyed anything that Douglas loved or valued.

I was still living and nursing in London and had rich doctors and lawyers' sons interested in me. They were able to buy me expensive gifts and take me out to theatres and posh restaurants. I did all in my power to dissuade Douglas. I would even leave him in my flat and go out with another man. But no matter what I did, he would not stop loving me and constantly asking me to marry him, telling me that he wanted me to be the mother of his children. How does a young girl handle that kind of compliment? I never said no; I would just smile and give him no answer.

Most of the Chargot household smoked roll-your-own cigarettes, except for Uncle Daily. It was such a done thing in that era. Even during my nursing training days all the nurses smoked, and many of the doctors. I have always hated smoking and never even tried to give it a go. I had looked on in horror and revulsion inside the lungs of live patients on the theatre table and seen the foul-smelling black treacle-like substance that coated their lungs. That cured me of any desire to take up smoking.

However, Douglas smoked a lot. I'd tell him that I would never marry a man who smoked cigarettes. Later, when I accepted his proposal of marriage, he had to first make a promise to me to give up smoking. He kept that promise for a long time, but eventually relapsed. The regular sneaky cigarette has been a thorn in our relationship for many years. I had to put my foot down and enforce this promise much later. Smoking was very fashionable at the time and the health impacts were only just being fully appreciated. Apparently, I was ahead of my time.

Yogi and I were still playing our game of saving up money and disappearing to Europe until our funds ran out. It caused Douglas great distress when our money began to run low, as I would stop writing to him so as to save on stamps. On one occasion he knew that I was going to visit my brother, Stephen, in Hamburg. As I mentioned in the previous chapter, Yogi had returned to England early, but I stayed behind with my brother and his wife. They had a new baby, their first born, called Michael. I loved babies so I persuaded them to take a day off from parenthood, and go to Lubeck for an outing, and bring me back some marzipan (Lubeck was the place where marzipan was invented) and I would babysit.

I was going to enjoy looking after baby Michael. The baby was asleep, so I took the opportunity to go upstairs and wash my hair. The front doorbell rang, and I began wondering how I was going to say in German that Stephen and his wife were out for the day. I wrapped a towel around my wet hair and opened the door. There standing on the porch was Douglas. He had tracked me down which was amazing, because he never even had Stephen's address. But he used his skill of investigation to find me and to this day he is still very good at being a private investigator. Neither Stephen nor Ursula believed me when I said I had no idea that Douglas was coming. They thought I had sent them away so I could be alone with him.

Some months later, it was the 13th of October 1964. I was back in my London flat. It was a very special day for me because it was my twenty-first birthday. I had experienced so many new things in that one year. However, the one thing that stayed the same was the fact that no one had ever bothered to make my birthdays a special day for me, but this was my twenty-first. In fact, all my flatmates had gone out leaving me alone in the flat. There I sat in our flat, 86 St Georges Square, in an armchair with my back to the door, feeling very unloved and neglected and sorry for myself, when a bunch of twelve red carnations suddenly fell into my lap. It was Douglas. He had hitchhiked all the way from his college in Shropshire. He was a little upset that the gift he had posted to me hadn't arrived yet. It was a four-leafed clover marcasite brooch – it had cost him practically every penny he had.

With the loose change left over in his pocket, he had asked a man selling flowers if he could have a few red carnations. He told the man how he had been traveling for two days hitching lifts, just to get to see his girlfriend because it was her twenty-first birthday. The flower vendor threw in extra carnations to make it a full dozen. It had now been a full year that Douglas had never given up on me even though I had often been quite cruel to him. His love for me was amazing, and unlike the love of other men and I realised that with other men it was lust, not love. Douglas loved my mind, my many talents, like art and tatting, knitting, sewing, and all my domestic skills, as well as my body. He loved me for the person I was and treated me like a very beautiful precious gift, marvelling at my feminine form. He would make up songs to sing to me.

On one occasion he took me to Oxford and to his home, The Kilns in Headington, where Joy, Douglas' mother, and his brother, David, had lived. Douglas' mother was an American divorcee and had remarried a then little-known Oxford academic known to his friends as Jack. We were to meet Jack's brother, Uncle Warnie, and see Douglas' boxer dog, Ricki. Douglas was disappointed and embarrassed to find his Uncle Warnie severely drunk when he arrived with me. It was a sad and depressing visit. Warnie had been a fine gentleman but had struggled with alcoholism for many years. Sadly, after the death of Joy and then the death of his brother, Warnie took to drinking again and stayed inebriated for the rest of his life. He died in 1973.

Much has now been written about that household and those three amazing people. Jack, better known as C.S. Lewis, Joy Davidman/Lewis, Jack's wife, and Major Warren Hamilton Lewis, known simply as Warnie.

However, on that trip, I did get to meet Douglas' appointed guardian, Miss Jean Wakeman, who lived in Horton-Cum-Studley not far from Oxford. She was a remarkable and lovely lady, a great friend of Douglas' mother. Even though she was disabled from birth and found walking very difficult, she enjoyed her specially adapted car and would travel all over England working as one of the very few female motoring journalists. Jean had been given Joy's engagement ring; a milk stone opal surrounded by sixteen diamonds to be given to Douglas when he turned twenty-one. But she wouldn't hand this ring to Douglas who wanted it desperately to give it to me if I agreed to marry him.

That ring became a carrot used by Jean to goad Douglas into doing things like applying himself to his studies more, or not wasting his time on trips to London to see me. Douglas knew that it was rightly his so one day he just took it from Jean's desk in her study. She was furious. It did indeed become my engagement ring but sadly it vanished one day when we later lived in Tasmania. It had been taken out of its little ring box by someone. The box we still have, but we never found the ring. There were two possibilities that could explain its disappearance. One was that eighteen-month-old James could have removed it from the box and left it anywhere in the garden. Or a young girl who was staying with us at the time, to help me with the two small children and with the milkings, may have taken it. However, many years later when we were a little richer, Douglas had a replica made of it and therein lies another story for a later chapter.

Eventually Douglas was the proud owner of a BSA 250 cc motor bike. He would drive that bike for miles with me clinging onto his back for warmth. We would stay in cheap B&Bs. I would wear a ring and we would tell the owner that we were married. It was a wonderful freedom to be on our own and not under the watchful eyes of relatives or flatmates.

Once we travelled to Wales to a little seaside hamlet called LLangrannog where my Aunty Valmai and Uncle Jack had a holiday home perched on a cliffside. We especially made that trip because my brother, Stephen, and his wife, Ursula, were visiting them at the time. When it came time to leave, the weather had become very cold – there were inches of snow in places, so it was decided that I should travel in Stephen's car back to London and Douglas would take the motor bike. We kept close to Douglas to make sure he was okay. Halfway there Douglas was obviously suffering from hypothermia, so the bike was put on a train, and I massaged Douglas' feet, which were numb. His ears were frostbitten, and it took him several weeks to recover.

One of Doug's cleverest and most successful ploys to distract me from going out with other suitors was to buy me a hamster in a cage, complete with food and instructions. He knew that if I had such a thing in my possession other things would take a very low priority. It worked. I love little animals and I had never seen, let alone owned, a hamster before. It was my delight and fascinated me to no end.

During one stay at Chargot I rescued a baby fox cub and brought it back to my London flat. However, I had to part with it because when it got older it did its natural thing of rubbing a stink gland on the furniture to mark its territory. It was a very unpleasant odour similar to a skunk, so he was taken to Whipsnade Zoo.

On another occasion, I returned from Chargot with a very young female lamb. I bought disposable nappies for her to wear in the flat. I loved going for walks with that lamb. The lamb never

needed a lead and would follow me even through crowds of people. It caught the eye of a newspaper reporter when we were in Trafalgar Square. I was photographed and interviewed and the next day the lamb and I were in a London newspaper. I still have that newspaper clipping.

For a brief time, Douglas worked for Bertram Mills Circus in London as a stable supervisor looking after the beautiful Lipizzaner horses. I would love to visit him there and get special privileges to go behind the stage among the other performing animals. A tiger once made an angry swipe at Douglas and shredded one side of his circus uniform, but not making contact with his flesh at all. I sewed up those tiger claw marks, and that uniform hangs in his clothes closet to this day.

Still, at every opportunity, Douglas would ask me to marry him. The answer was the same, just a smile and perhaps a hug. I forget what my latest rejection of him was all about, but he left one day and never made his usual daily phone call. I was not too concerned till a week had passed and I had heard nothing from him. It was now 1966 and for nearly three years he had always been there for me. So, I got a bit worried and tried to find him. He wasn't at his usual haunts, and I began to panic. I thought to myself, *I've overstepped the mark now. I've lost the only man that ever truly loved me.*

I never thought he would leave me; he had become a major part of my life. *Oh dear, how can I ever get him back?* I thought. I realised that I really didn't want to lose him. I tried one more phone call thinking maybe he had gone to Chargot. But it was a long way away and he never went there without me. Aunt Iki answered the phone and called Douglas over. I heard him reply in the background, 'But no one knows I'm here.'

'Oh, don't be silly,' Aunt Iki said. 'Come and talk to Merrie.'

Doug would be twenty-one on the 10th of November. I had studied a toy rabbit in Hamleys toy shop in London and drew the pieces that made up the pattern of that rabbit, with the intention of making one considerably larger to give to Doug. When I first met him in 1964 at Chargot he was known affectionately as the *farm rabbit*. Apparently, all the agricultural students they took on were called farm rabbits. I organised a party at my flat, cooked a meal and invited the few friends that we had. I was going to give him another gift too, one he had been trying to get from me these last three years. I intended to say yes to his persistent question of, 'Will you marry me?'

It certainly was a memorable evening and one that brought about some quick changes. We were now officially engaged to be married and there seemed to be a sudden urgency to fulfil that action and to get away from everything. We would immigrate to Australia on the £10 assisted immigration scheme and buy a farm with some money that an American aunt had recently left him. It was I who approached Australia House in The Strand in London and persuaded them to give us the £10 passage to Australia. That turned out to be a challenge because I was actually Australian and held an Australian passport. Once in Australia, we would be known as *Ten Pound Poms*.

It was a 'let's get this over and done with marriage.' At the time we thought living 'in sin' was a better way than marriage – we said we only did it for the relatives and for any children that may happen. Even then, God was in control.

There was such a lot to organise and in the midst of it all I made the quick trip to Dar es Salaam to rescue my mother. The boat to Australia was due to leave England on the 20th of March 1967 – we only had four months to prepare. Westminster Cathedral was a Catholic Church in the parish of Pimlico where I lived so we would be married there. I still considered myself a Catholic, although I never went to Mass ever again since leaving my training hospital in Hobart. I had taken a strong dislike to Catholicism, or any other man-made formal religion. But I believed in the God of the Christian faith. I knew I was about to make a lifelong promise to God and to Douglas, to love, honour, and obey this passionate, arrogant, somewhat immature, penniless young man for a lifetime. And that I did, even during the years of incredible difficulty. A vow to Douglas was one thing, but a vow to God was unbreakable in my thinking. I really believed in God, the supreme creator and ruler of our planet and all humans. To break a vow to Him would be a very foolish thing to do.

Douglas was required to take religious instructions and told he must have his children baptised into the Catholic Church. That didn't seem to be a problem for him – it was more of an unspoken problem for me. The wedding was booked for the 20th of February. As a formality, we sent invitations to all my relatives and friends and to Jean Wakeman who was really the only family Doug had.

We honestly didn't expect anyone to come, so we were rather taken aback when many said they would come, and we realised we needed to put on a show. I would need a wedding dress and Douglas a suit. My wedding outfit cost me 6 shillings. I already had a long white chiffon skirt with pale blue smocking around the waist that I had made, as well as a white lace blouse. All I needed to buy was a length of netting to make a veil. I put a yellow wattle blossom wreath around my head. Wattle, or mimosa as the British called it, is the Australian emblem flower. Douglas hired a morning suit from Moss Brothers. I caused the sales rep to frown while forcing out a polite smile, because I had made the cheque out to Moss Broth. He said, 'Excuse me, madam, but isn't this some kind of soup?'

No reception, dinner, or any sort of party was arranged. A photographer came but we never ordered any photos from him but kept the proofs that had his big black stamp on them. Neither of us had money to spend on photos, but we were glad to have the proofs.

Strangely enough my father was also in England at the time. It was the first time he had returned since he went to live in Australia in 1947, twenty years previously. But he hadn't come to England to be at my wedding. For some reason he took an instant dislike to Douglas. When I asked him why, he said his head was too small.

He could have at least tried to be nice – this was an opportunity for him to reconnect with his daughter. How unkind words can wound and separate people, especially when spoken by a parent.

The ceremony was held in what was called the Mary Chapel inside Westminster Cathedral, officiated by the Right Reverend Monsignor Anglim. There was a surprisingly large crowd of people there. I walked up the aisle holding onto my father's arm. Douglas told me afterwards that he never even saw my father, only me. After we had said our vows to each other my father wanted to give me a kiss, but I withdrew from him and said I first wanted to kiss my husband. That remark wounded his pride.

Neither Douglas nor I had noticed that when we signed the marriage certificate at the registry office, that the name on it was David, not Douglas, his brother's name! It wasn't until years later when we were doing an around the world trip with all our four children, that we returned to that office with Jean Wakeman and were able to correct the error. Jean witnessed the signatures on

both occasions. She also gave us a belated wedding gift of a silver cutlery set in a wooden presentation box. That set has been very well used over the years and is still 100 per cent intact.

We were charged £10 for the marriage license. Doug didn't have £10 to his name so I paid it. Doug promised me he would repay me, and he did on my thirtieth birthday. He had 10 English pound coins formed into a necklace connected by gold chains made for me. He kept his promise.

For our honeymoon we spent two nights in the Park Lane Hotel, which was incredibly posh for us in those days. A new film called *Dr Zhivago* was being shown in a London theatre and Jean had bought us tickets to see it. Douglas had to go to the theatre in his wedding morning suit, for I had forgotten to pack a pair of trousers for him. Afterwards, we rented a flat in Oakhampton Road to stay in for the remaining month. My mother was our guest with her leg still in plaster, so she needed looking after. After the wedding my cousin, Lynette Stoddart, looked after her until we returned from our short honeymoon.

I continued to work night-duty as a private nurse right until the date of our departure. On one occasion when I returned after a night shift, I found the supper dishes of the previous evening not washed up. Doug looked on in amazement as I vented my disappointment while thumping a dirty plate with a fork, breaking it to pieces. He said he had been talking to my mother. No excuse. But Douglas seemed to get on surprisingly well with her. She actually liked Doug. The dishes were never left dirty till the next morning again. Jean offered to look after Mum when we left the UK, until she had recuperated. Then she too returned to Australia. Somehow, Mum actually arrived in Tasmania before us.

As I have said in a previous chapter, describing my arrival in Southampton from Australia, I had promised myself that I would take a big-wheeled English pram back to Australia with me. Well, that was a high priority job to be achieved. We went to Harrods in Knightsbridge and found the exact pram I wanted. It was white with a Wedgwood plaque on both sides. It was a delicate task to persuade the sales rep to crate it, and put it on the ship Aurelia at Southampton docks. He kept telling us it was quite impossible in the time available, until Douglas, whose persuasive skills I was only beginning to appreciate, said, 'You can't tell me that anything is impossible for Harrods to do.' The pram got onto that ship. We were so excited when we unpacked it in Tasmania. It was used by all our four babies and even by visiting grandchildren when we lived in Ireland. I have promised my oldest granddaughter, Rebekah, that she is to have it left to her in my will.

Chapter 11

Our first home

I had left Tasmania in November 1963 as a young girl of only twenty, for a six-month holiday in England, which lasted until the 20th of March 1967. Now, nearly four years later, I was no longer Miss Meredith Conan-Davies but Mrs Meredith Gresham. Only one month after our marriage, I was heading back to Australia, the land I had grown up in. And my husband was embarking on a life in a new country. Our few belongings, including the English pram we had bought from Harrods, had already been stowed in the ship that was to take us on that four-week voyage to our new life.

Carrying only a small suitcase and with the large stuffed toy rabbit that I had made for Doug on his twenty-first birthday tucked under my other arm, we took a London bus to Waterloo Station and a train to the Southampton docks. There we boarded the MV Aurelia, a converted World War Two German U-boat supply vessel. It had been rebuilt by the Australian Government for the sole purpose of carting immigrants traveling on the £10 assisted passage program to colonise Australia.

Although we thought of this trip as a sort of honeymoon, the shipping authorities were not sentimental about such things. We were shown to our cabins by a steward where Doug had to share with five rather wild young Irishmen, while I was put into a cabin some distance away, sharing with five other girls similar in age. When the weather became warmer, as we left the latitude of England, Doug and I would take our pillows and blankets out onto the deck, and so at least be together, and in the fresh air. The cabins were very hot and stuffy.

Life on board the ship soon became familiar. Meals were heralded by a loud bell. We chose the first sitting which meant breakfast at 7.00 am. But we often slept in, missing breakfast, and so by lunch time were very glad we had the first lunch sitting.

Every evening the crew entertained us in one way or another, either by showing a full-length classic movie or with a ball with a prize for the chosen Beauty Queen. Sometimes the crew themselves put on a pantomime or comedy show. For the Fancy dress ball, I dressed up as Alice in Wonderland and had the stuffed rabbit as a prop. Doug donned his Bertram Mills Circus uniform and came as a pirate complete with a Japanese katana sword that he had acquired from his mother.

On the 26th of March it was Easter Sunday. We were all given an Easter egg and that evening a grand ball was put on, but I couldn't enjoy it as the air was so thick with cigarette smoke. By the 28th the cold March English weather was replaced by hot sun, which meant swimming in the small on-deck pool. But it was usually too crowded for my liking. A notice went up on the notice board which I found amusing, it read, 'Blisters, like Misters, prefer blondes.' I didn't take heed and spent a few days with bad sunburn after lying out in the sun on deck. In those days there was no sunscreen.

Only eight days into our voyage we waited for hours at the entrance of the Suez Canal for a pilot boat to guide us through and I understood why. The canal was very crowded with vessels of every description. The water was very still and covered with an oil slick and floating debris. By midnight we were through the canal and anchored some distance from shore. Even at that hour there were merchants in small canoe-type boats heavily laden with assorted trinkets trying to sell their ware to the passengers. In the morning a fleet of ferry boats was planned to take us to the docks of Cairo where buses would take us into the city.

We were woken by the cabin steward very early and the whole day was spent in Cairo. We saw a museum, a mosque, the Great Sphinx of Giza, the pyramids, and lots of Bazaars. A turban-clad Arab in a long white gown offered Doug twenty-five camels to buy me. This was the second time that I had been offered to be bought, and I had appreciated in value by ten camels! Of course, Doug refused him. By 11.00 pm we were all told to be waiting at a certain spot where buses and another ferry ride would take us back to our ship. The ship set sail again at 1.00 am, arriving at Port Sudan at 3.00 am the following day. Doug took me out on to the bow of the boat at night to watch the phosphorescent lighting that danced and sparkled around the ship's bow as it ploughed through the still dark waters.

By the 4th of April we were sailing through the Indian Ocean. By the 7th we crossed the equator. For some reason that meant fun and games by throwing any unsuspecting person in the pool – I was thrown in clothes and all. We had become friendly with an aircraft carrier fighter pilot named Jim and his friend Pat, but both of their surnames I have forgotten. Also, a family called Wingfield and their six-year-old daughter called Joan. We gave Joan the big rabbit. It was greatly admired by her and had become a bit of a nuisance for Doug and me to cart around.

The ship planned to dock in Fremantle in Western Australia where a lot of the passengers were to disembark. This meant that Douglas and I would finally have a cabin to ourselves. As we gradually came closer and closer to land, I was overcome with emotion seeing what I considered my homeland again and had to force back a flood of tears. I think there was a bushfire somewhere, and that smell of burning eucalyptus trees wafted over the ship – a smell I had not known for years, the smell of my childhood.

We went ashore in Fremantle, and I bought Douglas a big T-bone steak. He had never tasted meat so delicious before. Our next stop was Melbourne where we disembarked and were taken to Essendon Airport – now called Essendon Fields Airport – outside of Melbourne. We were given red badges to wear to prove we were immigrants. At the airport we were given a free meal and from there we flew across the Bass Strait to Hobart. My sister, Bliss, met us and took us to her home in Berridale. I looked a mess as a few days previously we had been playing a game on the deck jumping over a rope. I had tripped on the rope and cut my lip quite badly falling on something on the deck. My lip and face were still swollen when Bliss met us. Bliss had five children by then, the youngest being about four, so the house was a bit crowded. This is where we caught up with my mother again as she was living in a caravan parked in the garden.

We were anxious to leave and be by ourselves – something that we hadn't been able to do for a very long time. We bought a Holden ute that had a canopy over the tray to carry our luggage and keep it waterproof. We also equipped ourselves with camping gear, two blow-up mattresses, and a small stove and cooking utensils. Then we set off to explore the north of the island, choosing the Lake Highway, a gravel road, to travel on.

Driving through farmlands, small villages with weatherboard houses, tin rooves and usually a veranda with wrought iron edging at the top looking like lace under the eaves, was so familiar to me, but very new and strange to my young American-English husband. Then we drove through kilometre after kilometre of dense virgin eucalyptus forests. Our destination was to visit some friends of my parents, the Rowels, who lived on the foothills of Mount Roland near Sheffield and my childhood home. This was a drive of about six hours from Hobart. I hadn't seen or contacted them since I was a child and didn't even know if they were still there. Thankfully the area was exactly as I remembered it, so it didn't take me long to locate their home.

Guy Rowel and his wife, Julia, welcomed us warmly and we stayed with them for two nights. While there, we met a man called John Anderson who learned that we were looking to buy a farm. He knew of a small 100-acre farm on the north-west coast that might suit us. He sent us to stay with friends of his, Mr and Mrs Mackay. Following his instructions, we easily found the place, and the Mackays were also very welcoming. We slept in their sleep-out accommodation for two weeks.

While there, Doug and I were taken night-time wallaby shooting by their son and his wife. We had to locate and shoot the wallabies by spotlight as they came out of the forest, and we collected them for dog (and human) food. But we got carried away with the excitement and ventured off the paddock and into the bush. Unfortunately, when we tried to return to the paddock, we simply couldn't find it! So, rather than risking getting totally lost or bogged, we made camp and spent the night in the forest. The men cut down lots of man-fern fronds and made a pad for us all to sleep on. When daylight came the way out was obvious. That was certainly a new experience and a valuable lesson learned for both Doug and I.

The farm that John Anderson told us about was near Smithton in the dairy farming area of Black River. We went and had a look at it, and both decided that it would do. But that was the only enthusiasm we could muster. The farmland was the best you could get – rich red volcanic soil, but everything seemed to need doing. The fences were falling down. The dairy was small and had never been fully set up, only milking two cows at a time despite having been built with four milking stands. The dairy was situated on the other side of the main entrance driveway to the house, which was irritating, as it would require always shutting gates and cow manure on the drive.

Twenty-three cows in calf and a small grey Ferguson tractor – like the one that my dad had purchased from England – came with the property. The house was a typical Tasmanian house – simple weatherboard with a tin roof. The interior walls were lined with hessian scrim and paper. It was a perfect hideout for the rats which we discovered would race around the house walls at night making quite a racket. But the price was right – only $16,000.

It was owned by Roy Smith, the only inhospitable Tasmanian farmer we have ever met. Rather than overstay our welcome with the Mackays, or pay for hotel accommodation, the Smiths reluctantly let us pitch our very small tent on the property till the day of settlement. May, June, and July are the coldest months in the southern hemisphere and, on the 22nd of May 1967 we braved the frosty mornings and moved onto our new farm. We had decided to call it Rivendell Farm. The house had four bedrooms and the Smiths could have let us sleep in the house but refused, so we pitched the tent and with the camping gear, blow-up mattress and sleeping bags, proceeded to set up our first home together. We found an old table in a shed which we used to keep our cooking gear off the damp soil and out of the reach of a black porker weight pig who was our first guest. Not a very polite or welcome guest either.

This enabled us to get a head start on familiarising ourselves with the farm and even work at some things that obviously needed attending to like repairing fences and making the hen house devil- and quoll- proof. I knew that to keep hens in Tasmania they had to be locked up in a secure hen house once they had gone to roost at night or a Tasmanian devil or a quoll (locally called a tiger-cat although they are not a cat at all) would kill the lot.

Initially we cooked our meals over a metho stove but later we found more warmth and comfort cooking on a campfire. Those

Our first visitor in our first home

meals usually consisted of a rabbit that Doug had shot and potatoes that we had gleaned from a nearby potato crop that had recently been harvested.

We even tried eating the wild moorhens but discovered that their meat was full of very tough sinews. They were strange birds, only using their wings to fly when in serious danger. They lived mostly around swampy areas and water holes, and they liked the creek below the house which had a dam on it to supply water to the nearby train station of Black River. The moorhens were very social birds, always congregating in numbers. They have a strange way of all working up to an incredible cackling noise and then stopping dead silent at exactly the same time. It was so sad watching their reaction when one bird would be targeted for supper and shot. The other hens would all gather around the dead bird and bow their heads while wailing loudly, as if mourning for their friend. We never shot any more of those birds after witnessing that.

The tent we were in wasn't very waterproof, so when the weather became wet, Mr Smith grudgingly let us move into the barn. And that's where our first son, James, was conceived. He had hair the same colour as dried hay and we always said it was because he was conceived in a bed made of hay bales. Once when it was raining too hard to cook outside – cooking with an open fire in a barn full of dry hay was unwise – they let us eat our breakfast in the house. And once we were invited in to watch something on their television. Otherwise, we fended for ourselves.

The other neighbouring farmers were very generous and kind, inviting us in to have a meal with them and, more often than not, to have a very welcome warm bath. We did a lot of work on the farm and spent a lot of time becoming acquainted with the neighbours over the twenty-seven days that we waited patiently in our makeshift accommodation. Settlement day was to be on the 17th of June. It was a joyful sight when a removal truck came and emptied the house of all the Smith's furniture and personal effects. The empty house was dry and warm and ours at last – or we thought it was. The Smiths made two trips back to the place to dig up plants from the garden, until I very angrily confronted them and told them to clear off and never return.

We went to a market in the nearby town of Smithton and bought a table for $2.00 and a three-piece lounge suite for $4.40. I later made fitted covers for them using my latest prize possession, a Bernina sewing machine that my father had bought for me as a late wedding present. The purchase of that machine even came with a tutor to give me ten lessons on how to operate it. I still use it today, fifty years later. We also bought a double bed for £2, 2/6.

Australia at that time had only just converted to decimal currency the year before. When I had left for England, we were using pounds, shillings, and pence, and of course England still uses pounds. It took a long time for me to get used to writing dollars, so my diaries often recorded things in 'old money'. We probably paid $2.25 for the bed.

That bed has a very funny story attached to it. Sometime later, on a particularly hot day, we had been out somewhere leaving the doors open to air out the house which still had an odour of the previous owners about it. On our return Doug went to have an afternoon sleep and flopped onto the bed. The entire bed, with Doug hanging on for grim death, jumped about a foot off the floor and headed across the room crashing against the bedroom door frame with a jerk and loud scream. It scared the wits out of Doug until he saw our big sow out of the window hightailing it across the lawn. The pig had apparently come into the house and had been asleep on the cool lino under the bed. She also had a nasty fright when the bed springs suddenly bounced down and hit her on the back. Pigs are very powerful animals and she immediately leapt to her feet and tried to escape as fast as she could, almost taking the bed with her.

The town of Smithtown was built mainly around the large Duck River Butter Factory, which employed most of the inhabitants. A store was attached to it which sold groceries and most household goods. It was very convenient for us. There was also a district hospital and schools for primary and secondary students. The sale yards were a place most farmers liked to gather on a Wednesday morning even if they hadn't taken in stock to be sold or never intended to bid. It was the meeting ground to swap farming stories and achievements and to seek advice from seasoned farmers. Doug spent many pleasant hours there sitting on a fence, watching, and listening and no doubt telling stories of his own.

We bid for two sows due to farrow at the end of the month. I helped Doug build two movable pig arks with seasoned timber we had bought cheaply. The sows both had eleven piglets three weeks later. One of the piglets was a runt. He would have died if we left him to compete at the milk parlour with the other stronger piglets, so I gleefully took him into the house to be hand reared.

The first of the twenty-three cows that we had bought with the farm calved on the 3rd of July and the rest of them soon followed suit. By the end of August, we were milking twice a day and selling cream to the Duck River Butter Factory and feeding twenty-two fast growing little piglets and their mums on the skim milk. When the piglets were porker weight Doug and I proudly loaded them into the crate Doug had made to fit on the back of our Holden ute and we took them to the market. I had grown very fond of those mischievous little piglets. When they were sold to a butcher, I even surprised myself by bursting into tears, much to the amusement of the hardened local farmers.

My diaries tell me that in November we were producing ten gallons of cream a day and receiving $350 a month from the butter factory. That was a lot of money in 1968. Once a month a herd tester would come to test the cows for a disease called brucellosis. It must have been eradicated because these tests are no longer necessary.

I was now more than a little bit pregnant, and it was no longer a secret, my rapidly expanding girth having given me away. We were given most things needed for our new baby by these kind people. But the big English pram we purchased in Harrods was to be the most useful child rearing thing we had. Often, I had three babies in it at once.

The dam below the house was rented by the railway to provide them with water and desperately needed to be cleaned out so the railway people sent a chap by the name of Vern Poke to do the job with his Gradall machine. Vern would usually eat his packed lunch sitting by the dam, but, on one occasion it was raining heavily, so I invited him to have his lunch on the veranda. At the time I was still rearing my small runt piglet by hand. I was using a baby's bottle and teat to feed it. In a fit of mischief, I wrapped the little animal up in one of the bunny rugs I had for my soon-to-arrive baby. Then I put a bonnet in its head covering up its ears and went and sat next to Vern as he was eating his lunch. He leaned over and not being a man of many words said, 'Give us a look at the kid then.' The piglet was greedily sucking away at the warm milk in the bottle. Well, poor Vern sat back abruptly and never said a thing. But word got around the village that Mrs Gresham had had the ugliest baby ever seen.

My due date was nearing. We had arranged for me to have the baby in the small local Smithton District Hospital. But farm work still had to be done, there were cows to milk and a paddock of oats to be planted. I was recruited to stand on the footplate at the back of the steel wheeled seed-drill and raise the lever to prevent the seed feeding out as Doug turned the corner of each new row. The little piglet that I had hand reared was now almost porker weight but still lived in the house with us. We actually have a photo of the pig, and our staghound dog, and the cat all sleeping on the hearth in front of the fire in the house. Pigs are by nature very clean animals. She never messed in the house. She knew how to open the kitchen cupboards by pressing the knob with her snout and would raid the breakfast cereal. She would follow me everywhere.

She trotted back and forth, back and forth following me perched on the seed-drill. My waters broke on the back of the drill and filled up my gum boots, so I waddled and sloshed my way home, but Doug couldn't come with me as it had started to rain, and he had to get the wet seed into the ground otherwise it would have swelled and been impossible to sow. I trudged home emotionally distraught, my tears mingling with the rain and that little pig faithfully at my heels. Being a midwife, I knew nothing was amiss. Neither the baby nor I were in any danger, and it would probably be many hours before the baby was born. But the happy soft squealing noise that piglets make when following suddenly stopped. I looked around. Piggly Wiggly had dropped dead! It was all too much for her. There was obviously a reason why she was so small and weak when she was born. She must have had a weak heart.

Doug drove me into the Smithton District Hospital where our first child was born on the 15th of March 1968. A 7-pound 4-ounce baby boy we named James Edward Lindsay Gresham. The name James was our choice, Edward after Uncle Daily, and Lindsay after Doug's father, William Lindsay Gresham. James was the beginning of the replacement of Douglas' family line. Cancer had claimed most of his immediate family, and much of his extended family had been murdered in the concentration camps in Germany during the Second World War. We visited Auschwitz in Germany a few years ago and saw on a plaque the names of many of his relatives who had lost their lives there.

Within a week I was back home from hospital. Being a mother and a wife at the same time was a new experience for me. Up to this point, Doug had been the sole focus of my married life. Now I noticed him a little sad as he felt he had taken second place. We talked about this, and he wrote a small piece and called it *And Baby Makes Two*.

I had handled lots of newborn babies, but this one was mine. I was totally fascinated and absorbed with this perfect little human life that came from us – a wonderful gift from God. However, I made a special effort not to let the baby eclipse Douglas. We would strap the big pram onto the carry-all on the back of the tractor so I could still accompany Doug with his farming chores.

I breastfed James for only three months as my milk suddenly seemed to not be sufficient to feed the hungry baby. I thought it was because I was working very hard on the farm and having broken sleep at night, but that wasn't the reason at all. I was pregnant again. James was only three months old.

We were both amazed but delighted, nevertheless. The two children would grow up together. The two of them have been very close to each other all their lives and are still best friends to this day. However, the devil comes to steal and destroy what God loves best: His children. He tried once again to destroy me and, thus, would have also terribly harmed Doug and James as well. I see this so clearly now. I also see how God rescued us from this deadly scheme.

I was eight months pregnant with our second child. James had only just turned one and Doug was doing his best to provide for his new family from the meagre income that the farm could bring in. One particular day, he had returned to the ploughing that he had started the day before. The tractor had been left in the field overnight, the plough in the furrow. Meantime I was left in the house to look after the baby who was now very actively crawling and getting into mischief. I developed a tummy ache but thought little of it. It intensified and I felt nauseated. A neighbour knocked on the door, but I foolishly didn't answer because I was about to vomit. So, after knocking hard and enthusiastically, he left.

How foolish I was, but I had not yet realised the seriousness of my condition. The plough which had been turning the soil very nicely for Doug, suddenly stopped turning the soil. Doug needed a tool to adjust the angle of the disks. I expect he vented his annoyance with a few swear words but unhitched the plough and with a strange sense of dread drove the tractor home fast. There he found me unconscious on the front lawn with baby James only eleven months old toddling around me. I had grass and soil in my mouth because I had been biting the ground in my pain.

Doug quickly phoned Dr George White, the GP in Smithton, who came with his newly acquired VW Kombi van that he had personally bought to use as an ambulance. Doug sat on the lawn beside me gripped with fear with tears streaming down his cheeks while waiting for the makeshift ambulance to arrive. I was rushed into the Burnie Hospital and after pumping out my stomach, was taken straight to the operating theatre. Mr Heath, the resident surgeon, who had a little hobby farm and milked goats, came rushing to the hospital in his farm overalls. Once thoroughly scrubbed up and gowned, he made an incision in my heavily pregnant belly from my belly button right around to the centre of my back. My appendix had ruptured, and I was minutes from death as peritonitis would have quickly set in. I awoke with the Ryles tube still down my nose and throat, a lifesaving drip loaded with tetracycline in it, and a corrugated drain feeding into a bottle beside my bed. And an eight-month gestated baby kicking my huge incision and stitches from the inside.

The next day, when Doug had been thoroughly reassured that me and the baby were going to be okay, he went home to adjust the plough and get on with his work. But the plough worked perfectly and didn't need any adjusting at all. God had intervened by causing the plough to stop turning the soil – God had also sent the neighbour, but I had refused to open the door to him. Another kind neighbour, Peggy Atkins, had taken baby James from Doug's arms and looked after him until I was once again capable of doing so.

It was hard taking a baby to full term after having such a large incision. Every energetic kick of the baby was painful. Only a month after the operation I gave birth – natural birth – to our second baby boy and we named him Timothy George. George in honour of Dr George White who saved both our lives with his forethought of buying a Kombi van to double up as an ambulance. We were the first emergency patients to use it. Timothy was the smallest of all my four babies, only 5 pounds and 15 ounces, but grew to be the biggest of all our children. His baby teeth were an odd brown colour due to the massive doses of tetracycline I was on during his last month of gestation. But his second teeth were white and as hard as rock. Dentists would comment on their hardness, and he has never had to have a filling in his life. This is now recognised as a side-effect of tetracycline, and it has been adapted as a deterrent for tooth decay.

James was just starting to talk when his brother joined the family. However, James could never quite manage to say Timothy, so would call him Digitty. To this day that name has stuck, so to his family members he was, and still is, known simply as Dig.

Two babies in that big pram were no trouble. It would come everywhere with us when we worked on the farm. The big wheels covered the rough ground with ease, and the large spring suspension was a comfortable ride for the babies.

Peggy Atkins was married to Denny, and he was a great character. He kept bees and taught Doug the art of beekeeping. Doug would go off with him into the leatherwood forests around the area and help him. The honey from the leatherwood flowers brought a high price and was very sought after, oddly enough for making perfume in France, although it is very tasty as well. Later, Doug kept his own bees which gave us plenty of honey for ourselves and to give to other people – this skill has been handed down to James who also now keeps his own hives. Denny also had a pack of hunting dogs, and Doug would join him hunting wallabies. We ate a lot of wallaby meat in those days. Young female wallaby meat was delicious, but we soon learned to avoid the older ones and the males – their meat was very gamey and strong.

One day, Denny Atkins took Doug on a fishing trip to the mouth of the Arthur River. They returned quite late in the evening in high spirits. I jokingly said, 'No fish then?' The insulting connotation was too much. Doug emptied a large sack of big black-back salmon onto the sitting room floor. They thought it was funny but guess who had to clean up the fishy mess off the floor? The men were both a little too happy, having stopped at the pub on the way home and exchanged fish for beers over the bar.

It didn't take us long for us to become almost completely self-sufficient. The soil was fertile and produced lots of vegetables to eat and freeze for the winter months. We butchered our own beef and fried it in cream, something we had plenty of. There would be home-cured bacon sides hanging from the kitchen ceiling, cutting off a thick slice for breakfast each morning. The hens laid well. We even had free range turkeys, so roast turkey wasn't just a Christmas treat, we roasted a turkey whenever we wanted.

Our big turkey gobbler was twice the size of eighteen-month-old James. One day we watched with fascination as James tempted this big gobbler to eat corn out of his hands, but we weren't to know James' full intention. With remarkable speed and agility, he lunged and grabbed both legs of that big turkey and hung on tightly. Turkeys are powerful flyers and this turkey immediately flapped like mad and was just getting airborne when he crashed into the fence being unable to get enough altitude to clear it. James was to become an airline pilot and that turkey was the first thing he ever flew.

We made our own soap from the fat of the animals, our own butter from the cream, and we made jams and preserved fruit in Fowler jars. The floors had home-tanned sheep skins on them. The only things we bought were things like flour, sugar, tea and coffee. Our weekly grocery bill was about $12 a week. Each shopping day we would buy each child a 'dinky toy' matchbox car.

I now made all the children's clothes as well as clothes for myself and Doug with the Bernina sewing machine that my father had given me. I made curtains and padded and covered apple boxes to make furniture to sit on. Much later Doug and I would go to the Burnie dump and often find discarded shop remnants. One lucky find was a roll of awning material. I covered an entire old lounge suite with that. I used to say to Doug, 'Oh, I can't do that.' And he would reply, 'The only thing you can't do is that which you are not prepared to try.'

So, I ended up making him a mustard corduroy suit and lots of very flamboyant shirts and ties. All of which came in handy, it was the late sixties after all. But I digress.

Doug learnt a lot from the rough and ready farmers who were only too willing to talk for hours about farming to help a young

man from England. They too would enjoy listening to Doug tell stories of his farming days in 'Pommy Land'. I would get rather annoyed as I would be left to finish the milking or feed the pigs by myself.

One day I was lighting the fire in the sitting room, using the local newspaper, The Advocate, to kindle it with. I never, as a rule, read the paper but on this day, I glanced through the jobs available list. An announcer was needed to work at the local radio station 7BU. Half in jest, I said to Doug, 'You're always talking too much, why don't you apply for this job and get paid for talking?' And he did just that. Very shortly afterwards he was driving the 14 miles to Burnie early every morning to do the breakfast show on air. Doug has been gifted with a very lovely voice and knows how to use it and that was the start of his very successful radio and television career.

This new job meant new friends and other money-making areas opened up for him. His personality was always to be the centre of attention, so he found himself hosting local shows and nightclubs in Burnie – even singing with a pop group. It was the sixties and men's clothing were bell bottom trousers, platform shoes and floral shirts and ties. He already had a good supply of these from my Bernina.

Douglas would drive to Burnie early each morning to cheerfully wake up north-west Tasmania on 7BU radio with his breakfast show. He became a familiar voice for many dairy farmers who would listen to him as they milked their cows. I too would be milking our cows in our four-stand milking parlour. Dig would soon fall asleep again in the big pram listening to the rhythmic noise of the machine and his daddy's voice. For James it was all far too exciting, he would be alongside me wearing a tiny pair of gumboots. The cows were always very careful not to knock him over. Occasionally, when the cows were disturbed, I would stand him in a cream can, with only his eyes and nose visible and his fingers gripping the edge.

He would love to dabble in the thick froth that formed on top of the skim milk after the milk had passed through the cream separator. Once a week the cream truck would collect the five-gallon cream cans full of cream from the one-metre-high cream stand that was at the bottom of the drive and take it to the Duck River Butter Factory in Smithton. Taking the full cream cans to the end of the drive often became my responsibility when Douglas was on air. It was a fairly simple job using the hydraulic carry-all on the back of the tractor,

which would lift the cream cans to the top of the solidly built cream stand. This was provided everything went smoothly.

The train tracks crossed our driveway. These had become raised over time due to the erosion of the soil and gravel around them. It was a delicate job to slowly and carefully get over the lines without losing the cream cans. One morning the Ferguson tractor stalled with its back wheels between the lines. Try as I may, I couldn't get it to start again. Then, to my absolute horror, I heard the train coming. I think I must have had an adrenaline rush or, more likely, God sent me a strong angel to take most of the weight. I lifted that tractor clean off the line and pushed it out of harm's way – something I normally would never be able to do. The train driver gave me a friendly wave not knowing what a narrow escape we had had.

About 200 metres from our house lived an unpleasant man. He had at one time worked at the Black River train station, but for some reason he had been fired. The train tracks also ran across his driveway and then up a gentle slope and past our house. In retaliation for being fired he greased the lines, making it impossible for the train to get up the hill. So, one day, when this neighbour drove to town, the railway men took a tractor with a front-end loader to his property and lifted away his steel cattle grid that was across his driveway. Of course, his car went headfirst into the hole when he returned.

He played a few of his nasty stunts on us too. One day our cows got out and instead of walking over and knocking on the door or making a phone call, he fired his 12-gauge shotgun at our house. The pellets spattered on the roof and the front of the house where our baby was sleeping. James was still very small, and I would push the pram onto the veranda to let him sleep in the fresh air. Douglas was not amused by this behaviour and deterred him from doing it again by shooting the chimney off his house with his Lee Enfield .303 rifle!

One night we had a big bonfire and bought some fireworks and crackers to entertain some youngsters who had been giving us a hand on the farm. A car came racing up the drive. It was Bill, another neighbouring farmer. He got out of his car, flung open the boot, which was full of ammunition and guns. He had thought the nasty nameless neighbour and Douglas were having a shoot-out, and had come to help.

It wasn't uncommon for us to have guests staying with us, including guests from England who knew Doug's parents. One such guest was Dr Gordon Sanders. He was one of the team that discovered penicillin with Alexander Fleming. Our fields were dotted with lovely mushrooms the week that he was with us, so we picked a basket full of them and Dr Sanders taught us how to make and bottle champignon a la grecque. It was delicious.

A boyfriend of a London flatmate also came to visit us. He was a fussy eater and would never eat anything new or strange. We served him up a wallaby steak telling him it was beef. He came back for a second helping, saying it was the best steak he had ever eaten. We kept it a secret for a few days, until we just couldn't resist telling him what he had eaten. He admitted that he would never have eaten it if he had known it was some kind of kangaroo.

Bringing the cows in for milking each morning and evening was usually done on foot. Cattle are lovely creatures of habit and in no time at all they would calmly amble most of the way to the dairy after simply being called. I would often carry baby Dig in my arms when I got the cows in, leaving James to play on the childproof veranda – especially now that our neighbour was no longer spattering it with shotgun pellets. But, at the time, we had an over-enthusiastic cattle dog called Shep. Shep would occasionally get out of control and cause the cows to gallop all the way down the cow lane which narrowed before it got to the yards. I was yelling at this over-excited dog to 'come to heel' when, to my horror, I saw my little eighteen-month-old golden-haired child up to his knees in the muddy narrowed section of that cow lane. He had escaped from his enclosure, and tried to get to me. The cows were racing towards him. There was nothing I could do but watch in terror. I could see no child, only trotting cows pushing into the narrowing of the lane, trying to escape from the madly yapping dog. The cows vacated the lane and came to a halt in the dairy yard. There, standing in all that mud, was James completely unharmed, covered in muck and laughing. The cows had carefully avoided him. James thought it was great fun. But for me, it was terrifying.

Our first tractor was the little grey Ferguson that I mentioned earlier. It was a magic little tractor and served us very well. I was often required to sit on the bonnet to keep the front wheels on the ground when we overloaded the weight it was carrying on the rear three-point-linkage mounted carry-all. Later, we bought a larger four-wheel drive Czech-made tractor called a Zetor. I missed my Fergy but at least I never had to provide ballast again. Four-wheel drive tractors were a novelty in those days and Douglas would occasionally be asked to demonstrate our new-fangled Zetor at shows and sales, a job he enjoyed hugely.

It was nearly four years since we had immigrated from England and had bought Rivendell Farm. I was pregnant again. The baby was due to be born in June which is mid-winter in Australia. James was almost four and would soon be school age. We realised that we really hadn't seen anything of the rest of Australia – even myself, I had only known Tasmania. Once the children started school we would be anchored to the spot. It was now or never, and we decided to explore the rest of Australia. So, we put the farm on the market. It sold remarkably quickly although not without some skulduggery from the buyer. Doug was still working as a radio announcer at 7BU in Burnie, so we bought a 22-foot Millard caravan. A friend of ours named Albert, who owned a photography shop in Burnie, kindly let us put our van on his small hobby farm. The idea was to stay put until we welcomed baby number three into the world and once he or she was settled into the routine of life outside the womb, we would start on a new adventure and explore the rest of Australia.

We were able to store a lot of our belongings at Albert's place and only take the essentials with us in the caravan. That turned out to be a big mistake. Albert moved our things out of his house and put them in a farm shed where some vandals broke into the shed and smashed everything. I had a carved camphor chest that I had bought in Dar es Salam. They took to that with an axe and smashed all my treasures that were inside it.

But the most tragic thing that was lost was a box containing all of C.S. Lewis' letters that he had written to Doug's mother, Joy Davidman, and her letters back to C.S. Lewis. I'm sure that today they would be of great interest and would be very valuable. They were blown by the wind around the paddock and soaked by every shower of rain. Completely destroyed. But perhaps that was God's providence protecting the privacy of two remarkable people. I often wonder, *what happened to this or that?* and just shrug and know that it was left at Albert's place.

Dominick Sasha Gresham was a 9-pound baby, my biggest, and he is now the smallest of our three boys. It wasn't easy for us all living in a caravan which we shared with Doug's latest acquisition, a lovely boxer dog, who we called Rindell.

A short distance from the van was the fast-flowing river, which made it impossible for me to leave the two older boys unattended outside. When it was impossible for me to watch them, I'd attach James onto the dog wire that stretched from one tree to another. He never minded that at all. It's amazing how permanent a caravan can feel when the grass grows up its wheels. I missed our home and the work on the farm.

There was also a growing concern in my mind, *is this man to be trusted? Am I to be trusted to be the caretakers of these three precious children? Here I am left alone, kilometres away from the nearest neighbour, no telephone, no transport.* I couldn't drive and it was before the days of second cars anyway. Doug seemed to be oblivious to all this as he gained popularity in his radio announcing job at 7BU in Burnie.

Dig was only three years old when he had his first asthma attack at Albert's. I put all three children in the pram to go to a neighbour's place to use their phone, but no one was at home. We never used to lock our farmhouse or take the keys out of the car when we were out, just in case someone needed to use the phone or the car for an emergency. But this house was locked. I pushed that heavily laden pram for miles. Rindell was pulling at the leash, so I tied her to the front of the pram to make the going easier. Finally, we arrived at a small country grocery shop. I phoned the radio station and Doug came to our rescue.

Dig spent some time in the Burnie Hospital, and we were made to worry over nothing because when we admitted him the staff initially thought he had rheumatic fever. Eventually, the doctor conceded that it was simply asthma which is scary enough. Shortly afterwards, James broke his leg just falling over and spent some time in a cast. And baby Dominick was below his birth weight at six weeks of age. It was a difficult period all jammed into a small caravan. I was so glad to get away from there.

Finally, we loaded the caravan with Doug's motorbike, the big pram that had to be dismantled to fit into the van and last to go in was Rindell. The caravan was pulled by a bright yellow Ford XT Falcon with black racing stripes that we nicknamed the Flying Banana Split.

And so began our next phase of life. Looking back on it now, I think we must have been mad, naïve, or just young and inexperienced; all three most likely. At the time though it was just getting on with the next stage. The going was hard but also dotted with some wonderful memories.

As I write it is 2.45 am on a Friday night, April 2020. I'm awake, trying hard not to be scared and worried. I tell myself over and over again, *Jesus is in control of this Coronavirus pandemic that has kept me and many others housebound since the 11th of March. When will it end? No end is in sight on this day, the 24th of April. How many lives will it take? Will it claim my life?* It would be easier not to worry and be scared if Doug was with me, but he is stuck in Australia. It's so lonely without Doug, alone in our lovely big villa, overlooking the blue Mediterranean Sea. We have never been apart from each other this long in the 54 years of our married life.

Chapter 12

Tasmania to Perth

The car and caravan were loaded onto the Tasman Ferry, the boat that made a journey each week from Devonport to Melbourne across the Bass Strait. Somehow it was good to be going somewhere and not just stuck at Albert's place. Our intention was to see a bit of Australia before the children reached school age. The experience certainly gave me the awareness of the vastness and seeming endlessness of the Australian continent. We would travel for hour after hour but, on the map, we had only covered an inch or two. We drove through the rich fruit, vegetable, and citrus growing land of Mildura, then through magnificent beef country, and then poorer quality sheep country. The land got drier and harsher as we progressed west, but we hadn't even gotten out of the state of Victoria yet.

Doug did all the driving. I did not learn to drive till we were well established in Perth a few years later. I sat next to him with baby Dominick on my lap – baby car bassinets and baby seats weren't invented in those days. I would change his nappy, feed him, and look after his every baby need on my lap. Once when I was changing a very messy nappy, he let rip and sprayed Doug most unfortunately. I was amused but Doug didn't find it at all funny. Ever after Doug would say, 'Don't point that thing at me. It might go off.' I thought it best to face Dominick the other way when changing his nappy.

James and Dig bounced around in the back with the dog. Children get very restless and bored on long journeys, especially a journey that seemed never-ending. But they were well-behaved toddlers and never gave us temper tantrums or fretful behaviour.

Every time we stopped for a meal or for the night, the big pram and the motorbike would have to be taken out of the van. The caravan was laid out very well. The kitchen and dining table –

which doubled as a bed for the older boys – was at the front. Then there was a shower room that had quite a deep tray at its base which I used as a bath for James and Dig, while Dominick went in the kitchen sink. Water was precious so the bath water would then be used as a washing machine. I'd put some detergent in it and add the nappies; I never once bought a disposable nappy. The ride over corrugated roads as we travelled got them beautifully clean. At the next stop, I'd give them a rinse and find a convenient tree to string a line on, and they would be dry by the morning. A very adequate double bed at the back of the van served as our sleeping quarters and also a romping area for the boys. A Porta Potti was disguised as a seat at the foot of our bed.

We avoided driving through Adelaide, and took the coast road through some spectacular scenery, but the boys failed to see the attraction. Being very active children, they were so tired of being cooped up hour after hour. The weather was getting much warmer and Dominick was getting dehydrated. He had always been a colicy baby but now with no air-conditioning and the heat in the car, and also in the caravan at night, he wasn't good and was causing Doug and me considerable concern. My breasts were getting engorged as he wasn't able to drink the usual amount. The engorgement caused my milk to flow much too fast and he would splutter, and gulp and of course, then double up with colic pain.

The next town we came to was Streaky Bay and we were forced to stop and deal with a dangerously dehydrated baby. The local doctor there was a German man by the name of Dr Giezler. He had Dominick taken by air ambulance to the Adelaide Children's Hospital. He was returned a week later but he was still unable to finish his bottle before he would draw his little knees up and scream with colic pain. I had reluctantly stopped breast feeding him; that way I could control the flow of milk by using a smaller teat on a bottle. But even that didn't work.

The poor little chap was in such pain that, in my desperation, I gave him 5mls of Panadol Elixir. I wondered if he would drink while sleeping, drugged on the Panadol. I tried feeding him with the remains of his bottle and he drank the lot! It was the best feed he had had in days. The next time he was due for a feed I gave him Panadol again, and again he drank the whole bottle while asleep,

with no colic pain. And so began probably an unconventional way of feeding this baby. He began putting on weight – the crisis was over. It had taken about three weeks of feeding him like this for the colic to completely disappear. Doug was horrified when I put him back on the breast. 'The milk will be bad by now,' he said. But Dominick never had colic again and I continued to breast feed him for another six months.

We must have stayed in Streaky Bay for two or three months. Money was running low. Doug first got a job with a gang of men whose job it was to dig a large trench for a municipal water pipeline to be laid. This meant blasting through rock with gelignite. Then a man named Mr George Schlink offered him a job on his large sheep property, welding steel cattle yards. This was a much better job because we were given a farmhouse to stay in. The house was very basic and sparsely furnished and the heat was oppressive. The boys seldom had clothes on so there was not much laundry to do which was good because the rainwater tank was getting very low. I used to wrap baby Dominick up in a damp towel and put him near the fan. England and Tasmania never reach those temperatures, so it was a new experience for us.

Another thing that distressed me a lot was the persistent little flies that loved to suck the juices from the corner of the children's eyes. I was told to put castor oil around their eyes to deter them. Every item of food could not be left one minute without a cover on it. The flies would gather in their thousands on the porch around the doorways, and bolt into the house at any opportunity.

We did get as much meat as we could eat. Doug would kill and dress a fat lamb with the help of George's son every few days. After the yards were made, Doug was asked to stay on and do other assorted farm work, mostly of which was done on horseback, which he loved, except for the ever-present suffocating heat and flies. The air was almost too hot to breathe, and any deep breath would usually include a few surprised flies.

When Doug and I were convinced that Dominick was well again, we packed our belongings back into the caravan and headed westward towards Ceduna and Penong. On the road to Penong someone had planted and maintained a cactus garden. The cactuses were of gigantic size and variety, and somehow this sight fascinated James. I wonder if he still remembers it; I expect so, because to this day he has always loved to grow cactuses.

We would drive for perhaps eight hours a day and find a safe spot to park. Then the pram and motorbike would be dragged out of the caravan which was a two-man job, and Doug would go around checking the car and van's roadworthiness: tyres, oil, water, lights and hitches to make sure everything was still intact. Once any repairs were made, he would then lie on the double bed and read the two boys a story while I would rinse and hang out the nappies that had been conveniently washed in the shower recess during the trip, and prepare a meal. If the potato eyes had started to sprout, I would cut them out and bury them in the soft dry earth on the edge of the road. I always liked to give every growing thing a chance. Then we would feed and bathe the children and put the latest wet nappies into the shower recess that still had the children's bathwater in. The dining room table would be lowered and turned into a double bed for James and Dig and, if it wasn't too hot, we all got a good night's sleep.

Ceduna and Penong were the last two towns of any size before the long gravel road through the Nullarbor Plain, also known as the Eyre Highway. This road is 1675km, mostly straight as an arrow and almost dead flat. The saltbush, treeless, featureless and flat country stretched 360 degrees in all directions as far as the eye could see. The road is used by long-haul road trains; big powerful trucks pulling sometimes three or four heavy-laden trailers. These powerful monsters would leave a trail of fine dust following them. The powdered dust would then settle back on the road like a liquid, filling up big potholes and making them invisible to other traffic. They were known as bulldust holes. We destroyed eight tyres by driving into those bulldust holes. Poor Doug spent many a hot sweaty hour jacking up the car or the van to replace a damaged tyre. Along the road at strategic intervals were a few roadside garages selling very overpriced second-hand tyres – we had to pay the price or call a halt to the trip.

Needless to say, by the time we arrived in Perth I think we only had $12 left. We longed to reach the sealed road at the Western Australian border at Eucla. There we could even stay the night in a powered caravan park and let the two boys run around safely. We might even find a shower that actually worked. Oh, what a blessing it is to have a shower after many days of conserving water in the caravan.

To finally be out of the dust of those gravel roads was wonderful. The dust seemed to find its way into everything. It would take me weeks to get it out of our lives. The bitumen road felt like we were silently gliding along, and at a much more reasonable speed. But the Nullabor had to have its final farewell. We had just driven into a caravan park in Norseman and unhitched the car, leaving Dominick still asleep on the back seat – we hadn't even taken the big pram or the motorbike out of the van – when someone threw a rock at the van. Bonk!

The noise startled us as it was thrown with great force, then another *bang*, then another, followed by more. The noise was loud as it hit the side of the metal van. We couldn't see who was doing it. Then the banging became thick and fast as hailstones the size of golf balls pounded one side of the van driven by a strong wind at a 45-degree angle. Every window on that side of the van imploded into fragments showering us all with glass. The boys were safe behind a section of furniture. Doug grabbed a blanket and wrapped it around me. Then he put on his motorbike crash helmet, dashed into the hailstorm and slammed the car doors shut leaving Dominick safe inside the car. He never even woke up. Rindell the dog had jumped into the boot of the car so Doug put the boot lid down on her. The onslaught only lasted a few minutes, but in that short time it had broken every north facing window in

Norseman, and pock-marked the entire side of the caravan. The car metal was a little less dented due to the fact that the metal was better quality than the van. Luckily, our insurance paid for the repair work that we eventually got done in Perth.

When I unwrapped the blanket that was covering me, we noticed I was standing in a pool of blood. The glass had sliced a gash in my leg. It wasn't deep and a few Band-Aids soon fixed it. The boys had wonderful fun romping around the piled-up drifts of the large hailstones. We had to get a glazier to replace the broken windows of the van. A task he did well and very quickly and charged us only the cost of the glass.

We left Norseman the next morning, and headed south to the farming district of Munglinup where my cousin, Hazi, was managing a large sheep station at Boyup Brook with his Australian wife, Julia, and their son, Charles, who they nicknamed Cem. The name Cem was for Charles Edward Malet. As I mentioned in an earlier chapter, Hazi was the one who had introduced me to Douglas as the *Chargot farm rabbit* in 1963 at Taunton Railway Station. He had immigrated shortly after Douglas and I had. It would be good to see him and meet Cem for the first time.

Hazi hadn't lost his looks and British charm, he was still the tall, dark, and handsome gentleman I had loved at Chargot, Somerset. I wondered how he got along with the rough-and-tumble Aussie men on the sheep station, but they all seemed to have accepted him, although they were like chalk and cheese. Julia, his wife, welcomed us and fed us royally. Cem was the same age as Dig, fair-haired and very polite compared to my boys. He enjoyed having some playmates. Doug helped Hazi weld up a roo bar for his car – something every outback Australian farmer needed. The kangaroos on the mainland were big, not like the smaller wallabies in Tasmania. They could do a lot of damage to a car if you didn't have a roo bar.

The reason we went to Munglinup was that the brother-in-law of George Schlink, who Doug had worked for in Streaky Bay, ran a farm there. Doug was told this man would surely find Doug a job. This he did, working on a sheep farm helping in the shearing shed and doing various tasks around the station. The worst job for Doug every morning was to heave dead flyblown sheep onto a trailer and dump them in a nearby swampy area. Apparently, the sheep had been mustered too early into smaller holding paddocks waiting to be shorn. There a lot of them died for lack of feed. There was no house available with the job, so we lived in the caravan and again, ate as much lamb as we wanted, as Doug was killing a sheep a day to feed not only us but the shearers as well, who were working flat out. They paid Doug well. Once we had enough money for the next hop of the journey, we left Munglinup and toured around the coastline of the south-west corner of Western Australia towards Albany, Bunbury and on to Perth.

Chapter 13

Perth, Western Australia

Hazi's sister, Mary-Jane, was now living in Perth. She was the youngest of Sir Edward's children. She had married an Australian man, Mr Bob Pickering. They lived in the pleasant garden suburb of Bassendean with their four-year-old son they called Cookie. I can't remember his real name; I think it's Charles. We both knew Mary-Jane quite well as she was often at Chargot, Somerset, when Douglas and I visited. After graduating from an art college in England she became a portrait and landscape painter. I was one of her practice studies that she painted at Chargot. Douglas never likes that portrait of me, although it now hangs in his Malta office. I don't think anyone could have created an accurate picture of me, his beloved, for he saw me through stardust eyes.

They had a large garden at the back of their house which sloped gently down to the riverbank. They invited us to park our caravan there which was lovely because it was a safe place for James and Dig to play in and I could relax without them escaping. We stayed there for quite a few weeks. Sometime later, Mary-Jane also painted a full-length portrait of Doug sitting, legs crossed, complete with his long boots, a polo neck skivvy, a

Greek fisherman's cap, and holding a bunch of car keys; the keys to his then pride-and-joy, a Jaguar E-type. This was his everyday style of dress at the time, and still is to this day. She was hoping to win the Parmelia Portrait Prize with that painting of, by that time, a well-known and respected radio and television celebrity. Sadly, it was unsuccessful. The painting has been with us many years now and also hangs in Doug's office.

The whole time we were at Bassendean, Doug looked for a job but with little success. But then two job offers presented themselves on the same day. One was a position as manager of a farrowing unit at a large intensive piggery. Doug had done this work in England and was a fully qualified swineologist – the only actual formal qualification he has. He often jokes about this as he has successfully held many jobs that had required various qualifications, none of which he had. The other job was as an announcer at a small country radio station, at a place called Katanning. Doug thought that BS was easier to shovel than PS but the job at the radio station had something else in its favour: a house was provided with the position. Off to Katanning we went in the Flying Banana Split, towing the caravan, that was now ruefully known as the Snail-Mobile, with two little boys, a baby, a boxer, a pram, and a motorbike all wedged in.

The house was unfurnished and with no kitchen cooking equipment, but we had the mattress from the caravan and the cooking equipment. The grass around the house was crunchy and the soil cracked for lack of rain. The ugly noise of white sulphur-crested cockatoos, and the musical warble of currawongs and magpies filled the air. The magpies had obviously been accustomed to meaty handouts from the previous residents, and would hop around near the kitchen door. I was quite mean when it came to giving magpies our hard-earned sausages, but they did get a few. They are territorial animals, and they would frighten the boys by swooping very close to them. I was told they could be quite aggressive and could peck the top of your head.

Doug started work as an announcer on 6WB, the country radio station of 6IX Perth. There were only three members of staff, the manager, his wife and Doug. We all became quite good friends. I resurrected the dry grass around the house by emptying the washing-up water and the bathwater onto it. Even a dead looking rose bush sprang to life. Fresh water was again precious as it came from a rainwater tank on the side of the house, and was not to be wasted on watering lawns and plants. Rindell, who was more of a liability than an asset, was caught red-handed killing a neighbour's sheep and received a lethal bullet for her fun time. The farmer was man enough to come and tell us. I was secretly relieved.

Our stay there, however, was short-lived. No sooner had we established ourselves in the community and settled into that house of bare essentials, when we were called to go to Perth. Douglas was to be a radio announcer on the parent station of 6IX in Perth. It was a big promotion; he had only ever worked in country stations and had never had any formal tuition in radio announcing. The managers at 6IX had heard his voice which was powerful but as sweet as warmed molasses, and very flexible. They wanted him. So, we packed up the van again and Doug announced on air that he was leaving. I was listening to him on our little portable radio and felt sad that no one thanked him or said they would miss him, so I phoned the station and put on the broadest Australian accent that I could and made a big show of appreciation and sadness to hear he was leaving us. It was a talk back show; anyone could ring in and say something, so my voice went out on air to the public in Katanning. It made Douglas' day. He never knew it was me but I told him much later.

At the time, Perth was a big sprawling city. Many people say it is a beautiful city, but I can never quite see the beauty of a city. I find much more beauty in God's untampered-with landscapes.

We found a lovely big caravan park away from any built-up area, called the Orange Grove Caravan Park, and settled our van into a powered site. All these happenings must have been in the one year of leaving Tasmania, for Dominick was still a baby just learning to walk and the other two children were not school age yet. It boggles my mind to think of the number of things we experienced in that one year.

Initially, our caravan was parked near the front of the caravan park. It was a noisy spot and had little privacy so, when Douglas was at the radio station one day, I had the manager hook up the van and relocate it to the very back of the park. A common complaint

of husbands about wives is that they like to rearrange the furniture and Doug thought he had solved this problem as the furniture in the caravan was bolted down. Well, when Doug got home, he couldn't find his home; the whole thing had been moved. But he did have to admit that it was a big improvement.

The park had a fenced swimming pool and a laundry with lots of automatic washing machines; what a treat that was. I'd been handwashing all our clothes and nappies for such a long time. The shower rooms were big and there was no shortage of hot water. There was a drawback though. Perth can get blistering hot in the summer months. We purchased a second-hand but good quality air-conditioner and even got a TV which we set up at the end of our big double bed. That quickly became a favourite place. Sitting on the bed in the cool with the TV entertaining the children with *Sesame Street, Play School* and local shows put on by 6IX such as *Fat Cat & Friends* was such a relief.

Another drawback that we overcame was the petty theft. Our children's toys would be carried off by unsupervised children, and tools and equipment disappeared regularly. We had bought James a wonderful shiny red pedal car. His first car. This was taken repeatedly, so we tied it to the van with a long rope. An adult must have cut the rope at night, and we never saw the peddle car again.

Also, a five-gallon can of petrol that we had chained onto the van was repeatedly drained. Eventually, Douglas added a pound of sugar to it and refilled it. That was taken too. It can't have done the thief's vehicle any good as they no longer seemed in need of our petrol.

I also bought a second-hand child's playpen, unscrewed one corner, and made a fence with it to stop strange children coming into the big canvas annex that Douglas had had custom built for the van. The annex was a great asset as now the two older boys could sleep in proper beds outside the van. This meant we no longer had to turn the van's dining table into a bed every night.

But another irritating thing about the Orange Grove Caravan site was that it backed onto a disused gravel pit which was the playground for hoons on motorbikes. They would roar their bikes up and down the slopes making a hell of a noise just when all the tired mothers were trying to get their little ones to sleep. Us mums complained to the manager, who only said he could do nothing about it. In desperation, we took the law into our own hands. We would confront the bikers ourselves, headed by me, carrying Douglas' loaded rifle. The day and the time were set. About ten of the mums banded together to make our complaint known in no uncertain terms to these noisy teenagers and I led the way.

'We' accosted the hoodlums, but I suddenly realised I was entirely alone. All the ladies had chickened out. It was all up to me. As the motorbike riders came around the corner where the track narrowed, I stood my ground and told them not to ride their motorbikes here at this time of the evening because we couldn't get our children to sleep. They just laughed at me. So, I carefully aimed and, more by luck than skill, shot the tyre of the leading biker, and threatened to do the same again if they came back. They must have taken me seriously for we had no more trouble from their noisy bikes.

The disused gravel pit and undeveloped land behind our van was also popular for people to ride their horses around. Driven to plant another veggie garden, I would take a bucket and child's seaside spade and collect all the horse manure. I'd dig it into the gravel and plant tomato plants, capsicums and lettuce and they grew surprisingly well.

One day Dig brought home a very lame red dog to see if I could help it. I noticed that all the pads of her feet were bleeding and raw. I presumed she had fallen off a farmer's ute and had run for miles trying to catch up with it. She was hot and very thirsty. I told Dig to give her some water and then I took her to the office, tied her to a rail and told the staff to call the dog pound to collect her. The dog pound van came but the dog was nowhere to be found. After they had left Dig showed us where the dog was. He had hidden her in his bunk bed in the annex. What could I do? The dog needed to be able to heal, and to do that she needed someone to adopt her. I should never have mentioned this to Dig who had already claimed her as his dog, as after all, he had found her. We called her Cherokee. That dog was a beautiful, calm, and faithful hound to us for many years, and she even eventually returned with us to Tasmania.

When Douglas started working at 6IX he agreed to be called Don while on air because it was easier to say than Douglas Gresham and there were already two Dougs broadcasting on 6IX. He rapidly gained popularity on both radio and television and was even given prime-time slots. He also hosted many shows that were put on by the station. One of these publicity events was an elephant race, riding real live elephants, which he won! It was probably a fundraising event for a charity.

His main claim to fame there was a radio show he managed, single handedly, called Night Line which ran from 9.00 pm till midnight. He got permission to make it a live helpline radio program. It was designed for people to phone in on air and air their needs, complaints or gratitude. Their needs were often met by other listeners who would be able to provide help or advice. One memorable occasion was a woman who phoned in to say goodbye because she had just taken an overdose. Doug had her call traced while he kept her talking on the phone and arranged for an ambulance to go to her immediately. Another call he had was from a man who phoned in to say he had just arrived home from work a few minutes ago with his little portable transistor radio, to find that his wife had stripped the house bare and taken herself and the children, leaving no note of explanation, only the telephone on the floor. So, he rang the Night Line. The general public rallied to his assistance, and he was helped and supported on every level.

There are many other stories I could tell about that show he managed. I would listen to it in the caravan at night when the children were asleep. He would return home at about 1.00 am absolutely drained. Unfortunately, when he left 6IX, no one was able to do that show. At one stage, Don (I'll call him Don while I recount his time there) was asked to take on an advertising job for a client who owned a chicken farm, selling tons of chicken manure by using 15 second ad-lib radio pieces. But, of course, he wasn't allowed to say the word 'shit'. He became famous for that achievement. He not only sold every ounce of the stuff but was branded with the name the Chicken Shit Man. Many years later when we were living in Ireland an American lady came to Doug during a function and asked if he had ever lived in Perth.

Of course, Doug said, 'Yes.'

She then asked, 'Have you ever been on the radio there?'

'Yes,' he said again.

She burst out laughing and said, 'I know who you are, you're the Chicken Shit Man.' She had recognised his voice.

During our time at the Orange Grove Caravan Park, Douglas' former life in England came back to haunt him. His step-uncle, Warnie, died. When we had left the UK, Douglas had effectively shut the door on that period of his life and had started afresh: new country, new wife, new family, new life. Now he had to return and once again enter that world that held so many sorrows. Before he left, Doug penned a beautiful poem that I still have:

As we part and say goodbye, weep not, do not cry.

Merely dip your finger in the sea

And the water that you touch,

Somewhere touches me.

For as I stand and watch you close the door,

The light of life and living dies in my heart.

That flimsy wooden barrier has left us once again apart.

Dry your eyes as you watch me leave.

Laugh and smile, do not grieve.

For now, that we are apart, and loneliness has come.

Every moment brings us closer, till again we will be as one.

I was left to look after the children and Douglas flew to Warnie's funeral.

He returned with three pale-blue bicycles for the children, even a tiny one for Dominick who was only three years old. The bikes were branded Gresham Flyers. I took lots of photos of the children's first efforts to ride their bikes. The two older ones soon mastered the art but little Dominick would push his bike around and cry with frustration.

Everyone who saw Dominick, whom we had nicknamed Pickle (because he was always in a pickle) would say, 'Oh, isn't he so cute.' And he did have the cutest little face you did ever see. These bikes had to be inside the van at night or else they would have been stolen. One day I saw James proudly straddling his bike leaning on the handlebars asking a group of onlooking children in a tough dominant voice, 'Do you know what space is?'

He never waited for a reply, but answered his own question saying, 'Space is more room to fight in.' I think he was trying to establish his pecking order.

The other thing Douglas brought back after attending Warnie's funeral was money. He was second-in-line after Warnie died to inherit from the will of his stepfather, Jack Lewis. It was a strange and somewhat frightening thing to suddenly have money to buy a house.

I had developed a skill of being frugal, and was almost proud of it. The strange thing is I have never lost the pleasure of not spending money on things. I still wash out plastic bags and reuse them and put the sides to the middle of worn-out sheets. I also darn socks, and mend anything broken. I have even mended some of the plastic pool furniture here in our Maltese villa by melting holes along the crack lines with a hot needle, so as to sew up the crack with strong nylon thread.

It wasn't long after Douglas returned from England that we had bought a house with a big overgrown garden on Kalamunda Road. It was walking distance from a primary school that we knew we would need soon. The children loved that place. I joined a spinning club and went weekly with our neighbour, Anne Williams, to different homes to watch the ladies spin and chat while they showed off their latest wool they had bought and dyed, or the garments they had made. I was soon the proud owner of an Ashford spinning wheel that we had ordered from New Zealand. It came with all the bits needed; carders, extra bobbins and so on. Week after week I would practice under the tuition of the spinning ladies. My work was knotty, thick, and thin. I ended up with a great deal of spun and plied wool from my first efforts at spinning. Later, when Doug also bought himself a wheel and had similar skeins of wool, I turned it all into a garment we called the Gyre-and-Gimble Jacket. It had tassels, a long hood and a belt at the waist. It was a garment that got many comments, some good, some humorous and others envious. Even Liberace, the flamboyant and hugely popular American musician, who Doug was at one stage interviewing on radio, wanted to buy it.

Once the children started school, I realised that I would need to learn to drive a car. Doug tried to give me driving lessons, but he is not a natural teacher. He used to terrify me by showing me how to do skid turns, and how to get out of a slide, oh dear. In the end I refused to be taught by him and I insisted on a professional driving instructor. Once he was satisfied, full of confidence, I went for my driving licence exam. Doug was with me. I passed the driving test, but I had gotten something very insignificant – I thought – wrong on the written test. It was horribly unfair, so I chucked an absolute wobbly, threw my handbag at the examiner and after explaining loudly how unfair I thought it was, I burst into tears. It must have amused everyone in the room as I remember on their faces a look of great delight and endearment – this pretty little long-haired blonde putting on such a show. I passed my exam the next time.

Doug was away from home a lot of the time. When he was home, he was trying to sleep, having got up before dawn, or having come home late at night. Either way, he wasn't much help with the children or company for me. As an up-and-coming radio celebrity, he had bought himself an MGB sports car, and then traded it for a bright yellow Triumph TR-6 and finally the very fancy Jaguar E-type. The E-type he never parted with, and it became a twenty-first birthday present for James. All these cars were toys, not family cars, and he loved them.

I was becoming more and more disillusioned about the so-called 'joys of motherhood' and marriage. Is this what it really is, just a person to look after the children, clean the house, pick up after everyone, while he had a social life, drove in his latest car, or was having a glass or two of beer with the men at the local garage, coming home only after I had got all the children in bed? The more I thought about this the unhappier I became. He had also joined the local fire brigade, a noble act, but that also meant more alone time for me and more time with his friends who I didn't know.

I began to feel giddy, and couldn't walk across a room without balancing myself on the walls. Doug sent me to our family doctor, a Scotsman, who told me I was suffering from depression and needed a break from the children. I was annoyed when he wanted to give me antidepressant drugs. I had done a little psychiatric nursing and dealt with otherwise perfectly healthy people with depression. I wasn't at all charitable towards them at the time, thinking, *why don't they just snap out of it?* I refused any drugs and thought, *I can snap out of this now that I know I haven't got a brain tumour or any other thing seriously wrong with me.*

Doug and I discussed all this, and we decided that I should take a holiday. When I had got my driving license, Doug had bought me the safest car he knew of, a 1969 automatic Volvo 164 that had been used as a demonstration model. It was a lovely reliable car that even had air-conditioning, an unheard-of luxury in those days. We kept it for years and it became James and Dig's first shared car. When we first got it, the boys were able to stand full height on the back seat without hitting their heads on the ceiling.

I could understand why Doug preferred to be away from home – outside the home he was admired and was the centre of attention because he could entertain people with his wit and humour and stories of his life. Everyone wanted to be his friend. After all, he was now a radio and TV personality. But inside the home he was asked, 'Where have you been? What took you so long?'

He returned tired and moody, easily angered, and irritable. He was unapproachable, yet full of expectation to be adored and cared for in a loving way by me. Where was the man I had married who delighted in nothing more than to sit and look at me and hold me in his arms? The children were a source of irritation to him as they disturbed his rest time. Oh, he did have times when he would love to wrestle with the boys on the floor, we called this 'Rampoojell' time. The boys adored their daddy, yet they felt there was something amiss.

Even Dominick begun to sense that something was amiss, for having been out of nappies for over six months, now started to wet his bed. I put a night-time nappy back on him. Still, he would wake in the night and want me to get up and change it for him. I did this for a few nights, until I realised how pointless it was. The night nappy never went on again and he was told that if he wet the bed, he would have to sleep in it as I was not getting up. That seemed to cure him as he hated being in a wet, smelly bed. He has always been meticulously clean and tidy; he never liked getting dirty. He was unlike his older brothers who were carefree, rough and tumble, seeking every experience even if it meant getting covered with mud or cow manure.

The situation at home gnawed away at me daily. I approached Doug about it, and he did try to change and stay home more often. One day he said, 'Have I stayed at home long enough? Can I go now?'

I replied, 'Yes, go.' But under my breath I said, 'Don't bother coming back.'

I would never actually say that for fear of total rejection which I never ever wanted to experience again. Instead, I began to secretly loathe him, while trying hard to seek his love and attention. A good recipe for bitterness, resentment, and depression to take hold. Yes, that doctor was quite correct. I needed to have a holiday but, more importantly, I needed to have time to think and formulate a plan to improve the way things were.

Doug took a week off work and stayed home with the children while I took my new Volvo and headed off on my first long solo drive to a place on the seaside called Margaret River, south of Perth by about three hours. The job of navigating there, using a road map, was very scary for me. There were no GPS navigation aids in those days. Doug always navigated; I had never done it before. But I was determined to conquer my fear. I got there, and never once did I take the wrong road.

I was delighted with the Holiday B&B we had chosen. It was set apart from other town buildings, nestled in amongst shady trees, with lawns and gardens. I would order a big English breakfast every morning, eat only a small amount and make sandwiches with the rest using the toast that was provided. That would then last me all day. We had arranged that Doug would phone me every evening at 8.00 pm and reverse the charge. If everything was okay with me, I would refuse the call. After doing this for quite a few evenings the lady at the telephone exchange started to plead with me to accept his call. She felt so sorry for this poor devoted man who kept calling every night only to be rebuffed.

The late afternoon November sun still had some heat in it but not too much. I decided to take a stroll along the sandy beach which stretched for kilometres on either side of me. With my socks in my pocket and the laces of my shoes tied together and dangling around my neck, the salt water and soft sand caressing and cooling my hot feet, my long loose hair being blown by a soft fresh sea breeze, I walked on and on, pondering all these negative thoughts in my head. There seemed no easy solution.

It wasn't until I came to a full and complete realisation of what it means to be a Christian, that I was able to give credit where the credit was due. From somewhere, a series of new thoughts came into my head. Up till now I had been defeated and afraid, but by 6.30 I felt alive and triumphant. I was ready to face whatever lay in my path as the mother of three small boys, and the wife of a man on the edge of a successful career and possible stardom. And face it with courage and determination. Looking back now on those times I realise that God had come to my rescue once again with yet another precious gift. For years I had credited these thoughts to my own intellect; now I know that it was God that had intervened and corrected my attitude. Let me try to explain the strange thoughts that went through my head that afternoon.

As I walked down that beach, in my mind's eye, I saw a large wheel a bit like the wheel on a bicycle. There was an axle, a hub cap, spokes, a rim, an inner tube tightly filled with air, a valve which allowed the air in or out, and, lastly, a tyre tread made of thick reinforced patterned rubber.

A thought came into my head that I, the wife, and mother, was the axel around which everything turned, including, in part, the healthy life of humanity and civilisation. The future generation was being formed under my supervision, love and care. Then the hub cap protects the smooth running of the axle – me – and it represents powers of Divine assistance, the Holy Spirit, sent by God to guide comfort and minister to His people. Under the protection of the hub cap were James, Dig, and Dominick: three precious growing and learning children who were to be the next generation. These children had the potential of being either useful and powerful citizens of future generations, or agents of hell, bent to destroy God's world. Their future depended on the strength and support of the rest of the wheel and me.

The steel rim is God Himself, the creator of the wheel, for it is God's design structure for humanity, and we are connected to Him by belief. The rim connects all the spokes to the axle. The spokes are the many support structures that enable me, as a mother and wife, to do my God-given job of raising the next generation. The support structure, the spokes, are easy to recognise and name. They are all the things that I need to bring up my children: their father's heritage and teaching, income earned by the father, Biblical teaching, security, a home, schools, hospitals and medical staff, food and water, fuel, transport, helpful friends, maintenance, protection, armies, governments, and skilled workers such as electricians, plumbers, and builders.

Around the rim is the soft inner tube tightly filled with air. This I saw as my husband and father of our children. He is so important that he is protected on every side: firstly, by the rim – which I told you was God the Father – and, secondly, by the outer tyre. The inner tube ensures a soft journey for what is being protected by the hub cap, the next emerging generation. Without my husband the road ahead is rough, bumpy, and difficult. He is tender and vulnerable himself and easily wounded, except that he is protected by the rim and the tread.

The tread of the tyre is made of thick rubber moulded with patterns on it for grip and safety. This is Jesus who is there to protect my husband and take the bumps and bruises and to keep us going in the right direction. Then I saw in my mind's eye that the road we travel on through life is full of difficulties, dangers, and temptations. The biggest of these is Satan's lies. Then there are cheats and thieves, sexual immorality, pride, fear, gossip, drugs and alcohol, depression (the Slough of Despond, from John Bunyan's famous allegory Pilgrim's Progress), hatred, envy, unforgiveness, and secrets and lies in a marriage, and any other nasty thing you would like to imagine. All these things can destroy the structure of the wheel.

The air that fills the inner tube, my husband, is belief and adherence to God and His ways. The more powerful it is, the more protection there is from the rocks and sharp things that litter the road. The last on my list is the valve; this lets the air in and keeps it in, or it can let the air out. This represents free will. Doug is free to choose his own way or to do things God's way. He can let the tyre be pumped up strongly with faith in God, or he can let the air out and be deflated and manage things his own way, without the guidance and protection of God.

These thoughts dominated my mind for the remainder of my holiday and during the long drive home. I borrowed a pencil and pad from the owner of the guest house and spent hours drawing the wheel and labelling all the parts that made it a functioning wheel and I perfected it when I got home. I still have the original

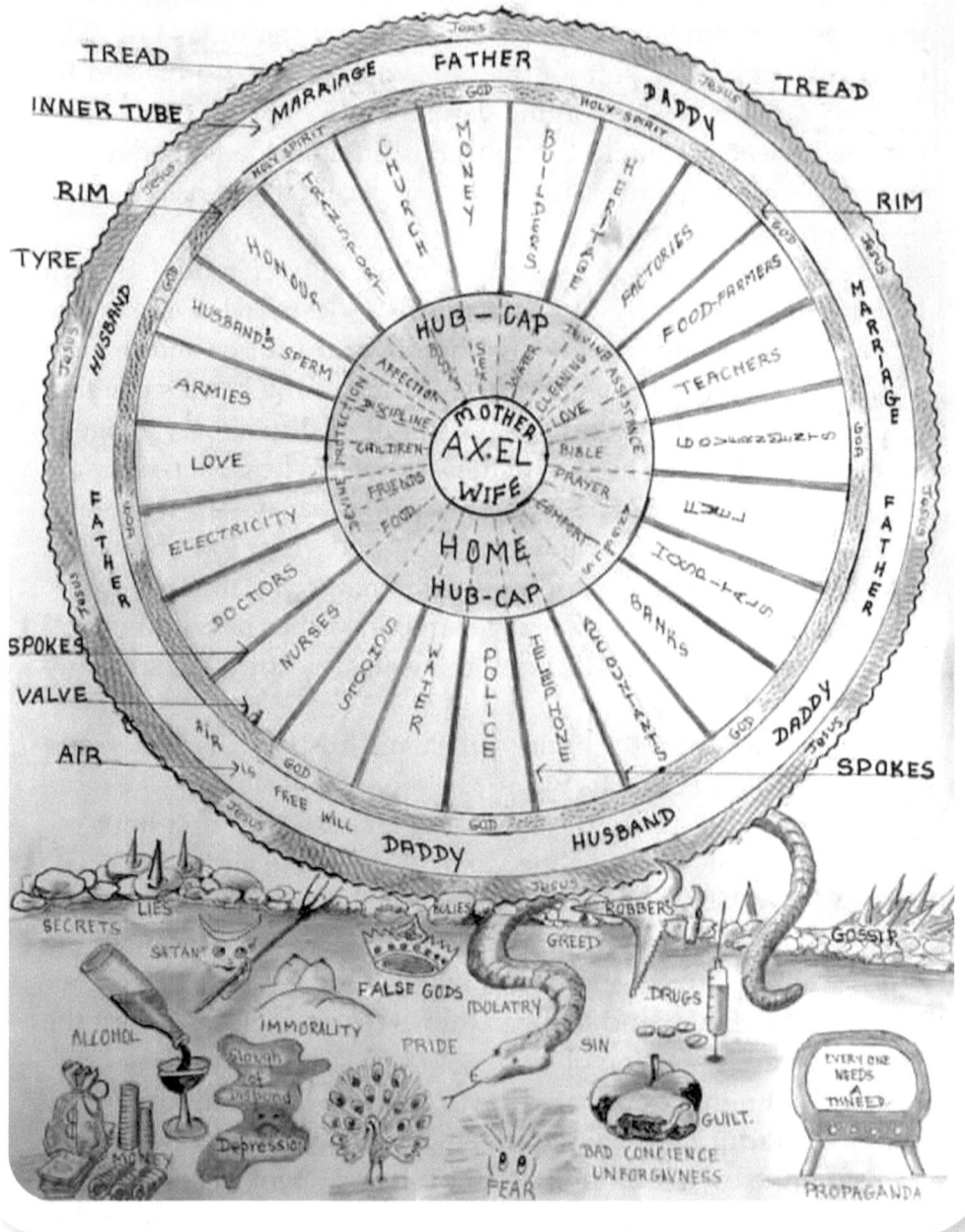

drawing. I will re-draw it to put into this book because that drawing is fifty years old now, and shows its age as it is worn and discoloured.

I returned home a different person. Gone was my long-suffering attitude, and depression. Now I realised that I was the most important structure in God's creation, and everything revolved around me to enable me to do my job of bringing up James, Dig, Dominick and any other children that God were to give me to raise for Him.

What I have written about – we shall call it an encounter with God – has of course been enlarged in my mind since I seriously took the teachings of Jesus in 1983. What completely flabbergasts me, is that even before I knew anything about salvation or being 'born again' I was given God's help in the form of a parable using the structure of a wheel, and He used this to snap me out of Satan's destructive vortex. For if I had not been shown my importance, I may have abandoned my marriage and my children to pursue my own happiness – Satan's cunning lie. But while the author of lies had many more temptations to put me through, that particular temptation and the lesson I was taught was of tremendous value through all the ups and downs in our marriage. It has always stayed with me and kept me stable.

Whenever I am with a mother with her newborn baby in her arms, and if the timing and situation is right, I will tell her of her privileged position, and the awesome responsibility she has been given; to care for God's child. And to also be a loving support to her husband, who works hard to provide for her needs.

Shortly after getting back from my break in Margaret River, Doug and I talked more freely about my role as stay-at-home mother. It was not an easy task. Small children can be very tiring, and I was missing interacting with adults with whom I could have an intelligent conversation. It was decided that I should take a part-time job doing relief nursing. We advertised for a flexible childminder who could fill the gap if Doug and my shift coincided.

A middle-aged couple living in Kalamunda answered the ad and they were ideal. Mr and Mrs Burns. They had reared their own four children and now delighted with the idea that they could look after ours. They came for an interview, we liked them, and the children thought they were wonderful and decided to call them Mumma and Papa Burns. I applied for two nursing positions. One at Kalamunda Hospital and the other at a Catholic nun's hospital in Bassendean called St Anne's Hospital, which I think is now closed.

The Kalamunda Hospital wanted me to start immediately. It had been seven years since I had worked in a hospital so I was a little apprehensive as I would be the only nursing sister on one of the small wards looking after some elderly patients, some with terminal cancer. The sister on duty showed me around and told me the routine, which was a lot to take in in one lesson. But, being night-duty, it was a quiet shift. One patient I remember was Mrs Plaistowe. She was the founder and owner of Plaistowe's Chocolate, now owned by Nestlé, and was quite a wealthy lady. But her wealth meant nothing to her because she was dying of terminal cancer. She told me she would give me all her wealth if I would give her my health. Health is precious, no amount of money can buy it. But that request made me appreciate my own wellbeing and health.

I enjoyed working there. Now I would have interesting tales to tell Doug when I came home and would also have a reason to take more pride in my personal appearance. I sometimes worked in the maternity ward there as well, and was the only nursing staff on duty at night. It worried me a lot because when I was attending a birth, the babies in the nursery were left unattended for long periods. Because it was a private hospital all the patients had their own doctor so there was no resident doctor. Our own family GP, Dr Swanson, often came in to attend to his patients or to deliver a baby.

I did not work there very long, because another vacancy came up at St Anne's Hospital. They must have kept my original application and they offered me the job which included more pay and better conditions. In addition, there would be other sisters, nurses, doctors and nurses' aides on the ward with me. I also knew one of the nursing sisters, Cathy Jones. She was a friend of our next-door neighbour, Anne Williams. Cathy said I could drive in with her, as we would both be doing the 5.00 till 11.00 pm shifts. I was only a new driver and the thought of having company when driving the 9 miles into Bassendean was a good reason to accept the job. I started nursing there on the 27th of October and worked three days a week until December a year later. I was paid $103 a week for those eighteen hours, and that was more money than I had handled in a long time. It felt good to be able to be a little bit more generous with gift giving and indulge myself with a few unnecessary frivolous items that took my fancy.

We developed a good routine at home. Whenever Doug was home, he would look after the children. Otherwise, Mumma and Papa Burns would come.

Memories are strange, wonderful, and sometimes frustrating things. My writing till now has been relying on my memory, with a little bit of help from Mr Google when I have to look up details on people, places and things to help me to be accurate. But it had never crossed my mind to check my five-year diaries. I never thought they went that far back in time. This morning I went into my little hidey hole, my office, which is a sort of small-almost-basement-type quiet corner in my Malta house. It has my personality strewn all over it in the form of pictures on the walls, a display of teddy bears, my original old Bernina sewing machine with various bits of sewing equipment around it, lots of art, painting and drawing things, and a small bookshelf full of gardening books, including knitting books, and Christian counselling books. And, my five-year diaries going back to 1966 right up to 2015. I am still working on the latest one, bringing that one to the end of 2020.

I developed a habit of keeping five-year diaries ever since my school days and seldom ever missed writing up the day's activities every evening. I had a great many of them. One of the most regrettable things I ever did in my life was to burn them one day in a bonfire that had been lit in the vegetable garden when we lived in Ringarooma, Tasmania.

Searching my memory, I began to realise that what I remembered the best were the emotional impacts about things rather than the detail behind the emotion. This was obvious when I review the day I burnt my diaries containing my memories of school, nursing training, my trip to England, nursing in London, my hitchhiking months in Europe with Yogi, and my courting days with Douglas.

At the time I burnt them I had been married about ten years and we were farming again in the north-eastern corner of Tasmania. For some reason I had had a ding-dong verbal fight with Doug. It must have been about those diaries, and some entries I had made in them before I even knew him. In a fit of rage, I threw those precious diaries into the fire. I was probably trying to demonstrate my indignation of him rubbishing some aspect of my life.

In burning them, I was saying, 'It's all water under the bridge, gone, now is the time to live and let bygones be bygones.'

All I remember is that I was furious at the time, so into the fire they went. It was only the diaries of our life together as a married couple that remained unburned. Those ones I found in my office cupboard – I now had facts to back up my emotional memories. A five-year diary only has a very small space to write in so I never wrote about my emotions or how I felt at the time thinking I would remember the emotions. And I do, but not the facts. Now I have both facts and feelings.

The ABC radio station flew Doug to Sydney for a training exercise – or something like that. As was our custom when we were apart, he would phone me every night, just to touch base. One particular evening I was given an unexpected challenge. The phone call went like this:

Doug said, 'Hello Grudle-Pug.' That was a term of endearment he often addressed me with. 'Guess where I am?'

'I haven't got a clue, tell me,' I replied.

'I'm in the Blue Mountains.'

'Oh, really, what's her name?' Doug is not an adventurous type and there could be only one reason why he would have left his paid-for hotel.

'Pam,' he said, somewhat sheepishly. She was sitting on his bed beside him, and was alarmed to hear her name spoken to his wife.

'Okay,' I said. 'Get some paper and write this down: "I, Pam, do solemnly swear that if I get pregnant, the baby belongs to

Mr Douglas and Meredith Gresham." Now make her sign it.' Apparently, she went off in a huff and didn't return.

'Well,' I said to Doug, 'I'm not having any baby of yours being raised by anyone other than myself.'

The whole incident upset me deeply, but I was actually amazed at how I had diffused or interrupted the situation. Those words I spoke were totally spontaneous. I know now it was God who had given them to me. Well, can you think of a better way to have reacted? Screaming, crying, ranting and raging wouldn't have had such a good outcome. Mind you, I did have words with him when he got home but I couldn't help feeling a certain amount of glee in spoiling his night and hers.

Summer in Western Australia gets unbearably hot, often up to 40 degrees and above. While we did have air-conditioning in the sitting room of that Kalamunda house, one can only keep small highly active children content for a little while with Lego or colouring-in. The Volvo was air-conditioned so one day I took the three children to Lake Leschenaultia in Mundaring to cool off and play in the decent playground. I didn't want to get into the water so I parked in a spot where I could watch the two boys, while baby Dominick and I both stayed in the air-conditioned car.

There is nothing more annoying than a bored child, so when children are not bored and are happily playing, the world is a good place. It was a moment like that. Suddenly, I noticed that there was a panic going on in the lake water where James and Dig were playing. The water was turning red around a bunch of children. A man who was in the water picked up Dig, and started carrying him out of the water. Dig was quite calm, but blood was pouring out of his left foot. He had trodden on some broken glass in the water and now there was a deep gash in his foot which was bleeding profusely.

I had nothing to bandage it up with, so I wrapped James' t-shirt tightly around his foot and told Dig to hold his foot tight. The doctor's surgery was open. Both older boys seldom wore shoes so the skin on the soles of his feet were like leather. The doctor had terrible trouble getting a local anaesthetic needle through his skin and even more trouble closing the cut with five stitches. For ten days Dig enjoyed himself like a king. We had to wheel him around in a babies' pusher, and fetch and carry everything for him. I think he thoroughly enjoyed all the attention.

We had become friendly with a South African real estate agent called Rod. Rod would inform us about houses selling cheaply in areas he knew would be fashionable very soon in the Perth suburbs. These houses usually had a lot of potential beauty but had become run down with overgrown gardens around them. We sold the house on Kalamunda Road for a considerable profit after only living there for two years, this was because during our time there I had made the garden a showpiece. It wasn't hard to do as it had a lot of beautiful established trees, shrubs and fruit trees to work with.

We moved into a house in the adjoining suburb of Lesmurdie that Rod had found for us and the two older boys could still attend the same school in Kalamunda. The house was on a small apricot orchard and was set off the road by a double drive with a rose garden separating the drives. The house itself was attractive and only needed a fresh coat of paint, but the garden would be its selling point. Doug bought a ride-on mower and in no time the long yellow grass around the house was turned into lawns. I established a productive vegetable garden and made use of many other neglected features to make that modest house into a desirable place to live.

The apricots proved a bit of a hassle. We never sprayed them and so by the time they were ripe they were full of fruit fly. The fruit all had to be disposed of as it was a finable offence to be caught with fallen fly blown fruit lying on the ground. It was a big job each year. However, fortunately, Rod had found another house for us to buy, so we never had that job for long.

It was while we were at the Lesmurdie house that our fourth child was born. When my pregnancy was in the last months, I resigned from my nursing job in St Anne's Hospital. Our Scottish GP had been monitoring my progress and would deliver the baby in the Kalamunda Hospital where I had once nursed for a season. It had been a very long, dry, hot summer. There wasn't a blade of natural green grass to be seen anywhere. There are two things I remember well about my fourth baby's birth. The first was as soon as the baby's head crowned the heavens let loose with a loud clap of thunder and the skies opened and let down a deluge of much needed rain that went on for days. The drought ended. The second thing was Doctor Swanson saying, 'This one has its seams tucked in.'

Yes, it was a perfect little 7-pound 3-ounce baby girl. We were all overjoyed. She was born on the 15th of April 1976. She remained unnamed for days, as we had no girl's name chosen.

There was a saying in the Gresham family line, that Greshams only sire male children. The saying definitely held true for the last 200 years until I broke this tradition. On that day, I held in my arms a soft warm bundle of sheer delight. A very precious gift from God who promises to satisfy the desires of the heart to all those who love and obey Him. Yes, I know that on that day I barely knew Him let alone loved or obeyed Him, but God, I found out later, is not bound by time like we are. He gave me my heart's desire, a daughter, a girl child to cherish, teach and enjoy.

Having worked in that maternity unit before, I was aware that the newborns were sometimes left unattended for hours when the midwife was busy delivering another baby. I upset the attending

PERTH announcer Don Gresham with wife Merrie, new arrival Lucinda Stormy Meredith Gresham and sons (from left) Timothy, 7, James, 8, and Dominick, 5. Lucinda Stomy is the first girl in 200 years of boys in the Gresham family. Stormy? The heavens turned on a severe electrical disturbance the night she was born. She weighed 3.2 kg (just over seven pounds).

midwife by refusing to let her take my baby into the nursery. The matron of the hospital was called, telling me it was hospital rules that babies are kept in the nursery. I put my foot down and still wouldn't let them take my baby from me, so I had to sign a paper saying that the hospital takes no more responsibility for this baby.

By now, Doug was a well-known public figure in Perth, so newspaper reporters came and took photos of us all with our new arrival who was still unnamed. I still have those newspaper clippings. We eventually did agree on a name: Lucinda Stormy Meredith Gresham. We put the Stormy in there because she was born during a tremendous thunderstorm. She soon become known as Hubsie-bubsie, and then simply Bubble. A nickname she carries to this day.

Shortly after baby Lucinda was born there was another birth in Perth that made headlines in the newspapers. The female orangutan at the Perth Zoo had had a baby as well. But there was a problem, this mother refused to have anything to do with her newborn. An urgent call was made to the general public to any breast-feeding mother to bring expressed breast milk into the zoo to feed this tiny baby with. I had plenty of milk, so with some encouragement from Doug, who loves orangutans, I phoned the zookeeper and told him I would feed the baby ape alongside my new baby girl. The zookeeper was very touched at the offer but said he had been supplied with a lot of breast milk and so the offer was declined.

Chapter 14

Daddles

We are all wonderfully and uniquely designed by God for a purpose. It is He who imprints onto our blueprint our characters, our abilities, and our outward appearances. I would often think of the deep meanings in that song *Where do you go to my lovely?* by Peter Sarstedt from 1969. Those two children in the song longed to be free from the stigma of poverty and to excel with the gifts and abilities God had given them. One of them achieved that by using her God-given beauty, but her brother knew the poverty she came from. Sometimes God places us in an adverse place where our abilities and talents can't be certified with a university degree or diploma. This was the case with my beloved Douglas Howard Gresham. He was and is a man of many God-given talents and has successfully put them to use over the years. But let me tell you where he came from. The combination of the blueprint of his parents will give you a better understanding where Doug gets his unique qualities from.

Douglas was born the second son of a highly intelligent Jewish woman, Helen Joy Davidman. Born in 1915, she grew up in the Bronx in New York. She was known by her middle name Joy. She was the second generation of a Polish/Ukrainian couple who had immigrated to America in the late nineteenth century, the one small surviving branch of a family that was almost completely wiped out by the Nazis during World War Two.

Both her parents were school teachers, therefore they were employed in those hard times, and Joy was provided with a good education, including piano lessons. She was found to be a child prodigy with an IQ score of 150, and possessed exceptional critical, analytical, and musical skills as well as a photographic memory. She was a very active child and far more intelligent than her parents who thought she was hyperactive. They took her to a doctor who put a wooden collar around her neck embedded with uranium needles to treat an overactive thyroid, which was thought to be the cause of her hyperactivity. As a result, her thyroid gland was destroyed and she had to take thyroid tablets for the rest of her life which was cut short, most likely, by that wooden collar as I am sure you can imagine.

Joy married William Lindsay Gresham in 1942 (the year I was born), and had two sons; the first was David, and the second son they named Douglas. Bill and Joy Gresham both tried to make a living from writing, but it was hard in those days to sell their work. Joy's best-known work is the book called *Smoke on the Mountain: An Interpretation of the Ten Commandments* which was published in 1954. Her first novel, *Anya*, was published in 1940 and, at the time, received critical acclaim, but is little known now. She also won several prestigious awards for her poetry.

During the Great Depression, and being brought up by atheist parents, Joy grew disillusioned with the American capitalist system and joined the communist party where she was quite active. For a short time, she somehow wound up working for Metro-Goldwyn-Mayer (MGM) in Hollywood. There she wrote at least four movie scripts, none of which were ever used, but she did help rear the lion cub that became the MGM studio symbol. The same one you see roaring on screen before a movie.

Doug's father, William Lindsay Gresham, was an equally fascinating person.

Known as Bill, he always claimed he was part Cherokee Indian. His facial structure confirms this. He had very high cheekbones and a chin that moulded into his neck and was not at all pronounced. He was born in Baltimore, Maryland, but moved to Brooklyn, New York, as a child where he became fascinated with the carnival show on Coney Island and became friendly with a man with no legs. This man became his mentor and taught him many of the secrets of the carnival and sideshow business.

After he left school, he drifted from job to job. Like his eventual wife, Bill was also a talented musician; he sang and played all the popular songs but particularly enjoyed folk music. He loved to be on stage and had charisma, charm, a good strong singing voice and a handsome physique. He was always a showman. He also found work as a magazine editor and supplemented his income by singing as a radio show host and doing magic shows.

Like Joy, his mind and heart moved towards communism which led him to volunteer as a medic in the Spanish Civil War. He returned to the USA in 1939 with a bad case of PTSD, tuberculosis, and alcoholism.

While in Spain, he was encouraged and inspired to write, eventually producing a fictional piece called *Nightmare Alley* and a non-fictional book called *Monster Midway*, both about the carnival sideshow scene. *Nightmare Alley* was his most successful work and was even made into a major motion picture starring Tyrone Power and several other big names of the day. On its release in 1947, it was not terribly well received due to some of its scandalous and risqué content, but today it is considered a noir classic. Doug's father also wrote a biography of Harry Houdini, short stories and magazine articles, and a haunting semi-autobiographical work about a tuberculosis hospital called *Limbo Tower*. At present, *Nightmare Alley* is being remade as a full-length feature film.

Unfortunately, while in Spain, he became a heavy drinker, and at times abusive. At one time, in an alcoholic frenzy, he hit Douglas over the head with a small fragile bottle which shattered on impact. Eventually he joined Alcoholics Anonymous and was sober for years. When Douglas was about seven, Bill was found to be having an affair with Joy's first cousin, Renee. Bill and Joy decided to divorce, leaving Bill free to marry Renee. Having gotten on top of his alcoholism he was, by all accounts, an excellent husband and father to Renee's two existing children, Bob and Rosemary. By this stage, he had also abandoned communism and turned his attention to spiritualism and Scientology but gave those up too saying that they were just another spook show.

After the divorce, Joy took her two children to England. She too had abandoned communism, and had been corresponding with a university lecturer, author and noted Christian apologist called C.S. Lewis (also known simply as Jack) and she longed to meet him. A friendship developed and, after a long, convoluted, and complicated series of events, the two were married. It is a remarkably beautiful and tragic story and has been told several times in several books, including in Doug's own autobiography,

Lenten Lands. In 1993, the story was made into a major motion picture called *Shadowlands* with Anthony Hopkins and Debra Winger, directed by Sir Richard Attenborough. Doug was asked to be a consultant to Sir Richard, something that he greatly enjoyed.

Suffice it to say, Joy and Jack were married as she was lying sick in a hospital bed with terminal cancer. Miraculously she went into remission and was given four more years of marital bliss before the cancer eventually claimed her in 1960. Ironically, several years before he met Joy Gresham, Jack had penned and published his own autobiography and titled it *Surprised by Joy*. For Doug, the death of his mother was utterly heartbreaking. He was only fourteen years old, and Jack was equally heartbroken. She was a wonderful person, a loving and caring mother, and the joy of Jack's life. Jack didn't really care to live much after she died. He did, however, write the very valuable book called *A Grief Observed*, which was the telling and working through of his own grief.

In 1960, shortly after Joy's death, Doug's father, Bill, came to England to visit his two boys. By this time, Doug had bonded with his new stepfather and feared that he hurt his real father by not being more loving towards him. A year later, back in America in 1962, having been a heavy smoker of cigarettes and pipes for many years, Bill developed cancer of the tongue and throat and, soon after, ended his own life rather than inflict himself on Renee and his family. Then, on the 22nd of November 1963, Jack followed Joy to the grave. History buffs may recognise that as the exact same date as Aldous Huxley died and JFK was assassinated.

So, Doug's mother died when he was fourteen, his father took his own life when he was fifteen, and his stepfather died when he was sixteen. Doug was devastated and essentially without family. Thankfully, as I've mentioned in an earlier chapter, Jean Wakeman, a staunch friend of Joy's, had agreed to be his guardian, so at least he had a roof over his head. Except for Jean, and the poor, sad and equally bereaved alcoholic Warnie, I never met any of Doug's remarkable family.

However, through all the above, I have hardly mentioned David, Doug's elder brother. David was the cause of a lot of emotional and psychological trauma to Doug. One time, while the family were still living in America, David stood on his smaller five-year-old brother's chest under the water in a swimming hole in a field near their upstate New York home. Douglas realised that if he didn't do something he was going to drown. He locked his little legs and feet up and behind David and pushed him away as hard as he could and ran screaming to his parents. They wouldn't believe what he told them. They could see no wrong in their oldest child who would flatly deny that he had done anything to hurt Doug. To this day, Douglas thinks that David had some serious psychological issues.

Doug also told me of a time when he was fourteen years old where David doused him with petrol then tried to throw a lit match on him. Doug knocked the matches out of his hands and escaped to change his clothes and wash off the petrol that had soaked him.

When the English farthing was due to be removed from circulation, Doug realised that they would eventually be collectors' items and worth quite a lot, so he had collected a bag full of the little quarter penny coins. He had been saving them for months. David threw the entire collection into the clay-bottomed lake behind The Kilns. Anything Doug valued or loved David would steal, hide, or destroy.

Other times, when Doug was small, David would physically injure Doug who would run to his mother for protection and comfort. David, following close behind, would deny the whole thing and say Doug was telling lies to get him into trouble. I can't imagine the impact that this relentless victimising must have had on Doug, who is the most truthful person I know. Today, to even suggest to Doug that he is not telling the truth, will anger him.

David always posed at being a scholar and intellectual. In rather typical fashion, when living at The Kilns, which was a strongly Christian household, David chose to adopt Orthodox Judaism after having been through several other religions first. He took on all the associated dietary requirements, dress codes, loud chants, and observations. Admittedly, the Judaism was quite legitimate; he was in fact Jewish, because his mother was Jewish, but it added one more complexity to their already difficult life at The Kilns.

David was living in London when Douglas and I were courting, and occasionally I suggested to Doug that I would like to meet him. The look of horror mixed with fear and anger, followed by a blunt, 'No,' puzzled me, but was enough to stop me from insisting.

But one day I did make Doug very angry with me. I had found David's telephone number in Doug's address book, and, out of curiosity, I phoned him. Someone else answered the phone so I asked for David saying I was Douglas' girlfriend. When David came to the phone, he was angry and spoke to me in hushed undertones, telling me of his displeasure that I, a *Goy* (non-Jewish) woman, should dare to phone him. He then continued the conversation in German for a few seconds and hung up the receiver. I didn't understand much of what he said but got the message that he didn't want others in the room to know he was talking to a non-Jewish woman. That was the first and the last time I ever spoke with David.

When I told Doug what I had done he was furious and afraid, telling me that now David knew of my existence, he would now try to ruin me, or destroy our relationship. I was shocked and surprised at Doug's anger; he had never spoken to me like that, but it was obvious that he was genuinely fearful. The subject was dropped.

I am unsure of the details, but David eventually married an Indian woman and had two children by her, and for a while they all lived not two hours from us in Ireland. But again, Doug kept his distance from his brother.

I did, however, get to meet David in person shortly before he died on Christmas day in 2014. Although 'meet David' seems to be stretching the term a bit. He had advanced Alzheimer's and, at the time of our visit, was in a Swiss hospital. He was a heavily bearded frail old man, and his mind was completely gone. He was unable to recognise anyone, including Douglas. He was fearful and angry and was giving the nursing staff considerable trouble. That encounter shook Douglas to his core. I sat outside in a small garden area and held Doug tight as he sobbed and sobbed uncontrollably. I think he must have really loved his brother who he had had to distance himself from all his life. David was the last remnant of the family that was stolen from him, and I think Doug mourned the relationship that he had never been able to have with his brother.

We have, since become quite friendly with David's petit and lovely wife Padma, and her two sons, Ishmael, and Joseph. She is a sweetheart – loving, generous and kind. She often phones me to see if I am okay in this difficult time of lockdown. She never says a bad word about her husband, but we suspect that it might have been a difficult marriage.

....

Someone once asked me, 'What's Daddles like?' Without even considering the question I said, 'Daddles is infuriating, controlling, proud, and self-righteous. But, underneath his desire to control, is a man who has overcome most of his childhood traumas and has successfully turned it into a life to benefit others. He has rescued me and many others from bad beginnings. He has taught me about love and acceptance, charity, and building on the good in people, rather than condemning them for their past mistakes. I dislike him a little and love him a lot.'

My answer so impressed that person who had asked it, that he wrote it down. That's how I can now confidently repeat what I said. Daddles is fun-loving, yet quiet and serious with a gentle laugh. A lover of all things beautifully made, especially the beauty God has created in the female form and the beauty of poetry in motion in a classic car. Technological masterpieces from the old Concorde jet to the new Tesla car also delight him.

Daddles is a man of huge contrasts. He is greedy and selfish, and yet generous and giving. He is proud and arrogant, yet humble and thoughtful. He is brilliantly intelligent, yet sometimes infuriatingly obtuse, perhaps deliberately. People love him or loathe him. He is staggeringly confident and self-assured, yet desperately insecure and shy. He is bone-idle lazy yet driven to excel. There rarely seems to be middle ground with Daddles. I have often referred to him as an atom bomb with a marshmallow centre.

He loves the music of artists such as Neil Diamond, Max Merritt & the Meteors, Simon and Garfunkel, Roger Whittaker, Jane Oliver, Manhattan Transfer, Marty Robbins, Kenny Rogers and James Galway, to name just a few. Mostly music from his radio announcing career. His favourite classical piece would be Vivaldi's

Four Seasons, and Ludwig van Beethoven's Ninth Symphony. He himself loves to sing and has a lovely deep baritone voice.

His education was not extensive, and he holds no degrees or formal qualifications in anything except swine husbandry, yet he is very intelligent and extremely well read. He once told me, 'I never let schooling interfere with my education.' Yet he can converse with people of all walks of life. Like the line in Kipling's poem, 'If you can walk with kings – nor lose the common touch … you will be a man my son.' He is quite at ease, even with royalty, who we have rubbed shoulders with more than once. We spent an hour or so with Camila and Prince Charles at the Royal Albert Hall before the premiere of *The Lion, The Witch and The Wardrobe* in 2005. Doug chatted with Charles, and I got on famously with Camila, a lovely lady. Yet with any workman, be it a builder, a plumber, or a car mechanic, he is equally able to hold his ground. He gets on famously with them all because he speaks their language.

When I first knew him, Doug was insecure and afraid. Later, he was often practically kept housebound by terrible attacks of fear, depression, and anxiety, which left him unable to face people or to go places. Divorce, repeated childhood bereavement, and extreme sibling rivalry from a disturbed elder brother have left deep scars.

Another contributing factor was the fact that he slowly developed a condition that went undiagnosed for perhaps two or three decades. It is now known as systemic candidiasis and is an overgrowth of yeast in his intestine. The doctors would treat the symptoms but were unable to find the cause. His anxiety was treated by prescribing Valium, and his gut problems were treated with antibiotics. The antibiotics made him feel better, but the symptoms would soon return. Then it was thought he had allergies, a patch test was done, and he reacted to all of them! He seemed to be allergic to food, and I think his weight dropped as low as 60kg. It was a hard time for all of us.

We were running a dairy farm in Ringarooma, Tasmania, when this illness was at its worst. A lot of the time he simply stayed in bed. Every duty became an enormous effort for him. But he would force himself to do the heavy demanding manual labour that is required to run a farm. A lot of the work was done by me, and the boys were a great help. They drove the tractors and shared the milkings, harvested and fed out hay, or any other task, from a very young age. Inside the house we all had to be calm and quiet for any loud noise like the slamming of a door or arguing children would cause Doug to have a panic attack and he would sometimes fly into a rage. The illness caused him to be verbally abusive. That was the hardest thing to endure. It left a wound on all the children that they have carried into their adult years.

A talented doctor eventually found out why he felt so ill and explained how the illness had brought about the feelings of anxiety, fear, and anger. She treated him with a new drug called Diflucan. It took a long time but finally he was rid of the illness. But I'll tell more of his sickness and cure later.

But over the years he has slowly but surely become a mensch – a Yiddish word meaning a man of integrity and honour – who is capable of any given task, a leader, and a trouble shooter. Despite his handicaps, he was, for some time, the Chief Emergency Services Coordinator of north-eastern Tasmania and Captain of the fire brigade. This meant that in certain circumstances, he had authority over and above the ambulance staff and even, under certain conditions, the police.

Now he loves to be the centre of attention, admired, and sought after – don't we all love that to a greater or lesser degree? He loves to delight any guest with rides in his classic cars and with stories of his life and with jokes. Loyalty has always been paramount to Doug. If you become his friend, you will always be his friend. He tells me, 'I don't know how anyone can fall out of love. If I love someone, I will love them for life. I still love every one of my girlfriends.' I am living proof of this statement; through thick and thin he has always loved me.

He has a special rapport with animals, especially horses and dogs. In London, when Doug worked for Bertram Mills Circus, he was a stable assistant helping to manage the magnificent Lipizzaner performing horses, handling many of them simultaneously and leading them out into the circus ring. I really cannot share his love of horses, for me they are too big, too strong-willed and flighty. I'm afraid of them, and they know it. But we both love dogs. I've learned not to make a fuss over a stray dog, or I'll never be able to get rid of it.

He also has a passion for restoring once beautiful but neglected things like old houses, gardens, or classic cars, or even just a rusty pair of pliers or scissors will occupy him for hours as he cleans and polishes. This passion to restore also extends to people whose lives, marriage or relationships have been shattered by abuse or loss. We both worked very hard at this for thirteen years when we lived in southern Ireland, at a house we then owned called Rathvinden. We loved to counsel and try our best to help emotionally distraught people. One time we counselled a young woman we nicknamed Curly Appletop who was suffering from anorexia nervosa. Later, when she got rather tubby, we smilingly told each other, 'Oh dear, I think we overdid it.'

We were both eventually taught a wonderful Biblical approach to counselling by a Canadian doctor called Philip Ney. During the time we were under his tuition, we ourselves underwent some much-needed restoration as well. It was something of a turning point for both of us. But there will be more on this subject in another chapter.

When my Uncle Daily was alive, all his grandchildren called him Daddles. Somehow, Doug took on the name as well and to this day he is known as Daddles by his entire family and many others besides.

Chapter 15

Trials and adjustments
Homes in WA

We moved house three times in those six years that we lived in Western Australia. It was mainly a money-making venture, aided by our real estate agent. If a house was bought and sold again after twelve months of ownership, there was no capital gains tax to be paid.

A house with a lemon orchard on Crystal Brook Road, in the rapidly developing suburb of Wattle Grove in Perth, came on the market. It was a cement brick house with a tiled roof. Unusual, as most houses then were weatherboards with a tin roof. We sold the Wheelwright Road property we had been living in for a considerable profit. Gardening has its benefits for it was the garden improvements that helped it to sell quickly.

Our next living abode was shielded from the busy road by a grove of mature lemon trees. About four giant Jacaranda trees, with their wide canopy, kept our deep veranda shaded. These Jacarandas were vividly decked out with blue flowers before any leaves were even present. We made this area stunningly attractive, by simply turning the sandy soil under the trees into a lovely cool entertainment area by paving it with red bricks and placing nice outdoor furniture on it.

By this stage, Bubble was beginning to crawl. One morning I found Dominick under these trees carefully placing teaspoons of sugar from the sugar bowl, in little heaps on the brick paving. When I asked him what he was doing he said, 'I'm putting sugar down so when the ants eat it, it will rot their teeth and they won't be able to bite Bubble.' Dominick was school age by this time and joining the two older boys who we would drive to school in Kalamunda. Later, they all confidently caught a metropolitan bus at the end of our drive travelling to school and then home again at the end of the day.

Another feature of this place was the overgrown disused vineyard at the back of the house. We spent weeks dismantling what seemed like kilometres of eight-gauge wire off the posts and pulling out the old vines. We turned that area into a vegetable garden, and the far end into a field that held my heavily pregnant house cow called Rosanna. She was a Dairy Shorthorn and gave a full two-gallon bucket of milk morning and night. It was so lovely to have a never-ending supply of fresh milk. The milk raised her calf and our children. In the height of the summer when fresh grass was in short supply, I fed her on wild jam-melons that grew prolifically in the area. They are a sort of small nasty tasting watermelon. I would cut them up into small pieces with a spade so she could manage to eat them. Otherwise, she simply could not open her mouth wide enough to get her teeth into them as cows have no top front teeth, only bottom ones.

Our neighbours on either side also had small holdings and hobby farms with a variety of fruit trees, cattle, sheep, chickens and so on. One neighbour kept some pretty impressive large racehorses in his fields which the boys were forbidden to go near. But the temptation was too much.

Bubble was in her highchair chewing an apple core, which Dig 'borrowed' and used to seduce one of these horses. The boys slipped a scrap of rope around its neck and led what must have been a nice quiet horse down into a dry creek bed where James – who has since filled me in on the finer details of the escapade – was able to scramble up onto its back. But then the horse refused to budge. Dig was advised to take the rope off the horse, but it still refused to budge, so James suggested that Dig tap the horse on the rump with the rope – which he did – by whirling it through the air and bringing it down with a resounding whack on the surprised horse's bum. The horse, of course, took off like a rocket, cleared another dry creek and headed for a fence. James held on over the creek, and then quickly exhausted everything he knew about horse riding (nothing), saw the fence coming up and decided to abandon ship. Unfortunately, the ground was littered with hard ant mounds that are quite unyielding when hit by a small boy at a gazillion kilometres per hour.

In the meantime, I was in the house doing the usual household chores. I went into the boys' room to find James in bed – a very strange thing at that time of the day. He tried to pretend nothing was wrong. Later he was not hungry at dinner, and that evening Doug found a very sad boy hanging over the side of our above-ground swimming pool, floating a broken arm in the cold water. The truth then came out, and Dig was conspicuous by his absence. A trip to the doctor, an x-ray and a plaster cast soon put him right. However, when the cast came off, he was treated to a few half-hearted smacks from his father's belt for disobedience, but it was more of a formality than a punishment. Anyway, the arm soon healed with no lasting consequences other than a tiny bit more respect for horses.

We painted the exterior cement bricks white and did various improvements inside the house. At a certain time of the year the whole place was covered with purple lupins that had self-seeded. Along with the lemon trees there were also a few olive trees that produced quite well. We picked, de-bittered and brined our first olives at that place. We soaked them in a solution of weak caustic soda, and then put them into Fowler's jars, covering them with brine, and vacuum sealed them. They came out surprisingly well. Today we have many olive trees here in Malta including very rare white olives, and we have become masters at the art of making them edible and delicious.

The lemon grove gave us an annual job of laboriously picking lemons, putting them into sacks and taking them by the ute load to a local juice factory. The money they fetched paid our rates. A ute is, by the way, what we call a pick-up truck in Australia.

I became somewhat concerned about a habit that was being formed in our home. The children, and even Doug, never wanted to leave the TV to come to the kitchen table and have their supper. So, I would feed them like animals, putting their food on the sitting room floor in front of them and I would eat alone at the kitchen table. In those days TV sets were temperamental, and it could be difficult to balance the picture. We always got the latest, newest set available by simply renting one. If it played up, the rental company would replace it with a new one.

I tolerated this mealtime travesty for quite some time, simply because I knew Doug loved to watch it while eating – and he still does. But eventually I had had enough. I phoned the rental place and told them to come and take it away. 'But, madam, you have six more months rental paid up on it.'

To which I answered, 'If you don't come and take it, I'm going to put it on the street.' They came and took it.

The boys returned home from school that afternoon, threw their school bags on the sitting room floor and stared in disbelief at the empty spot where the TV used to be. When I sent them outside to play in the lovely cool evening air, all they could do was to throw stones at a tin shed. Well, I was very unpopular for a while, even with Doug. The children had forgotten how to play. Their inventive minds had faded. But soon they were playing cops and robbers, cowboys and itchy bums, hide and seek, and other games on their bikes or with skipping ropes. They made tracks to push their latest Tonka toy trucks along and stole the occasional racehorse.

What was even more fun was when Doug would play with them outside giving them piggyback rides or just walking quietly through the lemon trees in the cool of the evening. From that time onwards we did not have a TV in the house. Much later we got a set that would only play videos. The silly American movie *Smokey and the Bandit* was the first video we got. Doug and the boys watched it over and over again.

All the time we lived in the lemon orchard on Crystal Brook Road, Doug was working long hours at the ABC. He was becoming increasingly tired of living in Perth and longed to go back to Tasmania which he had grown to love and consider home. His dream was to bring the children up on a farm where they could learn useful life skills like fencing, hunting, ploughing, making hay, milking cows, how to kill and cut up meat for the freezer, and so on. He applied for a transfer with the ABC to Hobart, but it was refused. He also made two more applications which were also knocked back. We think the Perth ABC had a hand in their decision. Doug was popular and very versatile, too good an employee to lose to some out-of-the-way provincial outpost. He decided to fly to Hobart himself to see if he could persuade them to take him on.

Art, a friend of ours from our old stomping ground, the Orange Grove Caravan Park, gave him an address of a young woman he knew called Kay, who lived in Hobart and was finishing a Diploma of Education at the university there. Art suggested that Kay would be happy to give Doug accommodation in her flat to save on hotel bills. When the time was right, Doug got a flight to Hobart. He wasn't away long, maybe a week.

Because I was encumbered with four children, on his return, he caught a taxi home from the airport. It was wintertime. The big wood fired cooker was alight in the kitchen which was on the side of the house and had its own outside door. It was good to have him home again. I reached under his open jacket and wrapped my arms around him, and in doing so found a letter in his breast pocket. You may think it strange that I should open it and read it. Doug and I had two promises to each other on our marriage. One was that we would keep no secrets from each other. And the other was that we would not lie to each other. Lies and secrets break up relationships. The letter I had in my hand was from this girl called Kay. A letter that revealed the fact that after her time with him, she was besotted by him and freely and with intimate detail, proclaimed her love. Well, I wasn't expecting that, but it was actually no surprise to me.

When the silence in the kitchen became audible, in an undertone, I said, looking at the floor, 'I'd like to meet her.' My heart was heavy, and my mind was racing with all the things I wanted to say but couldn't. I wasn't going to rush into this situation like a mad bull. I needed time to think. So, I just said, 'I'd like to meet her.'

To which he replied, 'I can arrange that.'

I've forgotten how long it took him to 'arrange that.' Maybe weeks, maybe months. But the day came when she stepped into our Perth home. She was pretty enough, a mop of dark brown curly hair, very fair skin, an outstanding figure and a sweet face covered with freckles. The children were unaware of her significance, thinking she was just a guest. But it soon became evident even to them that she was more than just a guest as their father lavished his attention on her in a very familiar way. But she loved children and quickly won them over by playing games with them. All except young Bubble who, for some time, wouldn't have anything to do with her and would scream in protest if she tried to pick her up.

I was constantly struggling with what I called my Green Dragon: jealousy. But I was determined to win this battle, so I reverted back to my old deceitful self and became a great pretender, all the time wishing that Doug only had eyes for me. Never once did he exchange his love from me to her. He loved us both.

Children are adaptable and when they are young are always very happy to have the company of another adult who would play with them. In truth, it was a big asset to have help and company. We took the children to the beach to swim and play – something I was totally unable to do on my own. I could not manage a baby and keep track of three highly active little boys when all they wanted was to run off in different directions. Outings with the children with Kay to help was a joy, and not a nightmare.

I would sleep with Doug every second night. I was even able now to go to the supermarket without Doug's help. Kay and I would sit in a café, have tea and scones and chat while the children dropped ice cream all down their fronts. Doug hates that kind of thing and is always in a hurry to get home – life was becoming easier and more fun. All I had to do was keep my Green Dragon from raising his ugly head. Kay eventually went back to Hobart and her studies and life carried on.

As Doug's skills and talents, confidence and career had started to really take off, he had gradually become a god; hero-worshiped by many fans. This was a very dangerous position for both of us, for that was the necessary ingredient to fuel his innate pride, arrogance, and ego.

Daddles, like many men, had a high libido, which drove him to seek ways of gratifying it. He justified his behaviour and indulged it by rationalising about the stupidity of modern-day restrictions in marriage. After all, even Solomon and David had lots of wives, didn't they? And, he said, where in God's commandments does it tell us that we should only have one wife or concubine? It was the seventies, after all. We were modern people!

Despite being brought up a strict Roman Catholic, I was Biblically ignorant, having been indoctrinated with the catechism and Catholic dogma, and taught nothing of the actual Bible or the teachings of Christ. So, I swallowed the apparent logic of this and believed Daddles. After all, he pointed out, in many places around the world, men had as many wives as they could afford, and he was now making quite decent money. Now that I know what the Bible actually teaches about marriage, I realise that multiple wives were not God's actual intention for man, but it was man's own idea. However, at the time, it all made perfect sense and despite inner reservations, I condoned his behaviour.

The other factor was my own insecurity and low self-worth. I hungered for his admiration and approval. So, I taught myself to be tolerant which is often, but erroneously considered a Christian quality. What better way of getting his approval than agreeing with his modern liberated theory? I persuaded myself to enjoy the company of the women that he brought into our home. And another helping hand was appreciated to help me look after what was now four children, and deal with the household chores, and later even, the farm work.

Doug used to say, 'If I knew why women found me attractive and desirable, I'd bottle it, sell it and make a fortune.' It was true he did seem to attract women. They were usually educated and good-looking women of means and from good families, theoretically 'classy', but they made no secret of the fact that they lusted after him. Along with his growing celebrity status, he had become a very good-looking young man and had expensive cars and money. He also developed a distinctive dress code that enhanced his figure and his appearance. He wore white moleskin trousers, tucked into calf-high, custom-made boots and a white polo-neck skivvy with a blue ribbed Royal Navy jumper. When he was traveling, he would wear a handmade leather jacket pulled in loosely around his waist, accentuating his wide shoulders and excellent physique. To top it all off would be a Greek style fisherman's cap, with his long service fire brigade badge on it. I was his barber and kept his hair quite fashionable.

Before I married Doug, I had made him promise that he would give up cigarettes. I told him I had no intention of being married to a man who, later in life, I would have to nurse with emphysema or lung cancer. He gave it up for me. But, through the years, when he was out of my sight, he had been accepting cigarettes from other people. Especially now he was a celebrity working with the ABC, which was a very social life for him. I could always smell it on him. Smokers never seem to realise how much they reek of cigarettes to non-smokers.

He didn't deny it, saying, 'One won't hurt.' This distressed me a lot. As I have mentioned earlier, I had looked inside lungs and personally seen the damage caused by smoking and I had nursed patients who had poisoned themselves with tobacco. I was very concerned for Doug's health, particularly given his family's history of cancer. But, more significantly, he had disregarded the promise he had made to me before we were married.

The day came when, dressed in my best clothes and looking like a queen, I was escorted by him to the Parmelia Hilton Hotel where there was a social gathering of dignitaries, including members of parliament, Ernest Lee-Steere, the Lord Mayor of Perth, and the Australian Prime Minister himself, Goff Whitlam. We all stood around a large low coffee table sipping our glasses of champagne. I was just a listening ornament as the conversation was way out of my interest or expertise. Someone offered Doug a cigarette, or should I say, a red rag to a bull, me being the bull.

Doug looked at me with a look of defiance as much as to say, 'You won't stop me in front of this gathering.' I kept my eye on him as someone lit his cigarette with a lighter. I watched him as he inhaled deeply and took another draw and another. There must have been an atmosphere around that table, for the conversation had stopped. All eyes were focused on us. I calmly took the cigarette out of his hand and slowly, deliberately crushed it out on the palm of my hand. Then, calmly and slowly, scraped the ashes off my burnt palm into an ashtray on the table. The pain of that demonstration was excruciating but I never flinched. The silence was broken by some clown saying, 'Blimey, she's got you wrapped up.'

For years Doug had claimed that it was easy to give up smoking, he had done it plenty of times. Somehow, he never seemed to see the irony in that. While the physiological addictiveness of smoking is undeniable, the psychological addictiveness was probably Doug's weak spot, born out of a deep-rooted insecurity and desire to be accepted.

I can't honestly say he never smoked another cigarette. But the incident at the Parmelia Hilton Hotel made a strong impression on him. He curbed his foolish indulgence considerably from that moment. Eventually he never smoked again, except for a very occasional cigar after an evening out to dinner with friends. Even then it was usually a gift and not one he bought. I turn a blind eye to that.

Doug was still determined to return to Tasmania with or without a transfer with the ABC. He resigned from his job. The house was put on the market, and preparations were made to face that long straight flat Nullarbor Plain road once again. This time with four children, a dog, a Jaguar E-type, a Volvo, a house full of furniture and household goods, the same big pram, and, oddly enough, an entire spare bonnet for the E-Type.

Chapter 16

Tasmania, homeward bound – again

The dual cab Dodge truck was filled to capacity. This included two very heavy anvils that we had acquired. The space at the back of the truck, that was meant to be left free for us to sleep in, was usurped by a spare bonnet for the E-type that Doug had found and bought, thinking it may be needed one day. Forty-five years later it is still unused and sits at the back of James' workshop on his beef farm in Glen Innes, New South Wales. My Volvo and the E-Type had gone ahead of us, loaded onto the back of a semitrailer truck.

The new owners of the Crystal Brook Road house had already paid the $90,000 two weeks previously, for the house and six acres of land that went with it. A handy little nest egg for us to start a new place in Tasmania. We were obliged to pay $24 rent a week till we left. Years later, when Dig was a grown man, he had business in Perth and spent some time exploring old haunts. He found the Crystal Brook Road house with some difficulty, for the whole area is now a fairly tightly packed suburban area of Perth.

Some of my lady friends had come to help me clean the house so as to leave it nice for the new occupants. Most of the contents of the house were on the back of our five-ton Dodge truck. We had already sold a lot of things. The new owners bought the milking cow, heavily in calf for $150, and her two-year-old heifer for $100. The hens went for 50 cents each. The boy's bikes were also sold, and the ride-on mower fetched $450.

The week before we left, we stripped the trees of all the ripe lemons and took sixty-nine sacks of them into the juicing factory. It was also a blessing for the new owners that our stay was extended for two weeks as in that time Rosanna the cow gave birth to a fine big heifer calf. Being a very high milk yield cow, she immediately came down with hypocalcaemia, or 'milk fever', which is a dangerously low level of calcium in the bloodstream. If not treated immediately a cow will die very quickly. Being dairy farmers Doug and I recognised this and quickly got a Calcigol injection into her and saved her life. I was also able to give Mr Costello, the new owner, some lessons on how to milk a cow.

July and August are winter months in Australia so the season for biting flies and mosquitos, and the very numerous smaller flies, hadn't started yet. I explained to them that in order to milk Rosanna in the summer months they would have to first spray her with Aerogard – a human fly deterrent – otherwise the cow would fidget and swish her tail endlessly making milking very difficult. Rosanna actually looked forward to the application of this spray twice daily. It gave her some relief.

Doug's final parting crescendo with the ABC was a cleverly researched television documentary that he had done on the subject of life after death, called *The Last Taboo*. Many people who had had near death experiences and had been pronounced clinically dead and had come back to life were interviewed by Doug. He made it into a very interesting half hour of viewing. He was getting congratulatory messages and phone calls about this right up to the time we left. It was fascinating that most people he interviewed had had very similar experiences.

The 31st of August 1978 was Doug's last day with the Perth ABC. The following morning at 3.30 am we lifted sleepy children into the back seat of the truck, accompanied by a somewhat bewildered dog. Those six years in Western Australia were firmly imprinted on all our minds, except perhaps for Bubble who was only two years old. The sprawling area of Perth's many suburbs and small towns were silently passed by under the shadow of the night sky. When the children woke, five hours into the journey, we were already passing through green farmlands and vast areas of virgin forest. We stopped and lit a campfire and boiled some eggs, which we ate with buttered bread. By 2.00 pm we had already reached the gold mining town of Kalgoorlie. It was too early to stop for the night, so Doug drove on. We camped for the night on the outskirts of Norseman. We pitched our small tent, had something to eat, and all slept soundly, so glad to be able to stretch out flat and be away from the thumping bumping noisy crowded dog-hairy 723-kilometre ride in the truck.

The second day we drove from 6.00 am, after a campfire breakfast, till 5.00 pm and camped 60 kilometres outside of Eucla,

having covered 710 kilometres. We were on the Nullarbor again. Thankfully, the entire Nullarbor Plains road had been completely sealed by this time so that section was a lot easier than our first experience seven years before.

On the third day we were on the road again by 7.30 am having first had breakfast cooked on a campfire. Lunch was eaten in the cab of the truck. Doug's aim was to reach Streaky Bay before nightfall. We got there at 4.45 pm having covered 'only' 602 kilometres.

But as we pulled into Streaky Bay township, the truck brakes suddenly completely failed. Fortunately, Doug had a good friend in town who had worked with him during the time we had spent in Streaky Bay, waiting for baby Dominick to return to health on our original westward journey. His friend fitted brand-new copper brake fluid pipes. He wouldn't even let us pay him.

The following day we rested. Doug found a nice little seaside chalet that we could rent for $15 a night. Unfortunately, dogs were not permitted but someone Doug had known took her for the two days we were there. Meanwhile, the boys and I had a fascinating time mingling with dozens of bag-birds (pelicans) on the sandy beach; they had come to see if they could get an easy feed from us, but we had no suitable food for them.

Dominick had slammed his thumb in the truck door. Poor little fellow, it must have been terribly painful; I had never heard him scream so loudly – he was usually a very quiet child. His thumb was bent at almost a 45-degree angle. But, being very young, the bone wasn't broken, only bent. It healed back to normal very quickly.

We were on the road again. It was now the sixth day since we had left our home in Perth. We drove till we were about 90 kilometres outside of Adelaide. Thus, travelling near enough to 700 kilometres again. On this section the muffler fell off the truck, so it was a very noisy day. The exhausted children slept on the seats of the cab. We didn't bother to put up our little tent. Doug and I simply crawled under the truck into our sleeping bags and slept there with Cherokee the dog beside us.

On the seventh day Doug found a garage that fitted a new muffler. We then drove non-stop to Melbourne to my sister Bliss' place arriving at 10.30 at night. This was the longest leg of all at about 726 kilometres.

Bliss lived in an attractive home in a suburb of Melbourne called Blackburn with her six children: four girls and two boys, the youngest being about the same age as Dig. Her young teenage girls loved Dominick and kept swooning over him saying, 'Oh, how cute.' They played and danced with Dig, trying to teach him to be a nightclub dancer. My father was also there to greet us. He was now living quite near to Bliss, and she looked after him in his old age. It was like a little reunion as most of them hadn't seen our children for years. With our arrival, the house was very crowded, but Bliss fed up to sixteen people with skill and ease. She even took us in her Kombi van to Mount Dandenong for an outing. Despite her best efforts, it wasn't a very pleasant stay for I remember there was a lot of sibling jealousy and backbiting between all the children. But we were all grateful for the help, food, and accommodation.

The following day, being the eighth day of the trip, Doug drove to the airport to collect Kay. She had flown from Hobart to be a third driver for our vehicles. My brother, Tinker, joined us and was very helpful. He navigated Doug and Kay to the transport depot where the Volvo and the E-Type were waiting for us. From there the three of them drove back to Bliss' place in a convoy. We said our goodbyes and loaded the children into the three vehicles, Doug driving the truck, Kay driving the E-Type and me in the Volvo and headed for the docks where the car ferry, the MS Empress of Australia, lay in wait.

With both the cars and the truck loaded with all our worldly goods, the dog – who had to sleep in the truck – safely on board, the ship navigated the rough waters of the Bass Strait through the dark of the night. There was no way I was going to persuade James and Dig to sleep; it was all far too exciting. We had only paid for recliner seats in a covered area. Today Dig tells me about the fun of watching the wind, the roll of the sea and the ship derail unsuspecting adults. They thought it was a huge adventure.

The boat slowly edged its way against the Devonport dock at 10.00 am. It was snowing. Not heavy enough to settle but nevertheless it was bitterly cold after being accustomed to the milder weather of Western Australia.

Even in winter-time Tasmania is stunningly beautiful. There is something about it that the mainland of Australia hasn't got. The air is so clean, probably because Tasmania's air spirals off Antarctica and the island's electricity is produced solely by several massive hydroelectricity schemes on the central plateau. It is famous for the visibility of the stars at night – astronomers love to study the southern sky from Tasmania.

The cars and the Dodge truck were eventually unloaded from the ship. Poor Cherokee made a mad dash to the nearest patch of grass. She did not appreciate being locked in the truck all night. We drove in convoy, Doug leading in the truck with James and Dig, followed by Kay in the E-Type with Dominick to talk to her all the way – he had become quite a chatterbox at the age of five, 'jabberwocking' we called it. I bought up the rear with Bubble, now two, asleep most of the way on the back seat of the Volvo.

Our destination for the day was to get to Oatlands, in the Midlands, where my mother now lived in the small cottage that my brother Stephen had bought for her. It was a quick 200-kilometre hop through breathtakingly beautiful scenery. Quite a long haul by Tasmanian standards but nothing after what we had done in the previous week. We travelled through kilometre after kilometre of apple orchards, hop plantations, rich farming land and the convict-built towns like Deloraine and Westbury, and then turned southward through Longford which could be mistaken for a town in England. It had been one of the earlier settlements when Tasmania was first colonised, with British architecture and lots of English trees.

Now we were on the Midland Highway, the landscape changing to dryer farmlands, sheep stations and patches of virgin forest, past Campbell Town and on to Ross, another convict settlement, arriving at Mum's place in Oatlands by about 4.30 pm. Doug drove Kay back to Hobart in the Jaguar, which was another two-hour drive, and stayed the night there, returning the next day. It was the very first time my mother had met the children.

They were all very shy of her but fascinated by her inventive ways. There was a hanging fly screen made of the tubes of coloured biros. She heated the bath water by immersing an old electric heating element into the cold water. The TV had a broom handle connected to the on/off/volume knob, and another broom handle connected onto the channel control knob. Both dowels were supported at the far end by a string hanging from the ceiling right beside her chair. Remote controls weren't invented then, but she had nonetheless made herself a remote control. She had become quite disabled and getting in and out of her chair where she sat nearly all day was difficult for her. The house was dotted with pictures of Mary and the Catholic saints. Saint Teresa was one of her favourites, and even the pope got his picture hung on the wall. I thought it was very sad, not a single picture of her four children, any of her grandchildren, or even her husband was to be seen.

Doug had been in touch with Rod Stewart's real estate agent friends in Launceston and they said they would help us find and buy a farm. They also told us of a furnished house we could rent in the meantime in Campbell Town on the Barton Estate, a large sheep farm in the Midlands. We spent our first eight weeks there in that rental house. It was a busy time for all of us. As well as being driven from place to place by the agency, viewing various farms, Doug had been immediately pounced on by the ABC in Launceston and given a part-time job.

Kay often stayed with us and was a great asset as she helped look after the children while Doug and I were driven around viewing farms. It was early spring, the hawthorn bushes were heavily laden with cascades of white flowers, and the yellow gorse was in bloom. There were snow white lambs with their mothers dotted all over the lush green fields around the house. One night while we were there, Doug called us all outside to watch the amazing light display in the night sky, the beautiful Southern Lights, the Aurora Australis.

We began to feel quite at home in that idyllic surrounding. The children reluctantly went to the Campbell Town primary school on the bus each morning, where they struggled to get on with the rough and tumble farm kids. James was made to stand in the corner because he had mentioned that C.S. Lewis was his grandfather. Many years later, when we were living in Ireland and most of our children had left home, Doug was invited to be a guest speaker at an event. A middle-aged woman approached him and asked, 'Did you ever live in Campbell Town? And did you have a son called James?' Doug nodded.

'Well,' she said sheepishly. 'I was his teacher at the primary school in Campbell Town, Tasmania, and I made him stand in the corner for saying C.S. Lewis was his grandfather.'

Chapter 17

Merriedale Farm

The farm we both liked was on the north-east corner of Tasmania in the rich dairy farming area of Ringarooma, 325 acres for the sum of $75,000. The property was on gently rolling hills, with a deep flowing river as one of its boundaries. It had an established and operating dairy with a five-aside herringbone milking parlour, some uncleared bush land, and a house that would serve the purpose of raising the children and becoming a home. The village of Ringarooma was very small but boasted a pub, post office, primary school, one grocery shop, a haberdashery, petrol station, a mechanic repair garage and a few houses.

On the 20th of October 1978 we paid Mr Payne $8,000 as a deposit on his property. We had already decided to call the place Merriedale Farm. But it wasn't until the 10th of November that we actually moved from the Barton estate house to our farm and home to be. For the first fifteen days we set up camp in the barn, waiting for settlement day on the 24th when we would pay Mr Payne the remaining $67,000. The children loved sleeping in the barn, but I was so much looking forward to being in a real house of my own again. It was a beneficial time nevertheless because Mr Payne took Doug and me through the milking procedure and other things about the farm and community.

The 24th arrived. John and his wife moved out and we unpacked our truck for the last time and moved in. Kay drove from Hobart to help us get settled in. She and I did the evening milk together for the first time. We thought we were very clever to have accomplished that.

The ABC was reluctant to let Doug go, so they gave him longer shifts on air, which meant more money, so for many more months he would drive five days a week on the windy road through Scottsdale and over the Meredith Pass into Launceston and back. Thankfully, Doug loves driving, especially on that very picturesque windy mountain road in his faithful E-type.

It was times like that that I really appreciated having Kay with us. We were best of friends, so much so that Doug was getting jealous of my relationship with her! When she finished her studies, she left Hobart and took on a teaching job at a coastal town called St Helens, only an hour's drive from our new farm.

We soon mastered the art of milking in our new dairy and the other seasonal farm activities like hay making, planting spring feed for the cows, oats, or turnips and rape – types of brassicas – to be strip grazed using a movable electric fence. The boys would bucket feed the replacement heifer calves before going to school. Each year we would give them a gift of a steer calf to raise, always giving it the name of a cut of beef, like T-bone or rump steak. This was so they knew from the onset what that calf's purpose in life would be. As a two-year-old, their calf fetched a good price when sold and the money was deposited in their personal savings account at the bank. Dig bought his first car using his calf money. The children were happy, and the two older ones in particular became very skilled with farm equipment, driving the tractor or our little farm buggy, a flat-tray four-wheel drive Suzuki ute. They even milked the cows on the weekends. We had also bought them two Clydesdale draft horses. The stallion they named Clyde and Bonnie was the mare's name. When visitors came, James and Dig would delight them by taking them for picnics on the horse-drawn wagon.

At first, we were held at arm's length by the locals in the village. We were, after all, strangers – most of the Ringarooma people had been born there. Locals such as Len and Jeff Ranson's great-grandfather had ridden a bicycle through a bush track from Launceston with nothing but an axe strapped to the handlebars to this area and carved himself a farm out of virgin forest. It was fascinating to hear the quite recent memories from the older folk about their pioneering relatives.

During our time there we joined in the celebrations of the 100 years settlement of the north-eastern area of Tasmania. It didn't take those friendly salt-of-the-earth people long to realise we were fair dinkum Aussies, so they accepted us and helped us in many ways, despite us being a bit eccentric. They also weren't slow to make use of Doug's speaking skills and charisma. One year he was invited to give the ANZAC Day speech to a hall filled with all the locals from near and far. A few were in tears. He received a great emotional applause afterwards. He was also elected Captain of the local rural fire brigade and became the local State Emergency Service Coordinator for the region.

Eventually, Doug sadly resigned from the job with the ABC in Launceston, thoroughly sick of the steadily decaying quality of journalism and the long drive. He was now a full-time farmer, a lifestyle he loved. But he was having a lot of trouble with bouts of gut pain and diarrhoea, lethargy, irritability, and panic attacks. He told me it felt as though he was standing in front of a firing squad, waiting for them to pull the trigger. This resulted in him becoming, at the slightest provocation, very abusive to me and his children. We learnt to avoid these outbursts by becoming very subservient to him and not disturbing his rest time with loud noises. He would force himself to do a job that he alone could handle. He spent a lot of time in bed. It didn't occur to me that he was actually ill. I thought he was just lazy, because when someone came to the farm, he would suddenly come alive and bounce out of bed and I used to look forward to visitors for this reason.

Our family doctor, Clive Cawthorn, treated his symptoms with Valium and antibiotics which helped him a lot but never cured the cause. In the village he was known as the only farmer who ran the farm from his bed using his wife and kids to do all the work for him. After the morning milking, Kay and I would sit on the dairy step having a 'sanity' cup of coffee, as we used to call it, and bitching about Doug. It was a very hard time for all of us.

It was when this abusive situation was at its worst that I began to make what I thought was a meaningless prayer, more like an outcry of emotion, to the unknown entity I called God, saying, 'Oh, God, help us.' That misdirected prayer actually hit the mark; God was indeed listening and immediately began to help us.

Because we looked forward to Doug disciplining himself and being in a better mood when visitors came to the house, Kay and I, and even Doug himself, would pick up hitchhikers and, if they were interesting and seemed decent, bring them home. Hitchhiking was quite a common way to spend a summer holiday in Tasmania at the time. I once picked up an Irish dentist, I've forgotten his name, but we did go and visit him when we lived in Ireland years later. I can think of lots more, but time and space won't allow me to tell of them all.

It was Kay who brought back two couples from Bowral, New South Wales. A young married couple called Victoria and her then husband Peter Gordon and a second couple whose names I have forgotten. But it was Vicki who was instrumental in the diagnosis and eventual cure of Doug. Doug had been to an allergist in Hobart who had done a patch test on his back to see which foods he was allergic to.

As I have mentioned earlier, he tested positive to all foods. How could this be?

Vicki was such a live wire; she was a fun-loving but very serious little person and was sadly married to a man who constantly dragged her down. His very presence in the house would cause an atmosphere of tension for everybody. I forget the details, but Vicki stayed on while the other three left, including, oddly enough, her husband.

She enjoyed our company and we all enjoyed having her around. All the children loved her. She was quite at home in a pair of gumboots and bib-and-brace overalls as she helped with even the muddiest of farm chores. In her very early twenties when we met her, she was a petite and shy blonde with a deep love for animals and a desperate fear of spiders. At the age of fourteen her father had died, and she had had to drop out of school to help her grieving mother care for her younger siblings. We did not know it at the time, but when she came to us, she had only recently lost a child in a very late-term miscarriage.

We are still in touch with Vicki and visit her from time to time. Despite never finishing high school, this unassuming little girl eventually studied veterinary nursing, natural medicine and herbal remedies. But none of these satisfied her need for scientific rigour so she returned to school again and studied a Bachelor of Applied Science at the University of Tasmania, majoring in chemistry, biology and microbiology, with Honours!

She then went on to get a PhD at the James Cook University sponsored by the CSIRO and then became a graduate of the Australian Institute of Company Directors (Sydney), and, just to top it off, today she is in the process of completing a Bachelor of Arts in archaeology at the University of Leicester in the UK.

For a day job, Vicki is now the founder, Executive Director and CEO of a biomedical research facility in northern Queensland, with forty-four employees in five countries. She is internationally recognised, having researched and developed a cure for certain types of cancer, just approved and on the market for veterinary use and currently undergoing human trials!

Goodness ... the people you meet on the side of the road.

A few days ago, I emailed Vicki to ask her if I could tell her story. She not only gave me permission but answered in detail the questions I had asked her. Rather than try to paraphrase her words, I thought I would simply paste in some of her response.

I asked her to write about some of her impressions and memories.

> *Oh my, how can I put all of this onto a page?*
>
> *My very first memory was of us turning into the gate and driving up to the house. It was a farm, there were dogs, children, horses, cows – all which made me smile, and smile some more. We were introduced to Doug – confident, funny, a life force to be reckoned with. And then Merrie – warm and pleasant, but quiet and watchful, looking right through into our souls: 'Who are these people? Why are they really here? What do they want? Will they harm my loved ones?'*
>
> *I immediately felt drawn to Merrie. She was real, honest, someone to be trusted, someone who would not fabricate.*
>
> *And oh, my goodness, the generosity was overwhelming. By that evening we were ensconced in a farmhouse (Trenah – another of the Gresham properties) at the end of one of the most beautiful valleys I have seen, laden with treasures from Merrie's larder and a magnificent basket full of vegetables from the 'Merrie Garden' and gallons of fresh milk from the dairy.*
>
> *I was travelling with four companions, my husband Peter, a couple we knew and an Englishman we picked up during our travels. The others were content to stay at the house and not do much. For me I was drawn to the Gresham magnet. I couldn't explain it at the time, but I*

know now. My heart was broken, I was broken, and here were people who would fold me into their life giving me all that I needed to heal.

Doug was magnificent, fiercely intelligent, and larger than life. A humorous, mischievous man who was extraordinarily generous. But a complex being who was on his own path seeking healing.

Merrie was the foundation of the family. The rudder that kept the ship on course. She could be hard when needed but had a heart that was as soft as butter and a gentility to her that took my breath away. And how she worked! Tirelessly keeping farm, family and friends managed, nurtured and loved. And she taught me how to milk cows! Doug and Merrie let me take one of the tractors to Trenah so I could come and go between the farms.

Before I start on the stories, I must mention the children. Great kids, all lovely. But James was his mother's son. A gentle, kind, soft-hearted young man who I immediately felt a bond with. Not your usual teenager. A boy who saw the hurt in the world and felt it strongly.

Peter and friends eventually wanted to leave but I wanted to stay. So, we agreed that I would stay to help with the calving, and they all left – very happy Victoria! Doug and Merrie then bought me a beautiful Weimaraner puppy, Lance, who settled me even further into the beautiful life that these two wonderful people had laid at my feet.

I recall staying at Merriedale farm that time for three months (I think?) while Doug, Merrie and the kids did an around the world trip. Then the family thankfully came home (I missed them so very much). I then moved back to Trenah house for a while (months/years?), stayed at the old post office cottage for a while (many months?). I helped on the farm and had a wonderful time, so happy calving cows (I had good skinny arms for the problem presentations!), riding horses, milking, baling hay, feeding out – bliss! I then decided I was taking too much advantage of my dear friends and so rented a house just outside of Ringarooma.

Stories – so many! Many stories that involved Doug (what an outrageous fellow!), James and the other children, but this note is focused on Merrie so following are my 'Merrie stories'.

Merrie teaching me to milk her cows. What bliss! Such a joy to be amongst these beautiful girls early in the morning with this calm, ultimately capable woman. Her instructions were clear and comprehensive, and I could see that she quickly identified that I had promise – but she kept a watchful eye on me anyway. These were HER girls and woe betide anyone who messed with them! Merrie eventually trusted me to milk on my own and I loved it!

Merrie the gardener. Nothing was wasted at Merriedale farm. Cows ate the grass and produced the delicious, creamy milk. They also produced another valuable item, manure, which Merrie took full advantage of. Truckloads of this delightful stuff made its way to her vegetable garden which she tended with the fervour of a broad acre farmer. And the results reflected her dedication – organic produce that exploded with nutrition and that tasted beyond delicious.

Apple cider. Merrie and her merry band of helpers (children and Victoria!) with mounds of apples and a well organised process line – cutters, juicers, cleaners! The juice then went to Merrie who waved her magic wand and hey presto – cider! Merrie was amazing at producing food – she certainly could teach survivalists a thing or two. Cabbage into sauerkraut, milk into a marvellous array of puddings (the famous 'mud' – which thankfully did involve chocolate!), pickled onions, cakes, biscuits, family meals that would feed an army.

Meat packing. Doug wasn't the only member of the family who had a mischievous side. Merrie could also offer her challenges. I am a vegetarian and have been since I was seventeen years old. One day Merrie politely mentioned to whoever was in earshot that she needed help packing meat from a steer that had been butchered for the family table. She turned her serene face to me, and the challenge was silent but definitely obvious. Of course, I volunteered, I would do anything for this woman!

During my early days with the family, it was clear there were a number of personal challenges Merrie was facing. Doug, her husband, as mentioned previously, was a very interesting person with many excellent qualities. And his love for Merrie was palpable, deep and constant. But his demands of his wife were significant, and his needs were paramount. And Merrie met those needs with grace and a quiet acceptance of the way of things. She clearly identified what would be needed to keep her husband balanced and show him that he was loved and cherished. Merrie provided this support sometimes at great personal expense. And during this she always supported and addressed the needs of her children as well as the rag tag in their life, such as me. And there were others in the community that would come to Merrie, *recognising her as a stalwart individual who could solve problems and provide the salve needed for broken pieces – bodies and souls. Merrie's spirituality and love of God clearly was the basis of her strength and her personal support. This was incredible in itself as, if I remember correctly, her mother, was obsessively religious to the detriment of her beautiful daughter.*

And speaking of providing salve for a broken soul, Merrie certainly played a major role in bringing my shattered pieces back into alignment. Definitely Doug and the whole 'Greshamness' played a very big part, but it was the specific 'Merriness' that underpinned the process. Merrie is a complex character. As I mentioned previously, a gentle soul who could also be as tough and as uncompromising as iron when the need arose. Indeed, her love, care and generous spirit soothed and supported my healing.

But I believe it was the strong, resolute Merrie that silently challenged me to get on with my life and stop wasting my time as well as that of others. This woman led by example, she was a creature of substance, not of 'hot air'. And by being in close proximity to her, observing how she navigated her world and the myriad tasks and challenges she faced on a daily basis, a change was gradually initiated in me. She basically gave me a kick in the spiritual backside!

I honestly believe that Merrie provided the catalyst that set me back on the road of self-development.

Merrie, Doug and what I have referred to as their 'Greshamness' supported me to realise my potential and to grow into the capable, confident and productive woman that I am today.

Well, that was Victoria Gordon's impressions after interacting with us for six years of her life. When I read the complimentary things that she had said about us, I was delighted and slightly embarrassed to put her account in my book, but Daddles insisted that I put it all in. As complimentary as she is about me, I pale in comparison to what she has achieved. We are very proud of her.

Let me tell you a memorable story of our time with Vicki.

Shocking and tasteless baby jokes were one of the ways the young Vicki would get a strong reaction from Doug.

'What goes round and round and taps on glass? A baby in a microwave!'

Another one was, 'What's easier to pick up with a pitchfork, a pile of sand or a pile of babies?'

Doug eventually said, 'Vicki, if you tell one more baby joke, I will stop the car and roll you in a mud puddle.' They were both on their way back to the main house from checking the beef herd at a property in the nearby valley of Trenah, about 5 kilometres from Merriedale farm. We had bought that farm the year previously to use to winter the dairy herd for the three months of the year when they were not being milked and to raise some beef cattle.

Well, Vicki was warned but she just had to tell another shocking baby joke. Doug skidded the car to a halt on the wet Cottons Bridge that spanned the Ringarooma River, dragged her out of the car amidst giggles and screams of protest, and was busy rolling her in a muddy puddle when our neighbour Philip Atkins stopped his car alongside them and asked, 'Oi. What's going on?'

To which Doug replied, 'Just rolling this girl in a mud puddle.'

Philip saluted and said, 'Righto then.' And much to Vicki's chagrin, went on his way.

It wasn't long before even Vicki noticed Doug's mood changes and the fact that he spent a lot of time in his bed. She questioned him about this, and Doug told her how he felt most of the time and all the other many debilitating things he struggled with. Vicki knew of a lady in Sydney who had thrown her baby out the top story window and was convicted and gaoled. A doctor, who was investigating why perfectly sane people would be driven to such irrational behaviour, did a series of tests on this woman and various other prison inmates with similar stories and found they all had one thing in common, an overgrowth of yeast in the intestine.

When these people were treated with antifungal drugs like NILSTAT, their health and mental stability improved. This triggered interest from others in the medical profession and cause and effect was established. The onset of this condition is slow and can take years to become serious. Antibiotics would kill the natural fauna and flora of the bowel, allowing yeast to further invade the area. The yeast multiplies causing most of the things that Doug suffered from – weight loss, bloating, diarrhoea, allergies, irritability, anxiety, and anger.

Vicki put Doug in touch with a doctor in Sydney by the name of Dr Anne Swain. Dr Swain was familiar with this newly identified condition and Doug became her long-distance patient over the phone. The first thing she did was to put him on an elimination diet, eliminating all known food allergens. Initially, this caused Doug to feel terrible, but she had warned him this may happen. After the first week he began to feel much better, saying, 'I haven't felt this well in years. I thought it was normal to feel ill all the time.' He was to stay on the elimination diet until all his symptoms had gone and he was gaining the weight he had lost.

It was a good thing that we were farmers. Our freezers were always full of prime beef and lamb. For breakfast I'd grill him a big T-Bone steak with two eggs on a microwaved skinless potato. Bread and dairy products were not permitted. Lunch would be roast lamb or chicken, with lettuce and parsley and potatoes fried in beef fat and tinned pears with Rice Bubbles for dessert. We all became jealous of his large plates full of delicious foods. His appetite had returned, and also his energy level. He was very reluctant to come off the elimination diet.

Eventually the time came for the first 'challenge'. After many weeks on a diet with little variation, he was to be tested with capsules containing different food allergens. These would arrive in the post from Sydney. The capsules were numbered with instructions but had no description. A blind study. For instance, the first week, he would take capsules from bottle number three and take one every morning for three days. Then he would wait four days, while reporting each day on any side effects. If there was no ill effect, he could take the number four capsules in the same manner. And so on. He had had no adverse effect from any of them until we got to the second last capsule. It turned him inside out within an hour.

We had to wait till he was back to normal before taking the last capsule. This capsule had to be taken in our doctor's surgery as it could cause an anaphylactic reaction. He did react to it quite strongly – but not dangerously – with gut pains, bloating, and general malaise, which took almost a week to recover from.

By this process of elimination Dr Anne Swain was able to confirm her suspicion that Doug was suffering from a condition called candidiasis, an overgrowth of a particular type of yeast in his intestine. Also, after many years of loving to drink milk, it was also discovered that he was lactose intolerant. As you can imagine, Doug's health slowly but surely returned to normal with the help of antifungal drugs such as NILSTAT and later a more efficient drug called Diflucan. They were $10 a pill but the dose was only one a week. Beers, wines and fermented foods had to be avoided. The hardest for him was to curb his sugar intake, as he has such a sweet tooth.

I eventually got back the man that I had married. And the children once again enjoyed having a more stable father instead of a bear with a sore head. I see now it was another way how the devil tried to destroy us and the stability of our family unit. But the gift-giver intervened and sent us that young girl, Vicki Gordon. Doug wasn't such a lazy, abusive man after all. He was quite ill, but now, at last, curable.

However, it took a while for the children to not be afraid of him for, as with any father/son relationship, there had to be discipline. Perhaps Doug, in his effort to have perfect children, was a bit too hard with the discipline. Children can also try the patience of a saint, let alone two people who had had very little examples of how to be a good parent.

Still a deeper, darker problem lurked in the shadows in both of us that needed to be addressed. I'll say no more on that subject right now, except to quote Doug himself who said, 'If you set yourself up as God, you have a fool for a deity.'

....

One beautiful warm, sunny day, when the whole place felt just right, I was busy cooking in the kitchen, looking after Bubble who was only three years old at this stage. I had put her in a pretty little dress and told her to go and play in the garden, for the summer weather had at last arrived. Doug had just left to go to Trenah in the Suzuki farm ute to check the beef cattle. We had recently installed a two-way radio system connecting the house to the dairy, the Suzuki, and tractor. There were no mobile phones in those days. It was proving to be a very useful investment and I never realised just how useful it was about to be. The garden and lawn were fenced in with a sturdy mesh fence that had been set on a 30cm high concrete step. It was just the right height for a little girl to stand on, peer through the fence and look at the orchard and the road that ran past our property. Bubble ran through the open door of the house across the lawn and jumped onto the concrete step to see if her daddy was returning.

Moments later she was back in the kitchen, whimpering and showed me her arm. There on her forearm, 1cm apart, were two small puncture marks. I turned pale, not wanting to believe what I was looking at.

I asked her, 'Was it a snake?' She nodded and told me there were three snakes. We think what she had seen were three sections of the same big snake that had threaded its way through the mesh on the fence.

I immediately ran to the two-way radio and called, 'Base to mobile one.'

The welcoming calm voice of Doug replied, 'Yes, mobile one here, how can I help you?'

'Bubble has been bitten by a snake.' That was all that needed to be said. Doug spun the ute around and slid to a halt a few minutes later amidst clouds of dust in the yard. He made a quick call to the local police station telling them he was coming through in his E-type – which was well known by the local constabulary – with Bubble who had been bitten by a snake.

Mil per mil of venom, the Tasmanian tiger snake is among the world's most deadly of all snakes. But they usually won't attack unless trodden on or harassed. It is always wise to wear gumboots when walking through long grass. Even trousers help, because their fangs are grooved, not hollow like an adder, so a lot of the venom would be absorbed by the material of the trousers. But Bubble had been bitten on the bare arm.

By the time Doug had arrived, I had bound up the whole of her little arm in a crepe bandage. The E-Type paid for itself that day. The whole road into Scottsdale, where the doctors' surgeries were, was strangely empty of any traffic at all. Bubble sat on my lap as I sucked on the puncture marks on her arm and spat it onto the floor of the car. We travelled those 30 kilometres in twelve minutes; the car was airborne several times on the crests of hills.

Bubble was given an antihistamine, I think, and then an ambulance drove her, Doug, and me the 60 kilometres over the Sidling Range on the very windy, hilly road at breakneck speed to Launceston. Sitting in the back, it was difficult for me and Doug to stay on the small seats around the corners. Actually, I felt quite car sick, or it could have been fear that caused my nausea.

Bubble slept most of the way, drugged by the injection that had been given to her at the surgery. The hospital staff were waiting for us and sped our admission into the intensive care unit of the Launceston General Hospital. All I could think of was that only a week prior to this, one of our dogs had picked up a 15cm long tiger snake that had crawled out from under the black plastic on the strawberry bed where I was picking strawberries. The dog shook the snake hard and let it go. Ten minutes later the dog was dead.

Once inside the ICU, the attending doctor had a battle royal to try and get an intravenous drip in. Bubble screamed and fought with all her strength. By this time the venom was taking effect and she was quite delirious, not recognising either me or Doug. She clung to one of the nurses thinking she was Pickle (Dominick). The antivenin in the drip slowly took effect on the snake poison. It was a long night, but by the next morning Bubble was delighting all the nurses in the ICU unit with childish laughter and play.

Doug had to leave early that afternoon to get back and milk the cows. Bubble was now out of danger and would be alright. He got a lift to the outskirts of Launceston determined to hitchhike back to Scottsdale, but cars seemed to be few and far between. After walking for some time his feet were blistered in his gumboots as he was still in his farm clothes. A car eventually stopped, and the driver said, 'Are you alright, mate? Can I give you a lift?'

On the way, with tears in his eyes, Doug told him what had happened. The man told Doug he had heard about it on the radio and offered to take Doug all the way home. Doug thanked him and explained that he had to pick up his E-Type in Scottsdale. We owe that man a huge debt of gratitude for he followed Doug back to the farm and even helped him milk the cows. Such was the love and kindness of the Tasmanian country people.

We learnt afterwards that our whole area had been alerted and every roadside farmer had made it their duty to clear the traffic off the road. Even the Sideling was traffic free for the ambulance. Neighbours had come and cooked a meal for James, Dig and Pickle and stayed the night with them. The cows were milked and the calves fed. Their attentiveness and helpfulness showed us just how much we were now a part of the community.

Bubble recovered with no ill effects, but the Jaguar was now in a sad way. It had never been driven so hard. The drive from the farm to Scottsdale would normally take over half an hour, but Doug did it in about twelve minutes, including a brief fuel stop in Ledgerwood. The road was initially loose gravel and then mostly sealed but undulating, pot-holed and windy. Just outside Scottsdale there is what the locals called the 'Three Mile Straight'. At the end of that, just as it entered the township, Doug glanced at the speedometer and saw 155mp/h (about 250km/h) and the car was still accelerating. The police had the traffic stopped in town and we had skidded to a halt at the surgery only seconds later.

The car had been Doug's daily driving car for some time and was already showing its age, but that twelve minutes pretty much finished it off. Apparently, the clutch was slipping, and second gear had vanished, the front tyres were showing canvas and the front brakes were nearly on fire. The exhaust system had burnt completely off the car leaving two big burn marks on the rear license plate, but the engine was still running fine. Doug had that car completely rebuilt and put into storage. It is now stored at James' farm and has very rarely been on the road since. James still has the burnt Tasmanian license plate.

・・

Although Kay completed her Diploma of Education, she only used it for a brief time taking work as a music teacher at the two neighbouring towns of St Helens and St Marys on the east coast of Tasmania. Doug bought her an elderly Morris Major car, which enabled her to make the hour-long trip to the farm every weekend. Then Kay expressed her desire to run a restaurant instead of being a music teacher.

In the middle of Tasmania is the beautiful little convict-built town of Ross. And in Ross there is an old coaching inn, called the Scotch Thistle Inn, built in about 1830. Ross is at about the midpoint of what was once a gravel track that linked Hobart in the south, to Launceston in the north. Both these towns were shipping ports which supplied Tasmania with many much-needed goods from England and other places. The ships also transported British convicts to the penal settlements on what was then called Van Diemen's Land. Many of these convicts were people convicted of 'heinous crimes' like stealing a loaf of bread to feed their starving family in England in the early 1800s. Much of the early roads, bridges and buildings in Tasmania were built by the forced labour of these men, the Scotch Thistle Inn being one of them.

That gravel track has long since been sealed and then completely rebuilt with Ross no longer on the main highway but bypassed. Ross had become a sleepy little tourist attraction, noted for its wide streets lined with lovely English trees, and many attractive convict-built sandstone houses, several interesting old church buildings and a unique bridge over the Macquarie River which is one of the oldest bridges still in use in Australia. In a remarkably far-sighted move, the local council had at some stage passed an ordinance that there was to be no overhead power or phone lines in the town. This gives the town a very uncluttered and peaceful, old-fashioned atmosphere.

Doug bought the Scotch Thistle Inn. Kay was to run the inn as manager and chef. We designed period costumes to be worn by the waitresses. Full-length dresses with a white apron fitted neatly around the dress and were secured at the back with cross straps and a big bow. The idea was to have a venue for a lot of our excess farm produce – beef and poultry, preserves, jams, sauerkraut, vegetables, homemade smoked sausages, huge strings of plaited onions, and honey from our hives. Even butter and apple cider. However, we never quite mastered the art of making cheese. Our first and last attempt got used as a cricket ball by the children. I also made hand-drawn labels for the jam and honey jars. Doug would make a weekly trip to the inn to deliver the farm goods. Kay lived there managing the staff of about four people. The system seemed to be working well for a time, providing Kay with an income and us with a venue for our abundant self-sufficient produce.

Kay's only formal education was as a music teacher. Her cooking skills were really quite rudimentary although she had learned a lot from me about basic good old-fashioned farm cooking. She also knew nothing about managing the finances of a business. She was very much thrown in the deep end, but when it came to cooking, she must have had some latent skill as the inn soon became quite well-regarded and even won a few awards.

At intervals, James stabled his draft horse in the old coaching stables and would give tourists rides in the horse-drawn cart on school holidays. He noticed that Kay had begun to indulge in the readily available supplies of alcohol and would often sleep till midday with her other duties being neglected. The well-watered system was beginning to fall apart. I'm not sure how many years we owned that place but eventually it was sold.

⋯⋯⋯⋯⋯⋯⋯⋯⋯⋯⋯⋯⋯⋯⋯⋯⋯⋯⋯

Another venture Doug got into was selling highly valued possum and wallaby skins. Ricky Blackwell (whose day job was spreading bulk superphosphate fertiliser) and Doug would go out at night with a spotlight and a rifle. The light would pick up the red glowing eyes of a possum in a tree. Selling the pelts would require shooting it between the eyes so as not to make a hole in its skin. Brush-tailed possums were almost in plague proportion in populated parts of Tasmania. The possums would be attracted by the easy meals in people's orchards. It made it difficult to get a crop of fruit and even the vegetable garden came under attack.

Each time they went night shooting they would end up with about twenty or thirty possums and the same number of wallabies. They fetched $8 to $10 for a possum hide, and about $6 for a wallaby which was a lot of money in those days. James and Dig would start the skinning process by skinning out the hind quarters with their pocketknives and then Ricky would hook the carcass on a stout nail and pull the rest of the hide off. The old disused timber stables at the Trenah property were ideal for pegging out the skins with nails. All the old partition walls for the stalls were still there and these were covered in drying hides. During the day the European yellow-jacket wasps would come in their thousands and strip off any bits of meat that was left on the skins, leaving them in top condition to be sold.

The possums were noisy creatures making a horrible choking, coughing sound that sounded like a man being strangled. It was a frightening noise to hear in the middle of the night if you didn't know its origin. We were always on the lookout for possums in our orchard when the apples and cherries were ripening. One night James located a possum in one of the apple trees.

He said to me, 'Mompska, how much will you give me if I can catch that possum?'

There was no way he could catch a possum in the dark, and up a tree, so I put a high price of $20 on the wager.

Well, in a matter of minutes he brought into the house a very angry possum wrapped up in a blanket. He told us with absolute glee how he had simply placed the blanket under the tree and given the branch the possum was on a hard shake. The possum fell off its branch and in a flash James had him rolled up in the blanket. The mistake we made was letting James open the blanket to show us his catch. The possum made a run for it. But the house, with its closed doors and windows, provided no freedom. The thing now had to be caught again, no easy task. The poor panic-stricken possum ran up the curtains, across bookshelves and furniture causing havoc as it knocked everything off the mantelpiece amidst delighted yells and screams from the excited children.

Eventually I caught it under our double bed where it had tried to hide. But there was a problem: I couldn't lift it up. It had embedded its razor-sharp curved claws into the pile of the carpet. Doug was needed. He was the only one who had the strength necessary to release its grip from the carpet. When we eventually viewed our apple thief closely, we saw it had left its claws in the carpet, soft bleeding ends were all that was left of its tree climbing ability. It was a terrible sight. We all felt so sorry for that poor possum. We let it go into the night. James got his $20, and we learnt another lesson.

· ·

One day, I was busy with household chores, and had just taken a basket of laundry to hang on the line. Bubble, who was now about five years old, was using the Hills Hoist as a convenient climbing frame and had climbed into its topmost structure, when the local policeman, who was also our friend, came up the drive in his police car. I greeted him but couldn't help noticing the serious look on his face. He asked to see Doug. I told him that Doug was in Ross. Then he told me he had come with a warrant for Doug's arrest for non-payment of taxes! *How could this be?* I thought. Our accountant in Launceston handled all our farm accounts and submitted a tax return each year. I raced inside and phoned Daddles and told him about it.

After some time, it was discovered that, despite working for a large and reputable law and tax firm, our accountant hadn't actually submitted a single tax return since taking us on as his client. Our lawyer at the same firm, who was a good friend, said we had no option but to sue him and his law firm. So, Doug found another lawyer in Hobart to handle the case. We won hands down and it actually paid us rather well. It turned out that other people also had had the same thing happen to them. Doug was exonerated from failing to pay his taxes for the past year and was also granted a large amount of money to cover the legal fees. We did quite well from it all. Suffice it to say, we took our business to another accountancy firm and put everything in the hands of a young man, Melvin Adams, whom we nicknamed Nilverm. He became our life-long personal advisor and friend.

But quite soon afterwards Doug and Nilverm were presented with another mammoth problem; again, to do with tax. It was a complicated situation involving taxes on royalties of C.S. Lewis' books and reciprocal tax agreements between the UK and Australia. The system, as I understand it, states that whichever of the two countries' taxes on royalties was the highest, would be the one to be paid. England owed Douglas a large amount of money of the taxation that the Australian Government should have had, but the British tax authorities hadn't paid it to the Australian Government. This meant that the British Government had stopped the onward payment of the royalties in England, therefore Doug had not received them and the taxes that should have been paid to the Australian Government were not paid as they should have been.

After several failed attempts to get assistance, or even a reply, from the British end of things, we were in a quandary. They never responded to our letters or phone calls. Young Nilverm was defeated. He didn't know what else to do.

Doug said to him, 'Okay, I'll write to Her Majesty the Queen.'

This only received a disgusted look from Nilverm who said, 'You're mad, mate. What good will that do?'

But Doug went ahead and did just that. He wrote a delicate and carefully worded letter to Her Majesty the Queen describing the dilemma he was in and asking for her help. Then we waited.

And now comes an interesting twist to this story.

At the time, our letterbox was positioned about half a kilometre down the road at an intersection where it was convenient for the postman, but most inconvenient for us, and tempting for local vandals. Eventually, our letterbox (an old fuel drum) was pulled out of its hole in the back and thrown into the river! This meant that we had to pick up our mail from the post office and I used this opportunity to try and persuade the post office authorities to deliver our mail at the bottom of our drive.

I said to this man, 'We get some very important mail, you know.'

'Madam, what makes you think your mail is any more important than anyone else's?' he snapped back at me.

'Well, when did you last receive a letter from Her Majesty the Queen?' I replied, holding up a letter from Buckingham Palace. It had no stamp on it, simply the Queen's ER insignia with a circle around it. It was a letter from Her Majesty's Private Secretary, advising us that Her Majesty thanked Douglas for his letter and would have the matter investigated!

And the following day, quite coincidentally, I received a letter from my old friend, Yogi, in London. Yogi had married an English Earl, Lord Broke Mountevans, who sat in the House of Lords in Parliament. It was just a chatty letter that she must have penned from her husband's office, using his stationary. That letter also arrived in a very official looking envelope with The House of Lords stamp on it. The lady at the post office looked very surprised. We were too but acted as though nothing was out of the ordinary.

The post office agreed to deliver our mail to the end of our drive.

A short time later we received an envelope from the British taxation department with a curt note, saying, 'You did not have to involve Her Majesty,' and a cheque for the full amount. With absolute glee, Doug drove all the way into Launceston and smacked the letter and the cheque onto Nilverm's desk, saying, 'Do you still think I'm mad now?'

....

Now it is time to tell you of the second incident that was like the grand ending to that time of our lives.

Wheaton College in Illinois, USA is home to the Marion E. Wade Center, which, with American style energy, devotion, and enthusiasm, houses a collection of items associated with, and studies the writings of the following: C.S. Lewis, J.R.R. Tolkien, Dorothy L. Sayers, George MacDonald, G.K. Chesterton, Owen Barfield, and Charles Williams. They had finally tracked down the youngest stepson of C.S. Lewis, one Douglas Gresham, who was living in a remote part of the world in the backwoods of Tasmania, where the Tasmanian devil comes from. That was all they knew of Tasmania.

They contacted Doug and asked him if he would be willing to come to Wheaton and talk about his stepfather at their annual C.S. Lewis conference, all expenses paid. A trip to America with all expenses paid and an opportunity to be centre stage again, how could he refuse? So off he went, leaving me with the children and the farm to look after.

Much to their surprise, they found Doug to be a highly sophisticated, well-dressed, handsome young man who was well accustomed to captivating an audience with a microphone. He stole all their hearts with his memories of the seven years he had personally known the man they all so admired.

It was suggested that he could dictate these memories to a ghost writer and make it into a valuable book. But halfway through they realised that Doug himself could and should write the book. With the encouragement of the Wheaton academics, he set about the task of writing his first book, on a typewriter using Tipp-Ex and lots of swear words. Through frustration and many tears, he dredged up and re-lived those most painful times in his life: the death of his mother, the cruelty of his brother (he couldn't write much about that for David was still alive) and the death of his father and stepfather. This project kept Doug busy for over a year on his return to the farm.

We were all very excited when he came home from Wheaton, and we plied him with many questions. What did he talk about? What was it like in America? Why did they want him to talk about his stepfather? What questions did they ask? It left me with a much bigger unspoken question. Who is this man Lewis? Why do people in America want to know every detail about him, even the brand of tobacco he smoked? I realised I knew nothing about this man and had never even thought to ask Doug questions about him or even read any of his books. Had I missed something important?

I unpacked Doug's case and put the contents away neatly where they belonged. In his suitcase there was an unopened gilt-edged green and gold cassette box containing the unabridged audiobook *Mere Christianity* on twelve cassettes. It had been a gift from a Wade Centre staff member and was read by the British actor Michael York. I placed this among his other dusty unread C.S. Lewis books. I wasn't interested in listening to them, even though I loved to listen to tapes when I was sewing or cooking. But these tapes were all about religion, a taboo subject for me. Even the name on the cover made me recoil. I never ever wanted to have anything to do with religion ever again. 'Be nice to people and don't hurt anyone' was my motto. I thought the God I had created in my mind would be very pleased with me if I did that, and He would let me into His heaven when I died. And that's all there was to it and all I wanted to know.

Chapter 18

New outlooks

That summer had yielded a good harvest of fruit that needed to be preserved. The year was 1983. The fruiting season is a busy time. So much ripe fruit to harvest, which added to the already busy daily routine on a dairy farm. I would spend hours peeling and preparing our orchard crop to be placed into Fowlers jars for canning.

Being dyslexic, I seldom ever read a book but used to love listening to the classics on tape. These tapes I used to pick up at the Launceston Library. They were labelled *Tapes for the Blind*, but the librarian never seemed to mind handing them over to me. I had a laundry basket full of pears to bottle so I looked for a tape to listen to as I worked. The tapes I had in the house were ones I had listened to several times already. I needed something new to occupy my mind.

The *Mere Christianity* tapes that I had unpacked from Doug's suitcase, in the shiny new unopened presentation box, were very conspicuous amongst the other aged and faded books written by his stepfather. Reluctantly, I opened the box and put the first tape on. I did not pick up my peeler or pear corer, but instead had my finger on the stop button all through that first tape, for I wasn't going to listen to any of this 'Go to Jesus' nonsense from anyone, not even from Daddles' stepfather, the man that so many people at Wheaton College and around the world seemed to revere.

I listened to that first tape and even replayed it. It had captured my attention. It made sense. Jack, as Daddles referred to his stepfather, didn't use any churchy jargon in that first tape but spoke very simply and plainly about right and wrong and clues to the meaning of it all. Then he went on to tell us the obvious: that we, as humans, have a moral law built into us. We all learn very young that it is wrong to trip someone up, or to take what isn't ours.

I listened intently as I peeled and cored those pears and packed them into the bottles. I heard that there must be a designer behind all things, someone who had put into us this moral law. Furthermore, I learnt that there is an enemy of God and man. I recognised these two forces in myself. He explained what Christians believe. It was very different to what I had seen and had been taught from the Catholic catechism. Was I hearing about Christianity instead of churchianity or religion? It sounded strangely exciting.

It was now time to go milking. I reluctantly turned the tapes off, longing to hear more. The following day I made a trip into Scottsdale in the Volvo and bought myself a small Walkman cassette player and earphones. Everywhere I went I listened to those tapes. The children soon learned to leave me alone. I listened while I walked the fields to fetch the cows. I listened as I milked the cows. I listened while I was driving the car or collecting the hens' eggs. I listened to those tapes over and over again.

I felt an excitement that I had never known before. Was this all true? How wrong I had been in my own assumptions about things. How could the Catholic Church have it so wrong? I was right in one thing; I always knew there was a creator behind all things. What I didn't know was that I could know Him and have a loving relationship with Him. We were designed to know Him. In a sense I did know Him for I have the same attributes as Him, the same likes, and dislikes. I like what He likes, and I dislike what He dislikes. I love to be known and loved, so does He. I want to be appreciated, so does He. I hate it when people use me and don't thank me, so does He. The list goes on.

Jack explained so well how we can make contact with God and become a real live human being, the kind of being He originally designed before His enemy messed us up. I thought of it a bit like this. We see a nice car, it looks so perfect, but if we lift up the bonnet and find no engine, can we really call it a car? It can't do what it was designed to do and would go nowhere. The tapes talked about God breathing His life into us and making us fully human – like putting a functional engine in us. We have free will and can continue to run our lives our own way and be like unfertile eggs that will never know what it is like to be much more than just a decent egg. We need to become new men or women to be able to see Him and know Him and to receive His help to live this new life down here. Impossible to achieve by yourself, but so easy if we ask Him to do it for us. Not an easy task because we all want to run our lives our own way.

The one thing that troubled me about what I was hearing was this statement, 'He knows me and loves me.' Those two things seemed like a contradiction in terms for I thought, *how could someone love me if they really knew me?* For I knew myself to be full of bitterness, resentment, pretence, intolerance, and anger. Sometimes I'd drop my guard and these things would come out in fits of rage, although most of the time I hid what I thought was my real self. So, with regret and some sadness, I dismissed the whole subject and heaved a sigh of relief, thinking I had nearly been sucked into believing an illusion and a falsehood once again. Despite this conclusion, God now intervened in a dramatic way.

I had a very vivid waking dream. It was almost like an out-of-body experience. I was fully awake at the time. I experienced a succession of dreams which were like the acts of a short play. Through these dreams God showed me how through loving someone I could experience the 'Me' inside them. I could feel their pain or pleasure as if it was my own.

Then He showed me that He himself is at the centre of the 'Me' in every human being. I realised that God feels everything I feel, physical or emotional. He, like me, longs for my happiness and wellbeing. He even shares my longings to be loved and accepted and to be of worth and to be rewarded for my self-sacrifice and efforts. If I connect with Him, He can fulfil these longings much better than I can. I also realised that other people also have God at the centre of their 'Me' – whether they know it or not. If I hurt someone, God feels their pain. If I'm being nice to someone, I'm being nice to Him for He feels their pleasure.

So, I came to realise how and why God loves me, despite my angry moods, pretence and manipulation of people by sulking to get my own way. Even now, not many people can answer the question, why does God love you? I know the answer to that. Because He showed it to me. Through that understanding I came into a tangible awareness of Him.

At the very moment that I grasped the extent and meaning of God's love, something wonderful happened to me. It's hard for me to put it into words. I had never experienced such happiness and joy as I felt then. I was accepted and loved by the most important person in the universe, and I could drop the pretence that I had lived all my life.

Oh, the tears I shed and the remorse I felt thinking about all the people I had hurt, including myself, and all the relationships I had damaged in my life. I was deeply ashamed and asked Him to forgive me. I resolved never to behave like that again. I knew He was real because of the way He had turned my whole life around. I also knew He had been waiting for me to come to this point in my life for a very long time. As my wheel, He had always been with me, protecting me, and shielding me from many hazards as I travelled along the path of my life. He saved me from abduction and saved my life when I had a ruptured appendix at eight months pregnant. He had guided me through many troubled waters, misconceptions and false indoctrinations, and given me many gifts of strength and guidance along the way, this revelation of Himself probably being the greatest gift of all. I had accepted God's love and forgiveness. It was the most meaningful thing I had ever done in my life.

Another thing that Daddles had brought back from Wheaton was the Amplified Bible. I began to read it, something I normally would never have done. The only other Bible we had in the house was a very large family King James Bible, which had belonged to Doug's mother's parents. I would have struggled to understand that Old English terminology.

I've always been in the habit of writing things down, my thoughts or anything interesting that was said. I opened that Amplified Bible at John's Gospel quite accidentally – or so I thought. And as I read through the chapters I transposed all I could into the first person. For instance, when I came to John 3:16, I wrote down, 'God loved me so much that He sent Jesus to rescue me, so if I believed in Him, I would be alive and would not perish but live forever in heaven with Him.'

When I re-read everything I had written, I was head over heels in love, for it was the most amazing love letter I had ever read. What's more, it was from God to me. My family and friends noticed a difference in me. I was much happier instead of being long-suffering. I had lost my anger. I always used to feel angry inside. Just about everything had a different purpose now. I was nice to people to please God and not to make myself appear loveable.

My personal problems didn't all stop there and then. I still had, and still have, inward dragons to fight. But I know I'm not alone in my struggle. I know there is someone who feels my pains and my problems and understands where they come from and can help me through.

During the time I was learning and evaluating all these things, Daddles was away, but I can't remember where. All I know is, he wasn't there. That is why I had to handle my first big test on my own. A heavily laden Holden EH car came up the driveway. I watched from the kitchen window as a big fat man got out and came towards the house leaving his big wife and more children than I could count in his car. I knew who he was, he was Ernie Rumble. He had life figured out. If he had enough children, he could live on the government handouts and would never have to work again.

I opened the door to his knock wondering why he had come. He told me a sob story about how he had been evicted from his rental house in the village. He said he had heard we had a furnished empty cottage on our Trenah property and asked if he could live there. My heart sank. *Oh no, not that house, please,* I thought. It was my hidey hole, the place I went to when I needed to have a few days off from being a farmer, mother, and wife. I would take my Bernina sewing machine up there to mend or make clothes for the children, or to read or, more importantly, to have a few good nights' sleep and Daddles would look after the children.

Yet there stood this big ugly, dirty man asking me to give it to him. I found myself saying, 'Yes, when do you want to move in?' For I knew I was giving accommodation to Jesus, be it in a very strange disguise. A few days passed and Ernie appeared once more at my kitchen door. This time he said he wouldn't be needing the Trenah cottage after all, for he had found a house nearer the village that would suit him better. When he left, I danced a jig around the kitchen for sheer glee. No Ernie Rumble usurping my hidey hole, and I knew I had passed my first test of belief.

When Daddles returned, I tried to convey to him what I had learnt and how I felt. I probably did this without much tact, for his immediate impression was that I had become religious like my mother. He told me in no uncertain terms that if I became like my mother, he was leaving! Try as I may, I couldn't convince him that I was not. I told him about the daydream I had had, which I had called my *Theory of Me*. He told me the correct term was the *Theocentricity of the human id*.

Now that I had found a new managing director of my life that was no longer Doug or myself but Jesus Christ, my heart's desire was to do as He said. This meant finding out about His teachings. My decision to believe in Him wasn't really something I had decided to do; I had no option but to believe because of the conviction in my mind and heart that He was real. Not just a wishful thinking entity that I had formulated to suit my personal desires, but a real living being who not only was in charge, but had my best interests at heart. My decision to obey Him was harder and took learning and practise.

Chapter 19

Around the world in sixty-three days

The year was 1984. The two farms were at a low ebb in the months of May, June, and July. The dairy cows wouldn't calve till the end of July, and the beef cows at Trenah needed very little done with them at this time of the year, except feeding hay to them. Vicki was staying with us. She had been an on-and-off long-term guest and was familiar with all the barn yard animals, dogs, cats, hens and horses, and the running of the house. She agreed to 'hold the fort' allowing us to give the children a treat of a lifetime, taking them on a trip around the world. They were old enough now to be able to retain the memory, yet not old enough to disturb their schooling. James was in his last year at Scottsdale High School and the youngest, Bubble, would be seven in April. We also had a paid helper working on the farm – John Viney, a young local lad who came each day and attended to all the farm duties. The time was now or never. The date was set, the 25th of May, Dig's birthday, and home again on the 25th of July.

Kay was to come with us and was to be introduced as a child minder. Doug worked hard and ended up with a big folder full of airline tickets, hotel reservations and dates and places and relatives that we would visit. The airlines had a special offer for around the world travel, providing we did not back-track. Each child had their own suitcase and shoulder bag. Packing was difficult because we had to take clothes suitable for all seasons and times. The best outfits we bought were seven pale-blue and royal blue tracksuits to be worn by us all when we travelled on planes. Our little group of seven looked so sweet wearing them, and it made it very easy to keep an eye on our numbers when in busy airports. Lots of people commented on our appearance.

We left the house at 7.00 am all clad in our new matching tracksuits and piled into Doug's huge Austin Vanden Plas Princess limousine. The car had originally been brought to Australia for a Royal Tour. Her Majesty had visited and toured Tasmania in 1956. I was just a schoolgirl at Rowella at the time and I remember it well. Our school had been practising a drill of song and parade for months to welcome the Queen in her massive car. Ironically, Doug now owned it. I can't think why he bought it other than indulgence. The locals certainly found it convenient for weddings with Doug always being the chauffeur. However, after a while he got mighty tired of that job because it was a very large car, and it was a mammoth job to polish it.

The month of May is mid-winter in Tasmania, so when we piled into the Princess, it was covered with frost and very stubborn to start. It took quite some time to warm up enough to clear off the large windows. Vicki came with us because she had to drive the Princess back from Launceston Airport.

At Launceston we met up with Kay. Everyone was in high spirits as we embarked on the very first leg of our adventure, Launceston to Melbourne, where we then boarded a Qantas 747 to Los Angeles. On that flight, we had crossed the international date line, which meant that Dig had another day of his birthday. We were met in LA by Eric Christianson, a friend of Doug's father, who took us to the Sheraton Hotel. None of us needed rocking to sleep; we were all very tired.

The following day Dominick, Bubble and I parted company from the rest of the group and headed for Spokane, Washington, via San Francisco, arriving at 3.00 pm. We were met at the airport by two ladies dressed as nuns in brown and black habits. One of them was my mother! The other was Sister Mary Porter. Mary had visited my mother in Oatlands, Tasmania, and had come to visit us on our farm in Ringarooma. When she visited us, she had with her a wooden oblong-shaped box containing a statue of Mary. Doug had picked her up from the airport in the farm Suzuki ute and had decided to take a shortcut back to our farm using a bush track called the Mathinna Plains Road. Mary's luggage was put in the back. Over every bump in the rough road Mary had screamed out, 'Oh, mind my Madonna.'

For some time, my mother had corresponded with this order of Catholic nuns who had branched off from the Pope in Rome because of changes they wouldn't accept, like saying Mass in English and not Latin, and other things. I believe they had a pope of their own. But I'm out of my depth here. Anyway, they called themselves Discalced Carmelite Nuns. They had accepted my mother to join them. I suspect they thought she had money to invest in their order. Eventually they discovered she had no money of her own and was dependent on them. So, she was dismissed from their little club. I'm not sure how this timeline jigsaw puzzle all fits together. All I know is she was there in Spokane in 1984.

These nuns took us to their convent which was called Mount Saint Michael. At the convent we were met by a group of about twenty nuns all in full nun's habits. These nuns had made a name for themselves as the 'Singing Nuns'. They gave us a warm welcome with an impromptu concert, singing for us the song *Dominique* in multi-part harmony. They showed us to comfortable guest quarters where Bubble and Dominick were glad of an early night. I stayed up till about 2.30 am talking with Mary and Mum.

The next day we re-joined the family in Chicago, heading off in a hire car to Wheaton, Illinois, home of the Marion E. Wade Centre that I mentioned previously. We were met by Brenda Philips who took us to the house we would be staying in for the next three days.

A BBQ was held on the grounds of the Centre in our honour. We were introduced to wonderful Christian people who ran that Christian university. Peter Veltman and his wife, Marian, Ed and Ruth Cording, Marjorie and Steve Mead and their baby, and Mary Dorsett.

During those three days we were shown around the Wade collection where we saw lots of C.S. Lewis artifacts, including a wardrobe from The Kilns house in Oxfordshire and a letter from seven-year-old Douglas written to his daddy. It was a memorable time of swapping tales about life in Tasmania and the workings of an American university campus. Two very different worlds. I said very little, but soaked in the good company, their love, and the stories told by one and all.

New York was our next destination. We were on the road by 9.00 am in our Budget rent-a-car and a plane from Chicago took us to LaGuardia Airport. We were to go to JFK Airport by helicopter, but it was cancelled due to bad weather, so we got a bus to JFK and after a long wait caught a flight to Tampa, Florida. Eventually we came to rest in the Tampa Host International Hotel, and all had a good night's sleep.

The hotel shuttle bus took us to the Budget car rental place the next day. They provided us with a Lincoln Town Car, the only car they had big enough to fit us all in. When the girl behind the counter told Doug she was giving us a Lincoln Town Car, she was expecting Doug to show some excitement, instead Doug said, 'A Lincoln Town Car doesn't mean anything to me.' Meaning that he didn't know what it was.

Whereupon the girl replied, 'Oh boy, if a Lincoln Town Car means nothing to you, then I'm coming with you, baby.'

We still smile about that. The receptionist was busily filling out our details when she saw Tasmania as our home address. She was fascinated and said, 'Is there really a Tasmanian devil?'

Very quickly Doug said, 'Yep, sure is. You're lookin' at him.'

Years later, when Doug was in that same office again to rent a car, that same girl was there. She let out a happy shriek, 'It's the Tasmanian devil, he's back again!'

That Lincoln Town Car was massive. I'd never been in a 'Yank Tank' before. Doug, in his usual way, did a 360-skid turn with it in a car park, and tried it out on other manoeuvres and declared that it was underpowered and useless. But it did carry our entire family and luggage in quiet air-conditioned comfort with ease, which was probably more what it was designed to do.

We drove to Port Charlotte crossing the Sunshine Skyway Bridge. In Port Charlotte we met up with Renee and her daughter Rosemary, with her husband Jack, and two small children of theirs, Sean, and Erin. Renee was Doug's father Bill's second wife after he divorced Joy. The Florida air was so humid, Spanish moss hung from the trees, and I felt like I'd been dipped in jam, my skin wet and sticky all the time. Most of the inhabitants lived indoors in the comfort of dry air-conditioned air. It was totally impossible to dry clothes on a line outside. Not my idea of a pleasant place to live.

Kay and I were getting on each other's nerves, bickering, and arguing all the time. Doug had had just about all he could take and forced us to air our grievances and repair our tottering relationship.

How could I tell her that I resented her posing as one of our family? I'm such a coward when it comes to doing or saying something that will hurt and offend a person. Doug demanded that we love one another or else he was going home. So, I put an end to it simply by being nice to her, her benefit at my expense. Isn't that what love is all about? I had decided that love is not an emotion. It's an action. The emotion often follows. If I think of nice things about a person and do nice things to them, I will begin to feel love towards them. If, on the other hand, I think bad things about a person and do bad things to them, I'll begin to hate them.

We stayed with this family for six days in a house on a canal that had been lent to us. The canal looked cool and inviting so Dig and James went for a swim and swam the 40 metres across to the other side only to be warned by a man on the other side that the river was teaming with alligators. The nearest bridge back across the river was about '2 miles downstream'. The boys were not keen to walk that far in the heat, so they risked being an easy meal for an alligator and the two of them swam fast imagining snapping jaws behind them. They made it safely to the other side. They both suspected that the man had been pulling their legs until a few days later while canoeing they spotted a big alligator just metres away from them. Even in that canoe they felt unsafe.

While we were with Rosemary and Jack, we were taken to Disney World, walked around the Sarasota botanical gardens, watched water skiing events at the Cypress Gardens, and were taken to the beach to swim. I was expecting to cool off in the sea, but the water was as warm as a bath.

The next leg of our trip was to Burlington, Vermont, meaning an early start. By 4.30 am we were all in the Lincoln Town Car and off to the airport where we boarded a plane to St. Louis, another to New York and a third to Burlington arriving at 10.00 pm. It was a long day for a six-year-old child, but Bubble was very placid and easy to please. Chad and Eva Walsh, who were good friends of Joy's, met us at the airport and took us to our hotel where we spent the night in nice cool air-conditioning. A lovely change from Florida's hot humid air.

Chad's home was on the banks of Lake Iroquois, a truly beautiful place. We were lent a house and were able to cater for ourselves during our six-day stay. Doug paddled me around the lake in a kayak. By evening it was very wise to be inside for the mosquitos were large, numerous and voracious. We became friendly with a man who was building a wooden house without using nails or screws – no metal. He invited us to sample some good American wines at his home. Doug found a shop that sold fishing gear and set the boys up with a small rod and line each. They were thrilled to catch quite a few small fish which we ceremoniously ate for supper.

Another highlight of that place was the dairy farm, or should I say factory, that we visited. The cows were large and fat, never leaving their own small stall. They could lie down but not turn around. When standing or lying down their bottoms were over a gutter with running water flowing through it constantly, so there were no bad smells or cow muck. Having the cattle inside meant there was no need for fences. The fields were lush and green. The cut grass was fed to the cows on a conveyor belt that passed through their stalls. Also, the power lines were all underground. It was without a doubt the most beautiful farmland I had ever seen. But I did feel sorry for those cows. They never felt the warmth of the sun or the rain washing over them. Their environment was thermostatically controlled at a temperature that suited high performance cows to produce the quantity of milk required of them.

It was now the 13th of June, Dominick's twelfth birthday, and it was time to move on again after a lovely, interesting, and relaxing six days in Vermont. A plane trip took us to JFK and a hotel limo took us to the Statler Hotel in Manhattan. The two rooms we hired

cost $60 each for one night. The evening meal cost a great deal more at $180 for very little food. The children went to bed a little hungry and complained of the heat. None of us got much sleep. There were police sirens and even gunshots during the night. We had returned to New York to visit Doug's uncle, Joy's older brother, Howard Davidman and his wife and child. The conversation was interesting, reminiscing about Joy and Howard's childhood and life.

The next day we checked out of the hotel early and all seven of us went for a bird's eye tour of New York in a helicopter. It was quite hazy with smog but fascinating anyway. Daddles chatted to the pilot and asked him to orbit the Statue of Liberty. We floated around the famous lady at a very close range and took lots of photos. Other people on the balcony were taking photos of us as well.

We were dropped off at JFK Airport where we boarded a TWA plane and arrived in Heathrow, London, at 10.00 am the following morning. The children had slept most of the way, but the grown-ups found it difficult because the seats were small and uncomfortable.

We were met off the plane by my first cousin, Jonathan Price. He had been the best man at our wedding in Westminster Cathedral in 1967. We hadn't seen each other in sixteen years. He was now forty-five and I was forty. It took quite some time to collect our luggage and do the paperwork required to rent the Jaguar XJ6 for Doug to drive and another car, a Ford Fiesta, that was needed to fit us all in. No Lincoln Town Cars were available in England. Jonathan took us to his home where we met his wife Angel, and their baby son, Harvy. The others left to explore and do some shopping while Johnathan and I walked around Hyde Park and just talked. We had such a lot to catch up on. He was curious about Kay, and suspected she was more than a child minder. I told him about our de-facto relationship with her. Jonathan had always used his eyebrows a lot to express himself. That day I'd never seen his eyebrows quite so active and expressive. He was not judgmental but concerned.

On our second day in London, we took the children to the London Zoo in our hired Jag where we once again met up with Jonathan. Bubble was paraded around the Zoo on Jonathan's shoulders, a very high vantage point, Jonathan being 6-foot and 3-inches tall. Later that afternoon, we visited Yogi and her husband, Lord Broke Mountevans, in their Portland Square townhouse. Broke plied Doug with so much Scotch that he was not safe to drive. Kay had to drive through London traffic, and we got hopelessly lost. Eventually, we flagged a cabbie and had him show us the way to Jonathan's house. There was no GPS to guide us in those days.

After London, we spent a few days in a rental farm cottage in Gilford. From there we visited Christopher Price, Jonathan's brother, and his wife Margaret, at Morton Baggot. While staying in Gilford, we drove out to Doug's old stomping grounds around Oxford, popping in at Horton-cum-Studley to visit Doug's guardian Jean Wakeman, and introduce the children to her.

Most days in England were spent traveling from one relative to another and visiting friends and old haunts. It was lovely being able to introduce our children to friends and family. I was so proud of them. The visit to Chargot, Somerset, was probably a highlight for the children. It certainly was for me. Uncle Daily had aged a lot since the death of his wife two years previously. He gave the children a grand tour of all the gold, gilt-framed relatives that hung on the walls in Chargot and told them fascinating stories about them as he went. On one wall was a portrait of Lord Rochester with a monkey on his shoulder who tore up his bills. The children posed for photos beside the pictures of their ancient relatives. Hazi and Julia and their son Cem, whom we had last seen in Munglinup, Western Australia, were also at Chargot.

Aunty Valmai gave us a warm welcome and a lovely lunch at her black and white Tudor cottage in Cradley near Malvern. The house was surrounded by a beautiful typical English country garden. Kay at this time had gone off on her own to visit friends, and it was a relief not to have to explain her presence. But the relatives who did meet her suspected something strange was going on but were far too polite to comment or ask prying questions. But I'm sure there was a lot of talk behind our backs.

We drove in convoy to London the next day, arriving at Jonathan's place mid-afternoon. Doug went to talk with his publishers who wanted him to expand his book on C.S. Lewis, *Memories of a Compassionate Man*, into a full autobiography about his own life. He did just that and changed the title of the book to *Lenten Lands*. It was published by Macmillan Publishers in 1988.

Kay and I walked with the children through St James Park and past Buckingham Palace, the Horse Guards Parade, to Trafalgar Square. James climbed up onto one of the giant lion statues and I took his photo with his head in the lion's mouth. They were fascinated by the pigeons who would quite fearlessly sit on their outstretched arms or on their heads. A visit to Hamleys toy shop in Regent Street was a must. It took quite a while to get the children out of there. Bubble saw a doll in Hamleys that looked just like her. I bought it for her, much to the protest of the boys who said I hadn't bought them a gift. She named that dolly Hamley, and she still has it.

When we got back to Jonathan's place, he had prepared a scented bath for Doug and me and told us to relax while he entertained our children. He was such a sweetie, I have very fond memories of him.

The next day we drove from London all the way to Wales on the far west coast of England. It was a seven-hour drive, visiting Solva on the way, where Doug had spent childhood days with his mother and Jack. They would all go there for holidays together. Doug was disappointed; he said it had changed a lot. Our destination was Craig-y-don, the holiday home belonging to Aunty Valmai and Uncle Jack, shared with Christopher Price and family. The house was perched very conspicuously on the cliffs overlooking the small village of Llangrannog and the sandy beach below. We bought the children fish and chips for their supper and Doug, Kay and I had a pie and a beer at the Pentre Arms served by a moody Welshman who was obviously having a bad day. We stayed two days at Craig-y-don. The children loved it there. Bubble had even become friendly with a little Welsh child her own age and they played on the beach together for hours.

It was now the 4th of June and we left Llangrannog. It took us hours to travel the 170 miles, about 270 kilometres, to Morton Baggot, the home of Christopher and Margaret

Price. Their son Sebastian, who the children knew and called Basco, was also there. A couple of years previously, Basco, then in his very early twenties had spent several weeks with us on the farm in Tasmania. We all had supper in the garden at Morton Baggot because of the heat of the day.

Another highlight was a day spent at The Royal Show at Stoneleigh Abbey. We all fell in love with the purebred Dexter cattle. These are a miniature breed of cattle, only coming up hip high on me. One exhibition after another of the finest that Britain could offer in the line of agricultural machinery, cattle, horses, pigs, and domestic animals were on display. I took far too many photographs.

By the following evening we were in Paris. We had driven to London and returned our two hired cars, the Jag and the Ford Fiesta, which had cost £2,000 for our three-week stay in England. Then we took a plane to Paris and a taxi to our Hotel François in Montmartre where we ate a meal costing 700 francs on a very noisy hot night.

Daddles organised a helicopter flight around Paris the next day. It cost $500 for a 20-minute flight. In the afternoon we were all very tired and so we all slept for a few hours. Kay took the children out to get a meal and Daddles and I were left alone for the first time in a very long while. We found a nice restaurant and enjoyed each other's company, talking about love and family and the trip so far.

Three nights in Paris was our limit. Again, I took far too many photos on our scenic trip on the River Seine. Bubble and I both wore identical grey dresses that I had made. They had small pink flowers imprinted on the material, both of us looking very sweet with our long hair in bunches. In the evening we had to find a restaurant that would take American Express cards to eat at. We were a little apprehensive by the amount of heavily armed policemen everywhere, but nothing bad happened.

Our last day in Paris was spent sightseeing. Daddles spent most of the day in bed as he had an upset tummy, so Kay and I walked to the Louvre with the children. They weren't very impressed by the Mona Lisa. At 6.00 pm we piled into two taxis which took us to the Charles De Gaulle Airport. There were rabbits hopping around all over that airport; they must have developed a knack of avoiding the planes landing and taking off. We boarded a Lufthansa plane for Rome eventually arriving at, ironically, the Oxford Hotel at midnight.

While in Rome we went on a bus tour around the city, saw the Galleria Borghese, and joined a crowd of people for a guided tour around the Vatican, where we saw Michelangelo's Pietà and the Pope himself, who blessed the crowd of tourists and supposedly prayed for us. Doug took the children out at 6.00 pm to find a restaurant to feed them. Once they were fed and in bed, the three of us adults found a lovely restaurant and had a first-class Italian meal. The best food we had eaten in days.

Our stay in Rome was all too short. The following day we left for Greece and Athens, arriving at 3.00 pm. A taxi took us all to the Titania Hotel which was right in the centre of the city. We were informed by the hotel receptionist that the taxi fare from the airport should have been 800 drachmas, but we had been charged 2,000. Tourists are a prime target especially with currency changes. Recently, here in Malta, a bartender tried to charge Doug the equivalent of $20 for a beer. Doug just laughed at him and told him, 'Don't be stupid, I live here.'

Athens was a city of unrest. The heat was overpowering and not conducive to sightseeing during the day, so we preferred to stay in

the cool of the hotel. The streets seemed to be full of passionate young men demonstrating and loudly chanting the name of a political leader, Papandreou, over and over again. The children even called one of their new pups by that name when we got back to the farm.

It was still daylight at 8.00 pm so James and I took Bubble for a walk in the cool of the evening but soon returned because Bubble was drawing too much attention from the men who kept following us and expressing their admiration for her. She probably did look like a young Greek goddess – her fair complexion and long blond hair crowning a very sweet little face. But the men were creepy.

An air-conditioned bus took us on a grand tour of Athens. We spent about three hours walking around the Acropolis and looking around the museum there. Occasionally the delicious smell of sweetcorn being roasted over hot coals would waft our way. These sweetcorn merchants were on most street corners, and we just had to buy some, a cob for each of us. It smelt delicious but it was very dry and difficult to chew.

Daddles had an interesting encounter with a man who wanted his long boots. Without any warning, a man grabbed his right boot and frantically started trying to pull it off. He was either high on drugs or intellectually disabled. Daddles used his left boot to give him a sharp kick in the ribs and the man let go and disappeared in the crowd without his prize.

One day we went to the Greek Islands of Hydra, Paros and Aegina on a boat packed with Arabic, English, and Australian tourists. Market people begging us to buy their goods followed us around and made the experience unpleasant. Also, the air pollution made the sky look thick and grey even far out to sea. However, Dig now tells me he loved Greece and the Greek Islands. He thought the place was magical. The statues of naked women and naked fighting men seem to have made a lasting impression on my fifteen-year-old boy.

When we returned to the cool of our hotel rooms, James was angry and upset because his backpack with all his treasures had vanished. Each evening before the children went to bed, they were required to write about the day's activities in a journal and to stick in any interesting artifacts such as travel brochures or train tickets or menus. Anything that would be interesting to show people back home. James' journal was in that bag. Of course, the hotel staff were very unhelpful. Even getting our laundry back from the hotel laundry service was a hassle. All in all, we were glad when our time in Athens came to an end, and we were pleased to leave. Our next destination was to be Hong Kong, via Bangkok. Hopefully this next place would be more pleasant because it was to be our last stop. From there we would fly home, back to our life on the farm.

It was an overnight flight from Athens to Bangkok, 17th of July. None of us got much sleep on the plane which arrived at 6.00 am. By 9.00 am we were on board a Thai Airways flight to Hong Kong, arriving at 3.00 pm. A hotel coach took us to the Hong Kong Hilton. We had a quick look around the area then all of us fell fast asleep in our hotel rooms. The children had a room service evening meal but Doug, Kay and I had planned to eat at the Eagle's Nest restaurant on the top floor. However, something Doug had eaten on the plane had upset his tummy again, so Kay and I ended up eating by ourselves.

Our first full day in Hong Kong was packed with interesting events from dawn to dusk. The first half of the day we all sat in a clean air-conditioned bus and had a wonderful tour around Hong Kong. The narrator on the bus spoke multiple languages and seemed to prefer entertaining the children as he added humour to his explanations of buildings, the people on the streets, and the districts we passed through. We bought 'coolie hats' for the four children. A cable car took us to the top of Hong Kong, past the dwelling places of many people who lived perched on the steep slopes in houses made of plywood, sacking and even cardboard. The view from the top was amazing.

We were shown around the Tiger Balm Gardens and Excuse Me Beach. Its name alone conjured up interesting stories as to why it was called by that name. Walking around the residential area of the waterways was such an eye-opener for the children seeing how these people lived in their floating sampan homes. The poverty and the conditions they lived in silenced the chatter and the play of the children. As mentioned, Bubble was only seven, yet she still remembers it and told me today that she felt ashamed of her wealth. Strangely, despite the poverty, all the children there looked clean and well fed. Visiting a school was a highlight for me. All those little Chinese faces smiling up at us. They even sang us a song.

The next day was considerably quieter. Poor Daddles was still having trouble with his anxiety level which meant he needed to stay near the bathroom all day. One floor of the hotel was devoted to expensive shops and restaurants. One of these shops was a fabric shop and tailor. Doug had me measured for two silk dresses to be made to my design which I drew for the tailor. He promised to have them both completed before we left in five days' time. I still have these two dresses and can proudly say, at the age of seventy-eight, they still fit perfectly and look good on me.

We left the children in Doug's care. It wasn't hard to entertain them because there was a large swimming pool at the hotel and two friendly English girls the same age as James and Dig who provided plenty of fun and flirting. The children soon learnt how to book any of their food purchases to our room number. Kay and I caught the metro to Tsim Sha Tsui shopping centre. We bought three tablecloths for our large round 2-metre diameter dining table at home, and an embroidered blouse for Bubble. The hotel doctor visited Doug in his room and prescribed an antibiotic for him. So, by the next day he was feeling much better and able to come shopping with us. We bought gifts to give to people at home and camera equipment for us.

Before we left Hong Kong, we took a day trip across the border into Communist China. That was also an eye-opener for us. At the border we spent about an hour getting through about five checkpoints. An enterprising Chinaman was passing from one person to another giving them neck and back massages and expecting money. A battered bus then took us to the town of Shenzhen. The place looked filthy, with open gutters in the streets. There was very little decoration like neon lights, decorative shops, or flowers. Tiny slum hovels crowded around the plain concrete high-rise buildings which were spouting up all over the place. All in all, it was so drab, and a spirit of depression and fear could be felt. The people would stare at us with blank expressionless faces.

By 6.00 pm we were glad to be back in the luxury of our hotel, but we were all strangely silent. Apparently, Shenzhen is now a glittering metropolis.

By the fifth day we were all packed up ready to catch our Qantas flight home. My silk dresses fitted me perfectly. Every seam had been bound to prevent fraying. James and Dig said a fond farewell to the two girls that they had spent many pleasant hours swimming with in the pool. A courtesy hotel bus took us to the airport. We had a two-hour wait in Manila and then on to Melbourne, Australia. Another two-hour wait then a quick flight across the Bass Strait to Launceston where Vicki met us with the Austin Princess car. The last of our sixty-three-day adventure was over. Hong Kong had been a very happy ending for all of us.

The biggest treat of their childhood is now remembered by each of them differently. The daily reports in my five-year diary were a great reminder to me of the events and the different things we saw and experienced. For the children the trip was educational and interesting. For myself, a mixture of the above, but also fraught with anxiety and emotional turmoil.

I remember the group dynamic changing for the better when Kay parted from our company and went her own way for a short time in England. Yet it must be said, she was a great help to me. Doug was prone to anxiety which would manifest itself as 'upset guts', as he would call his bouts of diarrhoea. Whenever he was unable to accompany us on a tour or simple outing, Kay filled the gap, and we would venture out together and enjoy ourselves.

I know it was an awesome responsibility for Daddles, who had single-handedly pre-booked every event, visiting relatives, hire cars, tours, airline tickets, hotel bookings, and the finances for it all. He had done it all remarkably well. Each day had been planned and organised. Quite a feat considering that in those days there were no websites, emails, or mobile phones. No wonder he was occasionally uptight. I would have been as well if I had had that kind of responsibility.

In 1988 Daddles and I did a similar four-week trip again. It was partially business combined with pleasure. We travelled to Hong Kong and spent six days, while Doug attended to some business and I relaxed, explored and shopped.

We then visited Iw, in Phuket. She was the Thai exchange student whom we had hosted for six months at our Ringarooma home. Because she had mastered the English language while with us, she now had a prestigious job in a posh hotel. But I'm afraid our visit embarrassed her. The Thai people have a very strict ethical code of behaviour, and we broke every rule by being too friendly and familiar with her. But we did have a lot of fun exploring in a hired 4x4 open Suzuki. It was the rainy season, and the roads were very muddy.

Doug had business to attend to in London. While in England we re-visited lots of my favourite relatives and spent a lot of time with Jean Wakeman in Horton-cum-Studley, Oxfordshire. We attended a memorial service in Magdalen College with a high Mass and a choir with liturgical dancing girls. We had had a lovely time with Yogi and Broke in London, and visited another cousin, Yolandi, and her husband Brendon. They lived in a circa-1200 manor house in Teigngrace in Devon. The house had very low ceilings and you had to duck to get through the doorways. There were a lot of wonderful nooks and crannies with arrow slots in the walls, and secret passageways.

From my diary notes I couldn't help noticing how often Doug was suffering from overwhelming bouts of anxiety, fear, and an upset tummy. On one such occasion we drove to Chichester to meet up with William (Bill) Nicholson, the writer of the stage play *Shadowlands*, and Brian Eastman, the producer of the eventual film version. *Shadowlands* is a retelling of the meeting of C.S. Lewis with Joy Davidman and their love and marriage. As I have mentioned in an earlier chapter, it was later turned into a full-length movie with Anthony Hopkins playing Jack, Debra Winger playing Joy, and Joseph (Joey) Mazello playing Douglas. These two men were so looking forward to meeting Doug but sadly he was completely unable to converse, and I had to carry the conversation.

We also visited A.N. Wilson, who was writing a book about C.S. Lewis.

Then from Heathrow, London, we flew Concord to New York. An amazing experience. In just under four hours we were in New York where Doug did live TV and radio talks with CBN.

We visited Renee, Jack and Rosemary in Florida again, and even went to a Navajo Indian reservation in Chinle, Arizona, to visit an exchange student who we had been friendly with in Tasmania.

This time our visit to Wheaton College was very different for me. I was able to tell them of the impact that the *Mere Christianity* tapes had had on me, the tapes that they had given to Doug in 1983. I was asked to repeat the story many times to different people.

Chapter 20

Moving on, time of change

While we were on the farm in Ringarooma, Doug had decided to give Kay and me a gift. Doug had my engagement ring, the one that had vanished in the first year of our marriage, replicated. The mistake he made was to have two replica rings made. One for me and one for Kay. I was thrilled with my present but as soon as I discovered that he had also given one to Kay, I was devastated. I felt that this was treading on sacred ground that belonged to mine and Doug's love, relationship, and marriage. This act, although made in an effort to include Kay, had seriously backfired for me. I was so hurt. In my usual manner I said nothing but harboured and stewed on this gross injustice in my heart and there it smouldered. My resentment of having to share Doug with Kay grew. At the time, I did not make an issue of the rings as I was still obsessed with being in Doug's favour.

One of the first things I had looked up in God's instruction manual was His commands on marriage. Lines like, 'The two shall become one,' and 'man shall leave his mother and father and cleave to his wife,' (Matt 19:5, Ephesians 5:31). All was in the singular, there was no mention of multiple wives or husbands. On the *Mere Christianity* tapes, I'd also been listening to the chapter on Christian marriage. I apologised to God for having made up our own rules regarding marriage and ignoring Him, and asked Him to forgive me. Doug would have to do the same.

Kay was still running the Scotch Thistle Inn but was drinking the profits and costing Doug a lot of money. Doug continued to drive down there with the excuse of delivering produce. Eventually, I gritted my teeth, and phoned Kay. I told her that the relationship between my husband and her had to stop. Doug was honouring an adultery not a marriage. Kay was hurt and angry, and understandably so. She had invested youthful time and energy with Doug, myself, and the children. Years that she herself should have used to find a man that she could marry and start her own family with. She had indeed worked hard and contributed a lot. I felt ashamed and deeply sorry for her. She asked over and over again, 'What's in it for me?' A question I couldn't answer. With fear and trepidation, I told Doug what I had done and was surprised that he seemed strangely relieved. He promised me not to have sex with her anymore.

By this time, we had moved into a brick home in the village of Ringarooma. A sharefarmer and his family occupied our farmhouse and did the farm work. It was such a relief not to have to get up early every morning and milk those cows, and then repeat the whole process again in the evening.

It was about 10.00 am one morning that Doug returned from an overnight stay in Ross after having delivered meat and vegetables to the inn. I went out to greet him as he got out of the car. I needed to know something. My question was immediate, blunt, and straight to the point.

'Did you have sex with Kay?'

'Yes,' he said.

I went back into the house and sat on the toilet with the door locked for some time. I had to regain my composure. *Now what do I do?* I thought. I was so angry. I cried out to Jesus. In my mind and heart, I had already shut the door on Doug. I didn't even want to look at him, let alone look after him. I smile now as I remember when I would only make my side of the bed and never set his place at the dining room table or served out his food. I even resolved not to do his laundry anymore. Arguing, screaming, and ranting would be futile. I knew he could always argue circles around me with fine sounding words and rational sounding reasons.

A few days passed. I was the only one in the house. Doug was out somewhere. The boys had left for school on the bus and Bubble had walked to her school which was only about 200 metres from our new house. Once again God came to my rescue with another waking dream.

Without any conscious awareness that anything unusual was happening, I found myself feeling very apprehensive. I was walking down a long corridor with closed doors on either side, for the school bell had rung and the other children were already sitting at their desks in their classrooms. I couldn't remember which was my classroom. Panic, aloneness and lostness dominated my emotions. I turned the handle of the next door and entered the back of a classroom. I quietly sat down at an empty desk. In the front of the room stood the teacher on a slightly raised platform. He looked at me. I understood in that one look that he knew everything about me and delighted in me. He said to me, 'It doesn't matter what other people do to you, it's how you react to it that you must account to me for.'

When I woke from this odd dream, I noticed I had done some very strange things. I must have still been walking around the house tidying things up. Doug's slippers were in the fridge, the dirty gumboots were neatly lined up in the sitting room, I even found many of Bubble's toys in strange places.

I wondered what the meaning was behind what I had felt, seen, and heard. I realised, *yes, it's true, I'm just a frightened little girl, pretending to be grown up. And, yes, life is like a school. And, YES, the teacher was Jesus.* That sentence He spoke to me has become 'my safety rail' which, to this day, I cling to. Ultimately, I know I have to account to Him for my behaviour and not the behaviour of others.

Eventually the Scotch Thistle Inn was sold, Kay made a life of her own and the situation slowly resolved itself. I believe Kay opened a restaurant in Hobart. As far as I know, she never married. Over a matter of time, we lost track of her. And Daddles and I returned to being 'The two shall become one.'

When we moved out of the farmhouse, and the sharefarmer moved in, it was, in a way, heartbreaking for me. We had spent seven very interesting years there from 1978 to 1985. And the boys had learnt valuable skills that have been an asset to them throughout their lives. But there were things that I also wish could have been different. A farming lifestyle, in particular on a dairy farm, is intensive and time consuming. Farms are lucrative but also very greedy. No sooner did the money come in than it was demanded again to buy things such as superphosphate fertiliser or seed, fencing materials, expensive machines, or vet bills. I always did the accounts and paid the bills once a month, a job I hated.

Needless to say, our farming days were coming to an end as the children left home. Our interests were now elsewhere. In hindsight we should have sold the farms straight away, but we made the mistake of moving into a lovely house with a big garden in the village of Ringarooma and putting on a succession of two share-farming couples. Jeff and Jan, and then coincidentally, a second Jeff and Jan.

The new house was very comfortable. It had big picture windows looking out onto the spacious garden, and beyond onto lush green pastures, a picture of tranquillity with (someone else's) black and white Friesian cows grazing. In the distance were fields of pale-purple opium poppies, peas, and potatoes.

The soil in the area was rich red volcanic soil, I was told 2 metres deep in places. No wonder the trees were so gigantic. Along the drive leading up to our house was an avenue of huge elm trees, tall and majestic and untouched by the Dutch elm disease which was killing most of the elms throughout Europe. These dead trees stood like ghosts against the night sky all over England. I grieved to see their stark white limbs and branches, when other magnificent English trees were displaying brilliant foliage.

One of the most fascinating things in that garden was the humble little snowdrop. In January, very early spring in England, where these little bulbs came from, they would break through the cold soil, sometimes still snow covered, and they would be the very first garden plants to herald the coming of warmer weather. But January in Australia is very hot, being mid-summer. Still, these brave delicate flowers would appear, in the heat of mid-summer January, only to be scorched by the heat of the sun. They are the only plant I know of that is not dictated by the soil temperature and season to grow and bloom but seem to remember the calendar month.

Doug was now interested in a new project: an ultralight aircraft which came in a kit with instructions. He spent many hours with the local mechanic's son, Marcus. Together they assembled this aircraft. He actually bought two kits but only ever assembled one. When working in Perth in previous years, Doug had got a restricted private pilot's license, so he had a bit of experience with flying. But he only flew the ultralight a few times. He claimed that the area, being surrounded by hills and valleys, was unsuitable to fly an ultralight plane. But I think he frightened himself too much. Both planes were eventually given away, the second kit still in unopened boxes.

With only one child at home now during the weekdays, I applied for a job at the local hospital to do shift work or night-duty. The Scottsdale district hospital was small, only about twenty-eight beds, a geriatric ward, and five maternity beds. I was placed wherever I was needed, mainly in the maternity ward for not many of the nurses there were double certified. It was a bit daunting for me because during my absence from the nursing profession it had become quite high-tech and computer oriented. You could monitor a patient from the sisters' station by simply bringing the patient up on the screen. But it lacked the hands-on personal touch that I was used to. I didn't like it but somehow, I eventually learnt how to do it. I was glad that there was always another nursing sister on duty with me.

I was impressed by the honest display of kindness to me, the patients, and their relatives from the staff at the Scottsdale hospital. And I found myself being strangely cold and indifferent, which appalled me. The truth was that despite being highly trained, I was now out of my depth and very self-conscious. Sister Gresham was woefully out of date.

Barb, one of the nursing sisters I worked with, was aware of this, I'm sure. She was very intolerant of my newness and unfamiliarity of new techniques. She would throw the chart at me and roll her eyes with contempt, to such a degree that I dreaded working with her. I would look at the roster weeks in advance to see if I had been given a shift with her. By the time the day arrived I was trembling. Then I came across a phrase in the Bible that said, 'Bless those who spitefully use you.' To bless someone is an action, not simply a request for God to 'bless them'. We, personally, must do kindness to them, that will bless them. The *action* to bless seems to have been forgotten.

Love is another word that is action-based, yet so many just say 'I love you' while giving no action to validate it. The word 'love' can be an adjective (a description of a mental state), or it can be a noun (the name of an emotion), but it is mostly a verb. It is something you do. One of Daddles' very best phrases of wisdom he ever came up with is a definition of love: 'Love is your benefit, at my expense.' The most amazing demonstration of this was when a thirty-three-year-old man allowed Roman soldiers to drive nails through His hands and feet and suspend Him naked from a wooden cross. He could have called 10,000 angels to come to his rescue. But He didn't because it was for my benefit and yours that He allowed it: 'Love is your benefit at my expense.'

So how could I bless Barb?

I picked beautiful roses from my garden and gave them to her. I complimented her and asked about her family. All to no avail. Finally, I took a bar of our home-made soap wrapped in gift paper to her and oddly enough, that got her attention. She was very interested to know how to make soap, so I put on a soap making demonstration in our home for her and invited all who wanted to come. Our relationship was revolutionised. It was magic how it worked to diffuse a very volatile situation and make life much more pleasant for me at that hospital.

· ·

On the farm, I regretted not having more time for the children, to go to their school plays and attend speech nights or graduations where prizes would be handed out. There was always something that seemed to be more important to do. But was it? It certainly is a sad note in the hearts of all the children. I thought that when we moved away from the farm and that workload, *I'll have more time to do things with the children*. But by the time we moved, I had missed the opportunity. School days, for them, were turning into college days and boarding with other families in Launceston.

James and Dig finished at Scottsdale High School and then moved to Launceston and did their HSC at Launceston Community College boarding with a variety of families. After his HSC, James enrolled at the University of Tasmania in Hobart, to study engineering, but after a year moved to Texas in America to do a degree in aviation technology and aircraft maintenance. It took him twenty years to get back to Australia, bringing with him three 'souvenirs': a wife and two children.

Dig moved to Canberra and attended the Australian National University (ANU) where he undertook a Bachelor of Science majoring in biochemistry and molecular biology. He married a lovely girl and started a family. Later, he moved to Ireland for a while and completed an MBA at Trinity College Dublin. He now runs his own medical devices company.

Dominick went to a boarding school in Launceston and then attended Launceston Technical College to study architecture. Dominick married his sweetheart and together they now have five children. For a while, he also worked in Ireland but now they live in Brisbane.

As I previously mentioned, we hosted an exchange student from Thailand called Iw, but most of the time, Lucinda enjoyed being an only child.

I had three beautiful, gifted sons but to me Bubble was different. And she fulfilled the longing in Doug's heart as well. As a child he had always longed for a sister to delight in and protect and show to the world. Now he had a daughter to protect. One who would stand by him through life and proudly proclaimed to the world, 'This is my daddy, so don't mess with me; I'm his most treasured possession.'

Bubble also fulfilled the longing in my heart to have a close female companion. One who loves me and gives to me more than I could possibly give her. She was flesh of my flesh, bone of my bone. One to be with me in mind and spirit, in all that life can give.

Sons have a special place in a father's heart, I know, but a baby girl has a very special place in the heart of a mother. Not only was Bubble my daughter, but she was my last child. After her birth I had my tubes tied. The door was shut to me having any more children. I was determined to enjoy every moment of her development, her first smile, mastering the art of sitting unaided, crawling, walking, and talking, motor skills, learning the alphabet, reading, writing, drawing her first pictures of her mummy. Monitoring her progress at school right up to the day when she would graduate in her desired path in life. She was to obtain diplomas in gold-smithing, engraving and stone-setting, with added credits for wax-working and pearl-stringing from an academy of world-renowned teachers in Florence, the school of Perseo Scuola per L'Arte della Gioielleria, Firenze, Italy. She is also qualified to teach in these areas.

She was our treasure and our joy. Perhaps we lavished our attention and care too much on her, giving her privileges and gifts over and above her brothers. A familiar cry from her siblings was, 'Mompska, you would never let us get away with that.' A pony to ride and call her own, dancing lessons, jazz ballet classes, karate, storybooks, and story tapes to play on her own portable cassette player. Pretty clothes and more toys than the boys all put together ever had.

She excelled in all she did. In jazz ballet she was a star and an example to others. In karate she outshone other students and got as far as a green belt with two stripes. Even in sport she won every race. At the Ringarooma annual show she was decked out in a riding costume and proudly displayed her skills on a horse, clearing every hurdle. During one of these show days, she ran into the kitchen where I was busy preparing sandwiches for the canteen and asked me, 'Mompska, would you like $20?'

'That would be nice,' I said, and she ran off. An hour or so later she put $20 in my hand. She had signed up for a 5-kilometre cross-country race, which had the $20 prize. Most of the village kids had joined in. She was so confident that she would win. I was so proud of her. But in the Show Beauty Contest the prize went to the daughter of the show manager. So unfair, we thought.

As a young girl she had a small fat dappled grey pony she named Bilbo. We had bought him for her when we were still at the farm. It was a gift for her eighth birthday, I think. That little pony was incredibly placid. Early in the morning of her birthday, we walked the pony into the house and right into her bedroom. It was the first thing she saw when she woke up. Her playmates in the village would all scramble on its back together. I remember seeing three little girls on Bilbo's back, trying to get the horse to move. But Bilbo was far too interested in the fresh green grass on the roadside where the road was elevated with a ditch alongside. Bilbo just had to reach that tasty grass growing in the ditch. All three little girls slid down the horse's neck, over its ears and landed, giggling, in a heap in the ditch with the horse quietly grazing around them.

We never required her to do manual labour on the farm, or even help with the household chores, but she came with me wherever I went. As a toddler I would piggyback her while getting in the cows for milking. During the milking she would sleep in a cot encased in clear plastic under the milking parlour table. As soon as the milk was flowing, I'd fill a baby's bottle with warm milk straight from the cows and give it to her. Often, she fell to sleep lulled by the rhythmic sound of the milking machine and the easy listening tunes of 7SD radio station.

When I went to a party or BBQ, I'd take a thick-piled sheepskin rug, place it under the chair I would inhabit for the evening, spread my long full-length dress to cover the sheepskin and chair and there she would stay, peering out from behind my skirt or sleeping soundly. Her early life was a life of play, toys, music, stories, and pretty clothes. She was, and still is today, a delight to her parents.

In her formative years of primary school and social development, we listened to all her heart's desire. But one such desire we were unable to fulfil. That desire was to stay with me and to not be separated from me which posed a problem for her schooling. Home schooling would have been the way to go, but at the time it was unheard of.

The real difficulty came when her primary schooling was completed, and a decision had to be made regarding her secondary schooling. Scottsdale High School, which the boys had attended before going to college in Launceston, was out of the question. The boys had been teased and taunted there. We didn't want Bubble to have the same experience. The only other option open for her was to be a weekly boarder at a prestigious ladies' school: Methodist Ladies' College in Launceston, known simply as MLC. It was the same school that my parents had put me in at the age of five when we first arrived in Tasmania in 1947.

The first day of our parting was one I'll never forget. She clung to me, unwilling to leave me. I had given her my favourite soft worn-out old grey nightdress to take to bed with her in the dormitory. That way she could cuddle up to it and feel and smell me nearby. I literally had to prise her off me and left her standing alone amongst a group of noisy carefree children and supervisors. With a heavy heart Doug and I drove back to our empty house in Ringarooma. That parting broke my heart and was certainly a turning point in her life, and not for the better I'm afraid.

She learnt to adjust. But I fear we had broken her trust in us. Bravely she forced herself to become part of the school community. When she complained to us about the conditions for the boarders, we found alternative accommodation for her with the Tysons who were friends of ours. She was the only child there and would listen to the story tapes that I had given her, over and over again. To this day she can recite *Alice Through the Looking Glass, Ludo and the Star Horse* and *Lark's Castle* from beginning to end.

Eventually she went to Launceston Church Grammar School. I'm not sure now why that was. There she excelled in sport and became a key player in their hockey team. Each weekend Daddles or one of the boys – if they were home – would drive the 90 kilometres to Launceston over a mountain range to bring Bubble home. When collecting her from that school, Doug would stop his car outside the girls' dormitory, get out of the car and wait for her to appear. Bubble would race down the stairs through the open door and leap into her father's arms, wrap her legs around his waist as Doug would spin around in an effort to keep his balance. Not an easy feat when leapt on by a well-grown thirteen-year-old girl. Often, she would bring a friend home with her. She would prattle away non-stop telling her daddy all she had done that week. Then on a Sunday evening we would drive her back. She never told us she was unhappy.

Chapter 21

Yachting and a fifth child

I keep trying to move on from this period of our life, but there is still so much to tell. Through all the above I have so far made no mention of our fifth child, Melody.

Doug was approached to organise a fundraising campaign for a global charity organisation called World Vision. The plan was for a '40 hour famine' bus ride. Forty school children would be asked to volunteer to go around Tasmania fasting for forty hours on a bus, collecting donations from town to town as they went. A bus company donated the use of a bus, and two drivers volunteered their time. Even the fuel was donated. It was to be well advertised and even televised. Doug agreed. First of all, it entailed visiting many schools and speaking to the children about the work of World Vision and signing up volunteers to go on the bus. It was a great success, and a considerable amount of money was raised for children in impoverished parts of the world.

This experience set a train-of-thought in progress with Doug and shortly after the World Vision bus trip, he told me that it seemed counterproductive to send money to help children in their own drought stricken or politically depraved countries. These children needed to be relocated to safe stable affluent countries. He said to me, 'How would you feel about adopting an orphan from a third-world country and raising it as our own?' At that moment I felt as if the bottom had fallen out of my world. I was struck dumb. I just looked at him as big tears welled up in my eyes and went unhindered down my cheeks. Every fibre in my body was yelling, 'No, no, no.'

I was hardly listening to Doug as he excitedly went on about the fact that most of our children were on the verge of leaving home and we had enough energy to raise one more child. I was remembering the promise I made to God when I was twenty years old, that if ever I saw a baby on a doorstep, I'd take it in and raise it as my own. I saw, in my mind's eye, that baby on my doorstep.

Now that I had experienced first-hand the amount of sacrifice, hard work and painful love that went with raising four intelligent and adventurous children, I was reluctant to start again and take on that responsibility for yet another baby, especially as my youngest child was almost fifteen years old. I had begun to feel a certain amount of freedom again. I had a job at the hospital that I loved, and I was good at. That job had become more an outlet of my service to the community, than the money it brought in. *Must I again become a house mum?* I forced a smile on my face and said to Doug, 'Yes, okay.'

The wheels were set in motion and Doug contacted one overseas adoption agent after another until he eventually found one in Korea that was willing to cooperate. There was a lot of paperwork and interviews with authorities to see if we were fit parents – strangely, they never did that when I was having my own babies. They even interviewed all our children. The process was very slow. I had a pit of anxiety about this because we had actually put our names down for a special needs' child, which meant she could be blind or have Down's Syndrome or any other condition requiring special care. I was apprehensive, but ready for any child the Lord would give us.

In the meantime, Doug pursued another of his many passions: boats and sailing. There would always be a few sailing magazines cluttering up the house along with car and flying magazines. One day a 44-foot steel sloop came on the market. It was moored in Georgetown, not far from us. Doug and I went down to have a look at it, and, for Doug, it was love at first sight.

The boat had been built by two brothers who owned an engineering firm. They had built two identical hulls side by side. One had been fitted out for cruising, and the other was built for racing. It was the racing boat that we looked at. It was very strong and had a huge mast and sails fitted but no interior whatsoever. Doug traded his precious Jaguar XJS as part payment for that yacht.

The next two years or so were dedicated to overhauling the yacht and fitting the interior, using our own blackwood timber from trees felled on the farm. Two men were employed to do the job under Doug's supervision. When the yacht was ready there was still no news of whether we would be adopting a child, so we decided to put a caretaker in our Ringarooma home and go on an extended sailing trip up the east coast of Australia and return when a child was allocated to us and was ready to be collected. We were told it could take months.

A family who had recently moved into the area needed accommodation, so we agreed to let them rent our house while we went sailing. It was all quite friendly and informal, and no lease agreement was compiled or signed. When they asked how long they could use our house, Doug, in a fit of foolish excitement said with a laugh, 'Who knows? We could be gone forever.'

Prior to our departure date Doug spent days reading the weather forecast, and I prayed. Our first challenge was to cross one of the most unforgiving stretches of waters in the world, the Bass Strait. And do it in the middle of winter. The Bass Strait is at a point where the Indian Ocean in the west meets the Pacific Ocean in the east. Between them are Tasmania and the Bass Strait. The seabed between the mainland of Australia and Tasmania is raised, causing dangerously rough conditions for a small craft. It has sunk many vessels and not just small ones.

On the 2nd of June 1989, shortly before our planned sailing trip, the welfare office in Launceston summoned us to a meeting. We smiled when they told us that we had passed the 'Parent Test' which made us a suitable family to adopt a child. And we were then handed the adoption details of a four-and-a-half-year-old child together with her photo. The decision to accept her was still ours. We looked at the sad little face in the photograph of that child sitting alone on the steps beside a big pot plant, and my heart melted. Her name was Hyun Joo Choi. There was no thought of refusal. Tears were already blurring my vision. Doug and I hugged each other and agreed.

On the 6th, Doug made another trip into Launceston to have the official papers signed by a notary. We posted those papers together with five photographs, one of each of our existing children with their names written on the back and another one of Doug and me together and requested that they should be given to Hyun Joo. It only took till the 13th for the welfare office to hand a new passport over to us for her to travel with. We were advised that it would still be some months before she would be formally released to us.

The time to go yachting was now or never. The newly finished yacht, now christened Merriemaid, was provisioned and, with practically no experience, except for the sailing lessons that Doug had studiously taken, we set sail on the 17th of July 1989 to cross the Bass Straight accompanied by a young navy cadet called Paul. Paul was a relative of the people we had rented our house to. We thought he would be a help with navigation and other things, but he turned out to be a liability and a nuisance.

But it was amazing. I swear that we sailed smoothly across those treacherous Bass Strait waters in a calm ray of sunshine during the day and over smooth waters at night. Perfect conditions seemed to encapsulate Merriemaid for that whole crossing. It took us three days, taking turns on the night watch, with a favourable wind in our sails. The month of July is mid-winter in Australia. Sitting in the open cockpit under the night sky was bitterly cold, even dressed in our Baileys survival suits that we had purchased in America.

Our plan was to sail up to the warmer waters off the Queensland coast and explore the coral reefs, Whitsunday Islands and marinas until the adoption authorities told us that Hyun Joo was ready to be picked up.

Our first port of call was at the small fishing village of Eden on the south-eastern tip of New South Wales. From there we coast-hopped up the eastern side of Australia to Wollongong for the night. We then spent another night at Rushcutters Bay where we got a poor reception and had to anchor about 500 metres offshore. The next day we sailed to Birkenhead Point Marina in Sydney Harbour, where we were able to tie up at a pontoon jetty with lots of other yachts and sports fishermen.

Dig was still at uni in Canberra, so he bussed to Sydney and joined us on the 25th to the 27th of July. By the 13th of August we arrived at Mooloolaba just north of Brisbane in Queensland, where we rested for sixteen days having visited Port Stephens, Coffs Harbour and Southport on the way. Here our hitch-hiking crewman left us, and we actually danced a jig on deck. We were so glad to be rid of him.

The weather was warmer, which was such a joy to me as I dislike the cold. We hired a small car and explored the area. We saw long train carriages filled with bananas or sugarcane. All around the countryside were banana and pineapple and sugarcane plantations, tropical vegetation, and wonderful frangipani flowers, which I love.

During our time in Mooloolaba, Bubble and Dominick planned to join us to sail further up the coast to the Whitsunday Islands. However, at the time of their visit there was an Australia-wide airline strike, so they had to boat and bus all the way from Tasmania. Quite a lengthy trip.

Another thing of note happened at Mooloolaba. On the 24th of August my niece, Mary-Anne, tracked us down and phoned the marina looking for us. An office worker came and knocked on our hull to tell me that my mother had passed away during the night at a Melbourne hospital. My grief, after hearing the news, was unexpected, and took me quite by surprise. But it didn't last long because I had two hungry teenagers to feed and keep entertained. I was oddly grateful for the airline strike because I couldn't be in Melbourne in time to go to her funeral and the strikers had given me a perfectly reasonable excuse.

We set sail again through the Great Sandy Straits, a two-day journey navigating through shallow water and sandbars which could hold a yacht in its grip for days if we went aground and the keel got stuck. Map navigation was crucial. Bubble became our greatest spotter for cardinal markers at night and during the day.

We berthed the yacht at the Gladstone Marina for two days. Doug hired a car and took the children on a trip to Mount Hay 180 kilometres away. I had time alone which I desperately needed to contemplate and complete my grieving memories of my mother.

We kept sailing north reaching the Whitsundays on the 5th of September. We explored the safe anchorages, and the children would dive into the crystal-clear waters and go snorkelling, or paddle around in the tender, a small dinghy we kept on board and used to go ashore. We saw large turtles, dolphins, and a myriad of colourful fish among the coral. Sharks were not uncommon, so a close watch was required. On the 13th of September, Bubble and Dominick caught a bus from Abell Point Marina back to Tasmania, sleeping and eating on the bus.

After the younger two left, Dig and his friend joined us on the 20th of September for nine days. During this sailing adventure period, James was in the UK working at various farms and other short-term jobs. I would often write to him. James spent time working at Chargot House in Somerset for Uncle Daily and Hazi who was back in the UK by this time as well. For a while, he also worked at Glympton Park in Oxfordshire. The exact same places where his father had worked in his late-teen years and even under the same managers.

Dig, and a friend of his called James, were with us on the first leg of our southward journey from Great Keppel Island as far as Gladstone. Doug took me and the boys grocery shopping in a rented car. It was great to see him in such a good mood, joking and being the life of the party. That night, being their last night with us, we cracked open a bottle of champagne and I cooked a really nice supper. At 8.45 pm we took them to their bus bound for Sydney and on back to their studies at ANU in Canberra.

We stayed nine days in the Gladstone Marina, during which time Doug was reading a lot of Christian books by the author George MacDonald. His preferred reading had usually been science fiction stories. I tried hard not to express my delight that he was at last getting some real Christian input. The boat was also having some repairs done. One day we drove 300 kilometres to Monto and Biloela where we looked over a cotton gin. It was absolutely fascinating watching 10-ton slabs of raw cotton being vacuumed into the processing machines. The countryside was not unlike Western Australia – dry, sparse trees, brahman cattle, and a few crops irrigated by bore water. No banana trees or sugar cane here. Just fields of cotton. The roadsides were strewn with the puffy white cotton fluff. Back at the marina that night, I discovered the beautifully ugly cane toads. I sat and watched them for some time in the torch light.

On the 8th of October we set sail again and got as far as a small coastal town called Pancake Creek. It was a very nice anchorage and easy to get to. Unfortunately, for some unknown reason, Daddles hit emotional rock bottom and went into deep depression and a state of anxiety. He couldn't eat. We talked about it, but he could come up with no explanation. We could have left Pancake Creek the next day, but Doug's anxiety continued. He felt quite unwell, so we stayed put and both read. I got him to read that day's entry from the daily devotional booklet that I was working my way through. Later, I found him reading the Bible. He drew my attention to Matthew 18:19: 'When two agree on something, ask the Father in His name and it will be done.' Straight away we prayed that he would be rid of his emotional torment. It was done and we both thanked God.

Some months previously, just prior to our departure from Ringarooma, I had had a very vivid dream. I dreamed that Doug and I were on Merriemaid in a tremendous storm at sea. I had, very theatrically, stretched both arms out and had commanded the sea and wind to be still in the name of Jesus. The sea had instantly become calm, and I woke up with a fright. It was an awesome feeling to realise what had happened. I actually woke up Doug and told him about my dream. He was annoyed because I had woken him up for something so silly. I thought no more about it but the memory of it never faded, which turned out to be a good thing.

At 5.30 am we hauled up the anchor, and departed Pancake Creek, setting sail for Bundaberg. Doug was feeling better and was even able to eat something. The forecast was favourable, no mention of bad weather. We were making good progress with the wind in our sails. Doug was chatting on the radio with other south-bound yachts that we were sailing with. Then, without warning, the wind suddenly blew up and the sea became very mountainous. I was at the helm. Neither of us had a harness on. I feared for Doug's safety as he was fighting to reef in the sails, shouting at me to keep her pointed into the wind. But I couldn't even see the wind instrument which was only about 1.5 metres away from me because the waves were now drenching me with torrents of angry sea water, and my glasses had been knocked off my face. I had no idea that a storm at sea could be so loud. The nearest I'd ever been to a storm of this nature was watching it in a movie. The engine, which had been giving us forward momentum and steering, had to be stopped as nearly all the sheets (ropes) had been washed overboard and would get tangled around the prop.

I was sitting up to my waist in water in the cockpit despite having two 4-inch drains either side of me. The radar was no help. We were at the mercy of the wind and sea, not knowing if we were being blown out to sea or dangerously near land. The yacht was being tossed at very uncomfortable angles. At one stage I swear I saw the keel out of the water and the mast touch the sea on the other side. All I could do was cling tightly as I could to the wheel. I'm not sure how long we were battered by the ocean, but it felt like hours.

Doug was at his wit's end. He stood in the companionway and shouted to me, 'What shall we do now?' At that precise moment I remembered my dream. There was nothing else we could do, so I did what I had done in my dream. I couldn't stretch both arms out or I would have gone overboard, so, with my left hand stretched out, I yelled in a loud but quavering voice, 'In the name of Jesus, sea be still.'

The sea on that side of the boat completely flattened! I repeated the command with my right hand extended. The sea went quiet, the wind dropped to almost calm, and the boat was still!

The first thing to do was try and find out from the radar where we were (moving map GPS displays were still the stuff of science fiction movies). The other yachts around us came up on the radio. 'What happened?' was the question everyone was asking. The consensus was that we were caught in a mini cyclone type of windstorm, and we were at present in the eye of that storm. So, we must brace ourselves for yet another onslaught. This time we put our safety harnesses on and secured everything and waited. But there was no aftermath. The whole thing remains a mystery. But I smiled to myself and said, 'Thank you, Jesus.' There was a big mess to clean up inside the yacht. The thing I regretted most was that an open can of baked beans had ended up in my box of Christian music tapes.

So, Doug and I continued south, arriving at Mooloolaba on the 23rd of October 1989 where we arranged to leave the yacht and return to Tasmania. We had still received no news about when we should collect Hyun Joo from Korea but felt we needed to get home and prepare.

At one stage Daddles actually put Merriemaid on the market. I think he realised that yachting was too stressful for him. He suffered a lot from fear and panic attacks. But by the time we had packed the yacht contents into boxes to be shipped to Launceston and loaded up a second-hand Datsun Bluebird car for our journey south, he changed his mind and pulled the *For Sale* sign from the hull of the yacht.

That yacht trip hadn't really been a pleasant one for me. Doug had never handled a boat this size before. Doug had thought that sailing would be idyllic, with the wind in the sails and miles of ocean in front of him. It was his romantic idea of perfect freedom, but I don't think he had realised the amount of careful decision making and the risk factors of the sea. The learning curve was very steep and stress levels were often high. He was usually impatient and irritable and being Captain felt he had to have rigid control. His levels of anxiety would also often make him feel quite ill with bouts of gut problems and headaches.

To me, it felt more like a gaol where I was confined to the boat, unable to get off.

It was the 10th of November 1989, Doug's forty-fourth Birthday. The last day of Doug's dream yachting adventure. We had been away from home since the 17th of July. We spray wiped all the Lexan windows, polished the woodwork, and loaded yet more stuff into the car, in 35 degrees temperature. The sweat was running off us and stinging our eyes. We had been invited to the home of friends we had made earlier on – the Beilz's – for a farewell party. It turned out to be a birthday party for Doug. They gave him three music tapes of Gheorghe Zamfir to listen to in the car on our long trip home. It was a very pleasant way to end our yachting trip.

Yet we still hadn't been summoned to go to Korea. We set off in the heavily laden Datsun and drove via Brisbane onto the New England Highway, on through Tenterfield, Glen Innes, Armidale, Tamworth, arriving at Muswellbrook, where we spent the night in a comfortable motel. The next day we drove nine hours through the Blue Mountains on the Putty Road through Windsor, by-passing Sydney, and then joining the Hume Highway at Mittagong, arriving in Canberra at 5.00 pm where we were to visit Dig at his university for a few days. It was so nice to relax for four days in the comfort of the Pavilion Hotel and be entertained royally by Dig who, one day, took me on a 17-kilometre-long bike ride around Lake Burley Griffin.

From Canberra, Daddles started to phone around to find out what had become of the child we were to collect. The authorities in Korea told us to fax them our travel arrangements. At least now progress was being offered. But first, we had to get back home and then book a flight.

Another two days of travel and motel rooms overnight, on through Melbourne and onto the Abel Tasman car ferry across the Bass Strait to Devonport arriving at 8.00 am. It was the 18th of November.

We had intended to return to our lovely home in Ringarooma which we had rented out. We expected very soon to be bringing a small five-year-old Korean child who spoke no English into our home. But there was a problem. Despite plenty of notice, the tenants refused to move out! They argued that no agreement had been drawn up and Doug had said that he might never come back. They tried to claim squatters' rights!

So, our temporary accommodation had to be one of our ramshackle old farmhouses at Trenah. The house hadn't been lived in for years so there were possums in the roof, the paint was peeling off the walls and the bare floorboards would let the cold wind in through the cracks. But there was power, and water and we had a roof over our heads.

While it was not what we were expecting, it was such a relief arriving at our little Trenah house after being away for four months. Dominick, and Jed and Jeanie Crispin were there to greet us and welcome us home. They had decorated the place with welcome home signs and streamers.

Regarding the squatters, Doug sought legal advice and I prayed. I often tell people, 'If you don't know what to do, do what the Book says.' Again, I had to look at the problem from a Biblical viewpoint, as I had done before. It says, 'Bless those who spitefully use you, bless them, don't curse them.' So, I began to pray that the Lord would bless them. I also blessed them personally by taking them hot scones and cream from the dairy with a bottle of my homemade jam and other food treats. But they still wouldn't budge. I kept up my relentless prayer effort.

The Trenah house was a rather typical old farmhouse – weatherboard clad, with a corrugated iron roof and timber lined with no insulation at all. The toilet was outside and freezing cold. It was right at the head of the valley and only 100 metres or so from the dense forest that surrounded the property. It was very private and very quiet and at night the whole area teamed with wildlife.

On the ferry across the Bass Strait, we had met a tourist, a young German chap by the name of Michael and had invited him to come and stay with us, and shortly after our return, he took us up on the offer.

That evening Doug shot a wallaby which we hung on the garden fence where it could be illuminated by the powerful outdoor floodlight. We turned the inside lights off and from the dark kitchen window we were able to let Michael watch the Tasmanian devils. These shy antisocial, highly territorial, and quarrelsome creatures put on a grand display of their character and eating habits. The big Granddaddy Boss Devil ate first till he was so full he could hardly waddle. Then, in order of rank, the others were allowed to eat. There were a lot of very ear-piercing screams and fights, till at last there was nothing left of the carcass. Even all the bones were gone.

The Tasmanian devil has extremely strong jaws and is able to crunch up an entire carcass, leaving no trace. They will even clean up a fully grown dead cow, leaving only a well-chewed plastic ear tag. Devils are scavengers and will not bother a healthy creature, but solo hiking in the Tasmanian wilderness is not a good idea. Any nasty misadventure, a broken leg perhaps, and after a few days, the locals give up searching. The devils would have completely devoured the hiker. Their technique was to never let you relax or sleep, day after day, night after night. They can easily be kept at bay with a stick until eventually the victim would be overcome by cold, fatigue and hunger, and then the devils' feast begins.

Chapter 22

Hyun Joo Choi

We were getting absolutely nowhere with the orphanage, the Eastern Social Welfare Society, in Korea. Once again, they were telling us to wait, even though they had told us to fax our travel arrangements through when we had phoned them from Canberra.

Someone told us of a couple in Launceston called Pat and Bert Howard who had adopted ten children from seven different countries around the world, as well as the one child of their own. I have an article that I've kept for years; it's from the Woman's Day magazine, with a double-page spread photo of this group. I have it in front of me right now. When I phoned them and told them the problem, I was told it was a common occurrence and we should just go to Seoul and say, 'Here we are. We have come to collect Hyun Joo Choi.'

Taking their advice, we flew to Korea the next week arriving on the 16th of December 1989. It was mid-winter there and by 5.30 pm it was already dark. Looking out of the windows of the plane as we approached, I could see a city illuminated by neon crosses on the rooves of all professing Christians. A taxi drove us to the Swiss Grand Hotel through streets decorated with Christmas decorations. The trees all had their bare trunks and branches protected from freezing by wrapping them in layers of padding. The next day Doug phoned the Eastern Child Welfare Orphanage and told them we had come to get our adopted daughter. We were told to come at 1.00 pm the following day, which we did.

My heart was so full of joy and emotion, I was having difficulty not bursting into tears. After what seemed like a very long ten-minute wait, the sweetest little five-year and three-month-old child was brought to us. She held up her arms to me and said, 'Um-ma,' meaning, 'Mummy'. I lifted her up, cuddled her and cried. She stroked and pulled at Doug's beard. Korean men don't grow facial hair, so a beard was new to her. She was so little, so cute, alive, and sensitive, alert and totally accepting of us. Doug and I loved her at first sight, and she seemed to love us too.

In her hands she was clutching the photos we had sent her of her siblings-to-be and a photo of her new parents. She very slowly and deliberately explained to us who each person was. The assistant lady translated what she was saying as she only spoke Korean. Her head was bound up in a turban with an orange beanie on top. We were told not to touch her head as she and many of the other orphans had sarcoptic mange, which was highly contagious. We had given her a gift of a toy koala bear and some chocolates. Other toys were in the room. For about an hour we sat on the floor with her, entertaining her the best we could with toys and a colouring-in book and pencils. But we were not permitted to take her with us quite yet.

Back at the hotel the next day a Korean woman called Oni came with us to act as an interpreter when we went shopping to buy clothes for Melody. Melody was the name we had chosen for her new life in an English-speaking world. It was the name my mother used to call me when I was very little. That name suited her well. Oni chose six children's story tapes in Korean, and six children's music tapes. Our idea was that if we regularly played these Korean tapes to her, she wouldn't lose her mother tongue. But when we did get her home, she simply refused to listen to them. Again, we spent an hour with Melody under supervision at the orphanage. Each time we parted from her she would become very upset and was usually taken out of the room screaming in protest.

The following day at 2.00 pm, Melody was brought to us in our hotel room. We entertained her for an hour, or rather she entertained us. When it was time for her to leave, she had an absolute temper tantrum and screamed and tried to bite Doug for carrying her out of the room. The minder who had waited for her in the lobby had a major battle with her as she refused to walk or be carried. We watched helplessly but were mildly pleased.

On our last full day in Seoul, we were shown around the orphanage. Melody, clutching her koala bear, followed us closely. Lots of children had turbans on their heads. I took photos of all the little faces looking up at us and felt sorry that I couldn't take them all home.

Part of that orphanage had a large, heated room with a waist-high shelf along both walls. We had to put on gowns and a mask to enter the room. On these shelves were lots of premature babies, all struggling to live. They were naked except for a tiny nappy held on with a rubber band around their hips. Each baby had an intravenous drip inserted under the skin of their scalps to keep them hydrated. When I asked for an explanation, I was

told that if a young woman got pregnant out of wedlock, she was thrown out of her home having brought great disgrace and loss of face to the family. There was no help from the government for these unmarried mothers or their children. So rather than bring that disgrace to their families and poverty on themselves, they would abort their babies at about the seventh month and leave the live infant on the doorstep of the orphanage.

That bit of information triggered another question that I asked. What was Hyun Joo's story? The answer shocked me. Her mother was an unmarried girl from a well-to-do family. She was forced to leave home but refused to abort her baby so lived for three years working on the roads and feeding herself and her baby with what little food she could find from garbage bins. Eventually, she was found unconscious and suffering from malnutrition outside a shop with a three-year-old child clinging to her. When she was rescued, she was advised to give her child up for adoption.

Melody can clearly remember the time she was handed over to the adoption agency. She told us she had been told by her mother to wait outside a fish shop while her mother bought some fish. While the mother was in the shop a lady from the orphanage picked her up. She had screamed and fought to get free. Melody saw her mother watching through the window, not coming to her rescue. She first went to foster homes and was only at the orphanage for a short time before we picked her up. That last impression of her mother has remained in a heartbroken little corner of Melody's soul.

That evening we took her back to the hotel and into our lives. One of the first things I did was to put her and myself into a bubble bath in our hotel room. I took off her turban and washed her hair. There were great bald patches on her scalp.

That turban never went on again. Although the condition was supposed to be highly contagious, I was on a mission for God, and I knew He would protect me from the mange. I washed her all over. Then she took the flannel and soap from me and proceeded to wash me. I guess we both felt we needed cleansing to belong to each other. I have a lovely photo that Doug took of that special bath time.

We ordered a room service meal and to our amazement Melody ate the scorching hot chilli kimchi and the anchovies and even drank the soy sauce.

An early wake-up call to our hotel room, a quick breakfast, and the joy of dressing that petite little girl in the new clothes we had bought her, and a shuttle bus ride dropped us off at the Gimpo Airport. We were warned that there may be some animosity from the Korean people when they saw 'two white devils' taking one of their children out of Korea. I sat on the floor in the queue to the check-in desk and let Melody unbraid my hair and brush it. This may have helped to distract any aggressive protest.

At Taiwan Airport, Taipei, we had to wait forty-five minutes with Melody asleep in my arms the whole time, for our connection to Hong Kong. Then a very long wait of eight hours sitting in Hong Kong in the first-class lounge entertaining a very excited little girl. At 10.00 pm we boarded a Cathay Pacific flight to Brisbane then another hop to Melbourne.

By this time Melody had had enough of planes and when we went to board our last flight to Hobart, she didn't want to get on another one and I can't blame her. She chucked a complete wobbly as we called a 'give me my way or I'm going to scream blue

murder' demonstration. We bought her a toy kangaroo with a joey in its pouch. That seemed to distract her enough to get her onto that last flight. The language barrier didn't help. Once in Hobart we rented an Avis car and drove to Launceston where Dominick, Bubble and Mary-Anne met us. Then there was the windy road over the Meredith Pass to Scottsdale and that was the last straw for a very weary five-year-old. The poor child vomited all over the interior of the car.

Finally, we arrived back at our humble little farmhouse in Trenah. But not, as we were expecting, to the comfort and gracious living of our home and gardens in the village. That in itself, turned out in itself to be a blessing and an advantage.

Melody settled in well, but we soon discovered she was a very headstrong little girl who liked to get her own way. Dominick said, 'She must have ruled that orphanage with an iron scream.' When she didn't get her own way, she would give us an ear shattering demonstration of her disapproval. Doug would simply carry her out of the house and sit with her in the field where we could keep an eye on her from the kitchen window. She would scream and tear her clothes off and actually bite herself! But eventually she would realise it was futile and calm down. We couldn't have coped with that in our house in Ringarooma.

A bed was put in our bedroom for her, but one of us would have to lie with her till she fell asleep. Once in bed she would cling to us and repeat the same word in Korean, '*gajima.*' There was a shopkeeper in Launceston who had married a Korean lady, so we went to visit them with Melody. We were curious to know what this word meant. When this lady spoke to Melody in Korean, Melody was terrified and wouldn't come out from behind my skirt. She told us that Melody had been saying, 'Don't leave me.'

The scalp condition she had was not improving, so we had a biopsy of her scalp tissue done and it was quickly diagnosed that she did not have little parasites under the skin of the scalp but a fungal infection which was causing the bald patches. She was put on an oral medication called Griseofulvin. Within a matter of weeks there was healthy new hair growing back.

It was a full-time job for me from early in the morning till her bedtime as I was her only playmate. I was getting no time to have my daily quiet time with God, which I was accustomed to having. I only managed to get a few hours of breathing space, by getting up before dawn, sneaking out of the house by torchlight and sitting in our old Bedford truck that was parked in the yard. I had run an electric cord to the truck for light and for heating there was a small blow heater. I could watch the frost on the windscreen, melting and slowly sliding off, as the cab warmed up. There I would sit and do my Bible readings and write my prayer journal. It was Doug's job in the mornings to dress Melody and get her breakfast when she woke up.

The people were still refusing to get out of our Ringarooma home. I kept up my cry to God asking him every day to bless the Lipscombs and get them out of our home. We had moved out of our Ringarooma house on the 14th of June 1989. For nearly five months we were at sea, returning back to the Trenah cottage on Christmas eve with a frightened little five-year-old Korean child. It was not until the 2nd of July the following year that we eventually got our home back, during which time Melody was isolated from human contact except for our company.

The Trenah farmhouse was in a cleared fertile valley of flat farmland surrounded by hills of dense virgin forest on every side. The name Trenah meant 'basket' in the language of the old Aboriginal people of the area, and it described it very well. On a still night the silence was so complete that you could hear your own heartbeat without using a stethoscope. The wallabies are mostly voiceless animals but communicate by thumping their powerful hind legs and tails on the ground. This noise could be heard clearly.

Dominick, now nineteen, and Bubble, fifteen, would come to stay most weekends and on school holidays. Melody loved her siblings. Bubble's favourite game to play with her was to lie on her back and brace Melody with the soles of her feet on her hips and with Melody lifted high on extended arms, Bubble would pretend she was an aeroplane and give Melody an aeroplane ride. They called this a 'behungi' ride – *bihaeng-gis* being the Korean word for aeroplane. Dominick would give her kangaroo rides which meant carrying her on his back and hopping everywhere he went. She still hadn't met Dig, who was at uni in Canberra, or James who was doing various interesting jobs in Europe. The isolation must have been strange for Melody as she had only ever known life in a big city, amongst crowds of people.

Sundays were the days she looked forward to because I'd take her to church with me in Ringarooma. There were always children there for her to play with, and lots of attention from the admiring grown-ups. She was very cute. On the 12th of June, the beginning of a new term after the school May holidays, we thought that she had mastered the English language enough to attend school. Either Doug or I would drive the 12 kilometres into Ringarooma on weekdays to take her to, and fetch her from school. There was no problem getting her to attend school; she enjoyed every moment of it. But she had to be demoted to kindergarten from grade one 'to learn some social graces' we were told. I can just imagine the trials they had with her if she wasn't getting her own way.

By the beginning of July, the Lord answered my prayers, on both counts. He certainly blessed the Lipscombs, and He got them out of our home. A job became available for a resident couple to take over the Ringarooma Post Office. The post office house went with the job. They moved out of our home, and we moved back in. We even bought a brand-new cherry pink lounge suite to celebrate the occasion. Now Melody had playmates on tap and her school was only 200 metres from our house. All I had to do was walk her over the main road.

Many view life's gifts and blessings as coincidences. How would you feel if you stopped to help a stranded driver on a cold rainy night by providing him with enough petrol siphoned out of your car to enable him to reach his destination only to have your kindness ignored and passed off as a coincidence? Lots of people treat God's gifts and answers to prayer that way, and never stop to thank the giver of the gifts that are often received every day. It could be passed off as a coincidence that the post office job and house happened to be available, and we were able to get our house back. I looked at it as an amazing gift from God who answered prayers and thanked the giver of gifts many times.

Also, the year spent in isolation with Melody was a gift for it enabled us to develop an intimate bond with our new God-given charge, that would never have been so strong if lots of other people shared that time with her. Difficult? Yes, it was, but the benefits far outweighed the difficulties. I realised this also as a God-incidence, and again thanked the gift giver.

Life became much more pleasant for both of us once we were back in the village. I will have to admit that I did struggle a lot with feelings of rejection towards Melody because of my loss of freedom. When these feelings gripped me and my joy was far away, I would try and compensate by being ultra-attentive and sweet to her. By doing that my love for her would return. I complained to The Lord about it, saying to Him, 'She is taking up all my time.' Only to be reminded that time was not mine; it belonged to Him.

So, like the petulant child told not to take the biggest slice of cake, I would say, 'Okay, I won't have any then.' And I would then spend hours playing with Barbie dolls or colouring in with her. The compassion and sweetness of the Lord amazes me. The very next day my friend Hillary came by and said, 'Merrie, you just never get a break; let me take Melody for the weekend.' No one had ever offered me such a thing before. Hillary had two boys of her own who were a little older than Melody, but they had a great time together. My fifth child was now well settled in.

Chapter 23

Ringarooma

After I had discovered real Christianity, it still took me some time to pluck up courage to attend a Christian church service. When I eventually did, the pastor was a tall jovial man with a twinkle in his eye and a ready smile. I had encountered him before. He had come looking for the woman who had 'single-handedly taken the devil by the horns.' That's how he addressed me after I had put handwritten notices on many peoples' doors in the village, inviting them to come to my house and listen to the *Mere Christianity* audiotapes.

I naïvely thought that once people heard what I had heard, they too would be convicted of the truth about God. People came, and they politely listened, and I learned my first hard lesson in evangelism.* But when Pastor Jed Crispin and his wife Jeanie came to visit me, it was like heaven's door was open to me and I spoke to two people who were on the same wavelength as myself and also had this same intimate personal relationship with God that I was experiencing. That was what gave me the courage to enter his Anglican church one Sunday morning.

I sat at the back of the church hoping not to be too conspicuous. Pastor Jed saw me from his raised level and welcomed me loudly and bid me come to the front. I hesitated to go up to receive communion when the time came, but again he bid me come, saying I was very welcome to dine at the Lord's table. I had discovered I was not alone, and that there were other seriously committed Christian people out there. Jed and Jeanie are still two of my dearest friends.

After the service I asked Jed why there were so few people in the church. I had counted only about twelve. He seemed offended by my question and said, 'Give me time; I'm only one person.'

---

* - Isaiah 6:9 'They will listen and listen but not understand...' (EXB)

I replied, 'People won't come into the church unless they hear about Jesus.'

This must have got Jed thinking. He did some research and discovered a very simple six session course for individuals or groups called Christianity Explained which covered the basic foundations of Christianity.

The course had been compiled by a pastor called Michael Bennet who lived in Brisbane. Doug and I later became friends with Michael and his wife. Christianity Explained had circulated to many countries in the world and had gained a good response from a lot of people. When we were living in Ireland I wrote to Michael and asked his permission to teach it in Ireland. He was delighted and said, 'Now I can say it has reached Ireland.'

Anyway, Jed summoned all the committed Christians from his congregation to his house. He sat on a big beanbag in the middle of his sitting room. We all took our places in chairs around the perimeter of the room. In one afternoon, he took us through all the six sessions of that course, placing the visual aid flashcards in front of him as he rotated the course around his beanbag and onto the floor in front of him.

The first session was 'Jesus the Son of God.' In it we were shown the seven areas in Jesus' life where He had more authority than anyone who has ever lived, authority in teaching, over evil spirits, in healing, forgiving sins, in nature, death, and over people. At the end we had to say who we thought He was.

The second session was about Jesus' crucifixion and what it means to us today, if we accept it. This was a really powerful revelation to me. I'd never understood it so clearly before.

The third session was on the Resurrection, and the question was, why did God have to raise Jesus to life, and what this means to us today. These first three sessions were likened to a three-legged stool; the rest of Christianity rests on these three solid points.

The fourth session looks at the various ways people try to get right with God by their own efforts. They can't succeed and God, as a just judge, must judge you. No amount of good works or church rituals can cancel even one sin. That could only be done by Jesus through His life-giving sacrifice on the cross and His resurrection. Good works don't lead to salvation but accepting Jesus' free gift of forgiveness leads to salvation and life in heaven with Him when we die.

The fifth session is about how to go about receiving His forgiveness and making a decision to turn from your ways and to embrace God's ways by putting Jesus before your own will, ambitions, popularity, or anything else, such as pride or fear.

The sixth and last session talks about belief and behaviour and offers the listener an opportunity to make a decision to accept or refuse what they have learnt. An assessment sheet with questions to answer is handed out and each participant is taken aside privately to talk with the teacher.

All through the course, the Bible readings confirmed what was being explained. After Jed had finished the six sessions I was like a stunned mullet. I had no idea of the enormity and beauty of the grace and truths that I had hitherto just skimmed the surface of. The love and value Jesus placed on me that He should endure so much for me, rather than be without me for eternity. It gave me much more gratitude and understanding. I couldn't wait to take people through Christianity Explained myself.

Jed placed us in pairs and gave each pair a copy of the six sessions. We were encouraged to go and knock on peoples' doors and offer to take them through the course. I was paired with Phil Hammond. There was no force on earth that could have stopped me. I felt at last I had the ammunition I needed and I could now make an impact. Phil was just as enthusiastic as me. Daddles said once, 'It would be easier to put a lid on a volcano than to stop Merrie.' We did that teaching course in homes with entire families present, with individuals, in pubs, in churches, in restaurants, and even around a swimming pool. I still take people through it today.

Phil was a colourful character. I first encountered him and his wife Hillary on the road. I previously mentioned Hillary; she was the lady who offered to give me a break and look after Melody for a weekend. When I met them that first day, they were in a horse-drawn gypsy caravan home with two snowy blond little boys. He was a farrier by trade and would travel the roads putting shoes on horses. He often shod our horses. However, there wasn't enough money in his trade, so he was obliged to go on the government dole system. Later, they lived in a converted barn. Phil would have one haircut a year. Depending on when you saw him, he either had long hair or a crew cut. He had been a bit wild in his youth – a rogue, thief, and opportunist. I once asked him what he had done wrong. His answer was, 'You name it, I've done it.'

Anyway, Phil had had an encounter with God and turned his life over to Christ and His teachings. Jed would sometimes ask him to take the congregation through a teaching in church. He would wear L-plates front and back whilst teaching, explaining that he was just a learner.

He told me of the time when God had told him to trust Him and to cancel the government unemployment benefits. Phil argued with God that the money he received paid for his groceries and his electricity bill, and it was impossible to live without it. But God kept telling Phil, 'I won't bless you unless you cancel the dole.'

Phill shouted at God, 'Alright, You have it Your way.'

To make it more difficult for God, Phil now refused to take any money from anyone for the odd jobs he would do in the neighbourhood. He came to shoe two of our horses. When I handed him the money he usually asked for, he refused to accept it, so I threw it into his car as he was driving away. He threw it straight out. So, I put the money, plus a little more, in an unmarked envelope and put it in his numbered post office box at the post office. I had no idea that other people had been doing the same thing as well.

Phil gained a reputation as being a helper in times of need for any occasion. On school holidays he would take the tractor and trailer from the primary school and drive through the village like a Pied Piper collecting children. He took them to the swimming hole in the river and would spend the afternoons with them playing ball games or sitting around a campfire playing his guitar and singing Christian songs teaching the children about the love Jesus had for them. He would sit with the lonely, take ute-loads of firewood to the elderly, and many more small but noble jobs. He never had to get money again from the government.

On the day before his son John's eighth birthday, Phil asked John, 'What would you like for your birthday?'

John immediately replied, 'A bike.'

Phil simply looked up and said, 'Did you hear that, God?' And did nothing about it. The next morning there on the doorstep was what looked like a brand-new bike! A local farmer who Phil had helped some time ago, put new tyres on the bike his son had grown out of, gave the bike a fresh coat of paint and put a shiny new bell on the handlebars. By the time he had finished the job it was quite late at night so rather than disturb the sleeping household, he had simply left the bike on the doorstep.

I could tell you many more such stories that his wife Hillary told me. Phil was much too modest to boast about such things. If I'm allowed to boast a little now, Phil and I almost filled that small Ringarooma Anglican church with people who now not only knew about Jesus but knew Him personally after listening to the Christianity Explained course taught by Phil, myself, and others. Jed did the course with James, Dominick, and Bubble. In a matter of time all my family became believers except Dig who by now was living the life of a yuppie in Sydney working for a pharmaceuticals company. He drove around in a posh company car and had good looks that would turn any girl's head. Much later he did submit to the Lordship of Christ.

Let me now tell you how Daddles eventually, 'let go and let God.'

Daddles was still very suspicious of my new relationship with Jesus. I was now not only involved with Church on a Sunday but also a weekly Bible study evening that I had been directed to. It was the last straw for Doug. He said to me one Sunday morning, 'I'm sick of all the God bothering you are doing.' I calmly went into the bedroom, took off my Sunday church clothes and put my work rags back on. He asked me what I was doing, to which I replied, 'My relationship with God will not alter one bit if I don't go to church but my relationship with you will suffer. God wants you and me to have a loving relationship.' The next Sunday he changed his tune and encouraged me to go to the church service.

The year was now 1990 and although he had dismissed his concubine some time ago, he was still a little too friendly with other women. One of those indulgences backfired on him badly, and he was truthfully and forcefully confronted. This made him take a long deep look at his rules he had set as permissible for himself. God now moved in. Doug realised all the people he had hurt in his arrogance and indulgence, and he was deeply ashamed and longed to change.

He cried in bed for three days, eating and drinking nothing and just clung to me. He wouldn't even let me go and get meals or hang the clothes on the line. After three days I managed to get him into the shower. As the water washed over his sweaty body, I baptised him under the shower. He wanted to go to confession. I now knew it was unnecessary to confess to a man, and that he could go straight to God Himself, but I didn't stop him. He was reluctant to go to Jed, who lived only about six miles away in Derby, but insisted he phoned the archdiocese of the Anglican church in Launceston. Archdeacon Lechford answered his call. Doug, trying to control his voice and tears, told him he needed to make his confession *now*.

In an hour's time we were both in Launceston at St John's Anglican Cathedral. When it came time to go into the confessional box Doug refused to go in without me. No amount of persuasion would convince him otherwise. So, against all rules and protocol I went in with him. He was crying and I was crying as he apologised to me and to God for running his life his own way and for the harm and hurt it had caused me, his family, and others. This was the moment I had never stopped praying for. I knew it would at last lead to his eventual healing. I looked forward to the new creation in Christ that God was to make of my beloved.

As the months passed, I could see Daddles making an effort to be more pleasant to his family. We all noticed the difference in him. It was lovely to have him beside me at church on a Sunday and to even be with us on our Tuesday evening Bible studies in our home, where he soon took on a leadership role. His spiritual growth, prayer time and Bible reading was his private affair. We all looked for the fruits of his commitment. On the surface he would have many relapses, which made his children question his commitment to Jesus and His ways. I guess the restoration in a person's character takes time like any other restoration project. But this I can say, he has never indulged in an extra-marital sexual relationship again, although he remains to this day a little too fond of flirting and enjoying female company. His agonising bouts of fear and apprehension also came to a stop. He no longer felt the need to take Valium to quieten the anxiety of being responsible for a wife and what was now five children and all the livestock on a dairy and beef farm. He laid aside his kingship and often told me, 'I'm not where the buck stops any more, He is.' I can never stop thanking God for His gift of the transforming work He did and is still doing on my husband. And on me.

··

The little village of Ringarooma – jokingly, but fairly accurately referred to as 'Dial-a-gossip' – is set in the fertile dairy farming area of north-east Tasmania. Potatoes, peas, opium poppies and hops for making beer were farmed around the neighbourhood. Because it was off the main road it was a sleepy, quiet little haven. Hayward's grocery store, Barney Wise in the news agency shop – which also had a video rental shelf – and Paul Branch in the haberdashery shop were the only shops in the town. Of course, there was a pub and the post office. The petrol station and garage, run by Ronny Brown and his son Marcus, was another backbone of the farming community. Ronny also did the school bus run. I think Ronny maintained and kept everyone's cars, tractors, farming machinery, and motorbikes running in the whole neighbourhood. I know Doug, who loves to get greasy working on mechanical things, would often spend hours in Ronnie's garage.

Then there was the primary school, police quarters and the swimming pool. What more could a person need? The nearest town of any size was Scottsdale, only about 30 kilometres away.

The butter factory in Legerwood was only 5 kilometres away and employed lots of the locals. The milk tankers collected the milk from every dairy farmer for kilometres around, including milk from our cows, and took it to that factory. Doug was once chatting to the staff in the butter factory office. He was sitting on one of their desks when the office phone rang. Someone foolishly said, 'Doug you're closest, answer the phone.'

Doug picked up the receiver and said, 'Melbourne city morgue, you kill 'em, we chill 'em.'

The horrified staff member snatched the phone from his hand and began to apologise to the unsuspecting caller. It was the talk of the town for quite some time.

Then there were the farmers, who were salt-of-the-earth people. Geoff Ranson was our nearest neighbour. During the Second World War, he was a Bren gunner with the Australian Army and had fought in just about every theatre. Over the years we knew him, he told Doug many stories. The two of them would sit on a log, or any other convenient sitting place, after a day's cattle work. A tinny in one hand and a cigarette in the other, the stories would flow. Doug has always been a good interviewer and could get wonderful stories out of people who others found impossible to get talking. A skill he had put to huge use when he worked on TV and radio. Geoff told Doug of his life in the jungles in South-East Asia fighting the 'Japs', the horrors of the Kokoda Trail, and then fighting Rommel's troops in North Africa.

At one stage he was to be transferred to Crete by the Royal Navy but the ship he was on sank after being torpedoed. Another ship came alongside, and Geoff broke his ankle jumping from his stricken vessel onto the rescue ship. With great glee, Geoff told Doug that that was the only injury he received during his whole time in the army. When his ankle recovered, he was shipped to France where he took part in driving back the Nazi armies.

Geoff would tell of his army experiences with a twinkle in his eye and a smile on his face. He never showed any animosity for the enemy, with one exception. Somewhere in Europe, a hidden sniper took a shot at Geoff and the bullet went straight through his backpack. Geoff returned fire and shot that sniper stone dead. Unfortunately, the sniper's bullet had busted his Ingram's shaving cream jar and mixed it with his tin of 'bully beef' which was to be his evening meal. He was quite irritated about that.

I'll always remember Geoff with his very battered hat and his loyal little Jack Russell dog beside him. He called that dog Maggot. Maggot loved to chase passing cars and tear the mud flaps off. How he never got run over is a miracle.

There were a good number of World War Two and Vietnam War veterans in the area at that time. Unlike Geoff, many still carried the scars, both physically and mentally. One neighbour had had a particularly bad time as a Japanese POW. He refused to have anything that has been made in Japan in his house.

Geoff's younger brother, Len, was also a great friend of ours. Len had a well-equipped home with a butchering shed set up. He would kill, butcher, and prepare our beef for us. Doug nearly always helped. They would work away together, cutting up and bagging the meat, and drinking beer. The job would often take all day. His wife refused to let him drink alcohol in the house, so Len used every opportunity to enjoy a few drinks with his friends in his killing shed. He also had a smoke house that he and Doug had fashioned from a disused water tank. In this Len and Doug would cure and smoke the best ham and bacon from our pigs that I have ever tasted. Often, he would cure and smoke mutton as well – so delicious.

···

Marcus Brown, who lived just down the road and helped Doug build his ultralight aeroplane, had two young daughters who became great friends with Bubble. One day, the girls had been playing quietly for some time. I thought they were playing at Marcus' house under the supervision of Marcus' wife, and she thought they were with me. When both of us realised our error, we started to get worried. The three little girls, aged about six, were nowhere to be found. A few phone calls were made which also turned out to be fruitless.

At this stage, word went around the village like wildfire and in no time at all the entire town had turned out to search. Then, as evening was falling, and tensions were rising, a local farmer from some distance away arrived in our yard with three very miserable looking little girls in the back of his ute. He had found them sitting in the middle of his paddock crying. That morning the three girls had hatched a plan, packed their little sparkly backpacks with some essentials (Barbie dolls), and had run away from home. It is still sobering to think that they had managed to cross the fast-flowing Ringarooma River without any of them getting drowned. They intended to get to the coastal town of St Helens where Bubble's little friend's aunt lived, and they chose to go by a cross-country route which is why it was so hard to find them.

Bubble was told how she had upset and worried the whole village as well as her parents by her behaviour. She was told she had to be punished, and asked, 'Would you prefer a spanking or to be gated for two weeks?' She chose the spanking.

Until you have had an experience like that it is hard to appreciate what a small-town community is all about. They were prepared to do whatever it took and for as long as it took to find the girls.

In the longer school holidays, our home in Ringarooma was always full of pre-teen and teenage children. Nina and Daniel would come to us from Hobart, and Penny and Melanie from Launceston, plus any others who happened to be staying at the time. Nina and Daniel were – still are – the children of Bob and Trish Herman. Bob was a builder and Trish a teacher. We had gotten to know them through Kay, and they became great friends of ours. We are still in touch. Penny and Melanie were the daughters of our lawyer in Launceston. Along with them, school friends of the boys, and various cousins and other relatives would come for sometimes quite extended stays. The children loved to be at our place. I kept a strict work roster pinned to the fridge to enable me to cope with everything. Each day, each child would be given a chore to do. There was only one rule. You were not permitted to join the rest of us for lunch if you hadn't completed your given chore to my satisfaction. I never had to enforce this law. The other children simply would not let them eat if their chore wasn't done.

At these times, Daddles was amazing, and the children loved his fun ways. It was not uncommon to see him lying on the sitting room floor with a stack of five children piled on top of him amidst a great deal of joyful laughter and giggles. When he sat down in his armchair there would be a rush to see who would get to sit on his lap. His armchair usually had a child on each arm of the chair as well as one on his lap.

I got the children to play an interesting awareness game. Each child and grownup had to write their name on a piece of paper. We all put our folded-up names in a hat. Then we had to reach up into the hat and draw out a name and pin it on our lapel. The name you had drawn was the person you had to be for that entire day. The child who drew out my name realised how hard I worked all day. The one who drew out Daddles' name got to feel what it was like having kids jumping all over you. The good and bad habits were mimicked. At the end of the day, we had to say what it felt like living someone else's life. There was a lot of self-reflection, and a sense of awareness was learnt.

When it was time for the visiting children to be collected by their parents and taken home there was often an amusing and embarrassing moment when our little guests didn't want to go back home with their parents. Doug and I would stand well away and silently watch as the tears and pleading would start, ending up with an angry word of authority from the parent and a silenced child reluctantly getting into the car. Helping out on a farm really was thrilling for city children who seldom got a chance to be out in the country. I expect it's now part of their best childhood memories.

Dominick, who was studying architecture at Launceston Community College, got involved in a Christian leadership group there, and would often organise outings for his youth group. James took charge of the beehives and rigged up quite an extensive honey extracting enterprise in the large six-car bay garage that Doug had built. My brother Stephen's son, Alex, and his new wife, Kavita, came one summer at haymaking time. Together with

all our children and Dig's girlfriend and her younger sister, they built a gigantic peak-roofed haystack under Doug's supervision. It caused a lot of interest in the community and people would come and photograph it. Doug had learnt the skill while working at the Glympton Park estate farm in England in his agricultural student days. Alex and Kavita said on parting, 'It's the best time we have ever had in all our life.' It was nice to provide somebody's 'best time' and their help was also much appreciated.

Shortly after moving into the village house and before we went yachting, I was taken by surprise at my own change of attitude. I was very new to the practice of living as a Christian. There was a disabled man living in the village. He was a hunchback and walked with two short sticks and he had a condition called acromegaly, which meant that his bottom jaw was grossly enlarged. I had been in the habit of avoiding this man because he embarrassed and repulsed me by talking with saliva running down his chin and onto his jacket. One particular day I saw him coming towards me and instead of crossing the street to avoid him, I walked up to him. In his usual way he looked up at me sideways and greeted me kindly. I was taken aback by my thoughts of *what a beautiful man* that, with all his deformity and difficulty, he was kind enough to greet me, whereas I, who was a picture of health and vitality, was so ugly that I couldn't even talk to him.

Three dogs and the biggest sheep I had ever seen came with us when we moved to Ringarooma, faithful old Cherokee, the dog we picked up in the caravan park in WA, and Molly, a black Kelpie-Collie cattle dog. Molly was supposed to have stayed on the farm as she was useful as a cattle dog. But each day when she was let off the lead to muster the cattle, she would run the 6 kilometres to the village to be with us. She was eventually permitted to stay.

We had also been given a Doberman-Rottweiler bitch called Chelsie. She was also very loyal and gentle although she looked very scary as you can imagine given her breeding. Her favourite thing in the world was cats. She would catch them and eat them, one end to the other, usually on the back doorstep. Not a nice sight first thing in the morning. Cherokee and Chelsie both fell prey to the village dog poisoner who would periodically rid the whole village of dogs by throwing strychnine-laced meat over the fences into peoples' yards. I don't know if he was ever caught. He certainly caused many broken hearts with families weeping over their dead pets.

And, as for the sheep, we had an orphan lamb that we hand reared and named Sir Basil Unspun. He was incredibly tame and would follow me down the road and straight into the shops. The shop owners didn't seem to object. Given the chance, he would amble straight into the house to say hello. Shearing him every year was a mammoth task and he would nearly give himself, and the shearer, a heart attack in the process. He was supposed to become lamb chops, but no one had the heart to do the job. He lived to a ripe old age.

Chapter 24

Time to move again

We spent four more years at the Ringarooma house after we got the tenants out of it. Those were good years. Daddles was becoming increasingly aware that his many God-given talents were being wasted. Although he enjoyed manual farm labour, he would often comment that other people could do that work. God intended him to now use his other gifts: public speaking, helping people and being of service to humanity and safe-guarding the Christian message in his stepfather's books, which were, by now, being made into films.

James had been offered a placement at LeTourneau University in Texas, USA, to study aviation technology. He had returned from two years in Europe and been with us for nearly ten months wondering what the next step was. So, when this opportunity came his way, he gratefully accepted it. Before his departure Daddles took him to the Whitsundays for a yachting holiday.

It was while they were under full sail making good headway that Doug's new-fangled portable phone rang. It was a call from Canada. A renowned professor and clinical psychologist, Dr Philip Ney, had been given his number as a possible help with his enterprises. He had heard that Doug was a strong supporter of the anti-abortion movement and was also a good public speaker.

That phone conversation was the opening of a brand-new world for Daddles and me. First was a trip to Canada for Doug where he learnt more about this amazing man. He wanted Doug to join him in his plans of helping people out of drug dependency, depression and futility because of damaged childhoods or abortions. All the doctors could offer was to dose the patient up on 'happy pills', never looking to heal the cause of the unhappiness. A seed was planted, and the soil must have been ploughed deep. The farms, which had become our life in Tasmania, were soon to be sold.

Dr Philip Ney MD, FRCP(C), MA, RPsych was born in 1935 and is a controversial figure. He is loved by many and hated by others because of his strong moral and Christian stands. He has spent a lifetime studying and compiling a very effective form of group therapy to alleviate the destructive rut many people find themselves in because of being abused in their childhood. The therapy program also addresses and alleviates the psychological damage done by aborting an infant. In addition, with the help of Doug he developed a therapy program called The Centurion to help ex-abortionists who find themselves guilt-ridden often leading to alcoholism or worse.

Philip was the founder of IIPLCARR, The International Institute of Pregnancy Loss and Child Abuse Research and Recovery. One of his goals was to train counsellors in countries around the world to use his programs and show them how to conduct group therapy sessions. The way he did this was to collect a group of willing candidates to be trained and then actually conduct the group therapy course on them. Because 'one must first heal the counsellor before they are capable of counselling or healing others.' Most humans have had some form of destructive abuse in their lives, which, with help, can often be overcome.

On Doug's initial visit, Dr Ney organised several speaking engagements for Doug. The talks were mainly about the damage that abortion does to the mother, the family and whole community at large. After one of his addresses, Doug was asked by Philip to talk to a young lady who had tried to explain to Philip why she had to abort her baby in her womb. Doug listened and sympathised with her predicament. Instead of counselling her he simply took off a gold dolphin ring that he wore on his fourth finger, and gave it to her, saying, 'Here, give this to your baby girl when she is born.' Many years later we received a letter from a young girl who became the owner of that ring and wears it every day. She was the baby that this desperate mother was planning to terminate.

The big question for us now was, where do we relocate to? I told Doug I was too little to live in America; it frightens me and still does. England? Well, I said, 'I'll never leave the house, there are too many roads and it's too crowded.'

'What about Ireland?' Doug then asked me.

I simply said, 'I don't know anything about Ireland.'

'Well, let's go and see.'

Melody and Bubble accompanied Daddles and me to Ireland. James, who was now studying at LeTourneau but on his first summer holiday, also joined us. Dominick and Dig were too deeply involved with their uni studies to come with us.

We contacted various Irish real estate agents, gave them a rough budget, and told them we were looking for a house that we could run as a Christian ministry. Ireland was lovely; it far surpassed all my expectations. *Yes, this is where we will settle and work at restoring people instead of things*, I thought.

We sat in the offices of real estate agents and flipped through brochures of large country homes for sale. The choices seemed endless, and we were stunned by how much our budget could buy. No one wanted to be lumbered with a big house anymore.

The heating bills alone would cripple anyone. A two-bedroom bungalow was eye-wateringly expensive, but it seemed that for much the same money one could buy a fourteen-bedroom mansion on 20 acres!

For several weeks we were driven all around southern Ireland looking at possible places and I fell in love with Ireland. Doug told me, 'England used to be like this thirty years ago.'

The first house we were shown was in Leighlinbridge in County Carlow, but we had to see them all so as to compare. But my mind kept flipping back to that first place so in the end we asked to revisit it. The house was called Rathvinden House.

When we returned, the first thing that struck me was that the house and grounds seemed bathed in light, even though it was an overcast day. It didn't take us long to offer Matt Sharky, the owner of Rathvinden, a price for his property. He told us he had had the furniture valued and it came to 23,000 punts – Irish pounds or *Punt Éireannach* in Irish Gaelic. Doug said he couldn't afford to spend that much more. So, Matt said, 'No, no, take half of it and it's yours, free, gratis.' I went around with Matt that day and put blue stickers on what I thought would be useful furniture, and when we added it up, the sum came to exactly half.

Before we left Ireland, we met with Matt's lawyer in his offices in Dublin to finalise the sales agreement. He was a compassionate but very shrewd man. He looked at Doug and me hard and with a frown on his face, warning us that Rathvinden House was cursed. Responding to the look of surprise on our faces and raised eyebrows he went on to explain that the place had for the last twenty years been owned by seven different people; each of them had experienced broken relationships and bankruptcy and few of them had lasted more than two years. Doug just laughed and said, 'That will not affect us in the slightest because we have dedicated the place for the Lord's service. Whatever we do there will be for His service, honour and glory.'

Now it was his turn to look surprised. He had never had anyone talk to him like that before. The sales agreement was read out and signatures were required in the correct places. Then the whole procedure came to an abrupt standstill. While reading through the fine print, another signature was required. Apparently, the property was in half ownership with the owner's wife. Her signature was required. He said he didn't know where she was or how to get in contact with her; she was living somewhere in England as far as he knew. The couple had parted company three years ago. It was a nasty complication to the sale.

Then, while we were all sitting there wondering what to do, the phone on the desk rang. It was the owner's ex-wife. Matt hadn't heard from her in years and neither had his lawyer. She had phoned on a totally unrelated subject. It was a miracle and a further confirmation to us that God was on our side and in agreement with all we were doing. She agreed to the sale and the transaction went through. 300,000 Irish punts was agreed on the price for the house stables, and 20 acres of surrounding farmland.

Now began the monumental job of selling up the accumulated Gresham enterprises in Tasmania. The farms were mainly sold by auction. With a lot of wheeling and dealing and negotiating they were all eventually sold, even the livestock and machinery. The only thing that hadn't sold was the big Bedford cattle truck and hurdles. On our last day, a local dairy farmer came to the door and offered $5,500, a good price for it.

....

As I write, it is June 2020. I started to recall my memories in February. The time was right because I was on compulsory lockdown. You may recall that I mentioned I had returned home to Malta leaving Daddles in Australia. He, however, was marooned in Australia and we were unable to be together again because the airports closed down. It has taken this long to be reunited. Daddles returned two weeks ago on special dispensation for expats to Malta. He took photos of the empty airports and the various precautions taken to prevent the spread of the virus. For two weeks after his arrival home, he was in quarantine himself. It's only been today that I have been able to hug and kiss him. Thank God he was able to travel through Dubai and Heathrow without becoming a carrier or infected himself. Now at last we are together again. Still, one must observe the rules of keeping at least two metres from another human, wearing masks, and frequent hand sanitising. Malta Airport and many others are expected to reopen on the 1st of July.

It took nine months to finalise the sale of everything. We hung onto the 53-acre property across the road from our home in Ringarooma that we had bought several years ago. It had a very basic house on it which we moved into prior to our departure. Christmas in 1992 was celebrated in that house and was the last time our whole family would be together for a long time. The fertile farmland around the house was rented out to a local farmer and the house became a place that Dominick could call home while he finished his studies in Launceston. He jokingly used to tell people, 'My parents left home.' We still own that house and the 53 acres in Tasmania. Daddles was reluctant to cut all ties to his favourite place in all the world. The house is rented out.

We were now living out of one suitcase each. Little did I realise that the contents of those cases would be our only possessions for the next seven months. All our other belongings had been packed into large shipping containers by the removalist company and had already started their journey to Ireland.

Our last night in Tasmania turned into a big farewell gathering of friends from across the whole of the island. We had told a few of our friends we would be spending our last night in the Launceston International Hotel. But word seemed to have gotten around. We never expected so many people to turn up. It was very emotional and unexpected. From 5.00 pm till well after midnight they came, stayed for a while and left. We talked, drank, ate, reminisced, laughed, and cried as we said our goodbyes. Even Bubble's boyfriend and family came. Melody and Bubble's school friends came with their families as well. I had no idea we were all so popular. Farmers, shop owners, cattle buyers, family doctors, local mechanics, lawyers, accountants, and our pastor Jed, and his wife Jeanie, all came. Even members of our church family and Bible study group were there. Many people were in tears. Phil had brought his guitar and the evening ended with praise, worship songs and prayer in the foyer of the hotel.

The next day was the 4th of January 1993, so Daddles and myself with Bubble, Melody and James (who had flown back from Texas for a few weeks to help pack) left Launceston airport early and flew to Hamilton Island where our yacht Merriemaid was moored.

The temperature difference was a bit overwhelming–40–degrees and we had no air-conditioning. The intense sun on the steel-hulled boat made the interior feel like an oven. The yacht had had a lot of use since I had last been on it and was beginning to look very worn and scruffy inside. Doug and James went off to find old friends and acquaintances they had made from previous visits. The others made a beeline to the resort swimming pool, leaving me to unpack and make up beds. My smile was very forced and my heart heavy as I felt left out and far too hot. I was also somewhat derailed, having left behind my friends and familiar surroundings.

James could only stay with us for six days, but it was great for Daddles to have a competent yacht hand. He left us on the 10th and stayed a few days with his brother in Canberra before returning to Texas. Dominick joined us two weeks later on the 16th.

We were on the yacht twenty-four days, sailing around the Whitsunday Islands fishing and swimming but the girls preferred to be at the Hamilton Island resort and swimming pool.

There was no big farewell this time; we simply packed our suitcases, and flew to Brisbane where we put Dominick on his plane back to Launceston and we caught a plane to Sydney where we spent the night. Dig and his girlfriend, Amanda, had driven from Canberra to come and see us and say goodbye.

Chapter 25

Rathvinden house, 1993

The next day we left Sydney and flew to Hong Kong and then on to London, finally arriving at our destination in Dublin at 7.30 pm. We rented a car and drove the 95 kilometres to Leighlinbridge and arrived quite late at Rathvinden House. Anne Kelly, a lovely lady from the village who had occasionally worked for the previous owner and who we had met on our first trip to Ireland, was in the house to greet us with a hot meal and a cupboard full of groceries.

The previous owner of the house was very generous; not only had he left all the furniture that I had chosen, but he also had left us a linen cupboard full of sheets and bedding, all the cutlery, crockery, cooking utensils, fridges, and many more household goods. The house was fully equipped and functional from the first day. We were wondering why we had bothered to put so much of our belongings into those shipping crates that would eventually arrive.

About 100 metres below the main house was the large stable complex, which was able to house about twenty horses. There was a large barn partially full of hay, and a workshop with big double doors. Also, a smallish double-storey stone building with arched doors and windows which used to be a chapel many years before. The area had been concreted at one stage but was now breaking up and in need of resurfacing. There was also a room with a glassed-in facade, and a stone slab floor, which would have been used as a tearoom for social events such as fox hunting parties. Finally, there was a large tack room with a fireplace, cupboards, and lots of saddle-holding racks along one wall.

Occasionally we rented a stable to someone to put their horse in but later found this was not advisable for security reasons. Then there was a strange double-storied building with no floor on the upper level. Much later we reinstalled the floor and converted the top floor of this building into a very sweet self-contained living area for one person. We called this apartment The Dovecot. It was very useful to put a guest in if they needed more privacy.

During the owner's short residence in Rathvinden he had lost a great deal of money by breeding and racing horses. Unfortunately, he bred and raced slow horses. It had also cost him a fall out with his wife. He had been using only a few rooms in the basement. We were told by the village people how he would have a few B&B guests to stay and when the electricity or plumbing failed, he would pretend it just happened and promised he would repair it the next day, but did nothing about the malfunction.

We were also told it was something of a 'house of ill repute' as many wild parties had been held there. We heard a particularly amusing story about one of the wild dinner parties that was held there. The chef was told his soup tasted awful and to remove the half-eaten soup bowls from the guests, so the chef put the pot of soup outside by the back door. Coincidentally, a passing car had run over and killed one of the owner's goats. Not wanting to disturb the party, the driver dragged the dead goat up the drive and left it outside the back door, right beside the pot of soup. Sometime later, the dead goat was seen by the half empty pot. The owner thought that the goat had drunk the soup and died, so he had all his guests taken to the hospital to have their stomachs pumped out!

Our predecessor hated anything to do with organised religion and professed to be an atheist. However, he was thrilled and somewhat bewildered to be introduced by Doug while at the local pub, the Lord Bagenal Inn, as the man whose generosity enabled us to run a Christian ministry at Rathvinden from day one, by leaving us the house fully furnished and equipped. One could see the quizzical look on his face as he seemed to be thinking, *now, why would I ever do that*? But we felt it was God's way of equipping us for the task at hand.

⋯⋯⋯⋯⋯⋯⋯⋯⋯⋯⋯⋯

Being the beginning of February when we first arrived, the weather was cold and damp, shrouding everything with a low mist which gave the place a mystic feel. The trees were all bare and the lawns looked more like uncut hay fields. No one had tended the garden for about six months or so. Bluebells and snowdrops were already heralding the promise of warmer weather. People from the village would drop by with cakes or flowers to welcome us and offer help if we needed it.

There seemed to be an urgency in the atmosphere. Doug had a mission: 'Get the place ready.' Ready for what? We weren't quite sure. We were now the owner of a large fourteen-bedroomed Irish mansion at the time of our lives when we should be thinking of retiring into a small two-bedroomed cottage. Three of our five children had already moved away from home and both of us were middle-aged. However, the Lord had shaped our lives and equipped us with skills and talents, moving us halfway around the world to Ireland and to this large house which turned out to be badly in need of repair. The idea of renovating something so large was daunting to say the least. We prayed and obeyed the command to 'Get the place ready.'

The house itself stands majestic on about 20 acres of elevated ground surrounded by sweeping lawns and landscaped gardens, all very neglected and overgrown. The grounds were studded with

tall beeches and oaks and surrounded by fields (which provided privacy) filled with sheep and their spring lambs. Large ornate iron gates, with the name 'Rathvinden' in wrought iron and gold paint led to a sweeping driveway and forecourt in front of the house.

Gardening has always been my passion. With Doug and Mark – a good man we employed to do the heavier work like lawn mowing and hedge cutting – I soon had the garden looking manicured and colourful. Mark rotary-hoed a nice big patch in the partly walled garden below the house which I planted up with various vegetables, only to discover that I had provided a feast for the numerous rabbits and hares. An electric netting fence soon stopped their thievery. But the newly planted fruit trees were being ring barked by something. The culprits were the hares. We had to bind each trunk with crepe bandages that had been soaked in sump oil, up to about one metre from the ground. The top storey of the house had windows which provided Daddles with a bird's-eye view of the orchard and vegetable garden. Early in the morning Doug would sometimes shoot a nice big hare or rabbit for me to cook up – jugged hare is delicious.

A contractor named Jim was given the job of overseeing the skilled workmen who were to completely renovate the interior of the house, as well as replacing the slate roof and gutters. The basement of the house had a nasty pervasive mouldy smell about it, due to the rising damp. Every basement wall and floor were systematically chiselled back to stone, sealed and refinished, making it as waterproof as the hull of a boat. That was the end of the musty smell. The walls were made of seventeenth-century brick held together with horsehair and lime. After the workmen left every evening, I would go down and sweep and tidy the chaos. The dust from those walls caused me to get a strange chest infection that was not responding to antibiotics. Finally, a sensitivity test was done and revealed a rare bacterium which was cured by the correct antibiotic. It had probably been caused by the ancient dust from the mortar.

Many years ago, Rathvinden House had been a bishop's manse. One day, when the men were pulling up the flooring in a basement room, what looked like a gravestone with carvings on it was found. Unfortunately, one of the work men had already broken it in two pieces with his jackhammer. The Irish workmen were quite on edge about the finding, particularly since that room was known as the haunted bedroom. That evening, Bubble, who had a streak

of mischievous humour in her and loved to play pranks on the workmen, placed a china skull from her goldfish tank under one of the broken slabs which Daddles had carefully levered up for her. The Irish are superstitious people and afraid of the supernatural so when the big strapping lad of a workman lifted the stone the next day, he got such a fright that he jumped through the windowless window and ran across the lawn still carrying half the gravestone slab with him.

Jokes aside, that night Doug knelt at the side of the slab and prayed that the soul of the ghost be laid to rest. Anne, my helper, once said, with typical Irish logic, 'I don't believe in ghosts, but they are there all the same.'

Sixteen workmen, and at times even more, worked five days a week for nine months on renovating that beautiful old mansion, before it was again liveable. During that time, we had made ourselves quite comfortable in the stables. I had a double bed and household furniture in the tack room and Melody and Bubble had beds in the stable chapel. A kitchen was set up in the old tearoom – it was very cosy with a pot-bellied stove that burned day and night in one corner, and any number of tables and chairs and kitchen furnishings out of the big house. All the other household furnishings that we hadn't carted down to the stables for us to use had been put into two very large shipping containers that sat in the courtyard in front of the house, leaving the house now completely empty for the workmen to do what they had to do.

Doug slept in various rooms in the main house to protect the men's tools and equipment from thieves, keeping his 12-gauge shotgun beside him. Electricity was rigged up only in the room that Doug would be sleeping in.

On the 5th of April the first of our shipping containers from Australia arrived with the cars that Doug wanted to keep. There was the brand-new Toyota Land Cruiser which we had bought just before we left and were able to claim back all the sales tax as we shipped it overseas almost immediately. That vehicle was considered very up-market in Ireland and served us faithfully for the thirteen years we lived there. Eventually James shipped it back to Australia to use on his farm, and again, there was no import duty required because it was originally an Australian-sold car! James still uses it to this day.

Also in the first containers was Doug's Jaguar collection: his original E-Type, a MkII, an XK-140 and an S-Type. A building that had originally been built to house a pack of hunting hounds was stripped and turned into a large four-car garage. A few days later the containers with furniture and household goods also arrived.

Bubble and Melody were enrolled in local schools. Bubble was attending a secondary school in Bagenalstown about 6 kilometres away and made new friends and collected a herd of male admirers.

Bubble only stayed with us at Rathvinden for two years. She was missing her life and friends in Tasmania and became restless, longing for a way to get back to her former life. She never really settled well into the school she attended in Bagenalstown. We thought she would be happier if she worked somewhere with horses, so for a while she worked in a racing stable owned by a good horse breeder and trainer. But after a horrible fall off a horse she was exercising and jumping, she quit. She had become very friendly with a young Irish lad who used to sometimes work for us in the gardens. Although it was a distraction from her longings, it didn't last. Daddles also bought her a horse to ride called Casanova, Cass for short. She would ride the horse along the old tow path that followed the River Barrow which was only about 200 metres below our house.

When she got her driver's licence, we bought her a VW Beetle which, at the first opportunity and at the age of seventeen, she drove all the way to Waterford on a secret errand of her own.

I was sitting in the armchair with my back to the door when she arrived home. Leaning over the back of the chair she dropped an incredibly soft black bundle of fluff into my lap. At first, I thought it was a shapeless black fluffy toy. Then I shrieked, 'It's alive!' It was the answer to my childhood prayer. As I mentioned earlier, many years previously, I had spent my entire term's pocket money allowance at boarding school and had prayed so hard to win the raffle for a black female Poodle puppy. And here it was. That little Poodle was my heart's delight. I called her Pitou for that was the name I gave to the puppy that I never won in the raffle. From Pitou I got a litter of five pups and kept one, whom I named Poocherina – spelt incorrectly, I'm sure. We had a girl from Lithuania helping us at the time and she told me it meant 'little black curly one' in

Russian. For years the three of us were inseparable – both these dogs came to Malta with us after we had sold Rathvinden, and both lived to a ripe old age. Not to be outdone, Doug bought himself a boxer puppy who we named Polly. It was a great delight especially for Melody and Bubble who took on the responsibility of caring for and playing with her.

In December that year, 1993, we left a very capable family, John and Sandy Muller and their two children Rebecca and Faith, to hold the fort of Rathvinden for five weeks, while Doug and I, Bubble and Melody went to Tasmania to attend our son Dominick's marriage to a lovely Malaysian girl named Wendy.

John was an American medical doctor and missionary in Romania. They had first come to Rathvinden after the tragic death of their youngest child who had died of an ailment that would have been treatable in their own home country. Their two girls, Rebecca and Faith, became very dear to us. Faith was Melody's age and the two of them would play with their Polly Pockets and Playmobil toys for hours on end.

John would also teach about certain aspects of Christianity and became quite well known among the Christian prayer meetings, who would invite him as a guest speaker. He held a class of three sessions in our basement kitchen at Rathvinden doing teachings on baptisms for anyone interested enough to come. I attended and after his first lesson on water baptism, my friend Anna and I both said in unison, 'I think you had better run the bath, John.' I had never had a water baptism. I had asked a pastor in Tasmania about it when I first became a follower of Jesus Christ, only to be told my infant baptism was valid. This answer never really satisfied me, and I still yearned to have an immersion baptism. That afternoon Anna and I were baptised in the big pink bathtub upstairs.

Most of the family came to Dominick's wedding. However, James couldn't attend. He was in his last year at uni in America. Our old friend, Pastor Jed Crispin, was the celebrant at the wedding. Dig was his best man and Alina (Wendy's sister) was maid of honour. It was a joyous occasion. After the wedding and visiting our various friends, when it came time to head back to Ireland, Bubble pleaded with us to be allowed to stay. She was now eighteen and in charge of her own life so, sadly, we gave her her heart's desire and left her behind.

Unfortunately, but not unexpectedly, she found that all her old familiar friends had moved on and the bond with them was no longer there. But when I visited her in Devonport the following year, I was pleased to see that she was happy and had a nice little house that she and one of her old primary school friends were renting and she was working as a vet's assistant.

A few years later she got a job in a jeweller's shop in Devonport and met and married a very nice young man. We also went to that wedding. Daddles rode with her to the wedding in a horse-drawn carriage. He told her, 'Bubble, you can still change your mind.' But she was determined. The marriage didn't last long and ended when they both moved to Florence, Italy, so Bubble could pursue her other love: jewellery manufacture and design. She became a qualified goldsmith and gem-setter. Her husband left her and returned to Tasmania.

Melody also quickly made friends at our new home in Ireland. She was excused from the Catholic religious classes at our request. One day she told us that when the Catholic priest came to hear the children's confession before they were to receive their first Holy Communion, Melody had slipped by unnoticed and joined the queue for confession. When she arrived in front of the priest, she was told she didn't have to confess to a priest because she could take her sins straight to God – and those words came from a Catholic priest! I smiled for days after hearing that.

On the 25th of May, James joined us again on his summer vacation from uni in Texas. This time he brought with him his American sweetheart, Lara. She had never learnt how to cook or sew, let alone grow vegetables or how to freeze or can fruit. James left her with us for an extended stay saying, 'Teach her, Mompska.' She joined us in our stable accommodation while James went to Africa with another uni friend. Lara became my right-hand man and helped me with whatever I was doing. With some pointers from me, she even made herself a skirt and waistcoat on my Bernina sewing machine. That skill she never lost and is today quite a skilled seamstress.

Dominick also came to visit us for a month during the time that Lara was with us. He spent time researching the possibility of transferring his uni studies from Launceston to Dublin. It was his first visit to Ireland. Being an architectural student, he was fascinated by the renovations, and came up with useful suggestions. His masterpiece was a design for a heated insulated greenhouse. This was eventually built to his design and was my pride and joy where I could grow vegetables all year round.

Our very first official guest was a German minister with his wife and two teenage sons. James and Lara knew the eldest son Peter from university in Texas. Lara helped me move all my bedding and gear out of the tack room, where I had been sleeping and into another stable room, making room for the pastor and his wife to sleep there.

We made up extra beds for the boys in another stable. There was a tense moment when Doug turned up one evening with three young tourists who were on a bicycling holiday around Ireland, and couldn't find a B&B to stay the night in. Doug had offered them a place to sleep in the hay barn. At breakfast time the next morning our makeshift kitchen was quite crowded. The pastor complained that this was their holiday, and the extra people were an intrusion. I told him that one had to practise Christianity even on holidays. James returned from his adventures in Africa on the 5th of August with lots of photos and stories. It was wonderful having him with us. He was such a help in many ways but two days after his return he came down with malaria.

James and Lara left Rathvinden on the 23rd to return to their studies at LeTourneau University where he had become quite a mentor and an inspiration to the students and teachers. He was Class President for three of his four years there, ran an international student organisation, and won several awards and prizes. We all went to their wedding in Memphis, Tennessee, in 1996.

Now fifty-two years of age, James gave up flying regional jets for Delta Air Lines in the USA so as to raise his two boys, Michael and Lindsay, on a farm in northern New South Wales, Australia, to teach them life skills. It seems ironic that he should now be encouraging his seventy-eight-year-old mother to write her memoirs, when it's him who needs to impart to the world the wisdom and understanding which he has mastered.

I'm surprised to see in my diary that yet another guest, Sophie Conan-Davies, my brother's youngest child, then in her early twenties, also came to visit during the time James and Lara were with us. She stayed for some time sharing the stables. We often went to the local pub to eat – it wasn't easy cooking for eleven people in that small stable kitchen.

Chapter 26

Pandora's box

Dr Philip Ney, who I have mentioned earlier, had arranged with Doug to hold a seminar at Rathvinden in October to train counsellors in his Hope Alive group therapy technique that he had developed and perfected. The restoration on the house was far from finished and the day was drawing nearer. The pressure to have the house usable by October was great.

All the carpets from the house had been lifted, rolled up, labelled, and stored in one of the larger stables. A team of ten carpet layers were given the job of completing the re-laying of all the carpets in one day. However, on that day it was raining heavily. I went down to the stables to see what the men were doing. There they all were sitting on top of a mountain of carpets calmly smoking their cigarettes, their flat tray truck waiting outside. The rain off the roof was falling unobstructed by any gutter, like a waterfall across the doorway. I asked a stupid question, 'Why aren't you men bringing the carpets up to the house?'

'We can't do that, Missus, the carpets would be ruined, so they would,' they answered.

Without hesitation or fear of embarrassment, I stood outside in the rain by the stable door and said to myself, 'Lord, if you want us to host this seminar then please let the men take the carpets up to the house.' I lifted my hands up and called on the name of Jesus, in a loud bold voice commanding the rain to stop. The rain stopped instantly, and the sun came out!

I told the men to load all the carpets onto the truck as quickly as they could and put them all into the house. I acted as though nothing unusual had taken place but inside I was shaking with awe and wonder. As soon as the carpets were safely under cover at the house the rain came down again. Well, I never lived that episode down. The men would come to me and ask me to pray for no rain for their football matches. And later on, the men tiling the roof would even look to me for fair weather.

The day after my fifty-first birthday, on the 14th of October, Doug drove to Dublin to fetch Dr Ney and led a convoy of three carloads of people to the newly restored ground and top floors of the house to commence the first of many Hope Alive training seminars. The basement was still under construction.

The upstairs restoration was completed only in the nick of time. Anne Kelly and I were vacuuming up the sawdust and arranging the rooms as the first lot of guests were shown in. There had been no time to rehang the curtains, but the house had no nearby neighbours, so privacy wasn't an issue. However, the workmen still had plenty of work to be completed outside the house and in the basement.

Philip wanted Doug and me to attend the training sessions. Doug tried to excuse himself from attending, telling Philip that he had to supervise the work, but Philip insisted that he partake in the sessions. I also tried to make excuses saying that I had to cook and cater for the guests but that also was unacceptable. Philip said I must get a lady in from the village to do that. Anne Kelly and another lady came in to relieve me, so I also reluctantly found myself being trained to be a Hope Alive counsellor under the tuition of Dr Philip Ney.

The house had a very large double-sided carpeted sitting room with a big bay window on either end. Two large chandeliers completed the majestic room. A series of sliding doors could divide the room in two if need be. There was comfort and ample space to accommodate all of Philip's invited trainees from around the world to be taught this new method of group counselling.

A lady with dyed red hair and long painted fingernails arrived from America, with a massive suitcase. Another lady from the Ukraine came with only a small carry bag. I was fascinated by what seemed like miniature paintings on the American lady's fingernails. However, she gesticulated so much with her hands I couldn't get a proper look at them, so I caught hold of her hand and asked to look at her nails. Exquisite artwork was painted on them. I asked her how much it had cost to get them painted like that. She mentioned the sum and the lady from the Ukraine, who was a senior physician in a government hospital, gasped and said that was a month's wages for her, and she hadn't been paid for three months.

I think there were about seven different nationalities represented. A little lady from Scotland sat in the grand, tall wing-backed armchair and exclaimed, 'I feel like a queen.' I loved her instantly, and thought to myself, *and I'll treat you like a queen.*

We were all given a lengthy talk from Philip about the course and handed written papers containing the information we had just received. We were also asked to sign an agreement consenting to the training and the rules it implied. I already felt uneasy but resolved to go through the course, just out of curiosity.

For seven days from early morning till late at night we sat in that room, only breaking for meals. We went through the life stories of everyone in the room in systematic order, while Philip taught us how to relate to and deal with each encounter. When it was my turn to be centre stage and under analysis, I was flippant and treated my experiences with jest and smiled through most tellings. Many things I simply omitted to tell. I needed to preserve my sanity by pretending that I was sound in body, mind, soul, and spirit and able to deal with anything life could throw at me. If I really let people know how I felt – insecure and living a life of pretence – they would put me in a straitjacket and lead me off to a loony bin. There was no way that I was going to open Pandora's box and expose all my insecurities, fears, hatreds, anger, and low self-worth to anyone – especially now that I was the leading lady of what could be a safe haven for troubled people. I was a master of the art of pretence. My very countenance and charm would cause people to look to me for advice and help. Little did anyone but myself and Jesus know that I was an emotional wreck.

But Philip saw straight through my charade, although he graciously refrained from drawing attention to the fact. I expect he knew it would be a lengthy and hard process for me to trust people that completely again. Also, because he would be returning yearly to repeat the process and train another group of potential Hope Alive counsellors, this probably made him feel sure that I would eventually let my guard down and allow myself to be healed of the resentment, anger, and low self-worth and become real, with no need to pretend.

Philip gently led us to recognise the fact that we could never be the person God originally designed us to be. We had not had the nurturing needed to be that person. But God, as a caring and loving father, has provided us with an alternative blueprint of strong remarkable abilities and strengths. We were actually required to draw a picture of the person we should have been if there had been no neglect or abuse and if we had received all the necessary building blocks. I knew this person very well and went about describing and drawing myself with gusto and passion.

Then came the hard task of putting that person to rest. We all had to dig a hole under the trees in the garden and bury the person we should have been and grieve the loss. Tears flowed freely as we held that memorial service. We all had to say final goodbyes. I said words such as, 'Here lies the body of Meredith Agnes Llewella, a remarkable person full of goodness and a skilled medical doctor, scientist, teacher and artist. The inventor of the cure of many diseases.' I then threw the soil over my picture.

Then came the task of discovering the alternative blueprint that God, in his love and grace, has provided, often using the rubble as the building blocks, which makes me the person I am today. That person I hope you have already had a glimpse of as I have been revealing my life to you. One thing I was determined to be was a very good mother and wife. I never wanted to inflict the same kind of damage on my children or husband that was inflicted on me or my long-suffering father. I have always wanted to help people who were suffering emotional trauma and loss. Becoming a dedicated nurse and midwife was the nearest thing I could achieve to fulfil my passion for anatomy and physiology. And here I was now at Rathvinden, attempting to be a healer, restoring other people's damaged lives. God had even sent me a tutor, who also contributed to my own healing, Dr Philip Ney.

I am about to write for you a short story that came to me one sleepless night, many years ago. It illustrates my life and many other peoples' lives. I believe the story came from God but at the time I was puzzled as to the meaning of it. Dr Philip Ney revealed the meaning through the exercise he took us through that I have just related.

It's a story of a very sad princess – which I saw as myself. The story is a parable of the expectation of one day doing great things with the talents (the gifts) that God had given you in your blueprint. Then realising the dreams could never be achieved because of traumatic experiences in your childhood and school days or from a lack of money, or from parents often pushing you in their chosen direction, not yours. I often wonder how many gifted people – potential Einsteins or Beethovens – spent their entire lives trudging behind an ox ploughing a field in some penniless third-world nation.

Grief, anger and a life of pretence often haunts you for years afterwards, as it did me. I have called this book *The Gift* because God has given both Daddles and myself back all that the locusts had eaten. He replaced the empty box with many material and spiritual gifts. The greatest gift of all was knowing Him. God identifies with the poor in spirit and broken-hearted. I see now that my sadness was, and is, a gift. Without it I possibly would never have known Him.

The Gift

Once upon a time stood a castle, and in this castle lived a very sad princess.

She shouldn't have been sad, because her creator had chosen her to be joint heirs with His own son in His kingdom in the sky.

However, this little princess could never forget the present her creator in the sky had once given her, with the promise that it would one day make her very happy and fulfilled.

This princess started life on Earth as we all do; so little that she couldn't even stand. With other peoples' milk she grew and was able to stand on her own two feet and look around.

She was happy for a while because the world was full of toys, other peoples' toys, which she always had to give back. She didn't mind that, for you see her creator had given her a very precious and wonderful gift, but had told her not to open it till she was a grown-up woman.

The princess grew quickly, playing with other peoples' toys, and feeding on other peoples' food. Some food she made for herself; but later it caused her pain.

Play-acting, and copying other people instead of being yourself can be very demoralising – peer-group pressure.

She was happy enough for she always felt different, carrying around with her the gift given to her by her creator in the sky.

The sweetest food she made for herself was in the shape of a beautiful man. For a while it gave her great joy, so much so that she forgot it wasn't really hers to keep.

Her gift from her creator in the sky grew very heavy, but it never lost its appeal, so she would carry it around with her everywhere she went, just waiting for the day to come when she would be big enough to open it and use it for herself.

A notion grew in her head that if she went far, far away, she would grow up quickly. So, she left her man and went in search of other food. Then, she thought she would be big enough to open her gift.

She saw many things and played with many toys, even toys that were dangerous, and she ate lots of other peoples' food.

The gift grew so heavy and the desire to open it so great, that one day she couldn't wait any longer, so with the great courage that she had obtained from seeing other peoples' gifts she ripped the gift open.

It was empty inside. She sat down and cried like a baby. All her hopes and dreams that were in that box had just shrivelled up and died. For you see, no one had ever told her that she had to have pure nourishment to feed that gift.

So, the box, the gift given to her by her creator in the sky, was empty. And she was so very sad. But she still kept the empty box, for she wisely thought to herself, 'I could obtain pure milk from my creator in the sky, and fill my box again.'

And this she did, and the box grew and was filled once more with new promises of dreams to come true.

Now this princess grew happier for a while, for her creator in the sky gave her so much milk, she was able to feed other people as well.

But the sadness returned, for you see, she could never quite forget her original gift, and how it had been killed by not getting the correct food that it needed to stay alive till she was big enough to open it.

It was this sadness that she carried with her for a time and a day, even though she knew very well that she was loved and chosen by her wonderful creator in His Kingdom in the sky. She also knew that one day she would see Him, and be with Him.

Deep inside she longed for that original gift that was lost and denied her. So, she resigned to live, always feeding others, and enjoying the leftovers for herself.

One day she met a very wise old man who told her to give the empty box back to her creator in the sky and tell Him that she couldn't carry it around with her any longer, and to ask Him to please take it back and put it in His own heart and treasure it for her, so she could be free from this insatiable longing.

So, this was done, and she was given strength to enjoy the replacement gift that had been given to her by her creator.

She now lives happy with the thought that her gift box is safe with Him, and she feels complete in the knowledge that her creator in the sky knows it wasn't her fault.

She also no longer feels angry with those people who didn't give her milk from above to feed her gift.

What's more, she knows that she is loved and delighted in and approved of, by the most important person in the whole universe, her creator in the sky, who is very proud of her.

The end.

When I first became a follower of Jesus Christ, over the years my cry to Him has always been, 'Lord, please take away my emotional pain.' And that's exactly what he was doing – although I did not recognise it at first. God sent into our home a Christian man skilled in the process of healing damaged emotions. His aim was not only to heal the individual but to stop the cycle of abuse. A person emotionally damaged in childhood will often inflict the same sort of abuse on their own subsequent children. His aim was to now train counsellors to use his proven techniques of healing, which took him years to perfect.

Through it all, I realised that my emotional pain was legitimate, and I had every reason to feel the way I did. I learned I was not crazy. I was deeply wounded. In fact, I had done very well by managing to uphold my integrity and present to the public a sane and normal intelligent person. My defence mechanism of pretence that I had used to combat my damage was understandable but incorrect. Philip led us through recognising our injuries and the perpetrator of them, but also acknowledging the observer who did nothing to rescue us and then attributing the percentage of blame to each one correctly.

Philip then taught us the correct response to our loss and damage, which was not to wallow in low self-worth, fear, aggression, withdrawal, or pretence, but to peacefully contact the perpetrator and the observer and seek reconciliation, not by accusing them, but by forgiving them. Often these people don't realise the extent of damage and emotional pain they had caused. All this had to be told in a letter. The letters were to be carefully crafted following a strict format – more like a business letter. The shock came when after the letters had been approved by Philip, we were told to post them! The reluctance to do so was very great.

Philip told us many real-life stories of the consequences the letters had had in the past – often reuniting whole families in forgiveness and reconciliation. I posted my letter to my dad, who was the observer, and waited for an answer with bated breath. My mother was already dead but nevertheless I had to write and post a letter to her, addressed to Rathvinden House. One of Philip's assistants answered my letter on behalf of my mother, but for me it was an empty gesture. I thought my mother would not have replied like that. The answer I got from my father was at first disappointing. He tried to justify himself and virtually said in his reply, 'Well, you weren't such a little angel, you know.' But after several more letters to him, explaining to him that I was only a child, he apologised in his own way, excusing himself, saying he was unable to do anything about it. I knew that. I had no problem forgiving him. Forgiving my mother took much longer.

We were also taught how to react to people who would hurt our feelings in the future. He called this non-aggressive, non-destructive self-assertion. For instance, if someone was to call us a liar, we were taught to look them in the face, with no expression, no raising an eyebrow or smiling or nodding our head, and simply saying with confidence, 'I am not a liar.' We had to practise this on each other out of class, insulting and accusing each other, till we got it right.

Then we addressed the painful subject of abortion, which was handled with gentle skill and resolve by Philip. We were given homework to write an essay, welcoming and naming the baby, making room for him or her in the family. Then visualise the baby's accidental death and burial. Then at the next session we had to read it to the trainees. Again, it was gut-wrenchingly emotional. It was one thing accepting God's forgiveness for aborting my baby but forgiving myself was much harder. When Philip came again the next year, I was able to tell him and the class of the visual daydream I had been given which enabled me to forgive myself. We re-enacted it as a role-play for each woman who had aborted her baby. I have also written about this in Chapter 7. It is now used by Philip and all Hope Alive counsellors. It's now in his training manual crediting me as the author of the role-play.

Those seven days of intense training were the hardest thing I had ever experienced in my life. I likened it to going to hell and back. All the time during the seminar I was still living down at the stable complex with Melody and Bubble, getting them off to school each morning and catering to their needs as best I could. Doug had moved his bed into the basement of the house where the men were still working. The top floor bedrooms were full of guests and the ground floor was used to cater to them and hold the seminar.

After all the seminar guests had left, we all moved back into our own bedrooms in the house. It was the first time in months that Doug and I had slept in the luxury of our own bedroom and with an en suite bathroom.

Although I had tried hard to be flippant and uncooperative through the training, I had been given a lot of understanding of myself and my parents. One of the first exercises we were asked to do was to draw a family tree of our ancestors as far back as we knew, parents and siblings, and tell the class what we knew of each one. That awakened in me a realisation that my mother was not the only person that contributed to my abuse. The way she had been raised was how she was also treating me and my siblings. For her it was normal in her days to send one's children to boarding school and leave most of their upbringing to paid helpers. The cycle of abuse replayed on myself and my brothers and sister.

Each year that we lived at Rathvinden, Philip returned having recruited a new lot of people to be trained. I not only cooperated by being honest about myself, but Doug and I ended up being

Philip's co-workers with the groups. I saw first-hand how therapy worked in a powerful way in not only healing the individual but how the healing spread through whole families. We were issued with certificates as Trained Psychotherapists under the tuition of Dr Philip Ney. We then were able to conduct the Hope Alive six-month healing program with our own groups of patients. We became known as the only residential healing centre in Europe. Because of this we were sent some very difficult cases to treat.

Chapter 27

Rathvinden ministries

Now that our children had mostly moved on, Christianity began to take a much more public and pronounced place in our lives. This was a period of intense practical Christianity. We met some wonderful people and had some bizarre times. Sometimes wonderful, sometimes stressful, sometimes downright scary, but always interesting.

The name Rathvinden means the Fort of the Fairies. Rath means fort, and Vinden is Irish for fairy. The place was a historical landmark going back to the eighteenth century. We were told that it got its name because, before there was even a house on the property, the mound was a burial ground for unbaptised babies. Some of the locals claim it to be haunted and would be afraid to venture there after dark.

In the thirteen years we were at Rathvinden, we never charged for any of our services or accommodation. It was on account of this that the Lord generously provided everything for us. We held onto His word which said, 'Cast your bread upon the waters and it will be returned a hundred-fold,' (Ecclesiastes 11:1). Meaning, do something good without any expectation of return and the Lord will repay you a hundred-fold more. This promise of God was fulfilled. We received much more than we gave. This was especially brought to our notice when we sold that property and moved to Malta. The sale of the place paid for all the extravagant necessary restoration works and for all other expenses, over and above what we had spent.

We had fruitful and very busy years there.

We were sent troubled people from all over the world. Some who needed constant supervision. People with suicidal tendencies who had made several attempts to take their lives already. Others who were defeated alcoholics or dependent on drugs. Some who just needed a safe place to escape from an abusive marriage or a difficult relationship.

At first, we really did not know what we were there to do. All we knew was that God had work for us to do and the very first job was obvious. As mentioned above, the house was non-functional when we bought it. Half the electrics didn't work, the roof leaked, the gutters were more like sieves and the place stunk of mould. It turned out that the drains from the house were mostly blocked by tree roots causing the grey water and rainwater to pool around the house at basement level causing all sorts of rising damp issues.

I'll not bore you with the day-by-day, month-by-month progress of the development and restoration of the house, but let me give you an overview of what the ministry did turn into.

Reproduced below are the notes, written by Doug and placed in a folder in all the guest bedrooms, with an invitation to take one. I have added a little for the sake of this book but it's almost word-for-word how Doug wrote it.

Descriptive notes about Rathvinden ministries
Run by Douglas and Merrie Gresham

Rathvinden House is a large old Irish country mansion which we obtained at a time of our lives when we should have really been looking for a small cottage. Three of our five children had moved out of home to start their own lives. We are both middle-aged. However, the Lord, it seemed, had been training us both with skills and experiences and moved us halfway around the world to work for Him in Ireland. Eventually He showed us what He wanted us to do in Rathvinden.

The house stands in about 20 acres of fields and is surrounded by a large garden of sweeping lawns, hedges, flower beds and studded with tall, majestic beeches and oaks under which an annual display of bluebells and daffodils bloom. Below the gardens are stables which are able to accommodate twenty-three horses.

We have also restored a three-bedroom cottage which we called the Narnia cottage, which stands about 200 yards from the main house to be used by people who needed more privacy. Also, there is a self-contained flat above a barn, which we called 'The Dove Cot', for the same purpose.

We became part of the International Hope Alive Counsellors Association (IHACA), an organisation dedicated to alleviating and redressing the pain of people whose psychology has been damaged as a result of either the loss of a pregnancy or abuse in childhood.

IHACA was founded and is headed by Dr Philip Ney and Dr Marie Peters of Canada.

The loss of pregnancy includes the following: miscarriage, stillbirth, cot death or SIDS, adoption after birth and abortion. The most common by far is abortion. Post-Abortion Syndrome (PAS) has a much higher component of justifiable guilt. This guilt can be masked and covered for a long time by environmental factors. In the end, though, it can be devastating.

The term 'child abuse' should be defined as any inflicted environmental factor which inhibits or detracts from the development of the child's potential. The term covers verbal neglect, verbal abuse, physical neglect, emotional abuse, emotional smothering (active), emotional neglect (passive), emotional rejection, sexual abuse, divorce of parents during childhood (under the age of 20) which in most cases combines most of the facets of the above. Our part in the program is that we are both trained in the Hope Alive group psychotherapy method that the institute teaches and conducts.

[Each year we would take a group of ten or twelve people through the Hope Alive Therapy course. Most of these people would be accommodated in Rathvinden for the six months which it takes to complete the twenty-eight sessions of the therapy.] *We do not charge anything for the therapy, but the patients are required to help maintain the house and gardens. The work in the vegetable garden and orchard being in itself very therapeutic.*

We also facilitate training seminars in Rathvinden House. IHACA also trains therapists in many other countries in the world. [Many of these training seminars overseas we attended, alongside Philip and his assistant Marie Peters.] *We also facilitate seminars for Christian counsellors under the teaching of Dr Stephen McAuley. And various other groups come here for various functions and reasons. Besides that, we offer a cost-free holiday place for anyone in full-time Christian ministry to come with their family.*

We have a ministry of Christian hospitality that tries to address the problems, with the help of the Holy Spirit, of those whom the Lord sends to us. Counselling is in many areas, including grief, anxiety, health, marriage, and even a healing ministry and demon deliverance. We are rarely without guests.

Merrie also teaches a course called Christianity Explained, which is a non-denominational introduction to the essentials of Christianity designed to bring people into a personal relationship with Jesus Christ.

To help with the workload we recruit up to four ministry volunteers for six months at a time, cost-free accommodation in exchange for help with the house and grounds. Many times, the Lord brings to us helpers who themselves need help, so they go through the Hope Alive counselling as well while they are with us.

In addition to that, Doug also talks about the institute and its work, in all kinds of venues and all kinds of occasions. He has an online computer ministry as well and spends many hours answering emails.

Together with Dr Ney and Dr Peters we have also helped to found a group called The International Society of Centurions (ISOC). ISOC was established for the help, treatment and healing of men and women who have worked in the abortion industry. People in this situation have one of the worst self-inflicted psychological traumas and are ridden with guilt, often resulting in alcoholism and self-harm which no one was helping them with.

In the early days people would often ask us, 'What is your vision for the ministry?'

We would politely tell them, 'We don't have one. We simply leave that up to God. Whatever he gives us to do we will do with His help.'

....

A lot of our guests were those in need of a cost-free holiday. Pastors and missionaries were often unable to afford a holiday while in full-time Christian ministry, especially if they had children. One such family of seven children used to come for the full month of October each year. He was a pastor of a church in England. We would give them the entire basement where they could be self-sufficient with their own kitchen and entrance way. The children were aged from four to sixteen. The oldest child, who was using her own beauty and feminine form to attract attention to herself, rang alarm bells in her parents. Daddles was sitting with this family around their kitchen table one day when the subject was brought up and from the top of his head, he addressed the girl and said, 'Pretty attracts boys. Sexy attracts animals. But beauty, and by that, I mean beauty of character, attracts real men. Now you go out and decide what you want from the world.' I, for one, was so impressed that I wrote it down and have had occasion to pass on those words of wisdom a few times myself.

I used to look forward with joy and dread every October because my orderly home would be scrambled. The linen cupboards, the lovely playroom full of toys and games, had to be completely re-organised, finding puzzle pieces and mending broken toys. They were a lovely family, but the children had little to no supervision. Once I spent hours picking grass clippings and prickles out of the blankets that the children had taken off their beds and onto the lawns.

Philip Ney started to come about every six months or so with another group of trainees. One early group I remember very distinctly was a group of ex-abortionist doctors, mainly from the Eastern Bloc nations of Europe. Philip had developed a modified version of the Hope Alive therapy and from this grew the ISOC program mentioned above. Doug helped Philip format the much-needed program to help these doctors who had been led to believe they had been helping women by removing their unwanted babies. As they performed maybe twenty-four abortions a week, the repeated visual memories of usually live foetuses weighed heavily on their consciences. They began to see not a piece of flesh, but a human baby entering the cold cruel world by their hands, only to die and be discarded as hospital waste. These doctors told us that they often couldn't perform the procedure without vodka to quieten their conscience.

In many parts of Eastern Europe abortion is the state sponsored method of birth control. It was compulsory for doctors to do them. If they refused, which many eventually did, they lost their jobs. It was these displaced, guilt-ridden, often alcoholic doctors, men and women, who came to us, through Philip, for help. We called the therapy The Centurion as a reference to the Roman soldier who, having crucified Christ, realised what he had done, and said, 'Surely, this was the Son of God.' (Mark 15:39)

But our generosity and cost-free accommodation was also subject to abuse by unthinking persons. We soon found ourselves overburdened and unable to attend to the ones who really needed help. A charming but foolish young American lad, who was studying at one of the Oxford colleges, somehow came to be staying with us. Unfortunately, he told all his friends at uni where they could get fantastic accommodation free of charge with these amazing people in Ireland. It was decided after that all requests to come and stay should be handled by me. Daddles was too generous and unable to refuse people.

Aside from a cheap holiday, many of the visitors, particularly Americans, simply wanted to meet the stepson of C.S. Lewis. Celebrity hunting, however minor, seems to be a particular passion of Americans. Unfortunately, Daddles had become a celebrity, not only because of his connection with C.S. Lewis but on account of his own personality and talents as a public speaker.

People from many countries, but mostly America, invited him to be a keynote speaker at their various conferences and such. They knew that if my Daddles were speaking, ticket sales would soar. Amazingly, he never prepared notes before taking the stage and the microphone. He delivered talks to sometimes thousands of people entirely ad-lib. He would simply say, 'The Holy Spirit will talk through me. If He has nothing to say to you, then I will be without words. Any wisdom you hear from my lips, comes from the Holy Spirit. The folly is entirely my own. May God give you the wisdom to know one from the other.'

We always tried hard to be gracious to our guests, even the celebrity hunters. We were convinced that God had His reasons for sending people to us. One such American was Stan Matson. Although he was more legitimate than most being actively involved in ministry and spearheading a C.S. Lewis society in California. But I must recount Stan's first visit to Rathvinden to meet Doug and me.

James happened to be visiting at the time and he and his sister, Bubble, in a fit of high spirits and mischief, and in spite of both being young adults, were actually in the throes of a wrestling match on the carpet in the hallway. At the time, we had a Jack Russell dog in the household belonging to a gardener. The little dog also wanted to join in the fun. He jumped onto the heap of siblings and began enthusiastically biting both of them! Bubble, tired of being nipped, jumped up, grabbed the little dog in one hand, flung open the front door, hurled out the dog, and slammed the door. Only then did she realise that she had thrown the dog at a man who was about to ring the doorbell! It was Stan, his wife, and his teenage daughter, dressed in their Sunday best. They had just driven up the driveway to the big imposing house. Stan was reaching for the doorbell when someone jerked open the door, threw an angry dog at him then slammed the door in his face!

James of course immediately went to the door and found the poor, flustered and slightly bitten man on the doorstep. He apologised profusely, explained the situation and we all had a huge laugh. Stan and his family became long-time friends.

....

Although I couldn't run the ministry on my own without Doug's help, most of the workload was on me and I kept high standards. The house and gardens always had to look good, and the meals and meal tables were as good, if not better, than many hotels.

When people wanted to come and stay, I'd ask questions like, 'Are you in full-time Christian ministry?' or 'Are you in need of emotional or spiritual help?' If the answer was yes, I'd invite them to come and stay. If no, I'd suggest a good B&B in the village and invite them to come and have afternoon tea and a chat one day. No one was offended and we were able to do our job.

One lady from Dublin phoned and asked if she could come and stay with us for two weeks. I asked her those questions. When her answers were no to all of them, I asked her why she wanted to come. She told me she was a mother of eight children and her sister had come from England to look after the children so she could get away and have a break. I said, 'Lady, you are in a full-time Christian ministry; come and have a holiday here.' She came and during her stay told us that her husband was a traveling salesman and she had found out that he had a lover in Paris. I shared with her my experiences, and how I had dealt with the same type of thing.

Later, her husband also came to us. Doug and I were able to counsel the husband with the help of the Holy Spirit and resolve the destructive issue in their marriage. The husband agreed to forward all his lover's letters from his mistress on to Doug. Doug actually answered her letters in an effort to also help her. We later had a mock re-marriage ceremony in my office where they reinforced their marriage vows. I even made up a decorated re-marriage certificate for them, using my gifts of art and calligraphy.

Many people wanted help for emotional problems. Some would tell us of other counsellors they had been seeing for a long period of time. These people were in fact often attention seeking and lonely. I never refused them but there was a price to pay. I'd tell them that we couldn't see or counsel them unless they agreed to first go through the Christianity Explained course with me and after that we could talk. Many refused to come on account of that, but others welcomed the idea.

The interesting thing about that was that after they had completed the Christianity Explained course with me, and had understood it, accepted Jesus, and made a prayerful resolution to submit to His love and rule and accept His forgiveness, there was often no need for counselling. I, of all people, knew that there is no real healing unless we get our lives right with God.

After many sessions with a professional counsellor, the biblical truth still remains: '... a dog returns to its vomit. A sow returns to its wallow.' (2 Peter 2:22). Too many times we witnessed people who had benefited from the counsel we gave them over many long hours and days, or even months, leave our place happy and determined to live a victorious life, only to find that in time they were back to their destructive ways. Willpower simply isn't strong enough to change a person. Without a relationship with God, often, all their efforts are futile. I could give you many examples of this, but it would take another book to fit them all into the story.

One afternoon, when Doug was away in America, the phone rang. It was a pastor from Northern Ireland and his de-facto wife. They were at the Carlow train station and wanted to be picked up. I was confused. Apparently, a friend of his from Dublin had told him she had arranged it all, but she had never contacted me. I wasn't expecting them and knew nothing about them. But I couldn't just leave them at the station, so I hopped in the car and collected them.

After listening to their story, I ascertained that alcohol and drug abuse was the reason they came. They hoped to be set free. Now, I knew nothing about rehabilitating alcoholics so I phoned the rehabilitation centre in Dublin and asked them how I should handle these unexpected visitors. Their suggestions set in me a resolve to attack this problem head on. I was to write out a set of ten rules for their stay, that they were to agree on and sign. The tenth rule was if they broke any of the rules they were to leave, no second chances. I can't remember all the rules I made on that list, but a few I do remember.

They were to sleep at opposite ends of the house, and not talk to each other as I noticed that they were constantly arguing. Bed was by 9.30 pm and up by 7.00 am. I was to personally unpack all their bags and take with me any pills or alcohol. I would administer their medications. After breakfast each morning, they were to attend my class of Christianity Explained. They were not to leave the property till their release on a pre-arranged day. Each day I would spend an hour with them individually and listen to their story and help if I could.

Their story was long and complicated. The pastor had been set aside and not given any pastoral duties on account of his unfaithfulness to his wife, and his affair with the lady who now accompanied him. She was half his age. Most of it I have forgotten. I tend to put things like that out of my mind unless I'm actively involved with them at the time. They were very well-behaved, and they kept all the rules. They benefited enormously from the fresh look at the Christianity that they both professed to believe in. After their time was up, they had made a lot of resolutions as to how to restore his pastoral role and live a Godly life. They would part company and reorganise their lives.

I was patting myself on the back for a job well done without Doug's help. We would always counsel difficult cases together. Well, on their train journey back to Belfast they both celebrated in the train bar and apparently were completely inebriated by the time they got home. David was his name. He treated me like his best friend for years afterwards sending me cards, gifts, and news of his life. I do hope he eventually got himself under control. He was such a charming man – he probably substituted charm for responsibility. Unfortunately, I haven't heard of him for years now.

A lot of my time and energy was taken up with weekly classes of Christianity Explained. Everywhere I went I was constantly inviting people to join my next class. Lots of the workmen on site, including the project manager, were taken through it. In the process, I discovered a valuable principle. If you reveal Jesus to others, He reveals Himself to you in various ways.

I look back at those years now with such longing to be there again. I had never felt so connected to God in a daily workable way as I had felt then. God graciously healed people through me and gifted me with discernment and wisdom. I even learnt about the bizarre and frightening world of demon deliverance and, through God, had much success in that area as well.

One of the Catholic ladies, who I had taken through the Christianity Explained course, told her parish priest about it, and suggested that I do the course in his church in Graiguenamanagh as a pre-lent teaching. The priest agreed, thoroughly trusting this dyed-in-the-wool Catholic lady's judgement. So, it was arranged. I couldn't believe that I was on the pulpit in a Catholic church with about forty to fifty Irish Catholics listening. The teachings were going very well; the people were interested, listening intently to every word I said. I got through session number one, which is designed to prove that Jesus is in fact God. Even the very powerful rendition of the crucifixion in session number two was received with awe and gratitude.

But, as I was halfway through session three, which is telling why God had to raise Jesus to life again after his death on the cross, Father O'Connor came in and sat down amongst his parishioners. Suddenly he stood up and asked me in an abrupt tone, 'Who gave you the authority to teach from the Bible?'

I simply said, 'Jesus Christ.' And I quoted the passage, which is at the end of Matthew's Gospel, where Jesus commands us to go and teach all people. The priest was angry and told me I needed to have gone through seminary college or have a degree in theology to be qualified to teach. I made him even angrier by asking, 'Where in the Bible does it tell us that?'

I was told not to return, and he took his followers with him and left the church. But a handful of them remained, and I was invited by one lady to continue the course in her home, which I did.

....

I learnt a lot about demon deliverance from a very holy Indian-South African man named Godfrey, and his wife, Muriel. How strange, we used to send missionaries to Africa; now the Africans were teaching the white people about God. Godfrey would always find welcome accommodation at Rathvinden as he travelled the land teaching, preaching, healing and casting out demons. He taught me that demons could themselves get addicted to alcohol, drugs, or nicotine. The only way they could take these substances was through inhabiting a human body and making that person take the drugs for them. So many people desperately want to stop smoking or drinking but find themselves defeated. It's the demon that hungers for the substance, not the human. This opened up a new understanding of demon deliverance for me. They not only want to destroy us, but they want to use us for their own gratification.

After a person had completed the Christianity Explained course with me, I'd always ask them if they needed prayer for anything. It was at this time that healing through Jesus seemed to be strongest, probably because their faith was also strong then. One amusing little story is of the lady who, after completing the course and being asked for prayer requests told me she never really felt a connection or love for her husband of thirty-five years. I led her through a prayer renouncing and asking God to forgive her for all her sexual encounters she had had before her marriage and, in the name of Jesus, I broke the bonds that tied her to them. Then I asked her if there was anything else. She clasped her hands over her chest and said, 'I've always wanted bigger boobs.'

'Well ... okay, let's ask the Lord to provide that,' I said, and prayed accordingly. This lady would write to me often telling me how she was now madly in love with her husband, and as the weeks went by, she would gleefully tell me her need to buy yet another larger bra size!

Every Thursday evening Doug and I held a Bible study in the sitting room for the people of Leighlinbridge and any guests that were in the house at the time were invited to attend. A group of evangelists called the Covenant Players, who travelled through Ireland and the UK performing short plays, songs and mimes to schools, prisons, hospitals, and any public venue, would stay with us when they were in the area and would join us on a Thursday night.

On one occasion the question was asked of the group, 'Can a born-again Christian harbour a demon?' All answers would have to be biblical; no 'I thinks' were permitted. The conclusion was that yes, a demon could have a strong influence even over a spirit-filled person. Well, one of the members of the Covenant Players group strongly objected to the decision and came into my office after the study to complain angrily to me about it. I asked her one question. 'Sue,' I said. 'Is there any area of your Christian life that you are totally defeated in?' She never answered and left in a huff.

The next day she came to me again, more humbly this time and sheepishly said, 'I think I have a demon that controls me.'

'Oh, what's his name?' I asked.

'I just thought I had a high libido,' she replied.

I waved and said, 'Hi, libido.' She didn't think that was funny. So, I asked, 'When did you let this demon in?' She knew the exact time and place. Strangely, many people do. When she was fifteen years old, she witnessed her sister making love with a man on the sitting room floor of their home. Ever after that she was obsessed with sex and led a very promiscuous life herself. She got married and still couldn't resist men and her husband divorced her because of her unfaithfulness. She was listening to a travelling evangelist and gave her life to the Lord, thinking now she would be able to control herself, but the temptation still ruled her. She met up with the Covenant Players group and joined them, thinking, *now I will be able to be a good Christian*. But she was far from free of the sex demon that drove her.

I asked her if she wanted to be rid of this demon. 'Yes,' she said.

I led her in a prayer of repentance for letting this demon in and entertaining him. I laid my hands on her and commanded the demon: 'Out, in the name of Jesus.'

Sue started to choke. She ripped the t-shirt off from around her neck. She went blue. Then she went purple and fell on the floor. I panicked thinking, *I'm going to have a dead woman on my hands soon.* All I could think to do was to perform the Heimlich manoeuvre for choking people. I clasped her around the chest from behind and gave a strong squeeze, all the time saying, 'Come out, you demon, in the name of Jesus.' She dry-retched – I thought she was going to vomit on my nice pale-blue carpet – and then she took a breath.

My two Poodles who used to always be at my side hid under my office desk and snarled most uncharacteristically. The whole room felt electrified. I commanded the demons (as now I realised there were many of them) to leave the room and to go to the place that God had prepared for them. They left and the room was clear, and Sue was laughing with joy and relief. She used to write to me for a long time after that, telling me she was still free.

The story doesn't end there though. One day, I was telling this story to a group of people and a man came to me afterwards, saying he needed to have the same demon removed from him. I was amazed because this man was in full-time Christian ministry. I asked him the same questions that I had asked Sue. He too had led a very sexualised life before he gave his life to Christ. He had even been convicted of molesting children and had spent time in gaol. He felt defeated, unable to control himself. When I was commanding the demon out of him, he clasped his hands over his mouth and ran out of the room into the nearby toilet and vomited into the bowl. I asked him if he had felt nauseated during the time of deliverance. 'No,' he said. 'My mouth was just suddenly full of vomit.'

Another of my mentors and spiritual advisors were Paul and Nuala. Paul used to be a Jesuit priest and Nuala a Catholic nun. They both had had a personal revelation of the truth of Jesus in spite of their respective religious orders. But when they were caught telling others about this, they were relieved of their religious position and ordered to leave their monasteries. They later met and got married. But that's the very short version of their story. Both of them relocated to Florida to escape the wrath of their Catholic families. For three months of every year, they would return to their Irish homeland, and teach and preach to mainly Catholic communities. They too would find a place of comfort and rest at Rathvinden. We became very good friends and I often went with them on their evangelistic rounds. I witnessed amazing things with them.

On one occasion, they had been asked to pray for a dying lady in a hospital in Kilkenny and asked me to accompany them. The hospital room was crowded with family and friends all waiting for the old woman to take her last breath. Paul looked around the room and told the onlookers that it was unlikely that God would heal this lady while she was surrounded by such idolatry. He made the visitors remove every Mary statue and relic, scapular, rosary beads, Mass cards, and holy water, from the room. He also told any offended person to leave the room. Only a few remained. Paul prayed and nothing seemed to change, but that dying lady walked out of the hospital, completely healed, later that same day!

Paul and Nuala were able to help me personally with an issue that had been growing for some time. Most of my children had made it through their turbulent teenage years with sanity and relationships intact. But Melody was struggling badly.

Melody was a master of the art of upsetting me and making me get very angry with her. I could never do anything right in her eyes. I always felt on the defensive when I encountered her. Perhaps she felt the same way about me? Even a simple question asked in love would receive a curt answer. For example, if I asked her, 'How are you today, Melody?', she would reply, 'What do you want to know for?' Or if I asked, 'Why are you late coming home from school? I was beginning to worry about you.', this would infuriate her and she would reply, 'Why? Don't you trust me?'

One day I asked her why she was always so angry. 'I'm not angry,' she shouted.

'Then who are you angry with?' I asked.

'With you,' was her reply.

'Oh,' I said. 'Why are you angry with me?'

'Because you are not my mother,' was her quick response.

'So, you are really angry with your mother?' I asked. With that she thumped her little fists on the table screaming furiously, 'I'm not angry with my mother, I'm not angry with my mother.' And she ran up to her bedroom slamming every door behind her.

After her outburst that day, when she had settled down, I went into her room and told her I was sorry, and if she would let me, I could help her with this hard time. She looked up at me with her big brown watery eyes and said, 'But, Mompska, I'm only twelve.'

'Later then,' I said, and gave her a hug.

Most of her outbursts didn't end that well. Paul and Nuala noticed our struggle. When I was alone in the kitchen with them one day, they asked me why I had adopted a fifth child when I already had raised four of my own. I told them about the time Doug had asked me if we could adopt a baby from a third world country, and how I had immediately seen a baby on a doorstep. I then told them of the promise I had made to God, when I had my abortion, that if I saw a baby on a doorstep, I'd take it in and raise it as my own. Paul and Nuala were quick to find the reason that Melody and I were not getting along together. I had used Melody as a reparation, an atonement for my sin. In other words, I was trying to pay the price for my sin rather than letting Jesus take the price. 'So, what can I do?' I asked.

There and then they led me in a prayer of repentance for bypassing His sacrifice, and I returned Melody to Jesus and renounced my adoption of her. Then I accepted her back again as a precious gift from God. A gift, and not a price for my offence to God. Our troubles didn't stop immediately but started to improve from that day on. Melody is now in her thirties and still lives in Dublin. She phones me often. We love each other with every ounce of our being. She is my joy and delight.

....

We were helped with the routine work by four ministry volunteers who would stay with us for six months at a time. They were usually young girls, although we did have young men sometimes. They came to us by word-of-mouth. Doug often had speaking engagements overseas and would mention our work at Rathvinden, and the role of volunteers. This would trigger a desire to come and assist us. Strangely enough, we never had any Irish girls asking to come and help, but mainly girls from America. We also had two from Lithuania and one from India. Some would come to go through the therapy as well as being designated volunteers. I would give them 20 Irish punts a week so they could buy their own toiletries and stamps and would give them each two days off a week. I kept a strict roster, which I rotated, sharing the various activities and responsibilities.

We later discovered that we needed to make application forms for them to fill out before being accepted. This had to be signed by their pastor or a responsible adult because some of those earlier girls were more of a liability than a help. But even this didn't spare us from getting 'help' from unsuitable volunteers, like the girl who had never peeled a potato in her life.

In many cases, Rathvinden became like a finishing school for young girls as I taught them about personal hygiene, tidiness, and manners. One girl complained and questioned the reason why she had to keep her room tidy and clean. After all, no one ever went into her room except her. From that day on I told her I would come into her room and have morning tea with her every day. Each room had tea making facilities and a jar of biscuits. We became quite good friends on account of those morning tea visits and her room was never untidy again.

I taught them how to prepare meals, bake cakes, and clean. I also taught them to correctly set and wait at a table, how to be courteous, how to harvest the orchard fruits and make jams and bottle the fruit or dry it. Each year we dried a lot of apples. They learnt how to sew and mend, grow flowers and vegetables, string onions, clean silver, iron linen, and prepare guest rooms to my high standards. These were many of the things that I had learnt when I was a school child in Hobart, Tasmania. Today, children don't seem to be taught such things.

I learnt that some of the girls were afraid of me. They would complain to Doug about my strictness and standards. All too often I would have to tell them that I had found several things wrongly set up in the guest room that they had been asked to make ready. I would send them up to find the fault themselves and correct it. Later I'd check the room again, only to find no toilet paper, or a dirty tea tray or the biscuit tin empty, or some such thing.

I personally did all the laundry because the washing machine was a large commercial one and expensive to run. Putting just four or five small items of personal clothing in it would waste money and meant the machine would run nearly all day. But the girls did the ironing with the big commercial roller iron that Dig had bought me in Bagenalstown.

It was a joy and a delight when we would be sent people who I could rely on to do the job without supervision. I found that girls over twenty-five were far more mature and not always looking to 'have a good time'. One such girl was Alina, the sister of Dominick's wife. Alina was a tremendous help and could turn her hand to any task, often helping Doug in his office with the piles of paperwork. She was a good typist and would type while Doug dictated to her. She was fun to be around and was always cheerful and helpful, seeing things that needed to be done and doing it without having to be asked. She stayed with us for over a year. We missed her so much when she went back to Australia.

Rathvinden became a safe haven for many of the ministry volunteers but when it came time for them to re-enter the big bad world and find a job or look for a flat, they would be very reluctant to leave. The idea was so devastating for one of the girls from Eastern Europe, that on the day she was to leave I found her in

the bath having cut both her wrists! I bound up her wrists, but she seemed to be in a non-responsive trance. Our local doctor stitched up her wrists without a local anaesthetic. I held her hand still for him but she didn't even flinch.

We did have some wonderful helpers, many of whom are still in contact with us today and email us regularly. I am so grateful for the ones who gave us their time and help at a very busy time of our lives.

As I have already mentioned, many of our ministry volunteers were first and foremost patients who had been sent to us to go through the Hope Alive therapy course. There was always a real awareness on our part that during the therapy they might commit suicide. Some of them were very troubled individuals needing a lot of love and help. I'd tell them to phone my room if they were upset during the night, and 'please don't jump out the top-storey window as it will destroy my flower beds below.' Often my phone would ring at 2.00 or 3.00 in the morning. All I'd hear was a sniff and a kind of groan. At a glance, I'd see which room was calling, don my dressing gown and, taking my box set of Beatrix Potter stories, I'd hop into bed with them and read *The Tale of Peter Rabbit*, *The Tale of the Flopsy Bunnies* or *Jemima Puddle Duck*. I would often nearly complete the whole series before they were relaxed enough to go to sleep. The last thing they or I needed at that hour of the night was to revisit their past traumas.

Chapter 28

Wendy's story

We witnessed first-hand how healing and reconciliation could spread throughout the family circle and even the world thereafter, like ripples in a still pond when a stone has been thrown into it. This was strongly demonstrated to us in the well-known Slazenger family of County Wicklow, Ireland.

In 1961, the Slazenger family (of sporting goods fame) bought the huge Irish Powerscourt Estate from the 9th Viscount Powerscourt, Mervyn Patrick Wingfield. The Slazengers lived at the Powerscourt House, which was a private dwelling, but the house was badly damaged by fire in 1974. Today the house is partly repaired, and the gardens are open to the public. It is absolutely breathtaking and well worth a visit. In 2011, the *Lonely Planet* voted Powerscourt in the top ten houses in the world, while in 2014, *National Geographic* listed Powerscourt as number three in the world's top ten gardens!

In 1962, Wendy Slazenger, the daughter of company founder Ralph Slazenger, married the Hon. Mervyn Niall Wingfield, 10th Viscount Powerscourt, the son of the former owner, and herself became Viscountess Powerscourt. When that marriage fell apart, Wendy remarried a kind, wise and stable man called Ray Watson. We came to know Wendy at a time when she feared that her second marriage, as well as her life, was in danger of crumbling. She saw no reason to live.

We are still in touch with Wendy and recently I asked her permission to use her story as a case history of one of the people who went through the Hope Alive therapy program with us. She not only gave her consent but also wrote it out for me from her viewpoint. I'm going to use the writing she gave me. But before I do, let me also include her own introduction of herself.

Wendy is the daughter of Ralph Slazenger whose father was the founder of the firm mostly associated with sports equipment. When she was eighteen, she married into the Wingfield family and became Viscountess Powerscourt. After the break-up of that marriage, she was deemed to be unstable. It wasn't until she came to Rathvinden and went through the Hope Alive therapy with Doug and Merrie Gresham that she came to realise that her childhood had been one of extreme neglect.

Although she had all the material paraphernalia, she lacked any sort of emotional nurture, no affection, and no affirmation. Wendy was miserable at school and was eventually expelled from what was, at the time, a very prestigious, expensive and boring school in 1957. That beginning derailed, taunted and haunted her adult years and left her unable to function. Thankfully, she made a full recovery and is now a Hope Alive counsellor herself. This is how it happened.

My Rathvinden Experience
By Wendy Watson

I had hit rock bottom for probably the third time in my life. The first time was an attempted suicide, and the second time a complete nervous breakdown, whatever that means. On the first two occasions I was not a Christian. The third time I was. I fully understood that suicide was not an option, and I was desperate. Throughout my life I had undergone psychoanalysis, psychotherapy, counselling and so on. Both secular and Christian, prescribed drugs for depression from the top specialists in England. The list is endless.

It was November 1997. I was fifty-three years old and had just suffered a massive disappointment, which I saw as a total failure. All the old recognisable symptoms were there; crying most of the time, a huge reluctance to go anywhere or leave our flat. One Sunday morning we were just about to leave for church, I was feeling wretched and inconsolable. I rang my brother, John, in Ireland. I remembered that he had recently told me he had gone for help. He said that the man seemed to know all about John's life and had been able to help him. I rang John that morning and asked if he thought this couple could help me. John said, 'Yes, they could.' If I would go over to Ireland, he would set up a meeting for me.

My husband, Ray, and I flew over and drove to Rathvinden. We were greeted by Doug and Merrie and taken into Merrie's study. They asked me some questions which seemed totally irrelevant. Of course, it turned out that these questions were extremely relevant. We were invited to join a group therapy course they would run called Hope Alive.

It would be difficult for me to describe how incredibly reluctant I was to take up their invitation. I did not want to go. The only reason I did was because I could see that Ray was, albeit silently, issuing an ultimatum and our marriage was in jeopardy.

There was a vague attempt to find someone running a Hope Alive group in the UK, but the next one was not due to start till the following year. Doug reckoned I would probably be dead by then. So Rathvinden it was to be. As I look back on all this, some twenty-three years later, it is crystal clear to both Ray and me that God's plan for us was to go to Rathvinden, not just for my healing but for the ripple effect that became clear over the following years.

Our time at Rathvinden got underway in January 1998. The arrangement was that in order to be in the group and live there as well, we had to work. Even although Ray was not in the group, he had to work too. Merrie asked us to meet her in her study where she would allocate our different jobs. I should explain that I love the outdoors and hate house-cleaning, and Ray hates the outdoors and would have been fine with an indoor job. We were both shocked when Merrie announced that I would be cleaning the house, twelve bedrooms and thirteen bathrooms, and Ray would be given outside jobs to do under Doug's supervision. I responded quickly by saying I would not be able to do that because I had asthma. Merrie was calm and assertive, as she always is, and asked me what medication I took for my asthma. I told her and she said I would be fine doing housework. I was also not aware at this point that she had been a nurse. Ray realised there was no point in arguing and was more accepting than I was.

I think it was a good thing that the Irish sea was between Rathvinden House and home. Running away would have been quite complicated. After the initial few weeks, we did settle into life with the Greshams *at their remarkable home and their extraordinary ministry. We even began to take pride in our work. Merrie, in her wisdom, made it clear that she would not be checking up on my housework. She explained that she would trust me to do a good job. Part of their ministry was to make their guests feel welcome, and part of that was to have their bedrooms and bathrooms clean and inviting. The strange thing is that with all the housework I had to do, it proved helpful to have a physical job to do which gave me lots of thinking time about the previous session. This made it easier to then settle down in the evening to do the set homework which was reviewed in the next session. I think Merrie also knew that doing household chores would give me no time to feel homesick.*

Winter turned into spring; I was making good progress with the therapy. We made friends and were welcomed into the little church in Carlow. We learnt from Merrie how to be gracious and understanding, that difficult people are just hurting people. Doug and Merrie are an awesome team. Doug is an incredible diagnostician and Merrie is one who puts her arms around you and picks up the pieces as you process the diagnosis and get on with the healing.

What I have written is a small fraction of my life at Rathvinden. I will end my small contribution by writing a bit of what I wrote as we were leaving Rathvinden.

Praise God! After fifty years of attempted self-destruction, God has healed me. He used Doug and Merrie to do it. I could write another ten pages trying to thank them for being so willing to do this. My hand is still firmly in theirs, but they have taught me to walk on my own. With God's help and not to mention Ray's, I believe I can do this. At times it will be scary, but I know I can always pick up the phone and talk to them, I know they will listen, they said they would, and I trust them.

I should probably mention that about a year later Ray and I went to Mountjoy College in Canada, the home of Dr Philip Ney, who wrote the Hope Alive program, to train as Hope Alive counsellors. We have run groups ever since. We are grateful to Doug and Merrie for being such good role models.

That's Wendy's personal description of her broken life and how God intervened in an awesome way by repairing her brokenness and blessing many others. By remaking a remarkable, now strong person who, together with Ray, has been instrumental in healing others using the same Hope Alive therapy that healed her. Praise God.

Wendy's son Mervyn Anthony Wingfield – who became 11th Viscount Powerscourt – also trained under Dr Philip Ney in Canada after he saw the healing it had achieved in his mother. He is also now a counsellor using the guidelines from Philip's teaching and experience. The ripples continue, breaking the cycle of abuse, and so saving other children from the same kind of traumas.

But before I get onto another part about life at Rathvinden, I should tell you of the real unsung hero of Wendy's story: her rock-solid and faithful husband, Ray. He also wrote an excerpt for me, so I'll let him tell it himself.

Ray's Story
16th June – 4th January 1998

I was born and bred a city boy and after having lived and worked for almost six months at Rathvinden, I'm glad that my home is a small flat in the middle of Bristol, UK. I have really missed the concrete, tarmac, and carbon monoxide fumes. Seriously though, my stay at Rathvinden has been quite an experience, very difficult at times, but nothing is wasted in God's economy, and I am sure that I have emerged a better person. I feel I have grown and matured as a Christian. I've been aware of God chiselling rough edges off me, and supplying me with patience, self-control, perseverance, meekness and grace; all the qualities necessary to sponsor Wendy as a Hope Alive patient.

I learnt many new, allegedly useful skills. Very traumatic for someone to whom DIY and gardening are an anathema: mowing, strimming, racking, weeding, hoeing, drilling, rotavating, burning, trimming, clipping, sowing, and barbecuing.

The highlights of each week have been worshiping at Carlow Presbyterian church, under the excellent ministry of Stephen Johnston, Sunday lunch in the big house (we lived in the Narnia Cottage), Thursday evenings' Bible study led by Doug and Merrie with music supplied by Kieran (J.T.) Ryan and amazing cakes baked by Alina, as well as morning coffee in the Coal Hole. Above all, we have established some really good friendships that have lasted long beyond our time there.

The Hope Alive course healed Wendy, praise the Lord. Thank you, Father, for leading us to Doug and Merrie just in time. And thank you for also helping me through this time of testing.

We arrived at Rathvinden in the darkness and cold of winter and are leaving in the light and warmth of summer. Words cannot express the gratitude I feel towards Doug and Merrie. God bless you both. Hallelujah!

Ray Watson.

Chapter 29

Interesting people, interesting times

It's a fascinating process looking back on one's life. For Daddles and me, it becomes clear how God has been guiding and providing for us in many ways – especially after we had both submitted our lives to Him. At the time things just seem to happen; it's the way they are. However, we became aware of the people that God had sent into our lives who have gifted us by guarding, guiding, supporting, and loyally helping us with what we are doing.

In Tasmania it was a young red-headed accountant called Melvin Adams who, after getting to know us, has devoted his life to protect and help us. He followed us to Ireland and became our legal advisor, looking after our finances. He is still working alongside us. We are his only client. Doug seldom ever travels without him when on a business trip. While dealing with some very heavy-duty business deals – like making the Narnia stories into films – the both of them seemed to be having such fun enjoying the Australian mannerism of jokingly teasing and rubbishing one another, much to the amusement of the other, ever-so-serious American businessmen sitting around the conference table.

It says in the Bible that, 'One man sows the seed and another man harvests.' C.S. Lewis sowed the seed in my heart, but when we were living in Ringarooma, Tasmania, it was Pastor Jed Crispin who cultivated and nurtured that seed to maturity, which later grew to encompass Doug and then all of our five children – which I have discussed in Chapter 24. God couldn't have chosen a more suitable person to come alongside us and take me deeper into the truths of Christianity that I had encountered. Jed was, and still is, a man of God with a ready smile, a streak of mischievous humour, a twinkle in his eye and a heart overflowing with love. His character was equally matched by his fun-loving wife, Jeanie. We not only learnt a lot about Christianity from them but had a lot of fun doing so. They became lifelong friends.

Then there was Alina, whom I have also already mentioned. She came during a very needed time at Rathvinden. Free of charge, she devoted twelve months of her life to helping us with her God-given skills of office and domestic skills, and social interaction with the many guests we hosted.

Mark McDonald was a man Daddles employed as a groundsman and general handyman at Rathvinden. He was a real Godsend. He was an Irishman who guarded his integrity and honour with an iron fist. You could throw stones at his large solid body, but don't ever dare to darken his character, or doubt his truthfulness, loyalty, and honour. He was 100 per cent trustworthy. A man of few words, he would have protected us with his life. He admired and loved Doug with all his heart and would do anything for him. I think he admired me a little also. He built me a lovely brick and stone henhouse with nesting boxes opening from outside the building so I didn't have to go in among the hens to collect the eggs. He also made a rat-proof building joining it to keep the bags of laying pellets in. When the building was completed, I went to inspect it. There hanging above the door was a hand-carved plaque that Mark had made reading, 'The Hen Hilton. For the love of Merrie.' He had a very thick Irish accent which sounded more like a muffled quiet rumble. I always had trouble understanding what he was saying.

I have already said a lot about the Canadian psychiatrist Dr Philip Ney. He was and is the man God sent to me to answer my heart's cry, 'God please take away my emotional pain.' Through Philip, I learned how to rid myself of self-pity and the life of pretence I had been living. And to also realise that the people I had blamed and held at arm's length for so long, were not entirely responsible for the things I had suffered as a child. There were many others who should take a percentage of the blame. I still live by a lot of Philip's guidelines. And now I also have tools with which to help alleviate emotional pain and bad responses in other people's lives.

As I write, we are now living in Malta. And again, we can see how God has sent good people to support and help us. Joanna Agius has become our legal advisor, helper, and friend. She cares for us over and above the call of duty. Then there is Zaru, a rock-solid Maltese man who took on the job of being our handyman-cum-groundsman. He multitasks as a gardener, mechanic, chauffeur, tractor driver and fix-'em-up-chappy. Zaru takes his job of looking after us and our villa a little too seriously. I feel safe here when Doug is away because I know he is near and will come to my aid any time, day or night. I can't not mention Robert Cassar who has become part of our life here in Malta. He first came to us looking for emotional help. Now he helps us. He became fascinated with Doug's life and heritage and has taken on the monumental task of making a film documentary about him, calling it *An Honest Life*. His assistant is his wife, Rebecca. A deep friendship has developed between all of us.

The small Christian church I joined up with in Malta, pastored by Ken and his wife, Carmen, has been a great help to me, both spiritually and physically. I refer to them all as my brothers and sisters in Christ, and the group as my church family.

Everything we do, and everywhere we make our home, God provides for us. At the holiday home that we have recently bought on the Isle of Wight there is 'Mr Beaver', Daryl Aukland, who has become our friend and helper. He was the only tenant left in the cottages that went with the property when we bought the house and grounds. He fully expected to be asked to leave when we took ownership, but as usual Doug got on well with him and saw his value as a caretaker and general groundsman. Ironically, Daryl, who has worked as a professional actor, once played Mr Beaver in a stage production of *The Lion, the Witch and the Wardrobe* in London and has always been a big fan of the Narnia stories, so there was an immediate bond. Again, God had provided for a need.

As I mentioned in the beginning of this book, for three months every year we go to Australia to visit our three sons and their families. So, we purchased a little tropical island sanctuary in Queensland where we can relax. James, Dig and Dominick also use it as a holiday place to take their families to. There again is the capable and trustworthy man called Pete Beswick who was the caretaker for the previous owner and who now looks after the island for us, and any guests that visit.

It is Doug that instils such loyalty and devotion from these people. His genuine love and interest and enjoyment of any employee of ours – or anyone else he encounters – results in them pledging their support and allegiance, not to me, but to him. He is so kind to them and shares his life's stories with them. He is a gifted storyteller and his interaction with them is always jovial and friendly. He loves to take a plumber – who came to mend a pipe – for a ride in his Tesla or his Ariel Atom. This friendliness with complete strangers – which all our employees were at first – often worries me. But without intending it, Doug works magic on the recipient. They love him for it and become devoted to him. I have often heard them say, 'Doug is different; we have never been treated so well by an employer before.'

But back to Rathvinden.

In the group therapy sessions at Rathvinden Doug would take the lead, and I kept very essential notes on the progress and story of each patient, adding a verbal observation or question where necessary. The Hope Alive therapy would venture deep into the darkest periods of peoples' lives and emotions were often at breaking point. We had been warned by Dr Philip that at this stage the patient may even kill themselves. That would have been tragic, but it never happened with any of our cases, thank God. But if it had happened the relatives would probably have been taking us to court, so the detailed notes were essential. The notes also helped us review the session together in private afterwards.

The ability Doug had of seeing and hearing beyond and between what we were being told often amazed me. His observations were often short and cut straight to the point. I believe this was a gift of discernment that God had given Doug. I had a different approach. We were aware that our guests who came to us were sent to us by God for a reason. So, when a guest seemed to be happy, charming, and confident, I would ask them a question in passing, simply, 'What's the matter?'

They would immediately answer, 'Nothing.'

The next day I'd ask the same question, always choosing a moment when they couldn't engage in conversation. Again, they would just shrug and say, 'Nothing's the matter.' The third day I'd put a bit more emphasis on my question. Then the floodgates would open, and he or she would burst into tears, and say, 'How did you know?' Well, the truth was I didn't know, all I knew was that they had been sent to us by God for a reason and we needed to find out that reason. Occasionally though, the reason was for our own personal benefit and their stay would make us feel energised, encouraged, or helped in some area.

Even when Doug was sound asleep his gift of 'hitting the nail on the head' was active. One night the phone beside our bed rang. It was a man from the USA who had not thought to check the time difference between Ireland and America. Even half asleep, Doug was kind and gracious and never even let the man know the error he had made. He had rung to interview Doug about his stepfather. I was fully awake and listened to Doug's answers to his questions. One answer he gave was so profound that I quickly wrote it down on the notepad that I kept beside my bed, so it wouldn't be forgotten. The man had obviously asked Doug what church he belonged to. Doug answered, 'I belong to no church, for 'The Church', which is the Body of Christ, belongs to me. Jesus gave it to me when He died for me on the cross.'

In the morning, Doug had no recollection of the phone call or what he had been asked or said. He had been fast asleep all through that phone interview.

Often, Doug had to leave me to manage on my own while he went to America with Melvin for business meetings. It wasn't unusual for him to be gone for a whole month or more. On the 22nd of June 1995, my diaries recall that he left on one of these trips and extended his time with a three-week sailing holiday on his yacht in Queensland, Australia, returning on the 27th of July.

It was during this period – which was the long summer school holidays for the children in Ireland – that I had Melody home from school. She was, in a sense, an only child, so I'd invite her school friends to come and play with her. Guests also came at this time and needed feeding and catering for. The village was full of bored teenagers who would be moved on from anywhere that they gathered in the village because of their noisy, destructive, and disruptive ways.

A small group of them asked me if they could play tennis on our court. I permitted that and told them they were to stay only in the court area and not invade the rest of the garden. They agreed. But before a week was up the numbers had increased and they were paying no attention to the boundaries that had been set for them. I was deeply concerned, while at the same time feeling sorry for them. But they really overstepped the mark one day when I saw them pulling the unripe fruit off the orchard trees and throwing them at each other. They had also begun to carve their names in the grand old oak trees that studded the gardens.

I gathered the youngsters and told them to leave and not to return. But then I said, 'If anyone would like to come back and do a course with me called Christianity Explained, meet me at the tennis-court hut at 2.00 pm tomorrow.' This caused quite considerable laughter and jesting among the youngsters. I saw and heard one of them nudge his friend and say, 'Why not? Just for the craic.'

Armed with about fifteen Bibles and all the handouts for session number one, I bravely went to the venue the next day. It was impossible. I took down their names first, and this in itself caused great laughter. Two lads, with Bible in hand, climbed onto the roof of the hut. They used pages torn out of the Bible to make paper aeroplanes to glide in at me. Somehow, I persevered and got through the session because I noticed that there was a small group who were actually listening.

That evening I phoned my friend, Nancy. She was a local Christian lady who attended our Bible study evenings and had grown up in the village and knew all the children and their parents. She agreed to come and assist me. Session number two was considerably easier with her there. To start with she told me their proper names, and a bit about their family. They had all given me made-up names. Hence, the hilarity when I was dutifully writing down their names the afternoon before. But there were still a bunch of them who were extremely disruptive.

The next day I had had enough. My anger arose to boiling point. Nancy watched in utter amazement (she had never seen this side of me before) as I ordered everyone who had no interest in having a personal relationship with Jesus to get off the property! About half of them left but we ended up with six very interested teenagers. At the last session they responded to the invitation to repent and do things Jesus' way and were all told they could keep the Bibles. They met with me for quite some time afterwards and we would talk about a wide range of topics, always relating to morality and how to continue living as a Christian among their peers and families. I knew it wasn't going to be easy for them.

One evening at about 11:00 pm, when the summer light was just fading, the doorbell rang. There at the door was a group of these children with tools, cushions, and other articles that they had stolen from the property. They apologised and said they had come to return them. Thieving was a popular high-risk sport for many Irish teenagers. They didn't want the goods they had stolen, just the thrill of looting.

On another occasion Nancy came to visit me with one of their mothers. She had asked Nancy if she could meet the lady who had caused such a change in her son. My heart was bursting with joy as she thanked me for the transformation in her child. It didn't take much persuasion to get her to agree to joining my next group doing the Christianity Explained course – Nan was her name. She was the lady who played the piano at the local pub, The Lord Bagenal Inn. She was a jovial lady and was well-liked in the village. After she herself had completed the course, whenever she saw me in the village, she would always race over to me and loudly introduce me to her friends saying, 'Come and meet the lady that led me out of bondage.' When Doug returned after six weeks away in LA, and his three-week holiday on his yacht, he had no idea of the time I had had with those rowdy teenagers without his help.

A year or so later I met one of those teenage boys in the village. He had grown into quite a handsome young lad. I asked him if he ever thought of the things he had learnt from me in the tennis-court hut. He looked at me intently and said very slowly and precisely, 'Mrs Gresham, I will never forget the things you taught me in that tennis-court hut.' It's moments like that that make life worth living.

The local Catholic priest came to see me. He questioned me as to what I was teaching his parishioners. Many of the people whom I had invited to join a group of the Christianity Explained course had said, 'I'll ask Father if it's okay for me to attend your class.' I suggested that he should see for himself and evaluate the teaching. I asked him to do the course and he agreed. I took him through the contents of Christianity Explained one session at a time. After

I had completed the six lessons, I asked him what he thought of it. In an almost insulting tone he scoffed and said, 'It's an excellent course to make born-again Christians.' That was all I needed to convince the Irish Catholics to do the course with me. I would tell them that I had taken their priest through it, and he had said it was an excellent course.

....

Bridget, known by all as Birdie, was eighty-five years old, the granny of Melody's best school friend, Aisling. I had heard about her daily attendance at the Catholic Mass, and her devotion to Mary, saying the Rosary every day. I met her one day on the fourteenth-century Leighlinbridge bridge, the town's namesake. We stopped for a while chatting as we watched the Barrow River waters' never-ending journey under the bridge, and the ducks holidaying on the banks, basking in the warm midday sun.

'Birdie,' I said, 'You have such a love for God and spiritual things, I'm sure you would love to hear about Jesus in the Christianity Explained course I do. Would you like to join my new class on Wednesday morning?' She was delighted and agreed.

After completing the course and accepting all its Biblical truths, she came to me and said, 'Mrs Gresham, you have pulled out from under me everything I have ever stood firm on. Now I have nothing to stand on but Jesus.'

Birdie became a regular attendee of our Thursday night Bible study evenings. She loved the Bible and was filled with wonder at each new revelation in it. It was a joy for me to watch, for it reminded me of the time I first discovered these wonderful truths.

We only knew Birdie for a short season of about twelve months. She died sitting in her favourite armchair, with a grandchild on her lap, while reading a story to her. 'Mummy, Granny has gone to sleep and won't wake up,' the child told her mother.

It was an Irish custom to lay the deceased in their own bedroom, which was decorated for the occasion by displaying all the condolence cards. Anyone who wished could come and pay their last respects to Birdie.

Nancy fetched me and took me in to see her. About eight other people were sitting quietly in chairs placed around the walls. All other furnishings had been removed from the room. Birdie looked so peaceful, even younger. In front of everyone Nancy carefully pulled open Birdie's cold stiff fingers and removed the Rosary beads that had been twined around them, replacing them with the Bible I had given her. She announced for all to hear, 'Birdie would far prefer this in her hands.' No one said a word.

Later, the hearse carrying her coffin was parked in the car park of The Lord Bagenal Inn prior to the burial. Inside the pub, invited guests were seated at a banquet table drinking wines and beer and seemed to be rejoicing about the life of Birdie rather than grieving. This was an Irish Wake. I had been invited and arrived a little late, after everyone else was seated. I think it was Birdie's brother who greeted me at the door and took my arm leading me to a place of honour at the table where he bid me sit. I was surprised, even a little taken aback. *Why me at the head of the table,* I wondered. The man introduced me to Birdie's family members as the lady who had made Birdie so happy in the last year of her life. Sometimes love and service comes with a very unexpected reward, even here on planet Earth.

1994 and 1995 were intensely busy years for us at Rathvinden. Reading through those two years in my diaries, I was amazed at how full our lives were. I was gifted, or should I say burdened, with an unstoppable urge to save the lost.

Doug and I had recognition and status; the C.S. Lewis heritage attracted many people to our place. Doug's email correspondence was also growing. He was asked to do a lot of public speaking in Ireland and all over the world.

As well as that, Rathvinden had become known as not only a place to unburden but to get a new start in life, and we were seldom without guests. There were seldom empty seats at our big Tasmanian Blackwood dining-room table that seats twenty people. That table was made by a very clever young lad in Launceston, Tasmania, from the Blackwood trees that grew on our farm. Doug felled the trees and had the timber sawn into planks and kiln dried. The stack of wood stood for many years in one of the farm sheds. When we were to move to Ireland, we had the timber made into furniture for Rathvinden, all of which now graces our house here in Malta.

We must have been given incredible strength and endurance by God to have done all that my day-by-day five-year diaries have recorded. The Lord had also given me the gift of healing. This too was adding to our workload as the word got around.

However, the enemy of our souls, the devil, was also busy. He was very concerned that I was snatching people from his hands. One day the pastor of the big Presbyterian church in Kilkenny, who was our friend, came to see me – he was concerned for my wellbeing. He said, 'You are bringing so many people each week into a relationship with Christ and salvation, the devil will attack you. You have your neck stuck out for Jesus. You need prayer coverage.'

His remarks put fear into my heart. I phoned up everyone I could think of and asked them to pray for our safety. John even told me of the possibility of having petrol bombs thrown through our windows! I knew I had angered a lot of people who had had family members or relatives who had chosen to leave the Catholic Church because of my Bible teachings.

Dr Philip Ney was to come in three weeks' time for his second seminar to train another group how to perform his Hope Alive treatment program. He phoned from his home in Canada and said, 'Sorry, but I can't come. You will have to handle the seminar without me.'

'Why?' I asked. He said he was in great pain due to a slipped disk in his neck. The only way he could get relief from the pain was to stretch his neck from a door frame. I confidently and arrogantly said, 'Philip, that will be no problem, I will pray over the phone for your healing, and you will be healed.' This I did. I covered all the bases and took him through repentance of his nation's sins, repentance of the sins of his ancestors, repentance for the sins of his wife, (the two become one), and repentance for his own sins. When healing a Christian person, it's always the blood before the oil, the forgiveness before the spirit's healing. After that, I simply called upon the power of Jesus and commanded any spirit of infirmity to leave him. Then, I commanded his spine to be healed in the name of Jesus. Philip was healed, and was able to come to the seminar as our instructor and mentor on the 22nd of May 1994.

But before that date arrived, I developed a strange numbness in my left thumb. I thought an insect or spider must have bitten it when I was gardening, so I thought little of it. However, the numbness spread to my arm, accompanied by pain. A lot of pain. I had to carry on, for Daddles was on his yacht in Queensland with Bubble and wasn't due back for another week. Within days, it felt like a horse was standing on my arm. No amount of painkillers would subdue the pain. But even through it, as my diaries record, I continued my classes of Christianity Explained. During the teaching the pain would mysteriously stop.

Three days after Daddles got home he found me one night lying on the lawn in the frost in my night dress. I had drunk half a bottle of his special Glenlivet whisky to numb the pain. I wanted the frosty lawn to be like a counter irritant. The pain didn't go, even though I was numb all over – even my nose was numb.

Over the next few days, he took me to a series of doctors. One even sent me to a person who did acupuncture. The last doctor we saw sent me with a letter to see a neurosurgeon in the Mater Dei Hospital in Dublin. I didn't get back home that day but was admitted for pain relief, an MRI scan, and tests which confirmed that I had a slipped disk in my upper vertebrae. I was given some injections of omnopon-scopolamine, a powerful opiate drug, for five days, while they assessed the possibility of surgery to remove the disk. They were also concerned because I had a chest infection. Five days of ampicillin got rid of that.

Poor Daddles was beside himself with worry. Crying a lot, he asked Jesus to help. Melody and Bubble were also very frightened and worried. The day was scheduled for the operation. Daddles had asked the surgeon what the prognosis was. All he could say was that it was a 50/50 chance. I would either be healed or a quadriplegic for the remainder of my life. Daddles had emailed the people around the world and asked for urgent prayer. He told me thousands of people were praying for me.

We had a small flip calendar on the breakfast bar in the kitchen. Each day would come up with a Bible quote. On the day of the operation Daddles was getting ready to leave for the ninety-minute drive to Dublin, so as to be there when I came out of theatre. He flipped the calendar page over and read the verse for that date: 'The Lord giveth, and the Lord taketh away, blessed be the name of the Lord,' (Job 1:21). That threw Daddles into emotional turmoil. He drove to Dublin with those words going round and round in his head. He had never prayed so hard before, tears of fear and hope blurring his vision as he drove.

He arrived at the hospital just as the neurosurgeon was coming out of the theatre. He hardly dared to ask how the operation went. The surgeon told him it was a textbook procedure, and I would be completely healed. This time he prayed prayers of grateful thanksgiving. A week later, I was back at Rathvinden just in time to greet Dr Philip Ney and the new group of guests who came from all over the world for his training seminar.

I was still recovering from a major surgery but fortunately many people turned up daily to help with the things that I usually took care of. Even Bubble helped in the kitchen and with the guests, something she wouldn't usually do. Melody waited at table with one of her school friends. Anne Kelly took care of the cooking with the help of another woman from the village. I found it all too overwhelming and often had to leave the room and go upstairs to the quiet of our bedroom.

On reflection and hindsight, I summed up the reason for this episode. First of all, that phone call from Philip, I had said, somewhat arrogantly and with *self*-confidence, 'Don't worry Philip, I'll pray for you, and you will be healed.' The devil immediately saw a chink in my armour. I should have said, 'I'll pray, and *Jesus* will heal you.' I took the glory and never credited Jesus with the healing power.

Secondly, I had lost my confidence in God's protection and had taken on board the spirit of fear. Our pastor friend had said to me that I had my neck stuck out for Jesus, and we were in danger of retaliation from the Irish public, and from Satanic attack. He was right and Satan got me 'in the neck'. I found out later that the disk that slipped in my neck was the exact number disk that had slipped in Philip's neck. You can call it coincidence, but I know that '... our struggle is against the powers of this dark world and against the spiritual forces of evil in the heavenly realms,' (Ephesians 6:12).

God rescued me once again and enabled me to stay and work for Him for another season. I was forgiven and given the gift of health and life once again. One day I'll know if my spiritual assessment of the situation was correct. The Bible states that after death '...we will know all things as we ourselves are fully known,' (1 Corinthians 13:12).

....

Although our lives were very busy and demanding, the Lord occasionally gave us a break when we found we had no guests or obligations to fulfil. When that happened Doug and I were quick to seize the opportunity and escape to our lovely little motor-cruiser boat, Corikin which we kept moored in Lough Derg in County Tipperary. Of course, we also needed a reliable person to hold the fort for us, to look after the hens and two dogs and keep the place safe. Alina or a reliable long-term guest often did this for us.

On the first day we would put food rations and bare essentials in the VW Passat station wagon and head off about 11.00 am and arrive about 1.00 pm. We would then board our old but well-restored and cared for twin-engine powerboat Corikin and head off from Lough Derg and tie up at an isolated mooring or jetty.

After a bite of lunch, we would lie down for an afternoon rest. It wasn't unusual for us not to wake up till the next day. I don't think we ever realised how tired we were. I enjoyed the slow pace on that little boat. We would choose a quiet inlet to anchor and relax. Dromaan Harbour was a favourite place where we could tie up to a small jetty and go for walks. It was unpopulated and enabled us to also have the solitude we both desperately needed.

I'd take with me my calligraphy set and all my art supplies to elaborately decorate the visitors' book that I kept while we were at Rathvinden. This is something I still do for our guests in Malta. Each guest would have a double foolscap size page for their visitors' book entry. One page was to write on, and the opposite page would have their photo that I had taken with their address on it. The book was handed to each guest with their page ruled up and their name pencilled in. Anna O'Rourke would develop the photos for me in her photography shop in Carlow. The book would come with me to the boat where I could use my artistic skills to decorate it and calligraphy in their names. I would really have fun with their photo page, and I enjoyed depicting things about their stay or their life.

In the thirteen years we were at Rathvinden I filled twenty-three books. They have become a wonderful way for us to remember our guests. Each guest would be given strict instructions that this was not a 'thank you very much' book, but instead I wanted them to write about themselves and their lives. Memories fade. When someone we had hosted contacts us now, we often find their page and give our memories a good jog.

The original yacht, Merriemaid, that I spoke of often in previous chapters, eventually found its way to the Mediterranean. John Sanders, the man who has done numerous solo circumnavigations around the world, was given the job of sailing it from Australia to a safe, reliable marina in Malta. Our intention was to use it for a holiday break, and cruise the warm Mediterranean Sea. The cruising we never did. Somehow, we would get so interested in Malta that we never wanted to go anywhere else. When we had time, Malta became our holiday destination.

Eventually, Merriemaid was sold, and Doug bought a lemon of a boat. A huge and fancy twin-jet powered ocean cruiser that he called Lady Meredith. Unfortunately, it was not well built and had endless mechanical issues. She was also way too big for us to handle by ourselves, so she was only ever used as a very comfortable apartment during our periodic holidays in Malta.

Christmas time at Rathvinden became a nightmare for me. So many people who were at a loose end would descend on us for their Christmas cheer. It became a time I dreaded. Most of the cooking, making sure a present was under the tree for each person, and decorating was left for me to do. In a flash of brilliance Doug decided that we would spend all the next Christmases on the boat in Malta and leave the guests to make their own Christmas cheer.

My first Christmas in Malta on that yacht I remember as magical. Malta is densely populated and can be very busy. But as

Christmas approached, the usual hustle and bustle vanished. On Christmas day, the water was very still. Not a car or person could be seen around the usually very busy marina. The world seemed to have stopped still. As Christmas morning broke, hundreds of church bells rang out, near and far all day long, all playing their distinctive chimes. The Maltese take Christmas very seriously.

The weather in Malta was considerably warmer than Ireland. The sun shone and the sky and sea were blue. It was so refreshing after the cold and misty days at home in Ireland. Our times spent on the boat in Malta influenced our decision to move here years later.

During our time at Rathvinden, Dig and his wife, Cath, with their toddler son, Jack, were with us for a season. They took up residence in the Narnia Cottage. Dig was studying for his MBA at Trinity College, Dublin, from 2000 to 2001. He would catch the train from Bagenalstown to Dublin every day and return each night. Their second child, Georgie, was born in Dublin. I bought a pink flowering cherry tree and planted it in the garden of the Narnia Cottage to commemorate her birth. That tree was so little when I planted it. I saw it again just a few years ago. It had grown to be a strong beautiful tree delighting everyone with its beauty. And I can say the same thing about Georgie. She is now twenty years old and also delights everyone with her beauty and grace. Another baby boy, Ashton, was born to them while Dig was working in Chichester, England. They all now live in New South Wales, Australia.

Dominick with his wife, Wendy, and their first child, Rebekah, also moved to Ireland for a time, and were able to use the Narnia Cottage as a second home. They had rented a flat in Dublin where Dominick was working as an architect. It was a happy time because Wendy's sister, Alina, was also with us and was able to baby sit Rebekah while Wendy gave birth to their second baby girl, to whom they proudly gave the Irish name, Sinéad. We were sad to see them leave when they decided to return to Australia. They settled in Brisbane and made their home there. Every two years

Wendy would give us another grandchild. Two more beautiful little girls, Sionnan, born in the year 2002, and Xanthe in 2005. In 2008 they had a fifth baby, this time a boy, and they named him Caspian.

Chapter 30

Stage, TV and film

Narnia was planted in Douglas' life as a small child. Although he grew up with the author of those books, the seed remained dormant for many years, but it started to grow when he was forty-two years old and married with four children of his own. His first trip to Wheaton College in the USA awakened his God-given responsibility to safeguard the Christian message in C.S. Lewis' children's stories which were now under review to become full-length motion pictures.

As I have mentioned, first came Doug's book *Lenten Lands My Childhood with Joy Davidman and C.S. Lewis*, published in 1988 by Macmillan Publishers, New York, then a year later in Great Britain by HarperCollins.

As I have briefly mentioned in an earlier chapter, unbeknown to Doug, two British playwrights living in Chichester, England, Brian Sibley and Norman Stone, had decided to write a screenplay about the love story between Joy Davidman and Jack Lewis, covering Joy's untimely death. It wasn't till they finished writing it that they came across Doug's book *Lenten Lands* and were amazed at how accurate they had got the wording and emotional impact. The made-for-television film was produced for the BBC starring Joss Ackland as Jack, and Claire Bloom as Joy, released in 1985. It was critically acclaimed and won several BAFTA awards. Later, William (Bill) Nicholson, who had been involved with the original BBC version, re-wrote the script as a stage play which premiered in 1989 in London with Nigel Hawthorne and Jane Lapotaire as Jack and Joy.

However, Doug's book *Lenten Lands* takes the story further on than did *Shadowlands*, to the death of C.S. Lewis, through Doug's years of loneliness and on to meeting and marrying me. He even introduces our four (we hadn't adopted Melody at the time) children in his book. The title, *Lenten Lands*, comes from the epitaph on his mother's grave written by her beloved Jack Lewis. It reads:

Here the whole world (stars, water, air,

And field, and forest, as they were

Reflected in a single mind)

Like cast off clothes were left behind

In ashes, yet with hopes that she,

Reborn from holy poverty,

In lenten lands, hereafter may

Resume them on her Easter Day.

Eight years later, in 1993, Lord Richard Attenborough made *Shadowlands* into a full-length film in which Anthony Hopkins played Jack, Debra Winger played Joy, and child actor Joseph Mazzello played Douglas. The screenplay was again written by Bill Nicholson. Doug was also a part-time advisor to it after having sent his book *Lenten Lands* to him.

Lord Attenborough invited Doug and myself to attend a showing of his new film *Shadowlands* in London at the Odeon theatre, on the 12th of December 1993. It was a special showing for only the cast and crew.

On the day of the film screening, I met Lord Richard Attenborough and shared an umbrella with his wife as we walked in the rain to the restaurant where I also met Bill Nicholson and Brian Eastman, the screenplay writers. After the showing of the film, which was heartrendingly beautiful, we were unable to stay and join the crew and cast for the reception as we had to meet Daniel Batts. He was the editor of the Australian Christian magazine *On Being* and we were meeting him at the airport in Dublin, to take him with us back to Rathvinden where he was to spend two weeks with us over Christmas.

The film wasn't released to the public till the 3rd of March at which time we were again invited to come to what was a Royal Gala showing in the Odeon Theatre, London. Prince Charles, the Prince of Wales, and Camilla, the Duchess of Cornwall, would be there. The dress code was to be formal attire – Daddles in a tuxedo and a ball dress for me. Bubble would also accompany us.

I was in a panic because none of my evening dresses fitted me anymore because I'd been enjoying eating well with our many guests. As a result, I'd put on a lot of weight. My once fabulous figure was, shall we say ... not so fabulous anymore. Bubble dragged me into Kilkenny where we tried on dresses in about twelve different shops. I hated them all. But the fact was it was not the dresses I was hating, but the shape inside them. I eventually chose one. It was full-length, pale purple with a black lace-like loose fitting garment that went over the lot. When I showed Daddles he told me I looked like an old lady. I was fed up, but it would have to do. I wasn't repeating the previous day for anyone. Bubble, however, looked stunning in her dress, aged twenty with the same figure I had at her age.

For years Daddles had been trying to tell me to lose weight. He eventually gave up because it always made me angry. I had tried dieting but always overdid it for two weeks, eating practically nothing and of course losing weight rapidly only to put it back on again equally rapidly. I felt defeated.

In my daily prayer letter to Jesus one morning, I tacked onto the end of it, 'Lord, I'm so sick of trying to lose weight. If You want me to lose weight, then You do it for me.' I thought no more of it. But two days later the phone rang. It was an annoying salesman asking me if I would answer a few questions for him. I immediately replied in a way I always did with such phone callers: 'Only if you will answer a question for me.' He agreed and asked me what I wanted to know.

I said, 'You ask your question first.'

To my surprise he said, 'Are you satisfied with your weight?'

'No,' I answered truthfully.

Then he asked me how much I weighed. Well, this was a strange opening to a conversation. I don't even know this man and he didn't know me. Again, I answered truthfully and told him I was 11 stone or 70 kilograms. Then he asked me what weight I would like to be. I knew that too. '58 kilograms,' I said. 'Because that was the weight I was in my twenties.' He told me that in three months he could get me to my desired weight, money back guarantee, if I did as I was told and kept to his program. He would join me as my personal trainer.

It sounded too good to be true. Wonderful, I wouldn't have to go to Weight Watchers; he would come here and show me how to do what I had been defeated trying to do myself. I balked when he asked me what questions I would like to ask him. *Oh no*, I thought. *He is going to write me off as a nutcase and not be prepared to help me.* But he asked again. So, I asked my standard question.

'If you died tonight and God said to you, "Why should I let you into My Heaven, what would you say?"'

He said, 'I don't know. Do you know what I should say?'

'Yes, I do know.'

'Then will you tell me?'

'No,' I said. 'But I will do your program if you will do mine.'

He asked me what my program was.

'It's called Christianity Explained,' I said. He was silent for a while and told me he would have to think about it and hung up the phone.

I was angry with myself all the next day. I didn't know his telephone number or even his name. I had just ruined a great opportunity. But he phoned back that week and agreed to my proposition. The outcome of that strange phone conversation, and my prayer letter request was that, following his weight-loss program, I lost all my unwanted fat and got my twenty-year-old figure back in under three months. But sadly, I was not able to lose it in time for the premiere of *Shadowlands*. But I still use those dietary principles. Today at the age of seventy-eight I can still get into the dresses I used to wear in my twenties. Michael was his name, but I called him my Slimming Angel. He and his wife, Kate, did Christianity Explained with me and now he knows the answer to my question, and I often hope he asks the same question of others.

On the 3rd of March 1994 we left Melody with the in-house guests. Daddles and I left for Dublin Airport taking Bubble with us. We caught a Virgin Atlantic plane to London City Airport and a cab to the Stratford Hotel, where we dressed up in our finery. A chauffeur-driven car took us to the Odeon Theatre as guests of honour for the showing of the gala performance of *Shadowlands*. I tried hard to ignore the fact that I was not happy with my appearance and put on a happy social face.

We were ushered into a line-up of cast and crew, and other people involved in the film, to be introduced to Prince Charles and Lady Camilla. Lord Attenborough himself did the introductions. When he came to Doug, who was standing next to Joseph (Joey) Mazzello, Lord Attenborough mischievously said, 'I hope you realise, sir, that this little chap,' he pointed to Joey, 'is in fact him,' and pointed at Doug. Prince Charles' face went blank as he looked mystified from Doug to Joey and back again. Doug thought he better explain things and looking down kindly at Joey said, 'I think you played the role brilliantly, Joey, but of course for you it was easy.'

Joey immediately bridled, as Doug had intended and said, 'What do you mean, *easy*?'

Doug replied, 'Well, you had a script to follow, whereas I had to ad-lib the whole thing.' At which point Prince Charles, Camilla, Richard, Joey, and myself all laughed out loud.

At Charles' invitation, we were seated in the same row with him and Camilla. During the showing I noticed that both Charles and Camilla were deeply touched, with Prince Charles mopping the tears from his eyes at particularly sad and emotional parts.

After the film was over, we were chauffeured to the Hotel Café Royal for the reception dinner. We chatted with Debra Winger, Anthony Hopkins and Joey. Melvin Adams and his wife, Jenny, and Bubble were placed with us at our table along with Nigel Goodwin, the larger-than-life actor, and Elizabeth Stevens, Doug's literary agent. The conversation was joyful and entertaining. Nigel was such a good entertainer. Unfortunately, I missed much of it, as Bubble was quite overwhelmed, and was hiding in the ladies' toilet clinging to me. Daddles gave her one of his Librium pills which helped.

The next morning, we caught an early plane back to Dublin as we were to meet Dr Philip Ney at the airport and take him home with us. Apparently, there had been a complaint about me in the village. Some people were refusing to come to Philip's training seminar because the word had gotten around that I was proselytising. But their real issue was that I was persuading people to leave the Catholic Church. That was easily rectified. I decided I would let myself be seen at the Catholic Mass on Sundays.

This I did and it was an eye-opener for me. It was cold and dead. Even after Mass the people hurried home without stopping to chat with anyone. There was no demonstration of love for one another. But it worked. I had been seen, so they no longer looked at me as an anti-Catholic. I love Catholics in the same way as I love any other human. I knew what it was like to live in fear of dying with a mortal sin in your life because you have missed going to Mass on Sunday, or to then be sent to hell because you hadn't confessed your sin to a priest.

Chapter 31

Narnia in film

When Doug was approached for permission to make the Narnia stories into full-length feature films, he purposely made it his business to get involved in the process as a quality control consultant. The audition filming of the cast came across his desk for his comments or suggestions, as well as the scripts and filming locations.

Daddles was named co-producer for *The Lion, the Witch and the Wardrobe* and made many trips to LA and New York from Rathvinden, and spent many an hour on his computer negotiating film scripts or locations for filming. There was a lot of legal stuff to get right as well. Eventually, towards the last few years at Rathvinden, we could no longer host Philip Ney's training seminars.

We both went to New Zealand to oversee the making of *The Lion, the Witch and the Wardrobe*. Doug won the heart of all the child actors. Lucy was played by Georgie Henley and Susan by Anna Popplewell. Skandar Keynes played Edmund and William Moseley played Peter. I loved being there and started to realise the incredible amount of work that went into setting up the scenes. The attention to detail was amazing. I really felt as though I was in Narnia. People were walking around in full costume waiting for their turn to be involved in some sequence or other.

But the repetition of 'takes' could get a bit boring. The take was repeated till the director was satisfied. I understood what it meant to be an actor when I saw the children were acting scenes with a ball on a long stick. The ball was representing the position of Aslan, who would be digitally added in later, so they had to make convincing eye contact with a tennis ball.

While we were on set, Dig visited us with his four-year-old son, Jack. Jack was completely taken in by the whole environment. He didn't even see it as a film making set, but as real. At one time he walked through a scene setting of the White Witch's castle, and looked up at his dad and said, 'Daddy, this place is really evil.'

Bubble also visited the set and stayed for a week. She was living in Devonport, Tasmania, at the time. It was lovely to see her again. I wanted to have her impressions of that experience from her point of view so yesterday I asked her for them. She sent me an email answer which I'll now include:

My impressions of The Lion, the Witch and the Wardrobe, set in New Zealand, was a place of magic and wonder, not just for the elaborate sets or incredible diversity of human life, but from the smallest to the tallest and every shape in between. I remember being shocked by just how small a human being could be, then turning around being nose to navel with a woman who was playing a centaur.

Then there was the technology, which was mind boggling to me, although I would understand it better now. The incredible landscape, and such well-spoken sweet English children. Aside from the helicopter trips and the small plane rides with one extremely nervous man – that surprised me as his job would have called for him to fly a lot – there was so much more I wanted to see, things that interested me alone but due to my restraints, having to stick to my parents, I was unable to. I wish now I had pushed harder as opportunities like that will never come again in my lifetime.

Signed,
Bubble.

The year leading up to the release of the first Narnia film (December 2005) was a year packed full of excitement. It was one of our busiest years at Rathvinden too. There was never a day that we were free of guests of one sort or other. Some just came for a well-deserved break from their own busy ministry lives and others who desperately needed help. I used any free time I had to keep the garden groomed and productive. Melody was now living in a rented apartment in Dublin where she was studying French and Italian at the University College Dublin. She would come home often whenever she needed her mother's love and support. I'm afraid I sometimes failed with this duty. All this and more had to also be fitted into our commitments to the making of the film and the running of Rathvinden.

Doug was in constant demand to promote the new film and to talk about himself and his stepfather on TV and radio. He made many public appearances. He not only was the genuine article, the stepson of the author of the Narnia stories, but he had a lot of charisma and experience in entertaining and charming an audience. He had a magnificent voice and had answers to many peoples' questions about C.S. Lewis.

I had decided the year before that I could manage Rathvinden without the help of four ministry volunteer girls, who in themselves could actually add to the workload. If I needed help, I could always rely on Anne Kelly from the village who would recruit her own helpers to help her with large groups that came. I continued to do the Christianity Explained course with groups of people and was still sticking rigidly to my newly taught way of controlling my weight. By my birthday in October, I could fit back into my silk dresses that Doug had tailor-made for me in Hong Kong the year we collected Melody from Korea. The weight loss and exercise routine had made a big difference to my feeling of fitness, wellbeing, and self-confidence.

As the date of the film release got closer, the family began to arrive to join us in London for the Royal Gala premiere showing of the film.

On 3rd of November 2005, James' wife, Lara, and our grandchildren, Michael and Lindsay, then eight and six, arrived from North Carolina where they had just sold their house. James and his family had always been regular visitors during our time at Rathvinden as they all had travel privileges on the airline James worked for. But James wanted his two sons to grow up, like he had done, on a farm in Australia. So, James resigned from the airline business, sold his house in North Carolina, and made plans to visit us in Ireland before eventually returning to Australia to find a farm.

Apparently, when he thought the time was right, he had walked to the roadside and hammered a 'For Sale by Owner' sign into his lawn. By the time he had walked back to the house, Lara already had someone on the phone enquiring! Over the next few days, three more buyers were interested and were trying to outbid each other. The house was sold much faster than they anticipated, which meant they were free to come to Ireland and attend the premiere of the film Doug had worked so hard on.

Lara and the two boys were the first to arrive. James had stayed behind to pack his household belongings and have them stored till such time he needed them for his eventual new home in Australia. It wasn't until the following month that James finally completed his tasks and fulfilled his obligations with the airline he flew for. He arrived at Rathvinden on the 17th of November for an extended stay.

I remember one of the first jobs James did was to comb out the matted dreadlocks that Melody had cultivated in her hair. I had attempted to do it many times. It looked and smelt disgusting, but whenever I approached the subject Melody would be defensive and abusive towards me. I looked on silently and never said a word. I was so delighted to see that hairdo gone.

I think I must have thrown Lara in the deep end for, two days after she arrived, she was asked to look after the house for a week while I went to a Hope Alive conference at Windmill Farm outside Oxford. Daddles was in LA. It was great seeing a lot of my old acquaintances there, especially Wendy and Ray Watson.

Daddles' had his 60th birthday while he was in LA. Someone must have spread the word around, for he hates people making a fuss over him on his birthday. Disney put on a big party for him in the dining hall of the Four Seasons Hotel. On a large screen, President George Bush appeared wishing Douglas Gresham a very happy 60th birthday and singing his praises. But it was actually comedian Steve Bridges who was known for his amazing presidential impersonations. Doug was given that recording so I actually got to watch it – it was hilarious. Doug was also given so many gifts he had to buy another suitcase to get them home.

All my children and their families would soon be with us at Rathvinden. A rare occurrence. They were gradually arriving from Australia and America to be with us for the opening night, the Royal Gala showing of *The Lion, the Witch and the Wardrobe* to be held in Royal Albert Hall in London on the 7th of December.

On November 19th, James was able to drive into Dublin to bring his father back after being away from home for six long weeks. But Doug wasn't home long before he was being called away again. This time by a chauffeur-driven car that took him to the airport to go to London to be interviewed on TV and by the press. Fortunately, he was only away for two nights. In that time, he did eighteen different radio and TV appearances. No wonder he was constantly exhausted.

Dig had arrived the day before and was able to drive into Dublin on the 28th of November to collect his wife, Cath, and his three children, Jack, aged seven, Georgie, five, and Ashton, only four. Only Dominick and his family, Lucinda and Melody were missing.

Dominick and Wendy, with their four little girls, had decided to meet up with us in London the day before the premiere. Wendy had an aunt who lived in Woking, not far out of London. The family would stay two days with them so as to avoid unnecessary time in airports.

Bubble was living in Florence studying jewellery manufacture and design and would meet us in London with her husband and return to Rathvinden afterwards. And, as I mentioned earlier, Melody was living in a rented flat in Dublin studying French and Italian at the university there.

Daddles was called back to America on the 30th for yet more interviews and press conferences. I wouldn't see him again until we met in London the day before the premiere. He spoke at the Crystal Palace Cathedral, which is now known as Christ Cathedral. The speech was broadcast widely all over America.

For us at home the rush was on to get everyone suitably clad for the big occasion. The boys were fitted with rented tuxedos, and evening dresses for Melody, Lara and Cath – I had already purchased mine some time ago, but when it came to showing off our dresses to the men, I had lost even more weight and a quick job of taking it in was required on the sewing machine.

Dig and James also had hired tuxedos. The excitement was electric. Four-year-old Ashton joined in with the excitement without really realising what all the fuss was about. He thought it was all such fun.

December in England can be bitterly cold. The balance to look glamorous and yet stay warm was challenging. I purchased a big white artificial fur stole and long, white lined gloves to wear with my very summery looking evening dress. I was told we would be outside the theatre for some time before we actually went in where it would be warm.

On the day before the event, quite a procession of Greshams headed off to Dublin airport, driven by various volunteer drivers who would return home with the cars. Michael and Kate McQuillan, my Slimming Angel, had offered to housesit for us till we returned. Daddles was waiting for me at the Goring Hotel – he had flown in from LA the day before. Melody, Bubble and her husband and I settled into our rooms at the Goring. The Goring Hotel is often frequented by Her Majesty the Queen. It's a place where one feels like living in decadent Victorian times. It is very elegant, and the staff are all immaculately dressed with manners to match. All the others stayed at the Buckingham Palace Gate Apartments. Dominick joined them there. Their two youngest children, one still a babe in arms, were looked after by Wendy's cousin, Steven, on the big night.

Daddles and I spent the evening at a cocktail party for the cast and crew. I met up with lots of the people I had met while on set in New Zealand twelve months previously. Many of them were also staying at the Goring Hotel. It was like a big reunion.

The morning of the day of the premiere was spent at hairdressers for Melody, Bubble, and the other girls. I always stay clear of hairdressers. Every time I've been to one, I have never liked the end result, so I prefer to do my own. My hair is very difficult, being thick and blonde. Daddles would prefer for me to wear it loose. But, at the age of sixty-three, I felt that to be a bit too ungroomed. I curled the edges and wore it in a high bun surrounded by a matching scrunchie; that way I felt more comfortable.

A chauffeur-driven car collected Daddles and me and took us to Royal Albert Hall. We were introduced to our minder, named Dora, who led us through the crowds to walk the red-carpet gauntlet with other members of the production team, to be interviewed by about fifty press reporters, in front of a grandstand of onlookers. The flash from countless cameras illuminated the falling snow as we made the slow procession along the line. Our minder would stop by each reporter and introduce us to him or her. I would normally have frozen to death, but I didn't even notice the near freezing temperatures. The hype and excitement must have kept me warm.

We were then led up to the Royal anteroom where we were introduced to Prince Charles and Camilla, and other dignitaries. Without intention on our part, we found ourselves conversing with Prince Charles and Camilla the whole time, as we sipped champagne, and tried to avoid the various delicacies that were being offered to us. Then, to our surprise, we were invited to join the Royals in their private box to watch the very first showing of that amazing film. I loved every moment of it. It was fascinating to see all those many scene takes I had witnessed actually made into a seamless film.

I wasn't expecting the party extravaganza put on by Disney in a giant marquee after the showing. The whole marquee was decorated as a Narnia winter. The entrance was through lots and lots of fur coats which we had to push our way through into a snow-covered Narnia wonderland. The power malfunctioned as we were pushing our way through the coats. We thought it was all part of the experience, but it was a genuine power failure. Many people illuminated the way using their mobile phones.

Once inside, we met up with the rest of our family and the guests we had invited. Katherine Butler was there, chatting to James and Dig who had known her as a school child in Tasmania. She was now living in London and had her own hand clinic specialising in the repair of damaged hands, mostly musicians. It certainly was a magic evening. Even the younger children seemed to have energy to spare. I expected them to be exhausted, as it was way past their bedtime.

The next day, before we went home, Daddles and I were taken to the House of Lords, where Daddles held an address to invited guests. The others had already caught an earlier plane back to Ireland. We were met off the last plane into Dublin by Dominick who had already made two trips back and forth picking up other family members. Bubble had returned to Italy but would re-join us again later and spend Christmas with all of us. We were all elated and shattered. The whole thing had surpassed our wildest dreams – I'll never forget it. No one needed rocking to sleep that night.

But it was by no means the end for Daddles. He was still in demand, first from the Irish who wanted him to attend the showing of the film in Dublin. We took Michael and Kate with us on that occasion as a thank-you gesture for looking after Rathvinden for us while we were away.

On the 15th of December Doug flew once more to America, this time to Washington, D.C., where he had been invited to the White House to attend a private showing of *The Lion, the Witch and the Wardrobe* to President Bush and his wife with a gathering of children.

At Rathvinden I plunged once more into putting food on the table for my own hungry grandchildren and my sons and their wives. Household and garden chores resumed. James and Dominick cut back all the dead tomato plants from the heated greenhouse (designed by Dominick) that had served us very well through the years.

Dig, Cath, and their children had spent a few days with friends of theirs in Chichester, after the premiere. They returned to Rathvinden on the 12th.

Christmas day was joyous, hectic, and exhausting. All the children were under the age of seven; lots of presents, laughter, crying and fun for all. Bubble handed out the gifts from under the tree and I had had lots of help cooking a Christmas ham with all the trimmings. Every bedroom and every bed were occupied by a Gresham – eighteen in all. The big Tasmanian Blackwood dining-room table was full to capacity. Lots of photos were taken. We even hired a professional photographer to come from Kilkenny to take photos of our entire family. It was the first and the last time we have all been together and accommodated under one roof. It was such a joy and a blessing. I expect it was the happiest time that that ancient house had seen in many decades.

Dominick and Dig returned to Australia and their homes and jobs. Bubble and her husband returned to Italy on the 1st of January. Melody, who was at school in Dublin, came and went. Only James and Lara and their two boys remained.

We were beginning to feel that our work at Rathvinden was over, and the Lord was directing us in another direction. It was becoming obvious that Doug's work lay in safeguarding other Narnia films that were already being planned. It simply wasn't right to expect me to run Rathvinden ministries alone. Once again, Doug would need to spend many days and months working on set and supervising the making of the other Narnia films, always with an eye to safeguard the strong but subtle Christian message that Jack had cleverly woven into the stories.

'Sneaking past the watchful dragons,' Jack had called it.

We were beginning to think about selling up and moving – Malta was high on the list of options.

Chapter 32

Relocating – again

As early as June 2005, six months before the premiere of *The Lion, the Witch and the Wardrobe*, Daddles had been in contact with a Maltese real estate agent by the name of Michael Mifsud who ran the Elite Housing Agency. We agreed to come to Malta to look at some houses that he thought might interest us. Daddles arrived first. He had been in London for a meeting. Michael picked him up from Malta Airport and drove him to the Grand Harbour Marina where we had our boat Lady Meredith moored. I arrived the next day. Both Michael and Daddles were at the airport to meet me. The sky was blue, and the sun warmed my heart and body.

Overlooking the marina is the gigantic fortress of Fort St. Angelo, originally built in medieval times, and rebuilt in the mid-sixteenth century by Jean de la Valette of the Order of St John (the Knights of Malta). It was an active military garrison right up until 1979 and, although being badly damaged during World War Two, it has been largely restored. It towers over the harbour with an air of unconquerable superiority. It was a great place to get exercise and go exploring. I was still on my weight loss program, and exercise was an important part of it.

We sat on the deck of the boat in the warm evening temperature of 24 degrees, such a pleasure after the misty 13 degrees of the Irish early spring-time weather. I had my evening diet shake, and Daddles enjoyed a beer. Both of us wondered what God had in store for our next step on our pilgrim journey. Neither of us had definitely made up our minds that Malta was to be our next steppingstone. We had considered many other places in the world where we could live and still serve the Lord. The only criteria were that we needed to be in easy access to an international airport as Daddles would still be required to make many trips if he was going to supervise the making of all the *Chronicles of Narnia* films.

On previous visits to Malta, when we would come and take a break here from the heavy workload at Rathvinden, we had liked the place a lot. The Maltese people were extremely friendly and would go out of their way to help and befriend us. The warmer temperature was definitely a point to consider. As I have mentioned, I dislike the cold, and am prone to chest infections, and arthritis was becoming an issue for me. The whole place was fascinating and steeped in centuries of history.

I loved the Mediterranean architecture of the old buildings. Sadly, a lot were lost in the Second World War. Malta is recognised as the most-bombed place in Europe. Facing imminent defeat and starvation, the people held their ground and Malta was never taken, although it was an extremely sought-after strategic place in Germany's quest to conquer the world. At one stage, the entire island and people of Malta were collectively and uniquely awarded the George Cross 'for acts of the greatest heroism or for most conspicuous courage in circumstances of extreme danger.' The Maltese are still quietly proud of their award and even today, international mail should be addressed to 'Malta GC.' Today we have bookshelves full of books written about battles in, around, and over Malta. Daddles, who loves to read such books, is quite an expert on the subject. I love listening to his telling of how and why Malta was critical to winning the Second World War.

Once we had got groceries and settled in, Michael Mifsud collected us. The job of being driven around and viewing houses for sale began in earnest. We were taken to the crème de la crème of Maltese villas. They were grand, majestic, exotic, and affordable once we had sold 20 acres of house and grounds in Ireland. But it seemed we would have to be content with a grand house on very little land, if any. Michael was beginning to worry about me as I rejected villa after villa. I just couldn't be happy in a built-up area where a next-door neighbour could overlook your swimming pool, and where one had no garden or the possibility of growing vegetables or olive trees (we always dreamed of making our own olive oil). So, Michael re-directed our attention to farms and even an abandoned Carmelite monastery for sale on the island of Gozo. We still found a reason to reject them all. Evening came and Michael took us back to our accommodation on the boat. I dread to imagine what he was thinking of us.

We had one full day left. In the morning I poured my heart out to the Lord in my prayer letter saying, 'Lord, you know my heart, and promise to satisfy our hearts' desire if we love and obey you. If you really want us in Malta, then show me a house that we can both be comfortable in.' And I'm sure Daddles was doing the same. I like to spend some time every morning in prayer. I write my prayers down in a letter to God. I have books and books full of prayer letters. Now, they augment my diaries.

Our time in Malta was running out. We cleaned up the boat and did a few loads of laundry and packed our suitcases ready for an early morning trip to the airport the next day. At 4.00 pm the real estate agent phoned us and said a house in Żejtun had just then come on the market and asked if we would like to look at it.

Michael collected us half an hour later and took us to the place. He warned us that Żejtun wasn't a fashionable area and this property had a dairy farm and a pig farm quite nearby. The road approaching this place was very narrow – not enough room for two cars to pass. We stopped at a set of tall wrought iron automatic gates and Michael pressed the gate buzzer. A rush of excitement hit me. We hadn't even gone a few yards along the drive before I knew this was the place. It was set off the main road. Another smaller villa on the left was shielded from sight by a tall stone wall and trees. Otherwise, only fields surrounded the two-storey sandstone house.

The interior of the house had a dining/sitting room big enough for our big twenty-seater Tasmanian blackwood dining-room table. Marble floors throughout. A big office for Daddles with big arched windows overlooking a view of the garden and beyond to the fishing harbour of Marsaxlokk and the blue Mediterranean Sea. There was a big swimming pool with stone arches of bougainvillea flowers surrounding it. The garden had many features including a fountain surrounded by paving stones and seats. A little further along was another area closed off by an attractive wrought iron fence with a matching gate; it led into a secluded paved walled off area in which a statue of Mary was enshrined in a grotto.

Very pretty but nevertheless against God's second commandment*. I kept my mouth shut. It wasn't the time or place to preach. Especially in this fiercely proud Catholic country.

On the right, as you entered the property, was an arbour of large shady trees with a twisting path through them and a gazebo. The place was perfect. Even the occasional smell of cows and pigs seemed right.

Though it had land around it, that land had been rented out to a tenant farmer for his lifetime and for generations to come. It wasn't available. This caused Daddles to balk at a hasty decision to buy it.

There was a lot of talk and we felt as though if we hesitated too long, we would miss out on the sale because it was by far the best place we had seen even although it wasn't in a fashionable area, but this didn't worry us at all. In fact, it was a plus. Before we left, Daddles told the owner we would consider buying if he could persuade the tenant farmer to let us have the small strip of the land that he had leased. He actually did get the tenant to release some of the land although I believe it cost him a small fortune.

On the 22nd of July, Daddles once again went to Malta with his right-hand man and financial adviser, Melvin Adams, to look at the place. Melvin was in agreement with our choice of property. He loved it.

He made yet another visit, this time with James who had flown from North Carolina using his flying privilege as a pilot, on the 15th of August. James had just put his North Carolina house on the market as mentioned above and Lara actually sold the house while he was in Malta!

The real estate agent took them to see the Żejtun house which was called The Seagull in Maltese. We had already decided on a name for the house; we would call it Tai Harendrimar meaning the Hill of Life in a language called Old Solar that C.S. Lewis had invented in one of his science-fiction stories. The Hill of Life, to us, represented the swollen belly of a pregnant woman. A real hill of life. It was an appropriate name as Daddles had campaigned on

---

* - Exodus 20:4-5 'You shall not make for yourself an image in the form of anything in heaven above or on the earth beneath or in the waters below. You shall not bow down to them or worship them; for I, the Lord your God, am a jealous God...'

many occasions for the anti-abortion cause. During this visit he made a handshake deal to buy the house.

James and Daddles had a great time exploring Malta in a hire car before they parted company. Malta is a difficult place to get your bearings as the entire place is a maze of ancient streets. The villages, which looked more like towns to me, had grown to the point where they more or less merged, so it was hard to know where one ended and the next one started.

The countryside was a patchwork of small stone walled fields interlaced with tiny roads or footpaths, which were lined on both sides with more stone-walls. They tried to find the house by themselves but couldn't locate it until James climbed up onto a tall wall and spotted the house only a few hundred metres away.

James went back to the USA to finalise the sale of his own house, and Daddles returned to Rathvinden.

It wasn't till the following month, on the 5th, that Melvin and Daddles actually signed the sales documents for the purchase of Tai Harendrimar. There was an air of finality for us at Rathvinden, but we would have to be patient. We had to launch the film Doug had worked so hard to protect and perfect. There was also a lot of unfinished ministry work to do – conferences, weddings, and holiday stays that had been booked months previously. Not to mention Doug's frequent trips to the States on movie business and other speaking engagements, and of course the upcoming premiere that I wrote about in the previous chapter.

Skipping ahead again, it was another extremely busy year for us. Life had slowly returned to normal after the premiere. All the other Greshams returned to their homes, and my last ministry volunteer eventually left. It was Lara who helped me with the last of the guests, and with cooking and cleaning and harvesting, freezing, or bottling the orchard fruits. I intended to take a lot of it with us to Malta. Most of it could be sent over with our household goods, but some, like the contents of the freezers, we wanted to go by air. And therein lies an odd story, that I will slip in here.

I had packed all the harvested vegetables into a big suitcase and put the whole packed case in the freezer. A second case was packed full of venison that had been given to us by our friend who was a sharpshooter with the Irish Army. It was his job to cull the wild deer in the forest country. He would give the meat to us as a donation to our ministry. These cases of frozen foods were eventually air-freighted to us in Malta but when we went to pick them up from the airport, one case was missing. It had accidentally been sent to Moscow instead of Malta and would be retrieved and delivered to us when it arrived. Daddles and I were so worried that it may be the case full of meat which would defrost and drip blood. When we got back to our new house, we opened the one case that got to the correct destination and discovered to our relief that the meat had arrived safely and was all still well frozen.

At Rathvinden, James took on the unenviable task of contacting all the various later bookings and, with much apologising, cancelling them.

Life at Rathvinden began to slow down. It was time to relax, be a family and begin to slowly sort through the mountains of stuff that had accumulated as we prepared to move. But just as we were getting organised to move, we realised that Doug's aging guardian Jean Wakeman in Oxfordshire was getting very frail and needed full-time care in a nursing home. She was a responsibility that Doug had assumed long ago. He had looked after her every need – now it was urgent. We decided to take our campervan via the Dun Laoghaire to Holyhead ferry and drive from Holyhead through Wales and on to Jean's place in Horton-cum-Studley just outside Oxford. The roads were treacherous, covered with melted snow and ice. The drive took us 8 hours.

We found Jean in a bad way, hardly able to walk. With the help of an organisation called Finders Keepers we were able to locate and arrange accommodation for her in a nursing home. It was a blessing to be in our own campervan which we kept toasty warm with a blow heater and two doonas on our bed. We catered for ourselves so as not to stress Jean. Once we had got her into the nursing home, we once again braved that icy trip back to Holyhead and home again.

•••

One day, when Daddles was off on one of his business trips and I was sorting through my office, I came across some old home videos of our farming days in Ringarooma, Tasmania. One video, from the early eighties, shows my boys unloading hay off a trailer into what we called the Butt House – many years before, old Mrs Butt had lived there but now the house was derelict and was used to store hay. In the video, Bubble was prancing around on the half empty trailer in a blue and gold leotard with her long loose blonde hair caught by every passing breeze.

But those videos threw James into a dark place which he had tried for many years to escape from, as he saw and heard again the derogatory and abusive way his father spoke to him and treated him when he was a young adolescent. There was no demonstration of love or thanks for his help, only sharp critical words, voiced with no concern for the video camera that I was holding in my hands.

It took me several days to get James back from those memories as he relived his childhood under his father's disapproval. This was probably because he still seemed to be under Doug's scrutiny as he helped with all he could around Rathvinden; a place that Doug was very proprietary about, claiming it as 'his property' – even though, I believe I owned half of that property! 'With all my worldly wealth I endow,' were the words he spoke to me on our wedding day. It wasn't an easy time and was often fraught with tension. The old saying is so true that 'absence makes the heart grow fonder.' James was experiencing the opposite of that saying. Even at the age of thirty-seven, James was still being criticised by his father whom he loved with all his might.

For me it was the same old thing. Was I to confront Doug about his attitude and face a barrage of verbal abuse, or just let time pass and heal the situation? In hindsight, I should have corrected Doug. But the truth was I was still afraid of his disapproval. He would think I was taking James' side against his and so not being with him in his judgement. I cringe now when I think of those times. I really don't know how we would have managed without James' help.

I admit that having James' two young very rambunctious little boys in our home wasn't easy either. One time they were playing cops and robbers in the garden and one boy threw a stick at the other, hitting him in the eye. It was a miracle that his sight in that eye was saved. It took many trips to the Waterford Eye Hospital and stitches in the poor boy's eye. All this was tension we could have lived without. The eye is 100 per cent today, thank God.

Also adding to the workload in that last year was Doug's newly published book called *Jack's Life* that was being launched. It was written for the younger generation and tells of the life of C.S. Lewis from birth to his departure. A book signing tour of the States was scheduled where Doug would also advertise and promote the book and the movie.

In the meantime, Lara had also succumbed to the persuasive powers of my Slimming Angel and was doing the weight loss program with me. We would meet each morning and go through our half hour vigorous exercise routine before we came downstairs.

....

Next, Daddles was invited to go to Japan to speak. He left on the 8th of January. When he came home five days later, he told me of his experiences. First was the fact that the hotel lobby was on the 14th floor and his room was on the 26th floor. The toilet seat was warmed and when you sat on it, and it played music. Also, if you accidentally pressed the wrong button, you would get sprayed in the face with a spray of warm water. Obviously, it was designed to spray your undercarriage, and not your face. The Japanese loved the Narnia film which made record amounts at the box-office there. It had now beaten the first and second Harry Potter movies. On his return, a beautiful $5,000 string of Mikimoto pearls was a present for me from my beloved. He had bought them in Tokyo.

Around this time, Melody was becoming a bit of a worry. She actually did the same kind of thing I had done in my gay-abandon of youth. She packed a few bare necessities into a backpack and took off to explore the world on her own. But the world was a very different place in the two-thousands than it was in the sixties.

We would occasionally get letters from her. The first one came from Scotland. She lived for a short time in France before going to stay with Bubble in Florence. That didn't last long. Bubble did not like the added burden of worrying about her when she would be out most of the night and asleep most of the day. She stayed on the Isle of Capri and worked there for a few months before eventually returning to Dublin to work, living in a flat with about three others.

We visited Malta one more time before moving there permanently. This time with Melvin who was to set up bank accounts and all the other bureaucratic necessities. The lovely lady Joanna Agius handled the legal requirements for us to live in Malta. She is one of the many people whom God has sent into our lives to look after our many diverse legal and financial needs in Malta. Little did we know on our first meeting that she and her husband Robert would become loved and loyal friends. We have had many social and business encounters with her. She is a star, a real gem.

We were put in touch with an architect in Malta whose job it was to draw out a scaled floor plan of the house we had bought. I spent many frustrating hours deciding what furniture to take with us and what to leave behind. James made little correct-to-scale cutouts of our favourite pieces of furniture, and they all had to find a home on that floor-plan diagram.

All these jobs and commitments meant we wouldn't be free to leave Ireland till the middle of the next year. And Rathvinden was yet to be sold.

....

Again, God's Blessing was with us. Rathvinden was never advertised but He sent a buyer at exactly the right time. An Irish property developer. A man whose heart was bent on making money quickly regardless of the environmental beauty of the place. We sat with him in Doug's office discussing the sales agreements.

I expected Doug to be defensive when I said to the potential buyer, 'This property and house has been used for God's service. If you are buying this place for your own self-aggrandisement and increase, it will destroy you.' Daddles thought to himself, *Well, there goes that sale*. However, Doug had himself asked for a very high price hoping to turn this man away because he didn't want him to buy the place. But the buyer's eyes could only see money and his heart chose to ignore such a prophetic warning.

He agreed to buy Rathvinden, however the sale was subject to a successful development application which took some time to be approved. Unfortunately, when it came time for us to move to our newly purchased house, the approval had not come through. So, James and Lara, who had no pressing obligations, agreed to stay on and house-sit Rathvinden after we had left to take up residence in our Maltese villa, until the sale of Rathvinden was finalised. That took nearly a year.

During that time, James and Lara remained at Rathvinden and explored Ireland making many memories for their children. They even joined an Irish set dancing club and became very good at that fast and energetic Irish dancing. It was a lovely time for the young family. James was instrumental in organising the packing up of Rathvinden artifacts which filled several 40-foot containers of furniture and household goods, several containers of cars and a whole container of garden tools and equipment – a mammoth task.

Once the property was finally sold, they flew to Malta to visit us in our new home for a week and then on to Australia to begin their new life. James bought a run-down beef farm near Glen Innes in New South Wales to raise his family on. The farm is now well-fenced and has good pastures. His cattle are fat and fetch a good price. He has also turned the farm hovel into a comfortable, attractive home.

The purchasing of Rathvinden did in fact ruin our successor. His de-facto wife and child left him, and he found himself living alone in one of the basement rooms in that big house. The place was back on the market in only a few years, leaving him broke and grieving his losses.

....

Looking back on the thirteen years we spent at Rathvinden, perhaps the deepest regret I have is how I didn't spend enough time with Melody. Today I feel sad that during Melody's very formative years, we were very preoccupied with other people. She was only seven when we arrived in Ireland, and studying in Dublin, as a young adult of twenty, when we left. I was so consumed with life at Rathvinden that she was often left to amuse herself. She would stay the night at the homes of her primary school friends, where there was social interaction. From her viewpoint it must have seemed that the guests and other ministry duties had usurped her God-given right to her mother's attention. It must have also seemed that the God I served and spoke so much about was more important than she was.

Today I am very quick to point out to would-be missionary couples that their primary duty is to their children, even if it means postponing overseas missionary work until they are at least college age. It was not an easy time for Melody. Life is a series of seasons.* I deeply regret not having spent more time with Melody. Perhaps I am wrong, but I feel partly responsible that she has till now, turned her back on Christianity. I hope and pray that one day she will look at Jesus and not me for confirmation of the validity of

---

* - Ecclesiastes 3:1 'There is a time for everything, and a season for every activity under the heavens.'

Christianity. Today, as I write, Melody is in her thirties. Her sweet nature shows no lasting resentment towards me or the lifestyle she was subjected to. And that is a blessing, a gift from both God and her.

As for the lasting achievements of our time at Rathvinden, they are varied and many. Lots of them we don't even know about. We, but mainly Doug, still get emails from various people we helped in those days. He is the scribe in the family; I leave most of the correspondence to him. Let me give you a few examples of the ones we do know about.

A young woman came to us, but I forget the reason she came. She was staunchly pro-abortion, quoting all the usual marketing slogans to justify the horrific procedure. After spending a week with us she had completely reversed her views on the subject. When she returned home to the States, she set up a van with an ultrasound unit mounted in it and she started visiting high schools in various states. Pregnant mums would volunteer to let the students view the ultrasound image of a live, healthy, fully-formed baby. This would hopefully educate the children and deter any of them later in life from being talked into aborting a child. She would also park the van alongside abortion clinics and invited the women to view their own babies in utero, and hopefully reconsider their options.

Wendy Watson's story is another classic example of a massive achievement. A desperately wounded individual now healing others and restoring broken relationships in her own family line.

Many people claim that their time spent with us has given them strength and the tools to live a healthy life, and not a life of self-destruction. Certainly, that is what I experienced under the counsel and training of Dr Philip Ney. Philip gave me a new perspective on life. The main point was, it wasn't my fault, or totally the fault of the people I had laid the blame on.

One lady said to us, 'I have travelled the world searching for God, but never found Him. It was here, at Rathvinden, that I found Him. The Pearl of Great Price, what a gift indeed.' I believe many people left with that gift.

The ministry volunteers who came and helped with the running of Rathvinden learnt skills that will benefit them greatly in life. Cooking, growing, and harvesting food, making jams, and preserving food, gardening, how to set a banquet table, cleaning, and general hospitality. I even taught two of them how to make clothes on my Bernina sewing machine. The Rathvinden finishing school. They were expected to attend our Thursday night Bible studies and to attend Church on a Sunday. I can hope that it also strengthened their faith and relationship with God.

I had better mention the example that Rathvinden had on a young, engaged couple who visited us. We had known Christina Sonneman and her family since she was a child in Tasmania. She was in her early twenties and was a talented harpist when she came with her fiancé, Peirce Baehr, and her mother, Margaret, to visit us.

Peirce is a very fine young man. With their permission and approval, I took them through a very valuable session called, Negotiations of Reasonable Expectations. This exercise is designed to iron out any potential marital disagreements before marriage. It is even a useful technique to resolve disagreements and disappointments in married couples and can also be a useful exercise when you are starting a new job – between you and your employer – or even between a parent and troublesome child. While they were with us, a seed was planted in their minds by God to run a ministry similar to Rathvinden Ministries.

After they were married in December 2007 they purchased a block of land on a picturesque hill in the Huon Valley, a fruit growing area in Tasmania, where they built a self-contained solar-powered home to live in with their children. They also rented out chalets to accommodate itinerant fruit pickers from all over the world who would come during the fruit picking season from Europe, Asia, and America. The chalet accommodations were advertised as run by Christians. The name Pilgrim Hill suits the place well.

In January 2020 Doug and I visited them. One of the Japanese girls there said to me she chose this accommodation because it was advertised as Christian. She knew nothing about the Christian faith and wanted to find out what it was all about. She had come to the right place. Twice a week all their tenants would eat with Christina and Peirce and their tribe of seven little girls in their home. Before and after the meal the Bible would be read and discussed. A lot of their food is home-produced and grown on the property, like we did at Rathvinden.

A month ago, Christina and Peirce were blessed with their first baby boy. He will be doted on by his seven sisters, I'm sure.

....

Before we ventured into the next season of our lives, many things had to take place. Those last four months at Rathvinden were crammed full of activities of various sorts. The most memorable one for me was visiting my mother's family home in Wiltshire, England, at the Wilbury Park Estate in Newton Tony for a large Malet reunion.

As I have mentioned earlier in this book, we used that occasion as an opportunity to take the big English pram we had bought at Harrods in 1967, to be restored to new condition by a restorer of classic prams in Lincolnshire. That gallant pram had raised five children in a farming environment and was still strong but had lost its lustre. The navy-blue canvas hood and cover had weathered many a rain shower and the intense rays of the Australian sun and therefore needed replacing, and the chrome work needed attention. We loaded it into our motorhome and crossed the Irish sea on the ferry from Dun Laoghaire to Holyhead. From there it was a twelve-hour drive to Holbeach, Lincolnshire, on the far eastern side of the UK, to deliver the pram for restoration.

The next day we visited Doug's former guardian, Jean Wakeman, on our way to the Wilbury Estate to make sure she was happy and being well looked after in the nursing home in Headington which we had placed her in. She looked very frail and tired but otherwise all was well.

Once at Wilbury we chose a secluded spot in the designated car park in which to place the motorhome and then mingled with the crowd of about 100 of my relatives in that grand old house. I had brought with me a large leather-bound photograph album from 1903 that I had inherited. That album was marvelled over by many people as they recalled and pondered over its contents. For me, it was a reunion with many of my mother's family members as well as an introduction to others I had never met before.

Before we returned to Ireland, Daddles took me to the Welsh fishing village of Solva where he, Jack and Joy would stay on their holidays in Wales. By nightfall the following day we were back home. James and Lara had held the fort for us while we were away.

Another notable occurrence that took place in those closing months of our time in Ireland was another epic trip to Australia. After the release of *The Lion, the Witch and the Wardrobe* film, local interest in C.S. Lewis had been aroused. Doug was invited to be the keynote speaker at a first ever C.S. Lewis conference to be held in Sydney. There was to be a whole week of lectures to an invited audience, all expenses paid.

A chauffeur-driven car collected us from Rathvinden and drove us to our Gulf Air flight to Sydney, via Bahrain and Singapore. We were met by our minders in Sydney, Australia, and taken to The Star Sydney apartments on Darling Harbour, which would be our dwelling place for the next week. We were allowed the first day off to recover from jet lag before Doug was required. Then it was back-to-back newspaper and media interviews for Doug prior to the conference booking.

However, the morning of the first conference day, Doug felt ill and unable to walk due to giddiness. The corpuscles on his face had erupted into what looked like an inflamed spider's webs of red tracks. His temperature was up, and he felt extremely unwell. A doctor came to see him and said he had picked up some kind of viral infection. It would be impossible for him to fulfil his duties. People from all over Australia had come to see and hear him talk and sign books. It seemed like an insurmountable dilemma, until Dig offered to take his place.

By this time, Dig had himself become quite accustomed to holding an audience. He was the golden boy of a pharmaceutical company and was an award-winning sales representative. I think I was more nervous than him as he took centre stage and held his own as C.S. Lewis' step-grandson. I was so proud of him. The audience loved him – he did a great job. Doug recovered in due time, and we spent the next week or so in a hired campervan visiting our sons and grandchildren before returning to the monumental job of packing up our thirteen years of life in Ireland.

Chapter 33

Malta – our new location

The packing started in earnest on the 4th of July. The company that James had recruited for the job was Careline Removalists. It took them eight days to wrap all the furnishings in bubble wrap and jigsaw them into containers. The job was made all the more difficult because the 40-foot containers couldn't get up the drive so everything had to be loaded at the gate. Daddles wasn't there for a lot of that time. He had flown to Denver, USA, for two weeks to attend a book award presentation, hoping to be awarded a prize for his latest book *Jack's Life*. Unfortunately, he was disappointed.

As my cosy home became progressively emptier, I felt an incredible sense of bereavement, emptiness, and fear.

Right to the very last day I was leading people to Christ. Melody's school friend, Aisling, had recently been through the Christianity Explained teaching with me and was keen for her boyfriend (whom she had designs on to marry) to go through the teaching also. On the day before we left for good, I completed the course with him. He accepted the rule of Jesus in his life and so now became a man worth marrying.

On the 28th of July 2006, Daddles and I got into our heavily-laden campervan to embark on the journey overland to Malta. I had even dug up some rhubarb roots to plant in our new garden. We left James and Lara to finalise things at Rathvinden which included selling our lovely motor-cruiser on Lough Derg and arranging for my two Poodles to be flown to Malta when their quarantine period was over. Eventually they handed over Rathvinden to the property developer who had bought the house and land.

We drove to Rosslare and ferried the van to Roscoff, France, arriving at 5.00 pm, and then drove another seven hours through France, stopping for the night at a campsite at Châtres-sur-Cher. The next day we were on the road again by 8.00 am and, guided by the TomTom GPS, drove twelve hours over the Alps into Italy. We left the motorway and asked the Lord to find us a campsite. A sign for a holiday camp came up so we followed that and asked the owners if we could camp the night there. They turned out to be avid Narnia fans and were delighted to have us stay and connect onto their power supply. That night we slept well with the air-conditioner on.

By 8.00 am we were on the road again arriving at Florence at 1.00 pm. The TomTom led us to a caravan park. Bubble was doing her second year of jewellery manufacture and design in Florence, living in a rented apartment. She rode her bike to the caravan park and took us shopping for groceries. I was impressed that she had such a good grasp of the Italian language. She and I walked into the centre of Florence, and she showed me where she worked and studied, under the tuition of a leading Florentine goldsmith and engraver. About ten students sat riveted to their workbench creating their assigned work pieces. We spent some time in her ground floor apartment. Her Boxer dog, Agnus, had had a litter of puppies which were nearing the time to be weaned and sold, so we were an exciting new toy to be pulled and jumped on and thoroughly investigated. I took lots of photos. Nearly everything in that city cried out to be photographed. A truly beautiful city. At

9.00 pm she escorted us back to the campsite and rode her bike home.

By 3.00 pm the next day, we arrived at a lovely caravan park amidst a grove of ancient olive trees in Sorrento, just south of Naples. Melody was living on the Isle of Capri nearby and had ferried over to spend the next day with us before catching the last ferry back to her abode and her place of work. She seemed very happy, and despite being covered in mosquito bites, she looked well and cheerful. The place was so lovely and even had a little grocery shop. So, we decided to spend three days relaxing there after our packing ordeal and long journey.

After that we drove to the harbour town of Salerno just outside Naples, to put our campervan on a ferry scheduled to do a round trip: Italy, Tunisia, Malta and back to Italy. We joined a long queue of cars waiting to board the ferry, and slowly inched our way forward. However, before we reached the boat there was an archway to go through; our van was too tall to fit through it. Poor Daddles had to back that big van very carefully through the cars to join another line. We had booked a sleeping cabin which was very sparse, but a great deal better than trying to sleep on the chairs provided. At 9.00 pm the following day the boat arrived in Tunisia. Lots of people got off the ferry which didn't set sail again till 1.00 am.

It was now the 6th of August, eight days since we had left Ireland. This was our last day of travel. The ferry docked in Grand Harbour, Malta at 1.00 pm. This time we had no trouble finding Żejtun and our new home.

The sun's heat was relentless and extreme. August is the hottest month in Malta. Our handy-man, Zaru, had already put the air-conditioners on in the house (however, many of them didn't work) so we were able to get out of the heat a bit. I went for my first swim in the big pool. It was wonderful.

The empty house, which was made of limestone, cement blocks and marble was loud and echoey. I had been used to the silent, soft-carpeted floors of Rathvinden. It felt like living in a shell. It reminded me of the sensation from my childhood, when we would go into an empty galvanised iron water tank, and a sibling would bang or tap gently on the side. The slightest sound was amplified.

The house was very empty feeling, with only very few items of furniture the previous owners had walked away from. The heat of the day lasted for hours trapped in the house's masonry. The only things that seemed to remain cool were the marble floors on my bare feet.

Mixed with the excitement of new beginnings was the sad nostalgia of familiar comforts left behind – the soft carpets, the pleasure of the warming sun in the cool of the mornings. Here the sun was to be avoided as an unwelcome guest. It was fierce and dominating, especially in this month. The windows and doors were kept shut, and the curtains pulled close in an effort to keep hold of the small amount of cool that the dark of the night had given.

Our furniture wasn't expected to arrive for quite a while yet. We made use of what we had in the campervan and even went to our boat Lady Meredith and brought back the small washing machine and some kitchen equipment and bedding.

Although it was the hottest month of the year, the garden was ablaze with colour. The bougainvillea archways that surrounded half of the pool area looked amazing with cascades of red, pink, purple and white flowers against the cloudless blue Mediterranean sky. Geraniums of bright pink surrounded the fountain and adorned many other parts of the garden. Lots of oleander bushes were also in full bloom.

The unruly heavy, chunky rows of prickly pear cactuses that surrounded most of our boundaries fascinated me. Their abundant fruits clustered together in hues of red, orange, and yellow, clinging to the large fleshy green leaves – if you could call them leaves. They were ripe and ready to eat but I quickly learnt the foolishness of touching them. The almost microscopic glochids, sharp-barbed spines, would bury themselves in your skin and trouble you for days. You had to remove each one with a magnifying glass and tweezers. Zaru showed me that they can also be removed by pressing a well-chewed piece of chewing gum onto them or even strong sticky tape.

Zaru had been the caretaker for the previous owner, and he agreed to stay on and work for us. He proved to be an enormous blessing. He showed me how to safely pick and prepare the fruit for eating without getting those small spines embedded in my flesh or clothing. Using protective gloves and a long-handled pair of secateurs, he cut them into a bucket of water. Early morning was the best time to do this as the night dew had softened the prickles. After an hour in the water, they could then be handled with caution and peeled. I watched him do this. The fruit was delicious. I love them but Daddles can't stand them. The Maltese make a delightful liqueur out of them called *bajtra*. One year I made prickly-pear jam, but it wasn't very popular.

I refer to Zaru as my fix-'em-up chappy. He is my Maltese gem with the same kind of practical intelligence I have. Although uneducated and unable to read well, he is able to install or fix almost anything, whether it be plumbing, electrics, gardening, or anything mechanical. Having installed most of the hidden underground drainage and electrics for the previous owner, he knows where everything is. There also doesn't seem to be an inch of Malta that he doesn't know. And so, he also became our trusted chauffeur and go-feur.

During the time we have been living here he has planted a huge vegetable garden and, between the two of us, we have a constant supply of fresh fruit and vegetables, over and above our personal needs. I give so much produce away. He also keeps the massive yearly growth of vegetation in the garden under control. Each year the bougainvillea and other plants would seem to triple in size. Not only is he a gardener, chauffeur, handyman, plumber, and mechanic, but he is my security whenever Doug is away. He keeps his mobile phone close in case I need him in the night and has more than once come when a water pipe has burst, or fuses blown.

On one occasion I was in dire straits. After working all day with two people who had come to help me clean up the place after a bad storm, I really overdid myself and was in great pain that evening. The next morning, I was unable to even get out of bed or walk. Doug was in Australia filming *The Voyage of the Dawn Treader*. I called Zaru. He helped me from my bed and to the much-needed toilet. Then he went out and bought two walking frames, so I could choose the one I liked. With the aid of the frame, I was just able to walk. Zaru looked after me until Melody was able to come from

Ireland and help me for ten days. After medical examinations and an MRI, it was discovered that I had cracked my pelvic bone. A bone density test showed my calcium levels to be very low.

The field that had been added to the property needed an entrance gate and a new stone wall on the boundary line. This was one of Zaru's first undertakings. He soon had it completed and the area rotary-hoed and ready for planting. Nothing grows in the vegetable garden in the heat of the month of August. But by the end of November, he had brassicas, tomatoes, garlic, capsicums and potatoes already planted. Doug entertained and exercised himself wielding his big Australian cane knife, cutting down the large overgrowth of prickly pear rows that surrounded that area on two sides, revealing a collapsed stone wall, which we later renewed.

Also, buried amongst the prickly pear, we found old grape vines which had managed to survive. These were carefully freed from the stranglehold of the cactus. Zaru later made a trellis for the vines. They now overhang a stone path along one side of the vegetable garden. Each year my hens would gorge themselves on the lovely big bunches of red grapes because they produced far more than we could eat or even give away. This year, 2020, I made 150 grape bags on my Bernina sewing machine and protected the bunches of grapes from the birds and wasps. We harvested two wheelbarrows full of the big beautiful juicy bunches of ripe grapes, and attempted to make our first batch of wine, using equipment we bought second-hand. So far it looks promising. It sits in two big vats with a fermentation lock letting out the gas and preventing any air-borne bacteria getting in. Next month we will bottle it and have our first taste of our very own home-made wine. I only hope it will be drinkable.

The majority of the inhabitants of Malta are religiously Catholic. Every town has its patron saint, and each saint has a feast day. On the saint's feast day, the villagers try to outdo the other towns by festooning their town with lights and extravagant decorations. While this is in progress, streets are closed in and around that town. I often have to take a detour which usually results in me getting hopelessly lost until I find an airport sign – I could always find my way home from the airport. At dark, the festival would start with a display of fireworks and continue often till midnight.

To begin, this was fascinating to us. We would run upstairs and out onto the flat roof to watch the display. But after a few months of fireworks illuminating the night sky, and their very loud explosions, it became a source of irritation. Maltese fireworks seem to be designed to be extremely loud. The reports would reverberate and echo around the stone walls of the townships in the most remarkable way. Daddles has a rueful theory for their love of fireworks and loud explosive noises. During the war, Malta was bombed relentlessly every day and night for three years. Daddles thinks they became so accustomed to hearing explosions that they now need the noise to get to sleep at night.

Shooting season, which lasts for two months of the year, is another aspect of the place that is extremely annoying. It involves shooting pretty much anything that moves. Rabbits were all shot out years ago, but any poor migratory bird that made the mistake of stopping for a rest in Malta often came to grief. Although it is permitted to target only specific types of birds, these restrictions are largely ignored.

Our new home is surrounded by tall trees in a farming area. The small fields are fenced with stone walls. The shooters would love to gather in these stone-walled fields that surround our house. At dawn we would be woken by 12-gauge shotguns as they blasted any birds that flew within range. The pellets often splatter on to our house. The bottom of the pool was littered with them. One year when we emptied the swimming pool to clean and paint it, we got about a kilogram of pellets from the bottom of the pool. I was told that to report the shooters to the police would only antagonise them as many of the shooters were policemen themselves.

Again, I looked to the word of God for a peaceful solution, '... Love your enemies, bless them that curse you, do good to them that hate you, and pray for them which spitefully use you, and persecute you,' (Matt 5:44). I cut a long bamboo pole and attached a white flag to the end of it. With this pole, and pretending to take my two Poodles for a walk, I went early one morning to find the culprits. I found five of them in a prefabricated secluded shooting hide, all with their guns pointed skyward, eagerly awaiting any unsuspecting bird to fly overhead from our trees. I introduced myself to them and said admiring words about their prized guns.

Keeping a friendly smile on my face I asked them their names, carefully trying to remember them and where they lived – not many of them lived in Żejtun. Then, still smiling, I said, 'Do you know what I do when you wake me up at 4.00 am every morning with your gun fire?' I never waited for a reply but said, 'I ask the Lord Jesus to bless you, because that's what the Bible said to do with people who spitefully use you.' They looked blankly at me till I added, 'I will tell you the blessing I ask the Lord to give you. I ask Him to reveal His love to you and that you will all come to know Him and follow His ways and be saved.' One of the shooters didn't understand English so everything I said had to be translated for him. The message was really rubbed in that way.

I parted by saying, still with a small smile on my face, 'If you wake me up tomorrow morning I'll come and give you all a good bum-smack.' Well, that did it. They laughed and laughed and then had to translate it to the chap who didn't speak English and they laughed again. I left them, still laughing. But do you know what? They never woke me up again. It worked – for the remainder of that season anyway.

At 8.00 am on the 23rd of August, just twenty days after our arrival in Malta, our household goods and furniture arrived from Ireland in two 40-foot containers. These were again too big to fit through our gate, so the contents were unloaded onto two small flat-bed trucks and bit by bit the labelled boxes were carried into the house by eight strong men. I stood by and told them which rooms to put them into. The bubble wrap was cut off the furniture which was then carried to the allocated rooms. The temperature that day was in the mid-thirties. By 3.00 pm the containers were empty, the house full, and the men were hot, sweaty, and exhausted. Doug and I stayed up till midnight unwrapping and sorting our belongings.

We hadn't expected the previous owners to have left two double beds and large wardrobes and cupboards behind so we found we had more than would fit into the house. We simply gave stuff away to various workmen who were still painting and installing new air-conditioners, or laying travertine marble around the house and garden.

Two more 40-foot containers arrived at the docks on the 2nd of October, containing four of Doug's Jaguars. James had arranged for them to be housed in the Malta Classic Car Museum. The XK140, the C-Type, the XJS Lynx Eventer, and the XJS convertible made quite a procession to the museum in Qawra that day.

The only things now left to arrive were my two Poodle dogs – Pitou and Poocherina, which James and Lara were looking after at Rathvinden. Six days after the arrival of the cars, James and Lara and their two boys arrived by plane with the dogs. The dogs were taken to the quarantine centre to be examined before we could get possession of them. Those poor little dogs had been in their dog crates for over twelve hours, and they were absolutely desperate to find a patch of grass to relieve themselves on.

James helped us re-assemble our four-poster bed and helped with the placement of the furniture. His carefully designed scale drawing of where allotted furniture had to go was not much use due to the attractive furniture the previous owners had left behind for us.

My big Wilson pram also arrived in a crate from the restorers in England. The royal-blue canvas, leather work and white wheel rubber had all been replaced. Also, the chrome work came back shining like new. I kept a sheet over it to protect it from the dust of the household renovations. During this time, Daddles was a bit distracted reading through script after script to be used in the making of the third Narnia film, *The Voyage of the Dawn Treader*, till the right one was decided on.

The garden and grounds of the house were hemmed in by tall stone walls so once we got the dogs home, we let them loose to explore. At first, they were very nervous, not wanting to leave our side, until they discovered the dozens of cats that the previous owners used to feed. Chasing cats was their favourite sport. However, this habit got them into terrible trouble for the cats would simply disappear into the prickly pear bushes. Of course, neither of my dogs knew what these plants could do. Soon I had two very upset Poodles not knowing which paw to walk on next. The glochids off the prickly pears had covered all four feet with painful little spikes which took days to get rid of. They soon learned the hard way, as I had done, not to go near these plants, but cat-chasing was just too much fun. The cats soon realised they were not welcome and relocated themselves, which was a blessing.

Zaru helped us plumb in a brand-new Westinghouse commercial washing machine that James had found and purchased in Kilkenny before we left Ireland. That faithful machine has lasted us fifteen years. It is only now beginning to give us trouble, but new parts for it no longer exist.

Shortly after James and Lara arrived, Bubble and Matty (Matthew Handy, Bubble's husband) came from Florence to view our new surroundings and to stay for a few weeks also. All of a sudden, the house of five bedrooms was full to capacity. The previous owners had also left an old Mercedes car for us. Maybe Doug bought it from them; I'm not sure. We lent it to Bubble and Matty to go and explore Malta, but it broke down often and caused a lot of frustration, so we quickly sold it.

James and Lara took their two boys to the Playmobil factory. They were even permitted to assemble and make a toy man each that they could keep. James also assembled one and gave it to me. It still hangs on my smart car keyring. By the end of October, the rooms in the house were empty again. Everyone had left. James went back to the land he had grown up in, Australia, taking his wife and two sons with him. They borrowed our mobile home bus and set off to find a farm to work and make a living. Farming was a much cleaner and more enjoyable lifestyle than his previous job of flying regional jets around America. Often, when James stopped his work on the farm, he would think he had to go to work. To him, farm work was like recreation compared to being an airline pilot.

Bubble and Matty returned to Italy where Bubble continued her apprenticeship learning how to make and design quality jewellery. By March, 2007 she had finished her apprenticeship and was now a qualified jeweller. Daddles and I flew to Milan and were chauffeured to Florence to attend her graduation and receiving-of-awards ceremony. We were so proud of her. She didn't have an easy time in Italy. She struggled with sickness and the break-up of her marriage, not to mention having to master an absolutely new language. Matty never could get used to Italy and was unable to get a job because of the language barrier. He began to drink heavily. He worked for a while in England but soon realised their marriage was as good as dead and returned to his homeland in Australia. They divorced but remained friends.

Chapter 34

Making connections

Now in Malta, Doug and I were trying out different churches, trying to choose one to replace our Irish church family whom we had grown very fond of. But after a few attempts of trying out different Christian churches on a Sunday, we gave up. Most of them were conducted in Maltese with headphones giving us the translation in English. Neither of us liked this; we would become distracted, and our attention would wander. One Sunday we hadn't chosen another church to try out, so we walked the short distance down from our house and into the fishing village of Marsaxlokk and joined the crowds of tourists at the market situated on the dockside. There were lots of very colourful little fishing boats with eyes painted on the bows, bobbing gently to the sway of the sea, moored along the wharf. I looked at Daddles and said, 'We are worshiping at the altar of Mammon today instead of worshiping in church; this doesn't feel right.'

We were wending our way through the crowds of tourists all walking along the stalls looking at the various Maltese artifacts designed to attract their eye and money. Much to my surprise, there were tatted tablecloths, doilies, and runners. Tatting is a technique of lacemaking that has nearly vanished. I have not seen it done for many years. My mother used to tatt, and she would make beautiful lacework – she also taught me how to tatt. Today it is almost a lost art. I know how labour-intensive it is. It must have taken many hours to make those tablecloths, yet they were so cheap. I bought a round tatted tablecloth to fit one of our small tables.

As we strolled along, I noticed a man with what looked like the stalks of a frangipani plant sticking out of a paper bag. I tried to catch up to him, but he vanished in the crowd. Malta was the first place I had ever lived that didn't have winter frosts. I knew my very favourite plant, the frangipani, which had highly scented white and yellow flowers, would survive here. Daddles suggested we try and find the stall that he got the plant from.

We nearly gave up hope until we came to the far end of the row of stalls. There stood a man with a few plants at his feet. Pointing to the leafless thick stalks of a plant, I asked him the name of it. 'Frangipani,' he replied, at which I raised my hands automatically and said, 'Praise the Lord.' When I said this, he looked at me and asked me which church I worshiped at. I told him we had just arrived in Malta only one month ago and hadn't found a church we could feel at home in. He told me he knew of a good church run by an Englishman and his Maltese wife. He asked for my mobile phone number and said he would get them in contact with me.

A few days later a Maltese lady called Liz phoned me and said she had been given my phone number and told to call and tell me of the church she attended, called The Good Shepherd Church. She promised to collect Doug and me next Sunday and take us there.

It turned out to be a house church in the pastor's own flat. The room was very crowded, but everyone was extremely friendly. Everyone wanted to kiss us and give us a welcoming hug. They were not at all like the stuffy reserved British, and I learned that this friendly behaviour was very Maltese. They love to show their emotions. They cry easily in public and laugh and sing and dance when they are happy. I'd love to be so uninhibited. The service was good, in English and translated by a young girl into Maltese. I wasn't going to make any hasty decisions but would give this friendly church a fair trial, closely testing their doctrine against the word of God. Daddles however disliked the hugging and kissing and the close proximity of the people in that small room. He was quick to find fault and after a few Sundays, refused to go there again.

But I returned many Sundays, always taken there by Liz. I never thought I would ever be able to find the place by myself in my new smart car that Daddles had bought me for my birthday. Malta is a maze of streets. I got hopelessly lost among that network of streets on many occasions.

Ken, the self-ordained pastor, was also checking me out to see if I was truly founded in God's word and ways. We soon discovered we were of one heart and mind. His house church in Gzira, which had started with only a handful of people, was getting so crowded that people were standing in the corridor. New premises had to be found. We found a place in Birkirkara and met there for a few years until the owners got us out by raising the rent too high. For a while that church met here, at our villa, for the Sunday service and also for a Bible study evening on Tuesdays. We eventually found another premises in Hamrun, where we still are today.

Ken Brigs gave up a highly paid job on the oil rigs as well as a life of sexual promiscuity and extravagance as an attractive 'man of the world' with money (he was married with three children at the time) to live a humbler life as a Christian. He invited others to join him in searching out the Bible truths. From that beginning he became a teacher and pastor of the Good Shepherd Church. He is dedicated to following Christ and shepherding His children.

Our swimming pool has been used to baptise many new believers. It's always a very joyous occasion with everyone loudly singing the song, 'I have decided to follow Jesus, no turning back, no turning back' after the baptism. Prior to me joining that church family, Ken's baptisms were either held at the seaside or in a bath. They all love coming here and it's my joy and honour to host them. The church often spends fellowship time here sharing a meal, swimming, and getting to know each other better. Often, they would bring a non-Christian member of their family or a friend along to join us. This was a much better way of sharing the gospel.

There are only two villas on the street we live in – both side by side yet not overlooking each other. Our neighbour, Joe, is a highly respected and well-known doctor. He and his wife Lilliana were very kind and hospitable to us when we first arrived. Their three children had all left home by the time we met them. Lilliana, however, was not at all well. She had cancer but was fighting it bravely, while always full of charm and ready to help. I persuaded them both to let me take them through Christianity Explained. We sat around their kitchen table in their home while I slowly revealed the Christian message as opposed to the religious Roman Catholic teachings that they were familiar with, being careful to never put down their beliefs but keeping only to the gospel.

Both enjoyed the teachings and readily accepted Jesus' salvation plan with joy. Lilliana and I spent many hours together after that, further discussing spiritual truths, especially about life after death. I had given her a Bible which she read at every opportunity she had. One evening, on the 23rd of April our front doorbell rang. It was Joe from next door. He was flustered and disturbed and vented his emotions to me. He told me I was not to speak to Lilliana about spiritual things from the Bible anymore.

'Why?' I asked. He told me Lilliana had given up the fight to live because of me. I gave no answer but simply told him I was sorry to have disturbed him this way. She died seventeen days later on the 10th of May. I, and many others, were sad to lose her. She was a fine lady.

What preoccupied us most in the first few years in Malta was the renovating, improving, and decorating of our home and gardens. Doug loves to restore beautiful old things that have been neglected or damaged. He had Rathvinden House and the gardens restored from the ground up. Now his focus was on this place.

Every day for weeks on end there would be workmen here undertaking some task or other. I'll run through just a few of the restoration jobs in that first year. The first job was to install decent air-conditioners in all the rooms. That installation went on till the following January. On the 11th of January the air-conditioning was turned on for the first time. But the heat of the summer had long gone. Travertine marble replaced the old crumbling sandstone around the entertainment areas, paths, and forecourts around the house. Water tanks were put on the flat roof top which was also being re-membraned. A new intercom telephone system and security alarms and cameras were installed. The TV monitors and intercom system were installed from the front gate to the kitchen, Daddles' office, and our bedroom.

We bought pool furniture, shade umbrellas, tables, chairs, and recliners. Stone walls and archways were repaired. New awnings replaced the worn and tattered awnings that shaded most windows. Later, we also resealed the drive and turned the cracked tennis court into a giant car park, often full of the workmen's cars and trucks. Also, the latest enterprise was to install solar heating and electricity to the house to avoid the large electricity bills that Malta inflicts on its inhabitants. This, however, has been badly installed and is still causing us a lot of trouble, which I won't even try and explain here. This house and grounds are now regarded, by one real estate agent, as being one of the finest villas in Malta.

On the 5th of August we left Winnie, my niece (my sister Bliss' granddaughter) who had come to visit us, to house-sit and look after my two dogs. Daddles and I had been invited to join a cruise on the sailing ship Sea Cloud II docked in Dublin. Daddles was to be a guest speaker along with Dick Stub, Jerry Root, and several others. Most of the passengers were American. The ship was magnificently decked out with luxury living and entertainment areas. Our cabin was amazing with twin beds side by side. We glided through the water, fanned by a gentle wind along the coast of Ireland under full sail. Stopping at Waterford and Cobh (Titanic's last port of call), and then on to Penzance in the UK.

Daddles had a captive audience that morning as he gave his initial talk about his life growing up with C.S. Lewis. And later that evening he talked about his newly published book *Jack's Life*. During the day we had a bus tour around Penzance and St Ives. We sailed on to Guernsey, Saint Peter Port and went for a walk to see Victor Hugo's house. That evening Jerry Root gave a very good talk about God as our creator, sustainer, and our lover. Then Doug talked about the making of the Narnia stories into film.

Everybody was very eager to hear my story. They finally persuaded me to come up front and answer many questions which ended up with me getting most of my life's story told. I'm not good at public speaking, particularly when Daddles is listening. I constantly fear his correction or disapproval. He had the grace to leave the room. I surprised myself at how well I did. I think it's a microphone that usually derails me. But this time there was no microphone, thank God. There was a big response afterwards to what I had said – many wanted to hear more. I was unaccustomed to having so much attention; it was scary and somewhat intoxicating. I'm so glad that it's usually Daddles in the spotlight and not me. I'm afraid I would become over-confident and lose my serenity and humility. Americans are so good at gushing over you with such enthusiasm, it's scary.

The next day we docked in Normandy at the port town of Caen and took a bus trip to the war museum and to the Longues-Sur-Mer, a World War Two German artillery battery and to the cemetery at Colleville. There were thousands of white crosses stretched out in perfectly straight lines in all directions, each with a soldier's name on it. Standing in the middle of all those little crosses, two ladies, who had heard of our ministry at Rathvinden, talked to me endlessly about their own abuse, completely oblivious to all those young lives cut short and under our feet. It didn't seem the right place or time, but I was too polite or shy to tell them to stop.

On all these excursions on land Daddles preferred to stay on the ship and rest. We caught a plane back to London and on to Malta the next day. It was a very exciting and memorable trip. We met so many lovely people, many whom are still in touch with Doug via email to this day.

· ·

Doug was still making many trips to the States, Prague and London during this time, overseeing and advising on the making of the next Narnia film *Prince Caspian*, which was nearing completion. He also squeezed in a trip to Australia to go and see the farm that James had a mind to buy.

Prince Caspian had its grand premiere on the 7th of May 2008 in New York – nearly two years after our arrival in Malta. Zaru had driven Daddles and me to the Malta airport on the 5th. We were sitting in the airport lounge when who should walk in but our friend and financial minder, Joanna Aguis and her husband Robert. They were also on their way to New York for a short holiday. Daddles was able to get them VIP invitations to attend the premiere. I believe it was the highlight of their holiday. We had also invited our dear friend Katherine Butler. Bubble also joined us from Florence, and we invited my niece, Winnie, who was studying in Oxford to come to the premiere.

After we had all settled into our rooms at the Mandarin Hotel in New York and were enjoying a drink in the sunken lounge with other cast and crew, Melody, the last of our group to arrive, made a dramatic entrance by taking a flying leap from the steps that led down into the lounge and landing in Daddles' lap. Not a very ladylike way to join a group of celebrities, but she got a grand applause from the crowd, as Daddles tried to rescue his spilt drink and return her affectionate greeting.

The next day Daddles was very much in demand and got through seventeen interviews. While the rest of us went shopping, Bubble took Melody to buy her a dress to wear. In her usual fashion she had come with only a backpack with bare essentials and no dress or shoes. The rest of us had a lovely day, walking in the parks and eating sticky donuts. We visited an art museum and bought a few frivolous articles from the big department stores. That evening we all dressed up and attempted to look our best for a cocktail party in the hotel. Andrew Adamson, the producer, was there – this was his second Narnia film. Melvin, with his wife and family and many others, were also there.

The premiere of *Prince Caspian* was held the following evening in the Ziegfeld Theatre. It took over an hour to pass along a line of hundreds of reporters and cameramen all eager to talk to the stars, the director and the producer, and Mr. Douglas Gresham. I accompanied Doug along the line while the rest of our group stood with the many onlookers.

I wore my long hair down, which was now touched with silver, and a white full-length fitted dress trimmed with pink and turquoise that I had bought in Perth thirty years ago, before Bubble was born. Try as I may, I couldn't find anything prettier in the shops, or more flattering. And it was also a statement of triumph for me. I had lost more than half my body weight. Daddles loved my hair down and he loved that dress on me. It was him I wanted to look my best for.

After the showing of the movie, we were all taken to a big party/reception. It was all very elaborately laid out with various displays, and an endless supply of drinks and finger foods. However, all was not a bed of roses. There was a dark, sinister atmosphere in our family group at the premiere of Prince Caspian. Bubble resented Katherine. She waited for me to be alone with her before she vented her indignation and disapproval of Katherine's invitation and presence among us. But we had known Katherine since she was a young schoolgirl. She had grown up with our children and was once James' sweetheart. She had been a part of our life for many years, a regular visitor and close friend to both Doug and I. Melody and I balanced and juggled the two sides. I thank God for Melody's presence. She spent most of her time with Bubble, leaving me free to chat with Winnie and Katherine and the other guests.

The tension put a damper on the whole occasion, and it has become an event that I would rather not remember. Time and distance heal grievances, and absence makes the heart grow fonder. No further damage was sustained. Only the memory of sadness remains.

The years of labour, headaches, and triumphs in making that film were over at last. But the long journey of making the next Narnia film was just beginning. We all returned to our various countries and abodes, and back to our routine lives once again. Zaru had done a good job looking after my dogs and the house and supervising the workmen who were still busy mending and improving Tai Harendrimar.

People still came to stay with us for various reasons. The training we had from Dr Philip Ney at Rathvinden never departed from us and we found ourselves helping many of our guests at Tai Harendrimar with the skills and techniques we had been taught. The couple I have already written about, Wendy and Ray Watson, came to stay for a week. As did Christina and her mother Margaret Sonneman whom I also mentioned.

Life in our new Malta house had settled into the familiar pattern of endless workmen in the house, gardening and housekeeping and a steady stream of guests for me. But for Daddles it was globe-trotting again, as he set about overseeing the making of the next Narnia film, *The Voyage of the Dawn Treader*. This time it was being filmed on the Gold Coast of Queensland, Australia. For me this was wonderful. Three of our married children were in the vicinity. Dominick was the closest in Brisbane, and James in New South Wales. For Dig it was quite a bit further but near enough for us to spend time with him and for him to bring his whole family to the film set and watch the process of a film being made.

A few years previously, we had bought a large bus that had been converted into a very comfortable home on wheels. James and his family had lived in it for about six months while they were looking for a farming property to buy. Now it was a mobile home for Daddles to live in on set.

We again left our home in Malta with the Poodles under Zaru's care and arrived in Queensland on the 8th of August 2009. Our bus home, which was usually garaged at James' new farm, had been made ready for us at Dominick's Brisbane home. We spent a short time with him and got thoroughly climbed on and generally loved by his four delightful little girls. The youngest one, Xanthe, was only three.

It took quite a bit of organising to find a suitable parking spot for the bus amongst the closed-off area of the film set. The bus became Doug's home for the next three months, as he took an active role in the quality of the filming procedure, proudly wearing his name tag with Executive Producer on it.

That bus became a favourite after-hours meeting point for cast and crew. They would arrive with a six-pack of tinnies (Australian slang for beer in tins) or a bottle of wine and the stories and jokes would go on for hours. One of the set makers made a wooden plaque with 'Artist's Bar, open 6.00 pm' carved on it and secured it to the bus. That plaque now hangs in our Malta home with their autographs on the back of it.

The Spit is a tiny finger of land at a popular resort area on the Queensland coast. It had been selected for filming as there was road access, and yet ocean views in almost all directions. A life-sized sailing ship, the Dawn Treader, was set up on the foreshore. It was mounted on hydraulics and could be moved in an alarmingly realistic fashion.

All our boys and their families visited us while we lived on set. James and Lara even brought Lara's mum and other family members who were visiting from America.

The filming area was closed off from the general public by tall mesh fences. Each day there would be crowds of people all trying to get a good spot along the fence to see the activity or, better still, to see some of the film stars.

Although Doug was very busy most of the day, I was free to mingle among the people or just watch and enjoy the surreal atmosphere of the normal mixed in with actors dressed in strange costumes walking around as they waited for their turn on camera.

I only stayed five weeks before returning to Malta. During that time, Daddles took me to see his newly-purchased island about a mile offshore from the northern Queensland town of Mackay. I'll never forget the wonderful feeling of being totally alone on that island. The first thing we did was to gleefully take off our clothing and go racing around *uchi boochi* (Swahili for 'naked'). But we soon put our clothes back on, and gave ourselves a good spraying with insect repellent, as we were becoming a tasty treat for the many mosquitoes and the horrible sandflies.

On the 15th of September I returned home via Singapore and London. I very nearly missed my last connecting flight to Malta due to a very funny incident, although it didn't seem funny at the time.

I'm a knitter. If there is any waiting around expected, a long car ride or plane trip, I would take my knitting. I'm always in a hurry to complete someone's knitted birthday gift. Knitting needles had been forbidden to be carried onboard an aeroplane so I simply tucked my plastic knitting needles along the bottom of my bra, disguised as bra underwire. I had done this on many flights and got away with it. No one even questioned me when I'd been on the aeroplane happily knitting away the hours of the flight. But at

Heathrow Airport, when passing through the security screening, I was randomly frisked, and the security woman detected my hidden plastic knitting needles.

As far as they were concerned, I was carrying a concealed weapon! I showed them my knitting and tried all I could to persuade them of my innocence. I even phoned Daddles on my mobile and asked him to talk to them, telling the security agents that he was making a Narnia film on the Gold Coast of Australia. I shamelessly name-dropped, pleaded, and almost cried. They were talking about locking me up, taking away all flying privileges and even making a police note of the incident in my passport. I must have looked pathetic because I was also carrying a very large stuffed toy elephant that Dominick's children had bought me. It was much too big to fit in any of my suitcases.

Time was passing. My connecting plane would be departing soon. I sat down while they decided what to do with me. Everyone was so serious. Why didn't I think of this earlier? I hung my head and prayed, 'Dear Lord, please give me favour in their eyes.' No sooner had the words left my mouth, they said, 'Okay, you can go. In future let your knitting needles be seen, it is quite legal to take plastic needles on an aeroplane now.' Then, with their official duties executed, they all clustered around me asking me questions about Narnia and the new film. Narnia fans are found in the most unexpected areas.

Daddles worked hard and long with the producer Michael Apted to make this movie close to the way his stepfather had envisaged it. Even now there is bitterness in his voice when he relates how his suggestions were routinely listened to and then ignored. For the closing credits he had come across a sixteen-year-old girl, Meg Sutherland, who had not only written but personally sung a very moving and beautiful song that perfectly complemented the message in the movie. He submitted it to the directors who claimed to like it but, in the end, ignored his suggestion and used a popular country singer to sing the closing song.

Suddenly a big omission was realised. This big budget movie had not been properly advertised to the Christian viewers of the world. To make an impact, they called on Doug to appear on radio, television, and countless live venues and lots of different countries to advertise it for them. Poor Doug was constantly catching planes all over the world. I saw very little of him during that time.

It was no wonder that on the 30th of November 2010, when the Royal premiere was held, he was completely exhausted and emotionally and physically drained. But he held himself together answering questions, blinded by camera flashes as we walked the line-up once again and were interviewed by many reporters and newspaper personnel outside the Odeon Theatre in London.

Again, it took about an hour to be slowly led along the line. The temperature was only about 2 degrees above freezing. I had a salmon pink satin dress on with a cream-coloured lace coat over it. It was a dress I had designed and had made to fit my reformed figure perfectly. My hair was worn up, in a bunch of curls on top of my head with a salmon pink scrunchie. The heirloom opal necklace, that had belonged to my grandmother, was around my neck. I thought I looked so glamorous, but I have never been so cold in my life before.

After that we were led to join a line up to be introduced to Her Majesty Queen Elizabeth the II. She was so regal and gracious.

After the film showing – which I loved, but Doug saw many mistakes in – we were taken to a reception room for drinks. Bubble had designed and made gold Aslan rings for all the stars and personnel involved in making the film and presented them to them. Daddles also got one which he wears proudly at all his public appearances.

The next day, I was alone in the foyer of the Goring Hotel, a favourite hotel of the Royal Household, when, over a cup of tea, I happened to fall into conversation with a lovely and friendly lady. We chatted about why I was in London, the Narnia films, and the fact that I had recently met Her Majesty the Queen. She told me she was a personal dresser to Her Majesty and in charge of her wardrobe. Many chapters ago, I related the story of our mailbox saga in Tasmania, and I now saw an opportunity to thank Her Majesty for a kindness she had done for us when we were simple dairy farmers.

I asked this lady if she would deliver a letter to the Queen, and she agreed. I raced up to our hotel room and woke Doug from his much-needed afternoon sleep. After a few minutes of thought, he composed a letter to Her Majesty thanking her for interceding on our behalf in a mix up between the Australian tax office and the UK Inspector of Foreign Dividends. It could have bankrupted us.

Later, the friendly lady told me she had given the handwritten letter to Her Majesty and the Queen apparently remembered the situation well and sent her warm regards.

Chapter 35

Today: 29ᵗʰ October 2020

We came to Malta in August 2006. It's now getting to the end of 2020. Thirteen years have gone by so quickly. It's probably a symptom of living eight years over the expected lifespan of a human being, which I was told is three score and ten. But the years have become so short. I'd prefer to think of it as God has put time on fast-forward because the battle over Satan has been won. The victory is His. He is eager to bring out the banners and rejoice and make all things new.

I like the Bible verse that reads, 'The Lord has assigned me my portion and my cup. My boundary lines have fallen in pleasant places. Surely, I have a delightful inheritance,' (Psalm 16:5). Yes, my boundary lines here in Malta have fallen in pleasant places. We have always loved restoring beautiful but neglected things. The house has reached near perfection of being aesthetically pleasing to the eye, and is now comfortable to live in.

Daddles has a lovely big two-roomed office with a big picture window overlooking the blue Mediterranean. This room reflects his character. Books, artifacts of wars, Narnia film props, two large glass-fronted locked gun cabinets full of guns, photos of Jack and Joy on the wall as well as other photos of his immediate family. At one end of his office sits his desk with his big Apple computer which he spends hours behind every day. Only one framed photo takes a pride position on his office desk – a photo of his wife of fifty-four years looking very sweet in her early twenties. I think he took that photo himself in my London flat.

All the rooms in the house have been given a facelift. The house inside and outside is now utterly beautiful, with marble floors throughout and lots of patios and balconies, which is a luxury feature of most of the bedrooms. The big picture windows around the house are shielded from the sun's glare by yellow striped awnings. All windows have attractive outlooks onto the garden or overlooking the sea. The Maltese architecture is characterised by many archways. Most of the doorways, windows and balconies in this house have arched surroundings.

The very best part of the house, in my opinion, is my secluded little office-cum-sewing room-cum-prayer room and art room. It's on the ground floor with a glass-panelled wall and doorway leading out into a secluded, paved garden area and the pool. I spend hours there now, typing on my computer trying to sort my convoluted life into a readable and understandable book. It's the first time I have ever undertaken such a thought-provoking task. If it wasn't for the COVID-19 pandemic I would have never had time.

The garden has taken shape. The trees are all bigger now, providing a paradise for the birds in an otherwise fairly treeless landscape of tightly packed villages built out of the hauntingly beautiful yellow ochre colour of the quarried limestone. Most houses in Malta have flat rooftops for added living space. The Maltese are very house-proud and keep their houses almost like a shrine. The first impression is the entrance from the street. When both my Poodles were alive, I would get up at 5:00 am and be at a particular butcher's shop by 6.00 am to collect a free bucket of boned out chicken carcasses for my dogs. It always amused me to see so many front doorways into peoples' homes being given a good scrubbing at this early hour, with buckets of water and a scrubbing broom. One had to be careful not to get drenched as the buckets of water were flung down and swept onto the footpath. Often the footpath outside the home was also scrubbed. A well-worn floor washing cloth laid in front of the door added the finishing touch to the job and warned any person entering the house to first wipe their feet. Being a culture of people who worship and revere Mary, Jesus' mother, many homes had little shrines or Mary statues beside their doors with a lit candle or electric candlelight switched on at night.

When you look at the night vista of Malta's glowing lights you have to wonder, as we did, why there were areas of red lights raised above groups of dwelling places and areas of blue lights over others. We asked that question and were told that the homes that have the red lights above them worshiped Joseph, and the blue lights were for the Mary worshipers. I asked what colour light was for the Jesus worshipers, only to get a blank stare in reply.

Even this house had a small stone grotto in a secluded corner of the garden with a statue of Mary in it. The grotto remains but now has a slab of marble with John 14:6, 'I am the way, the truth, and the life,' engraved in gold writing on it.

I try to keep the flower beds around our home with low maintenance flowers only. Each year I collect the seeds from the abundance of larkspur flowers and broadcast them under the trees in the arbour. In May and June, it is a sea of blue, purple, pink, and violet flowers. These seeds I also sow anywhere and everywhere that I think Zaru is not going to spray with herbicide. I even spread them along the sides of our road.

July, August, September, and even into October the place is decked in the brilliant flowers of the bougainvillea and oleander bushes. Lots of other flowers here that I don't know the names of, also vie for attention.

In the fields, Daddles has planted about forty olive trees. These have provided us with gallons of olive oil each year. Olive picking time in September is usually a time of hard work and lots of fun with the keen volunteers who come to help pick them. This year we had a young girl who came all the way from the States to help, even though she had to go into fourteen days of quarantine in Dublin and again for another fourteen days when she got here. She was our only picker this year. We were very grateful for her help. She also helped me pick hundreds of pomegranates, husked them, and put them through my big juicer. The deep freeze now has fifty-six bottles of pure pomegranate juice safely stored to be enjoyed throughout the year to come.

Our place is an oasis of tranquillity and beauty. I love it. But outside the gate and in the big bad world, it is very different. I speak now as it truly is and not as the tourist brochures advertising Malta do. Over two years ago the council dug a deep ditch along Triq il-Kotob, our street, to put in a water pipe. They still haven't finished the job or made any effort to improve the quality of the small strip of road left for the residents to access our homes. Many other roads also are a mess. With good intentions I'm sure, a road is selected for restoration, but the job could take years to complete. Secluded roads like ours are a favourite dumping ground for the locals to dispose of their garbage, even though there is a weekly collection of rubbish. The council will collect fridges or even old carpets or anything too large to go into the garbage trucks. All it needs is a phone call. And yet litter is dumped in nearly all unpopulated areas, completely spoiling the potentially beautiful landscape.

When we first came here the number of cars on the roads were manageable. Now it can take forty-five to sixty minutes to get to Valletta from here, which is only a few kilometres away. It used to take no more than fifteen minutes. Other places are even more congested. A familiar phrase when someone is late, is, 'I'm sorry I'm late; I was stuck in traffic.' I was told by a man whose job it was to unload imported cars off a freight ship that 800 cars were coming into Malta each week. Every family now must find parking space outside their homes for an average of five cars per family. Zaru's home has six people living in it. His three children all have their own car. Multiply that number for each apartment and house along any street. The mind boggles. There is no room to park. My pastor Ken lives in Gzira and often has to carry groceries three blocks to get to his home from where he found a spot to park.

I'm not into politics but I hear over and over again that the newly elected Labour Party has destroyed the place. Massive building projects dot the horizon with their cranes, as more and more hideous modern buildings are eclipsing the uniquely old Maltese architecture.

Each town has its parish church, or should I say, cathedral. These massive and ornate buildings dot the horizon in every direction with their towering steeples. I can well imagine the poor people's money going into the construction of them. A lot of Maltese Catholics leave their properties and inheritance to the Catholic church in their will in an effort to gain a higher seat in heaven. I know my mother gave all our valuables to the Roman Catholic church. So sad, and completely missing the gospel truth. Jesus said, 'I don't dwell in temples made by human hands; I dwell in My people.' We are the church, the body of Christ and His dwelling place.

Significant changes have taken place in Malta since we first came here. Firstly, in 2004 Malta joined the EU. That tripled its economy. The downside was that the population increased by 17 per cent, which borders on being unsustainable. The inhabitants no longer feel that they live in isolation. They have become more metropolitan and accepting towards others. Their strength lies in their human resources. It has also led to a record number of university graduates and an increase in salaries. The other change was in the currency. It used to be called Lira and cents. It changed to the Euro in January 2008 making it easier to travel and share a similar currency with Europe.

I've noticed also there are far more refugees here now. It seems to be a favourite place for them to come and escape the tyranny in their countries. The Maltese Government looks after them well, providing shelter and giving them mobile phones to make it easier for them to find work.

....

I have made some very good friends here. But the thing that puzzles me is that the people I interact with and befriend are usually in their early thirties or even younger. We often joke about the fact that I am often older than their mothers. I first met Stefania, an unusually tall and stately Maltese girl in her late twenties, when she ventured into our house church. I saw that she looked like a fish out of water, treading on very unfamiliar ground, so I engaged her in conversation. We became best friends and spent a lot of time together. I wasn't the one who had led her to Christ, but I certainly helped her along this new journey. That was twelve years ago. Although she is now married with two children, we still try and spend time together.

Lorraine was another young girl who enjoyed spending time with me. I later met her husband, Gabriel. I was instrumental in helping her, and later him, in making a commitment to follow Christ. I have never personally encountered aggression from these girls' parents or relatives, but I have been told that I was hated by them because I had led them to follow Christ, and not a set of man-made religious rules.

Lorraine was a schoolteacher and when she herself became a mother of two, she was reluctant to put her children through the Maltese school system, knowing the Catholic indoctrination that occurs. She longed to home-school her children, which is not permitted in Malta. Doug and I were instrumental in this family migrating to Australia. They continue to thank us for their improved lifestyle there. They moved from a cramped Maltese apartment to a large home in Brisbane. They now have a garden to grow their own veggies and a swimming pool, and many more benefits that were beyond their reach in Malta.

Every Wednesday I used to go with some members of the church evangelising in the streets of Valletta and other towns, parks, or shopping centres, handing out tracts that had a simple gospel message on them, and a contact number if they wanted to learn more. To me, somehow this method of telling people about Jesus and salvation seemed to be a waste of time. People were too busy or not interested. I had had far more success doing the Christianity Explained course in my own home where I could be more friendly and interested in the people. I slowly gave up on the street evangelising and returned to doing my Christianity Explained courses.

I'm often plagued with feelings of guilt, remembering the zeal and energy I once had to show people their ultimate destination if they rejected Jesus and His love and salvation. I'm very eager to talk to anyone about salvation but at the age of seventy-eight I feel too weary to walk the streets talking to uninterested strangers. My faith is a resting faith, confident that Jesus will complete the good work He started in me in 1983.

It's probably a sign of the times we are living in. Many people are convinced that the second coming of Jesus is imminent. It does say in the Bible, that as this approaches, there will be a falling away from Christianity and many people simply don't want to hear about it. I am seeing this happening more and more. The pandemic of the COVID-19 virus has certainly made people ask questions, and become more aware of their own mortality. But there is still a reluctance to accept and submit to the lordship of Jesus Christ. In Ireland, years ago, it was much easier to lead people to Christ.

What makes or breaks one's impressions of a country would ultimately be the native people of that country. Overall, the Maltese people are lovely. They are kind and very friendly and willing to help. They are also very family-oriented. I'll never forget one of my earliest heart-warming incidents of kindness. It was from a funny little Maltese man in his early sixties who was straddling a ride-on marble polishing machine. Going up and down, round and round for hours polishing and smoothing off the newly laid travertine marble at our home. He looked up at me and handed me a slip of paper, saying to me, 'Here is my telephone number. If you have any trouble or want any help, just give me a call, any time – day or night.' I didn't even know his name, or anything about him. I was a stranger to him as well. Such unasked-for kindness from a stranger is not often seen.

As said by the Irish poet William Butler Yeats, 'A stranger is often only a friend that you don't know yet.'

· ·

At this present time of life all our children seem stationary, busily raising children of their own, some of which have already left school and home and are either in the workforce or going to universities for a degree of their choice. Or like Melody, who isn't married, just studying, and working day by day in an effort to pay her rent and buy food.

To tell of their present status, I'll start with the youngest – our adopted gem, Melody. She is tiny, only about 4-foot and 6-inches, now thirty-six years old. She is full of life and vitality, with a loving and charismatic character. When you encounter her, you realise she is immensely interested in you and wants to know all about you. Children love her, although she always jests and says she can't stand them. Adults also like her. She seems to have settled into life in Dublin. But hasn't found a man she likes enough to marry yet but seems happy enough sharing a flat with four other young people who are mainly from Europe.

Melody has already accomplished much after her school days. She has a degree in French and Italian from Trinity College, Dublin, and a postgraduate certificate in English language which enabled her to teach English to foreign students for five years. She works as a volunteer with NALA helping adults with literacy skills, as well as teaching English to Somali refugee women in Ireland. She has qualifications as a holistic massager as well as qualifications in advanced aromatherapy in a clinical setting and cancer care. At the moment, she is completing a Delta postgraduate diploma in English language teaching. In her spare time, she volunteers on a telephone hotline to help people who are depressed, have bipolar disorder or anxiety. Because of the pandemic, however, she is not able to even work at her occasional job serving drinks in a Dublin pub.

....

Bubble is forty-four at present. Divorced and a single mum. She is lovely, warm, soft, and cuddly, but she struggles with fear, anxiety, and ill health. This unfortunately often causes her to be on the defensive. Saying things that can poison and alienate those who long for the love of a sister or the close companionship of a daughter, driving a wedge between those who could be her greatest asset and joy. She herself once said, 'This life is just a dream. One day we'll wake up.'

One day I hope she will wake up and realise that God has placed her in an amazing family. A family who loves her and wants to be loved by her. Maintaining love for one's family is very important, even if they are rat bags. Bubble is highly intelligent and talented in many ways. As I have mentioned, she has degrees in jewellery manufacture and design from a prestigious school in Florence, Italy, despite not speaking a word of Italian when she got there. She has since become quite fluent.

When still living in Florence, Bubble had been a little too free with her affections and found, to her delight, that she was pregnant. She had separated from her husband Matty some years previously. Bubble came to us in Malta with her two Boxer dogs for most of her pregnancy. On the 31st of May, Zaru and I took her to Saint James Hospital where she had a Caesarean section, and her delightful daughter, Velvet, made her entrance into God's world. Doug was overseas at the time.

Velvet is now eight years old. Bubble left Florence and now lives in England where she home-schools her extremely intelligent daughter. The school Velvet was attending was closed like all other British schools because of the rapid spread of Coronavirus. Now that the schools have reopened, Bubble still fears the virus because she herself is not at all well, still suffering from erythromelalgia which lowers her immune system. She is therefore very careful to avoid any contact with the virus for Velvet's sake, so she continues to home-school her. Her dream of having her own jewellery shop has had to be put on hold as she is, for now, housebound and is devoting her time and life to educating Velvet.

Because she finds walking and being on her feet for long periods very painful, it is difficult for her to find time to utilise her profession of making custom designed jewellery. Her father helps her out financially. She has become a house mum, tutor, and the sole companion for her little girl – a job she delights in. Occasionally she will become filled with sadness as she remembers her athletic years of free movement and vitality and social charm. At times like this she would phone me or Daddles and have a sob over the phone. Daddles has a knack of cheering her up and making her laugh again. On the other hand, I would let Bubble also pull my spirits down. I would feel so concerned and sorry for her.

Lately she has become very interested in her ancestral background and has even contacted members of my mother's aristocratic family line to learn more. This has resulted in her making a network of new acquaintances which has made her feel important and good about herself as she discovers that she herself has many of the genetic qualities of these amazing people, her relatives. Doing this, Bubble has also taught me a lot about my background. I regret not asking my mother questions relating to my family when she was alive. Children don't think to do that.

When our children were old enough to understand such matters, we never focused much on their ancestral background either. It wasn't until influential people got in touch with Daddles and his book *Lenten Lands* was produced and published, that the children learnt much at all about their family background. And that was only their father's roots. Our lineages didn't seem important compared to the running of the farms in those days.

When we were living in that large house in Ireland, I was asked to take the Malet family ancestral portraits after the Chargot Somerset house was sold. There was no other family member's house big enough to hang them in. But Doug refused. There were

already large ornately framed portrait photos hanging in our grand drawing room. They were pictures of the up-and-coming generation, our children. Something that people would comment about.

Dominick, our youngest boy, will be fifty next year. He was always our low-maintenance child when he was young. Always a delight, no trouble, sweet and gentle as well as being capable and practical. A perfect gentleman in every respect. All three of our sons value their commitment to Jesus Christ, and closely follow His teachings. All of them have amazing testimonies of how they became Christians.

Dominick met Wendy, his wife, while studying architecture in Launceston. He was the first of our children to marry. The ceremony was held in Launceston, Tasmania, in 1994. Our whole family attended it except for James, who was studying in the USA at the time. Alina, Wendy's sister, was a bridesmaid and Dig was the best man. It was a joyous occasion and a lovely break from our busy lives at Rathvinden.

Dominick and Wendy now live in Brisbane with their five children. He works as an architect with a big firm, and is a deacon at Grace Bible Church, which the whole family attends. Wendy also plays an active role at the church taking primary school children for their own Bible study during church services.

Wendy and Dominick have been model parents in every way. They home-schooled all five of their children up to grade 9. In the final four years of their schooling, they were sent to a prestigious girls' school to get their Queensland Certificate of Education (QCE). Daddles kindly paid for that part of their education. At that school they were found to be well above the other girls in knowledge and maturity and were highly regarded by their teachers. Dominick and Wendy have both done a magnificent job teaching their children and bringing them up with the knowledge and principles of applied Christianity.

Their oldest child, Rebekah, our first-born granddaughter, recently graduated as a civil engineer and is getting married this December. It's unlikely that Doug and I will be able to attend the wedding unless the restrictions ease on airline travel and entry into Australia. Sinead, the second oldest, is following in her mother's and her grandmother's footsteps and is training to be a nurse. Nursing training has changed so much since the days I trained – most of their learning is done at a university. Our training was primarily hands-on, in the wards under supervision – a much better method, I feel. Learning how to be a nurse in a university is like trying to learn how to drive a car using an instruction manual. Their other three children are all still school age.

....

As for Timothy George, commonly known by his family as Dig, he is my gold medal boy. He has a Bachelor of Science degree from the Australian National University (ANU) in Canberra and an MBA from Trinity College in Dublin. Today he lives in Mittagong, New South Wales, with his beautiful wife Cath. They were married in Sydney in August 1998. I was unable to attend their wedding due to the workload at Rathvinden which couldn't be left, but Daddles and Bubble went.

Now in his 51st year, Dig has excelled in many ways. He now has his own company called Temple Healthcare which imports advanced neurological diagnostics equipment from Italy, world-leading sleep diagnostics from Iceland, and the world's most advanced transcutaneous blood gas monitor from Switzerland.

He also imports a wide range of respiratory and neurological consumable items from the UK, Israel, and Germany and he has a large warehouse in Mittagong where he keeps stock to distribute to hospitals and private practices across Australia and New Zealand. Not only does he import all this equipment, but he also installs it and trains the medical staff how to operate and analyse the reports from these machines. A small team of employees help him with the running of the company, both in Mittagong and up and down the east coast of Australia.

Two of his three children have left home now. Jack, the oldest, attended a boy's boarding school in North Sydney and is now studying Chemical Engineering at the University of Newcastle. The youngest, Ashton, is at the same boarding school doing his final year and Georgie, who is now twenty-one, has moved to Brisbane to be near her friends. It's been difficult for her to find a job because of the restrictions forced on the city due to the spread of the Coronavirus. She is working in a restaurant now. Daddles was also able to help with the cost of Dig's children's schooling.

• •

James is fifty-two, only one year older than Dig. He is my pride and joy. A more intelligent, caring and hard-working man you would be hard-pressed to find. He loves and admires his Mompska to bits. It's he who has encouraged me to tell my story and edits it for me as I go. I eagerly await his comments after writing each chapter. So far, he has been very patient with me, making suggestions and pressing me to be more descriptive, as if I am painting a picture. 'It needs colour,' he says.

He spent his formative years growing up on a dairy farm in the backwoods of Tasmania, attending a very basic high school in the agricultural area of Scottsdale. He completed his schooling at what was then called Launceston Community College, LCC.

He then went on to have all sorts of interesting experiences with a variety of jobs in many different countries. From building scale models for the *Muppet Christmas Carol* movie in London with Jim Henson's Creature workshop, to salmon farming in Scotland, and traveling the canals of France as a tour guide and boatman on a luxury hotel barge. He also worked at Chargot in Somerset for my cousin Harry who was then running the farm for my old Uncle Daily. The same Harry who had introduced me to Douglas. And later he worked at the Glympton Park Estate, in Oxfordshire, where Daddles had been an agricultural student all those years ago. And under the same manager. He has had driving jobs in the USA, Britain, Australia, and Africa.

In 1991, he enrolled in a four-year course at LeTourneau University in Longview, Texas, to study aviation technology (aircraft maintenance and flying), graduating with Honours in 1995. He now holds an airframe and powerplant mechanic's certificate and airline transport pilot's licences in both America and Australia. He has done a lot of flight instruction, flew corporate aircraft for a while and then spent several years flying for a large American airline quickly being promoted to Captain.

While at LeTourneau, one of the classes he was required to take was machine tool. The designated project was to machine a model engine out of a solid block of aluminium. This same project had been assigned to students for years and no one had ever been able to get their engine actually running. James was the first, and as far as we know only student to get his engine going.

James won first place in the Le Tourneau design contest, submitting an oil accumulator – whatever that is. He also represented his school in a state-wide aircraft maintenance competition winning first place. The prize was a large set of Snap-On tools, which he uses to this day.

Not only did he excel academically, but he played an active role in helping to run the establishment, both socially and scholastically. He was class president for three years, dorm student senate representative, Master of Ceremonies at several events, and weekend dining hall manager. In the wider community, he had several different mechanic jobs and, at the other end of the spectrum, was Stage Manager for the Longview Symphony Orchestra.

At LeTourneau, he fell in love with a pretty girl by the name of Lara who was studying psychology and biblical studies. They married in December 1996 in Memphis, Tennessee. Our whole family attended the wedding except for Melody. We had her airline ticket purchased and her bag packed to come with us but on the very day we were to leave we discovered that her passport had expired. It was a horrible omission, and very upsetting for her. She graciously accepted it, assuring us that it was okay. It was too late to put it right, so she had to stay at Rathvinden with the house sitters. At the time, Dominick and Wendy were living in Dublin so they were on the same flight as us. Dig and Bubble arrived in Memphis from Australia on the same day we arrived.

The usual wedding reception was held in the church hall for family and friends. However, a second reception had to be held the following day. So many people had heard that Douglas Gresham, 'the stepson of C.S. Lewis', was to be at the wedding and people had been bombarding James and Lara and various members of Lara's family for an invitation. But it was Lara and James' special day. They didn't want Daddles to eclipse it, so the couple wisely held a second reception the next day. They put on a grand English tea party at a hotel and all those who wanted to shake the hand of C.S. Lewis' stepson, and ply him with questions and have their photo taken with him, were invited. Daddles gave a speech and signed their books and generally was very amenable.

Today: 29th October 2020

We made use of our family time together by having professional photos taken, leaving gaps in each photo to copy Melody in at a later date, which we successfully did.

Now to the present day. Despite being a highly qualified pilot in both America and Australia, and also a qualified aircraft mechanic, James has moved on and is now on his second career. As mentioned in previous chapters, James and Lara are owners of a 6000-acre beef property in northern New South Wales, Australia. James considers his primary job to be being a good husband to Lara and he tries to be an equally good father to his two sons, Michael and Lindsay. As such he is manager and fix-'em-up-chappy of the farm which carries about 500 head of cattle.

Lara is heavily involved with the community. For some years, she has spearheaded Australia's largest Celtic festival. She plays in the local pipe band (tenor drum), helps with the organisation and running of the local community agricultural show, is involved with several different council and community groups and volunteers at a local Christian bookshop which she was instrumental in establishing.

Currently, aside from the farm, James is Captain of the local Rural Fire Brigade, and secretary/treasurer for a local vintage truck and machinery club. He oversees operating and displaying all the vintage machinery at the local museum and is involved with several other committees including a local council 'Roads Committee' representing his community.

In his spare time, which he doesn't get much of, he owned a small flight school at Glen Innes Airport and taught a good number of people how to fly, including both his sons and his brother, Dig. Dig has now just recently bought his own little aeroplane and is enjoying it immensely, while James has shut down his flying school as he was simply not able to devote the time to it that was needed. 'Teaching people to fly is not something you can do in a half-hearted fashion,' he said.

Both of James' children have now left home. Michael will be getting married soon. His studies at the University of New England, Armidale, have been derailed by COVID-19 but thankfully he has a job with a retailer of domestic appliances. Lindsay is pursuing his fascination for firearm manufacture and design and is attending a college in North Carolina studying gunsmithing. Like his father he excels in all he does and is very highly regarded by the teachers.

Most years the three brothers and all the cousins spend a week or so together on the farm where many memories are made.

Today: 29th October 2020

Regrets

Now that we haven't got the added workload of running Rathvinden ministries, I should have time on my hands. As I've mentioned, I do write a dated prayer letter to Jesus most mornings and I love to listen to my Bible on my mobile phone when I'm dressing, gardening or alone in the kitchen cooking. Every Sunday at 10.00 am I'd be at church joining in the joyous praise and worship songs and eagerly awaiting something new in Paster Ken's talk. On a Tuesday evening we would gather again for Bible study or to watch a Christian movie.

But the promises I made to myself to mingle with people more, to befriend them and introduce them to Christianity – as opposed to religious adherence – have never been completely fulfilled. There is a convalescent hospital within walking distance from our home. That was high on my priority list, but I went there only once to visit the sick. I also tried once to get into the Malta gaols, hoping to take the Christian message to some of the young offenders but would only be allowed in if I was a Catholic nun or a priest.

I wanted to restore my stretched and strained relationship with Daddles which had drifted over the last thirteen years in Ireland, by both of us being too busy with other things, often not related. I needed to be more attentive to him now that I had the time. Perhaps even going out together alone sometimes. We had planned to take trips around Europe in our motorhome, but these things never happened. He was still heavily involved in the making of the next two Narnia films and was away from home often. He was also in great demand as a public speaker, mainly on C.S. Lewis related gatherings in the States. And there still is his daily commitment to answer dozens of emails each day.

The COVID-19 pandemic has ground our busy lives to a standstill allowing Daddles and me to finally spend time together, which has been lovely. We sit and talk for hours and help each other with jobs around the house. Today we took all last summer's frozen tomatoes out of the freezer and made twenty jars of tomato ketchup.

Looking back through my five-year diaries, I am amazed by the fact that Daddles was so frequently catching planes to the USA or other places, leaving me to look after the house and guests. I was reluctant to go with him because it was boring. I'd be left in a hotel room while he went to meetings. We would only ever eat in the room ordering room service meals. Yet he would go with other people to fancy restaurants, or to accompany him to watch a play or something. Despite some of the fascinating places he would go, Daddles was never interested in sightseeing.

It was also difficult for me to leave my two Poodles with Zaru. As they got older, they would pine dreadfully for me. I'm told they would sit all day at the front gate, waiting for me to return. Or would be locked up in the garage on the four days a week when Zaru wasn't working here. So, I preferred to stay at home and hold the fort.

I wanted to be emotionally confident, to stand firm about my needs and not be withdrawn and manipulated into taking a back seat and told to be grateful for my lot. Because I am very grateful, even to this day. I have a lovely home and gardens, and I know Daddles loves me dearly and endeavours to always give me my heart's desires.

I wanted to be real without pretending to be clever, strong, or holy. Instead, the days on the calendar were crossed out one by one and I did nothing but clean the house, make beds, do the laundry, attend to everyone's needs, including the needs of my two Poodles. I harvested the veggies that Zaru grows and picked the fruit, freezing, bottling, or giving away the excess. I kept the cookie tins full of Anzac biscuits. I kept the guest rooms ready for new guests with clean ironed bed sheets and pillowcases, with soft towels folded up neatly on their beds. I fed any resident guest with delightful meals that I prepared. Daddles usually entertained them, amusing them with stories of bygone days and adventures, or by taking them for sightseeing trips around Malta – often ending at the fortified city of Mdina, where they would have a meal at the Bacchus Restaurant.

And of course, I am now heavily involved with my church family. They love to come here and swim in the pool and have long drawn-out lunches or BBQs together. Often it ends up with singing Christian praise songs while gathered around Franz who plays the guitar. These musical sessions can become quite entertaining as lots of people grab whatever they can find to tap out a beat on. Saucepan lids, buckets, or rubbish bins. We laugh while we sing, and some dance around. It's amazing what high spirits these gatherings can exhibit without any alcohol at all.

I enjoy wandering up and down the supermarket aisles choosing groceries for the house. I'd always try to make the poor bored girl at the checkout smile and feel loved by asking her if she enjoyed the job or commenting on her skills of handling the endless queues of people. Just small talk. Others, I noticed, would completely ignore those poor 'check-out-chicks'.

Occasionally I'd have a class doing the Christianity Explained course with me. But not as much as I used to at Rathvinden. Wrapping and posting birthday parcels to our grandchildren is a constant job with eleven of them all waiting for a birthday gift parcel from Grompska and Granddaddles, which are their names for us.

Most evenings when Daddles and I are alone, if I hadn't gone to my Tuesday night Bible study, we would spend time together watching TV. That was both an irritation to me as well as a time to relax and be with my beloved Doug. I'm not fond of TV watching and find most of it trivial and pointless. When Doug is away, I never ever turn it on. I'm not sure that I even know how to turn it on. We have watched some very fine movies on that big screen in our designated TV/library on the ground floor, but also hours of complete nonsense.

I keep the garden looking groomed and tidy. Zaru does the heavy work, hedge cutting, rotary-hoeing and most of the tractor work in the fields. Daddles sometimes loves to get on the tractor with the big mulcher or rotary hoe and cultivate our small fields.

Lots of my ideas and resolutions were never fulfilled, but in this I have confidence: God will finish the good work he has started in me. Why? Because He values me so much that He let men crucify His Son so He wouldn't be without me in Heaven.

Chapter 36

Balance points

Balance points of life are the people or times in our lives that often are a focus. The thing that gives us a reason, a hope, or something to live for. Have you ever balanced a long pole on one finger? That point of balance is fragile. Any deviation will upset the balance.

I can think of seven points in my life that I have trusted in for my security, sanity, and balance. Most of them let me down with a crash, causing my emotions and outlook on life to crumble.

My first focal point was my black *ayah*, Tousi Binti Simba in Africa. When I first awakened to life, in those first five years, she was my security. Always there for me. I was too young to realise that her ability to care for me came from two adults who were also there – my mother and father. I found myself lost and frightened when at the age of five, I was taken away from her and found myself on a big steamship bound for Australia. I reacted by crying for days.

After many months with no secure hold on life, I found my balance again in family life with my parents and siblings. Although she always claimed to be no good with children, my mother became my stabilising point. The centre of my life and my balance. I came to rely on her to keep me from falling apart. Life was carefree and delightful when we all lived together on that farm in Barrington, Tasmania. I belonged to a family, but it wasn't to last. I soon lost that balance point when Mother became religious and fragmented our family unit.

Years followed years when I had no stability in my life. Forever changing locations and schools added to my feeling of being derailed and lost. I became a loner. My father would introduce me to people as, 'This is Meredith. She is the secretive one.' Why? Because I had lost myself and my trust in people. It was during this time I learnt the art of elective mutism. It was my hiding place where I felt safe.

The nuns and fellow nursing students at Calvary Hospital in Hobart got me back on my feet. My life became balanced once again. I became a useful member of an organisation and was valued as a nurse and midwife. Also, my transformation physically from being an ugly duckling to a beautiful swan also helped me a lot. There was music and a lightness to my step. I identified with that song in the musical *West Side Story*.

'I feel pretty. Oh, so pretty

I feel pretty and witty and gay

And I pity any girl who isn't me tonight.

See the pretty girl in the mirror there?

Who can that attractive girl be?

Such a pretty face, such a pretty dress,

such a pretty smile, such a pretty me!'

Those days ended after five years. No longer was my security and balance to be found there. I went to England, and again became alone and frightened.

Slowly but surely my balancing point shifted as I began to embrace another secure point in life. It was none other than Douglas Howard Gresham. For a long time, I had been his focal point. His whole life was balanced in a hope and longing that was me. Then it shifted. He became my all-in-all. I became dependent on his intellect, his financial backing, and his charismatic personality. But he, like me, had had many traumas in his growing-up years. He became a very wobbly tightrope for me to keep my balance on. We both went through some very rough and hard times. In our desperation, two wobbly people clung to each other.

God had created the world in seven days, and it took seven stages to make me whole. Seven things I had relied on to keep my balance. In 1983 on the 3rd of December at 11:00 am, He changed all my life's unstable securities and put me on an unshakable even keel. I'm sure it was Him who kept knocking me out of balance. He himself wanted to become my focal point, my secure foundation. What was missing in my life was someone other than myself, or another frail human being to be my stabilising strength. I asked Him to be my all-in-all. 'Christ within me, my hope of glory,' (Col 1:27). There is a popular hymn with the words 'On Christ the solid rock I stand. All other ground is sinking sand'. Thankfully, it didn't take long for Daddles to also shift his balance and stability off me and onto Christ.

Acting the role of God for another human is not peaceful or comfortable. Today we love each other more deeply than we have ever done. But Daddles isn't my God, and I am not his God. We are free to be ourselves and travel this road to Glory together. As Daddles has said many times, 'None of us are qualified to run our own lives our own way.' Thankfully God has provided a maker's manual, His Word. He himself is that manual. 'In the beginning there was the Word, and the Word was with God, and the Word was God,' (John 1:1).

In summing up the life story of one of God's most foolish and insignificant children, I can now recognise some of the things that I clung to for hope and stability. No doubt these were orchestrated by God to preserve me, until it was the right time for me to accept, through trial and much error, the only thing that could give my life true stability. An unshakable, solid thing to cling to. I discovered the hard way that it wasn't my breeding, education, beauty, intellect, husband, possessions, children, or achievements. It was Jesus who had a higher plan for me. He would never leave me or let me down or disappoint me.

Before I even knew Him, He had done such a lot to help both Doug and me along the way. He was, and is, our gift-giver, and the greatest gift of all. Knowing and following Him has healed us both. The road I took, with all its twists and turns, led to Him. All other ways to happiness and fulfilment in life are trivial, chasing after the wind. Foolishness, utter foolishness.

Epilogue

When Daddles was stuck in Australia and all the airports closed, I wrote about my feelings at the time. I came across it yesterday. It wasn't intended for the book but here it is as an epilogue.

Yesterday, Wednesday the 13th of May 2020, was a horrid day. It was a day like many others that I am experiencing during this time of lockdown.

The last I saw Daddles was when I kissed him goodbye in the Ibis Hotel near Sydney Airport on the 15th of February. He was to fly to Mackay that day and enjoy some solitude. Pete, our island manager, would meet him and ferry him in the Sealegs Amphibious Craft to his most loved island retreat, Little Green Island. The next day I was to fly back to our villa in Malta, via Dubai and Larnaca. Daddles was supposed to follow six weeks later.

Little did either of us know that we wouldn't see each other again for a long, long time. The date of our reunion is unknown, and terrifying. Up to a few days ago he would always put on a brave face for my benefit as we messaged each other every morning and evening on our mobile phones. He eventually revealed to me that he couldn't eat or sleep, he was missing me so much that he would die if he didn't get back to me soon.

At this stage it is impossible. The Dubai airports and the Malta Airport are closed – and many others worldwide. I phoned James and Dig on a video call. Both were prepared to go and fetch him, but in the end the outcome was that he was to leave his solitary confinement and fly to Sydney – both Brisbane and Sydney had been closed but reopened for a short time. Dig would then drive him to his home in Mittagong, till a flight to Malta became possible.

What terrified me was Daddles' insistence that he would fly to Heathrow Airport and stay at his Isle of Wight residence till the Malta Airport reopened. England had become one of the worst infected countries with thousands dying each day. Hospitals were overloaded and understaffed. A lot of the doctors and nurses were either ill or dead. I told him he would die if he did that. He said he would die if he was separated from me and was prepared to risk his life to be with me.

To make matters more frightening, Bubble phoned from her lockdown in England and was trying to persuade me to get him to change his mind and wait till a vaccine had been tested and approved to be used on humans. She told me that a different milkman delivered her milk this morning because the previous one, a man in his thirties was dead. He had been infected with the virus. I fought back tears as she spoke urgently for a long time, but my voice couldn't conceal the fact that I was distraught and crying. 'I can't do a thing, I'm powerless, he wants to be with me and is prepared to die in the attempt,' I said.

The rest of the day I couldn't operate. I made a jobs list for the day but found myself just aimlessly wandering around the house. As I fought back tears I cried out in a loud voice to my God, who had filled my mind and heart with promises to look after His children, 'Do something, stop this pandemic or keep Daddles safe.'

Then by evening, when I had composed myself and got my emotions under control, my other daughter, Melody, phoned me from Dublin. She confirmed to me the plight that England was in. I told her I didn't want to hear about it, I didn't want to talk about it. Again, I plummeted into fear and helplessness.

With my hands held high supporting my body against the front door, I again cried out to God in a loud voice – no one could hear me as I was completely alone in this large house. I reminded God of His promises saying, 'I haven't lost my faith, I know You are in control, so please help us and help others who are in this same predicament, of being unable to return home.'

Then I remembered what I had always advised people to do and was normally in the habit of doing myself. He had told us to cast all our cares upon Him, for He cares for us, and will guard our heart. I had asked him a long time ago to be the keeper of my heart and promised Him I would not try to handle negative emotions myself. I apologised to Him for forgetting to do that and asked Him to forgive me. I said, 'Take this fear and loneliness and give me that peace that surpasses all understanding.' And He did.

....

Epilogue

Daddles eventually made it home to me on the 17th of June. We had been separated for four months. He did have to wait a long time on the Isle of Wight for a repatriation flight to Malta. The airport didn't officially open for another month. He looked so ill and frail when he got home. For fourteen days he remained in quarantine in our guest wing till all danger of spreading the virus was gone. God had kept him safe.

www.ingramcontent.com/pod-product-compliance
Lightning Source LLC
Chambersburg PA
CBHW021427080526
44588CB00009B/454